PLACES ON THE MARGIN

Alternative geographies of modernity

ROB SHIELDS

LONDON AND NEW YORK

First published 1991
by Routledge
11 New Fetter Lane, London EC4P 4EE

Reprinted in paperback in 1992

Simultaneously published in the USA and Canada
by Routledge
a division of Routledge, Chapman and Hall, Inc.
29 West 35th Street, New York, NY 10001

© 1991 Rob Shields

Typeset by LaserScript Limited, Mitcham, Surrey

Transferred to Digital Printing 2002

British Library Cataloguing in Publication Data

Shields, Rob, *1961–*
Places on the margin. – (The international library of sociology)
I. Title II. Series
304.23

Library of Congress Cataloging in Publication Data

Shields, Rob, 1961–
Places on the margin: alternative geographies of modernity/Rob
Shields.
p. cm. – (International library of sociology series)
Includes bibliographical references (p.).
1. Human geography. 2. Spatial behavior. 3. Geographical
perception. I. Title. II. Series: International library of
sociology.
GF95.S55 1990
304.2′3–dc20
90-8264
CIP

ISBN 0-415-04091-4 (hbk)
ISBN 0-415-08022-3 (pbk)

FOR MY PARENTS AND FOR 'M'

The anxiety of our era has to do fundamentally with space, no doubt a great deal more than with time. Time probably appears to us only as one of the various distributive operations that are possible for the elements that are spread out in space.

(Michael Foucault 1967, Berlin lectures)

CONTENTS

CONTENTS

ILLUSTRATIONS

FIGURES

ILLUSTRATIONS

ACKNOWLEDGEMENTS

This book developed out of doctoral research at the University of Sussex made possible by a Commonwealth Scholarship. I owe a debt of gratitude to many colleagues, reviewers, and the patient audiences of numerous seminars where the theoretical groundwork of this study was staked out. Perhaps my greatest debt is to Pete Saunders, who for three years read and reread successive iterations while dealing with numerous extra advisors, puzzling ideas, and foreign theories in each chapter, slowly cajolling a comprehensible presentation. A host of other figures contributed at seminal moments whom I can never hope to thank adequately. Many, including my grandmother, Mrs Agnes Paterson, helped correct the proofs. John Urry, Mike Savage, Kevin Meetham, Myung-Rae Cho, Aya Okada, Joerge Dyrkton, James Barlow, the late Allon White, Derek Gregory, Peter Dickens, John Cosgrove, and Ed Soja provided patient counsel and wider horizons. Without the sources made available by the Brighton Central Reference Library and the Royal Pavilion Museum, Brighton; the Niagara Falls Tourism and Convention Bureau in the person of Stella Howlett and Rosanna Schincariol of Travel Lodge's 'Coral Inn' (Niagara Falls) the chapters on Brighton and on the Niagara Honeymoon would have been impossible. The Niagara Falls Library and the local Historical Society allowed me access to historical material which filled in gaps. The Department of Sociology at the University of Lancaster and the School of Urban and Regional Planning, Queen's University, who afforded me hospitality and a toehold in Canadian academia during the actual preparation of this book, richly deserve my thanks, as do my Canadian colleagues, Mireya Folch-Serra, Brian Osbourne, John Holmes, Charles Gordon and above all Marie Brisson.

RS, Lancaster, December 1989·

xiii

PART ONE

INTRODUCTION
Places on the margin

When we seek to make sense of such problematical topics as human nature, culture, society, and history, we never say precisely what we wish to say or mean precisely what we say. Our discourse always tends to slip away from our data towards the structures of consciousness with which we are trying to grasp them; or, what amounts to the same thing, the data always resist the coherency of the image which we are trying to fashion of them . . .
(Hayden White 1978, Tropics of Discourse, p.1)

MARGIN AND PERIPHERY

Marginal places, those towns and regions which have been 'left behind' in the modern race for progress, evoke both nostalgia and fascination. Their marginal status may come from out-of-the-way geographic locations, being the site of illicit or disdained social activities, or being the Other pole to a great cultural centre. In all cases the type of geographic marginality discussed below is a mark of being a social periphery. That is, the marginal places that are of interest are not necessarily on geographical peripheries but, first and foremost, they have been placed on the periphery of cultural systems of space in which places are ranked relative to each other. They all carry the image, and stigma, of their marginality which becomes indistinguishable from any basic empirical identity they might once have had. From this *primary* ranking of cultural status they may also end up being classified in what geographers have mapped as systems of 'centres and peripheries'. At the margins of these cultural classifications are the peripheral sites and regions which form the topic of this book. Brighton with its beach, for example, is at the 'edge' of the British Isles, lying on the south coast. Yet its accessibility from London made it an ideal site for socially marginal activities – carnivals of desire and explosions of unrest. The Canadian North, by contrast, forms the mythic 'heartland' of Canada but remains a zone of Otherness in the spatial system of Canadian culture. The North is the complete antithesis of the urban civilisation of the southern metropolises. Thus it is that places on the margins expose the central role of 'spatialisation' to cultures and nation-states.

The example of the beach illustrates the extent of the cultural categorisation of geographic spaces and places. As opposed to being merely a topographic margin, the development of cultural marginality occurs only through a complex process of social activity and cultural work. There is a broad literature which has emerged over the last decade on cultural categorisation. In particular, the theme of binary oppositions between the High and the Low emerges as characteristic of the cultures of European civilisation. In their book *The Poetics and Politics of Transgression*, Stallybrass and White (1986) note that cultural categories of 'high and low, social and aesthetic . . . those of the physical body and geographical space, are never entirely separable.' In a process of categorisation through binary oppositions

> the human body, psychic forms, geographical space and the
> social formation are all constructed within interrelating and
> dependent hierarchies of high and low . . . . The high/low
> opposition in each of . . . [these] four symbolic domains . . .
> is a fundamental basis to mechanisms of ordering and
> sense-making in European cultures.
>
> (Stallybrass and White 1986:2–3)

Furthermore 'This does not necessarily militate against subtlety since "above" and "below" may be inscribed within a minutely discriminatory system of classification, but it does foster a simplifying binaryism of high and low *within which* further classification will be made' (1986:3).

To this opposition of High/Low, the parallel, geographic dualism of Central/Marginal may be aligned. The social definition of marginal places and spaces is intimately linked with the categorisation of objects, practices, ideas and modes of social interaction as belonging to the 'Low culture', the culture of marginal places and spaces, the culture of the marginalised. In his book on *Orientalism*, the Euro-chauvinistic myths of the Middle East constructed by Europeans to bolster their own cultural status and legitimise imperial ambitions, Edward Saïd (1978) has demonstrated this simultaneous definition of the Low-Other and the categorisation of the Marginal as being at the 'edge of civilisation'.

The politics of this process of symbolic exclusion depends on a strategy of what Saïd has called 'positional superiority', one which puts the High in a whole series of possible relationships with the Low without ever losing the upper hand. This allows a series of ambivalent representations of and relationships to the Low or the Marginal. Stallybrass and White conclude that 'Repugnance and fascination are the twin poles of the process in which a *political* imperative to reject and eliminate the debasing "Low" conflicts powerfully and unpredictably with a desire for the Other' (1986:4–5).

> The 'Top' attempts to reject and eliminate the 'Bottom' for
> reasons of prestige and status, only to discover, not only that it
> is in some way frequently dependent upon that low-Other . . .
> but also that the top *includes* that low symbolically, as a
> primary eroticised constituent of its own fantasy life . . . . It is
> for this reason that what is socially peripheral is so frequently
> *symbolically* central (like long hair in the 1960s). The
> low-Other is despised and denied at the level of political
> organisation and social being whilst it is instrumentally
> constitutive of the shared imaginary repertoires of the
> dominant culture.
>
> (Stallybrass and White 1986:5)

This recurring pattern will be borne out in the case-histories which follow. The relation of centre and margin lies at the heart of the identity of the four cases below. The social 'Other' of the marginal and of low cultures is despised and reviled in the official discourse of dominant culture and central power while at the same time being constitutive of the imaginary and emotional repertoires of that dominant culture. But, even if this binary separation is clearly visible to the social analyst, the construction of marginality, the classification of the Low, and the exclusion of the Other are not final points of achieved stasis. In the case-histories which follow, marginality reveals its own states, a history of transformations

5

between being margins, near-sacred *liminal zones* of Otherness, and carnivalesque leisure spaces of ritual inversion of the dominant, authorised cultures.

Four places and regions are compared to examine the importance of place-images to the culture of modernity in North America and Britain. Through these demonstrations, a conceptual 'toolkit' will be built up, with which we should be able to discuss not only images of places and regions but also the impact of contemporary, so-called postmodern, trends in the cultural and spatial organisation of modernity. Sites are never simply locations. Rather, they are sites for someone and of something. The cultural context of images and myths adds a socially constructed level of meaning to the *genus loci*, the classics' 'unique sense of place', said to derive from the forms of the physical environment in a given site. Thus, to give a brief example, to the *genus loci* of central Rome – the seven ancient hills which formed the sites on which principal buildings were located in ancient times and which later provided the nodes which the great axes of the Baroque Rome of Pope Sixtus V would link – I propose to add the cultural identity of Rome as a great city in relation to other cultural capitals, to European cities and to the socio-geographic regions of Italy. This means fully locating it in the different emotional geographies of people as different as tourists and city dwellers, building up an image of the place through the events and activities it attracts and repels, mapping its function in language and its role as a pole in the gestalt field of Western historical culture.

As opposed to this being merely a matter of myths, each case-history builds toward a demonstration of the centrality of spatial conceptions such as place-images for daily life. These images and stereotypes, an imaginary geography of places and spaces, are shown to have social impacts which are empirically specifiable and located not only at the level of individual proxemics (as discussed in the late 1960s and 1970s–cf. Hall 1966) but also at the level of social discourses on space which (1) underpin the rhetoric of ideologues and politicians and (2) pervade and subvert even the rationalistic discourse of planning and regional development policy (e.g. Massey 1984; 1988). In particular, the collective weight of these 'discourses on space' will be linked with the symbolic creation of a sense of community (cf. Cohen 1986) and with nationalism (cf. B. Anderson 1983).

6

The spatial practices and figurative images discussed in this book are evidence of much more. I plan to argue not just for empirical impacts but to demonstrate the importance of spatial concepts and categories, of which place-images and myths are only one example, for the whole way in which we go about thinking about our world in conventional terms. To use more fancy terms, the spatial has an epistemic and ontological importance – it is part and parcel of our notions of reality, truth, and causality. As an initial hypothesis, we could suggest that a 'discourse of space' composed of perceptions of places and regions, of the world as a 'space' and of our relationships with these perceptions are central to our everyday conceptions of ourselves and of reality.

Understandings and concepts of space cannot be divorced from the real fabric of how people live their lives. To do so would be like saying that culture is made up of beliefs and traditions but has no impact on how people live. Their concrete, non-discursive, prac- tices are both informed by and go on to provoke modifications in this cultural discourse of the spatial. In Chapter One, following Michel Foucault, the administrative, guiding nature of these discursive understandings and beliefs will be argued to be the key in the transformation of purely discursive (i.e. ideational, sym- bolic, and linguistic) notions of space and of 'imaginary geog- raphies' into empirically-specifiable everyday actions gestures of the living persons, of the crowd-practices and emotional com- munity of affective groups, of institutional policies and political– economic arrangements, right up the scale to the 'imaginary community' of the territorial nation-state (B. Anderson 1983) and beyond to form geo-political alliances, rivalries, and spheres of influence. This overarching order of space, is reproduced in concrete forms and re-affirms as well as reproduces 'discourses of space' which constitute it. The term *social spatialisation* will be used to designate this social construction of the spatial which is a form- ation of both discursive and non-discursive elements, practices, and processes. Taking my cue from the French philosopher Henri Lefebvre, the spatial will be approached as a materially produced form, a 'concrete abstraction' like the commodity form which is both the material ground of labour and the result of the oper- ations and inscriptions of capital on territory in the form of land values and the property regime (Lefebvre 1981; Harvey 1982). To throw this into new light, we could adopt Heideggerian termin-

7

logy to note that the spatial has both an *ontic* aspect as the for-
gotten datum of social practices and at the same moment and in
those self-same practices an *ontological* aspect as th at which we take
for granted in the everydayness of lots, of my property and your
property, of real estate signs and of the proudly-trimmed plantings
in front of suburban split-level ranch-bungalows. The paradox
whereby the spatial is both a socially-constructed arrangement of
divisions and territories and the ontic medium of all such arrangements will be explored in the next chapter.

Such a paradox also serves as a warning that we must recognise
that we build our concepts and theories from within our material,
forever prisoners of our geographical and historical context.
There is no still, Archimedean point outside of society and the
world at which all forces might be weighed and called to order.
Hence, the *aporetic* nature of any claims to 'objectivity' or freedom
from context, and the 'situatedness' of social theory – society
theorising itself. Yet, remembering that the spatial is more than
the historically and spatially specific ontological arrangements
through which we live our lives, and by paying attention to the
specific technologies of manipulation and formation of everyday
spatial notions and practices, we can build a base in theory from
which to criticise these arrangements and to imagine other
arrangements, other worlds and, even, different experiences of
the lived body.

This base in theory allows a comparative stock-taking of
common spatial insights which are often noted but rarely followed
up. In each case-history, as often as not, what is 'discovered' in this
book has already been noted elsewhere, but not taken seriously
and passed over. The question becomes, what might have been
concluded by these previous researchers – in history, culture studies, economics, sociology, and politics – had the centrality of the
spatial to their studies been better acknowledged.

Several 'moments' in this discourse of space have been selected
which allow the relative stability of old stereotypes about places
and regions to be examined for change in case-histories. In
Canada the ideological notion of a 'True North Strong and Free'
is central to nationalist discourse and plays an important role in
cementing the far-flung regions of the country into a nation, and
more specifically a 'Northern Nation', wherein all share in a common cultural phantasmagoria which makes Canadians different

from Americans and similar to Scandinavians by virtue of their association with a northern frontier (Chapter Four).

In the United Kingdom another sort of north is found encapsulated in the popular notion of a 'North–South Divide' which gains currency in political discourse from time to time. Recently, it has been revived, despite many disclaimers about its appropriateness for describing the different levels of economic activity in the 'North' and the 'South' of England. It implies that economic activity, and indeed the very routines of daily life, are fundamentally different in the two zones, the 'North' and the 'South'. The questionable ascription of a difference in type, rather than just a difference of degree by the popular media will be examined (Chapter Five).

Additionally, the case of the British seaside resort of Brighton provides a view of popular leisure pursuits on the beach, the carnivalisation of that liminal zone between land and sea (Chapter Two). The Canadian honeymoon site of Niagara Falls provides a correspondingly faded geographical icon of the sublime which has undergone a series of historical mutations under the impact of the promotional efforts of opposed local interests (Chapter Three). Diverse 'windows' into each of these 'moments' will be used to lay bare the threads of these cases. A television serial like *Coronation Street* provides one keyhole view of the British North while the diffracted pattern of images of the 'True North Strong and Free' in nationalistic rhetoric provides a view of the continuing underdevelopment of Canadian North.

A noble line of Marxian social theorists – Adorno and Horkheimer, Marcuse, Mattelart among others – have often schizophrenically condemned in theory the mass cultures they participate in practically, preaching a 'pedagogy of displeasure' and ceding a deeper understanding of culture to more instrumental and commercial forces (Stam 1988). The case-histories below fall more into the line of analyses pioneered by Benjamin (1973a) which searches for the progressive potential in popular cultures. They draw on both statistical data (tourism surveys and regional socio-economic data) and primary historical sources such as popular literature, comic postcards, and cinema. These sources are used to paint a multi-faceted picture of not only the manner in which places have been 'labelled' but also how this has found expression and been actualised in locally-specific ways as *places-for* this or that in crowd practice, the built environment, and in regional policy. One text to be interpreted amongst others, census and other socio-economic data are 'questioned' for the hints and correlations they give regarding the empirically-verifiable elements of social spatialisation. However, they are not used to define or delimit the spatial phenomena to the empirical or the quantifiable. This seems the only prudent approach to a complex topic which in the past has escaped the attempts of any one language to 'pin it down' for dissection (for a survey see Shields 1986).

The cases provide an empirical basis from which the language and concepts necessary to a unified theorisation of the importance of the spatial is developed in a concluding, synthetic chapter. In this, the case-specific analyses are integrated into a wider theorisation of contemporary aspects of 'spatialisation'. With this conceptual framework in place, a discussion of the debates over changing spatialisations which have arisen in the context of discussions of community, nationalism, and modernity conclude the book.

This is an exploratory work, a book of reappraisals and re-readings of the taken-for-granted, which sets out to cover a great deal of terrain and to produce a workable mapping of the cultural importance of the spatial. The objective is not to provide a new, totalising theory. A spatial problematic does not displace problematics of class, gender, or ethnicity. Rather, it relativises most of the sweeping generalisations which have been extracted from limited case studies and reintroduces us to the complexities of the interplay between the different facets of social life. Problematics such as race, class, or gender are uninteresting and contribute little when isolated from the complex web of structures and arrangements in which people cope, cooperate, and compete in everyday life.

The concern is to create a space in academic discourse for a fuller discussion of the spatial than has previously been undertaken. As such, more questions will be raised than can be answered. Nor will this book provide a neat set of indicators to further the spatial technologies of this or that planning specialism. In fact, conclusions would be premature and would be to take these four case-histories rather too seriously. The theoretical elaboration of this project on social spatialisation has deliberately been kept to the simplest sketch so as not to foreclose on the case-histories which follow after the theoretical chapter. It is the subject of a forthcoming book. Nonetheless, grand theory and pompous hypotheses, modern, postmodern or of any other colour seem not to have been much help in the past. The fecundity of this speculative project for others will be a measure of its success.

EARLY APPROACHES: A REVIEW IN THE FORM OF CRITIQUE

The present work advances beyond earlier approaches to the meaning of the environment which have included work in the area of human geography, environmental psychology, and semiotics. It is important to recognise, however, the legacy of this positivistic, sociologically and culturally naive 'environmental image research' of the 1960s and 1970s and the contributions from hermeneutics and semiotics, even if there is space to outline only briefly this tradition of research which is well presented in Pocock and Hudson's *Images of the Urban Environment* (1978) or Gould and White's *Mental Maps* (1974, revised 1981) and critiqued in any number of other works (Jackson and Smith 1984). The focus here will be to re-evaluate several concrete examples of how social divisions are spatialised as geographic divisions and how places become 'labelled', much like deviant individuals. Habits such as spatialising important conceptual oppositions (for example putting one thing on the right, and another thing on the left, or classifying people by the places they come from: the 'right' or the 'wrong side of the tracks') have been studied as pathologically irrational forms of behaviour but will be shown to be an essential conceptual shorthand. These prejudices amount to a form of everyday knowledge which has been trivialised and dismissed by researchers interested in more 'serious' knowledge. Nonetheless it betrays a systematic 'disposition' towards the world (cf. Foucault 1980a; 1980b; 1982) coded into the framework of common sense.

There is a long tradition of sociologists and anthropologists interested in the spatial aspects of culture and society. Durkheim and Mauss devote sections in *Primitive Classification* (1963) to the study of 'social space' and the social nature of environmental perception and orientation. They argued that the territorialisation (Deleuze and Guattari 1976) of geographic space – its transformation from undifferentiated 'natural' space into the coded topography of 'civilised' territory – and its division into, for example, cardinal directions and areas, was culturally arbitrary and, in the case of the societies they studied, reflected social divisions (1963:10–12). The landscape is divided up in the image of its inhabitants. Giddens (1984) is only the latest in a long line that has included Sorokin (1943), Needham (1973) and Walter Benjamin (1978).

The generic term 'image' appears in connection with places in the English geographical literature as far back as the writings of Trowbridge in 1912, who commented upon some city dwellers' sense of orientation while others are 'subject to confusion as to direction when emerging from theatres [and] subways' (1912: 889). While some people appeared to have 'imaginary maps' centred upon the locations of their homes they became disoriented outside of their neighbourhood in unfamiliar areas; others appeared to have egocentric maps, seeing the city in relation to their personal position rather than the position of a particular landmark or point such as their home, and thus being less likely to become disoriented. Pocock and Hudson argue that this behavioural interest led inevitably to the study of environmental images: 'the modelling and understanding of spatial behaviour . . . a premise (tacit or explicit) of many image studies is that the environmental image underpins behaviour and forms a crucial link mediating between the environment and behaviour in that environment' (1978:9).

The behavioural focus led geographers to focus on individual perceptions and motivations using psychologistic research methods which proved difficult to generalise from. David Lowenthal's key 1967 article signalled an attempt to develop a geographical epistemology anchored in individual experience and imagination (Lowenthal 1967:260). While social custom was included in this research, it was custom as experienced by the individual. This methodological individualism, emphasising the uniqueness and subjective nature of environmental experience, was to burden 'environmental image research' with the problem of generalising from the individual to the social universe of shared meanings (Jackson and Smith 1984:21).

Despite their congruence with each other and with the world as it is, private milieus [sic] do diverge markedly among people in different cultures, for individuals within a social group, and for the same person as child and as adult, at various times and places, and in sundry moods.

(Lowenthal 1967:251)

Unlike the concern of this book, most work in geography has focused on this micro-scale: the 'private milieu' of an individual. Through the 1970s and even into the 1980s, research remained firmly within the orbit of the concerns of Lowenthal's benchmark essay, the contours of its assumptions and the parameters of its aspirations remaining unchallenged. A positivistic, schematic view of individuals' environmental surroundings emerged where there are as many images of any given scene as individuals apprehending it (Lowenthal 1967:249). Egocentric images were characterised as being in continuous flux but subject to saturation and fixation as a particular scene or set of surroundings became 'taken for granted' by a person. The issue of the social construction of categories of understanding into which objects would be sorted and dubbed with a culturally-inflected identity would have to wait for phenomenologically and hermeneutically-oriented researchers. The most devastating critique targetted the behaviourist assumptions that 'mental images' could be tied directly to observed, overt behaviour which researchers assumed provided a realm of 'solid, verifiable fact' for research. Mental images are only *hypothetical constructs* whose relation to behaviour is far from being a simple, univocal, causal linkage.

Lefebvre would argue that this typically visual approach merely reinforces the dominant logic and relations of capitalism (1981:Ch.3). It arbitrarily separates the individual (who is cast as 'Subject') from his or her environmental milieu (which is recast as 'Object'). Pocock and Hudson state this assumption clearly: 'Environment is taken to refer to anything external to the perceiver which influences, or might influence the perception process. . . . Awareness or interaction with the environment is achieved primarily by the visual sense experience' (1978:19). There are immediate consequences of such an ontology. The convenient separation of subject (perceiver) and object (perceived) led to laboratory research which substituted photographs for real environments. Environments are not analogous to images. Cosgrove (1982) has argued that they are interacted with, and one might

13

propose an even more radical emphasis by arguing that environments are participated in, being both an object of reason and a container of the thinking subject who does not so much 'interact with the whole environment' as participate in and depend on it. There is tremendous complicity between the body and environment and the two interpenetrate each other. So, what was really being referred to by 'image' in much of this research was the memory of a scene. More rarely was it the remembrance of an experienced environment, and even then, almost no attention was given to the socially-maintained *reputation* of a place or region which will be the focus of the case-histories below. A clear distinction must be made between research into people's existential participation in their environment and research into the culturally mediated reception of *representations* of environments, places, or regions which are 'afloat in society' as 'ideas in currency'. It is this distinction which separates the present work from this positivist tradition in geography.

In the best of this research any 'mental images' of places are considered to be conditioned by the mediation and intervention of conceptual systems, normative conditioning and socialisation. This 'cultural geography' (Claval 1980), by emphasising the development of a sense of place and territorial attachment, encouraged a proliferation of research on cognitive representation (Relph 1976a). Images of particular environments or places serve both referential functions (as memory aids, or frameworks for reconstructing events) and *anticipatory* functions (serving as a guide to future encounters at or in given sites and places). 'Contrary to what is often stated, studies on representations do not focus on the particular characteristics of images, but show instead that a place is nothing by itself, but depends on other places and practices to imbue it with meaning' (Bailly 1986:83).

The most interesting of the work on environmental images, from the point of view of the present study, comes from the research directed at establishing the degree to which and the manner in which fancy, fantasy, and wishful thinking play a role in the production of images of the environment. Appleyard's research provides the example of a European engineer in Ciudad Guyana who, although having no difficulty outlining the layout of the settlement, inserted a non-existent but much hoped for railway between his steel mill in the interior and the coastal port in his sketch map (1970a:112). Here projected plans and fantasy 're-places observation to extend the image from the datum of the known world to *terrae incognitae*' (Allen 1976 cited in Pocock and Hudson 1978:63). Place-images take on a prescriptive nature (Pocock and Hudson 1978:62–63).[1] But this predictive ability is strictly with the cultural context of the taken for granted logic of the structure of the world or city (for example, the 'right' and 'wrong' side of the tracks in many North American railroad towns). The seventeenth-century European presumed that the Nile ran East–West, in 'symmetrical sympathy' with the known course of the Danube (Pocock and Hudson 1978:63). In this manner, new experiences of new places are aligned with past experiences and old, known verities.

Phenomenological research into people's involvement with places and the 'lifeworld' explicitly attempted to overcome the subject–object dualism and discounting of emotional meaning imposed by positivistic approaches. Relph (1976b) incorporates Heidegger's ideas of 'place', and 'dwelling' (1968a), in his outline of people's 'deep' empathy with their place of dwelling, where they feel 'at home' within an environment of 'placelessness' and alien-ation which emerges from the attitude of domination over the world and a concentration on control over the environment. The inter-relationship of people's lives and the place in which they are lived is exemplified by Vidal de la Blanche's *genre de vie*, 'a lifeworld rooted in a particular land [*pays*]'. In such a relationship of 'total and unselfconscious involvement ... the person and place are indisociable [sic]' (Relph 1976a:78) becoming submerged or blurred in a continuous dialectical interchange where a person seeks to identify with and through his or her environment.

Yi-Fu Tuan has argued that this pre-reflective lifeworld of the immediate is in 'pre-intellectual' and authentic (1977). But, meaning has been widely argued to arise out of a linguistic constel-lation of words (Derrida 1974). If this is so, how can meaning exist prior to what certainly appears to be an 'intellectual' level of cognition? Initial, pre-reflective experience, while having sense (*sens*) is not *in se* 'meaning-full'. It is received perceptions or 'experience', but this is immediately structured as it is taken up in concepts organised through language.

The strong emphasis on the interpretative component of individual understandings of the world implicit in this humanistic approach de-emphasises the formative and compelling nature of social surveillance and 'discipline' (cf. Michel Foucault, see pp. 38–46). Harvey denounces the phenomenology of human geography as parochial (1973:24) by arguing that it cannot comprehend the objective social forces that lead to the destruction of place. But this 'easy' critique is anticipated in Heidegger's 'phenomenology of being' which rejects the search for a priori foundations of knowledge such as 'objective social forces' for a focus on understanding human existence and experience within the context of a historically constituted social world. Van Paassen argues that the implication of such an *existential* orientation for geographers is that

> the so-called 'spatial order' in fact is a societal order, which can be interpreted only as a social product resulting from the complex interplay of human perceptions, objectives and capacities, institutional rules and material conditions connected with human and physical material substances in space.
>
> (Van Paassen 1976:333)

Human geography is therefore an appropriate area of socio-logically-informed investigation: Ley speaks of the 'personality of place' being derived from the coherence of 'intersubjective' experience: 'any habitually interacting group of people convey a character to the place they occupy which is immediately apparent to an outsider, though unquestioned and taken-for-granted by habituées' (1977:508). 'Intersubjectivity' refers to the shared character of lived experience and meaning. But as such, it presupposes that experience has common characteristics across groups of subjects despite admitting the lack of 'a single, objective world; rather there is a plurality of worlds as many as there are attitudes and intentions of man' (Relph 1970:194). This assumption, while appropriate to initial investigations, now deserves refinement through critique and empirical investigation.

How is it that such meanings come to be shared? Is it through *socialisation* to group norms and conventions of meaning? Or is it through a environmental version of *labelling* whereby a place is 'labelled' as the place for such and such activities (e.g. worship of a local deity held to be responsible for crop success). As such it might acquire something of the meanings of those activities

16

(harvest, the fragility of horticulture) and may stand-in as a 'symbol' of those activities. Possibly, such intersubjectively shared meanings are acquired through mundane and functional processes of behaviour and activity (a behaviourist hypothesis)? Perhaps subjective experience is incommensurable and idiosyncratic, acquiring its propositional form only by being 'forced through' the mediating and structuring grid of linguistic systems of meaning (a structural–linguistic hypothesis)?

However, geographical phenomenology has naively subscribed to an eighteenth-century view that language provides a relatively unproblematic medium for the expression of sense experience. It is only a matter of lifting the veil of 'taken-for-granted-ness', to 'see things as if for the first time.' Thus Pickles's arguments for the adoption of a pure Husserlian phenomenology in geography presuppose a unique datum of human experience which remains unestablished in his arguments, against the by now quite important weight of psychological, linguistic, and ethnographic evidence which supports the postulate of a multiplicity of different frames of reference tempered only by the *force* of normative socialisation which structures and 'frames' experience for us (see Shields 1986).

The importance of language as the medium (if not the mediator) of any intersubjective meaning moves us to a consideration of hermeneutics which will establish the background research on the transfer of meaning. Its relevance here will be to the manner by which stereotyping images of places or regions are shared and communicated between people. Hermeneutics is closely related to the humanists' interest in subjective interpretations of the meaning of spaces and places. In its modern sense, it derives from Dilthey's rejection of Husserl's bracketing of everyday experience in favour of a method of understanding the world of experience which takes account of the fact that meaning is contextually located *in* the world, not found floating around as a transcendental essence outside of experience (Dilthey 1900). No understanding can be 'pre-suppositionless' but occurs through and with the mediation of past human experience in much the same manner that one might interpret a book, understanding the meaning of the words of the text through a reflective reference to one's own experience. The meaning is thus given to the text by the reader, the author's meaning is not something that resides within the book itself, otherwise there would never be disagreement.

Places and their images are not scientific 'objects' (assuming such things exist, even in the natural sciences). Place-images, and our views of them, are produced historically, and are actively contested. There is no whole picture that can be 'filled in' since the perception and filling of a gap lead to the awareness of other gaps. The 'filling in' of gaps is itself part of a particular cultural project, which must itself be included in our cultural 'mosaic', but *its* new presence raises new questions about, for example, why we are concerned about filling in gaps anyway. And, if individual place-images or even an entire 'culture' are not objects to be described, neither are they a unified corpus of symbols and meanings that can be definitively interpreted once and for all for every person. Culture is contested, temporal, and emergent (see Clifford and Marcus 1986:18–19).

The hermeneutic concern with the meaning-laden world of purposeful beings is thus precisely a concern with the phenomenologists' 'life-world' of everyday experience (Gregory 1978b:60). But here theorisation is regarded as the generation of what Giddens calls 'meaning-frames' (1976:143) which are *necessary* conditions for any understanding. Thus, the point of view of the observer cannot be bracketed out as is attempted in phenomenology. As opposed to a phenomenological suspension of the referential framework of conscious understanding to seek a pre-conscious or intuitive level of comprehension, hermeneutics advocates the reciprocal interrogation which comes about between two equally accepted frames of reference (Gregory 1978b:60).

> The interpreter is involved with but not enclosed by the life-world he [sic] is trying to understand . . . it presupposes that there is at least some common ground between the two, an arena in which the encounter can take place . . . the meaning ascribed to the one [meaning frame] constantly mediates the meaning ascribed to the other.
>
> (Gregory 1978b:61)

This occurs through reflexive circulation between subject and object, observer and observer – what Heidegger called the 'hermeneutic circle' between the two referential meaning frames (1986b). This takes place through the media of the body (tangible experience) and language (communicated experience). A *specifi-*

cation of discourses thus becomes essential. Who speaks? For whom and for what reasons? This is thus much more than a matter of making carefully limited social science claims. It is thoroughly *historicist* and *self-reflexive.* In the 'Introduction' to a recent anthology, James Clifford points out that this specification of discourses can be observed as a general 'dialogical' trend in ethnographies, built up as dialogues between participants, informants and ethnographers. This leads directly to the pioneering work of Mikhail Bakhtin (1981; 1984) whose categories of dialogism, heteroglossia, and carnival suggest a method of polyvalent analyses which leads beyond dogmatic, economistic, and totalising cultural theory:

> These fictions of dialogue have the effect of transforming the
> 'cultural' text (a ritual, an institution, a life history, or any
> unit of typical behaviour to be described or interpreted) into
> a speaking subject, who sees as well as is seen, who evades,
> argues, probes back . . . the proper referent of any account is
> not only a represented 'world'; now it is specific instances of
> discourse . . . [which] locates cultural interpretations in many
> sorts of reciprocal contexts, and it obliges writers to find
> diverse ways of rendering negotiated realities as multi-
> subjective, power-laden, and incongruent. In this view,
> 'culture' is always relational, an inscription of communicative
> processes that exist, historically, *between* subjects in relations of
> power
> (Dwyer 1977; Tedlock 1979).

> Dialogical modes are not, in principle, autobiographical;
> they need not lead to hyper self-consciousness or
> self-absorption. As Bakhtin (1981) has shown, dialogical
> processes proliferate in any complexly represented discursive
> space . . . . Many voices clamour for expression . . .
> monophonic authority is questioned, revealed to be
> characteristic of a science that has claimed to *represent* cultures.
> (Clifford and Marcus 1986:14–15)

This hermeneutic mode of investigation leads to an 'active dia-logue' between different constructions of reality. In making one aware of the 'preconditions built into our social practice and organisations that enable us or hinder us in understanding one

19

another' (Gadamer 1975:315 cited in Gregory 1978b:61) hermeneutics is a 'two-edged sword . . . cutting through illusions about
life-worlds on one side and through illusions about ourselves on
the other' (Gregory 1978b:61). Rather than regarding itself as the
privileged, scientific method, hermeneutics is proposed as the
basic mode by which people appropriate their world. Thus, it
ultimately argues that it transcends the division of the natural and
human sciences, the former being involved with a dialectic of
theory and observation (Lefebvre 1946) and the latter with a
double hermeneutic between social science theory, or people's
representations of reality to themselves (one pole of the dialectic),
and their world itself (the alternate pole).

The question of shared meaning thus re-emerges as a central
problem which will be considered in the next chapter. How is it
that 'reality' is constructed socially by and for us such that
meanings and meaningful experiences the emotional affect of a
place can be communicated? The work of Geertz, an anthro-
pologist, is relevant here and provides an important bridge into
European *semiology* (below) by way of its North American variant,
semiotics. Geertz sees anthropological work as essentially a 'semiotics of society' (literally, the study of social signifying practices and
meaning, but see pp. 22–24). In questioning the existence of
'culture' as an independent variable, he has focused on the
methods of ethnographic observation and description, arguing
that the diverse behaviour exhibited by people in social situations
cannot be taken as merely data for a hypothetical cultural entity or
process. In a famous line, he says, 'what we call our data are really
our own constructions of other people's constructions of what they
and their compatriots are up to' (1973:9). The characteristic
hermeneutic circle of social science or the 'double hermeneutic',
as Giddens would have it (1976:79ff.), involves both the 'entering
and grasping the frame of meaning adopted by the actors
themselves in the production of social life, and reconstituting
these within new frames of meaning according to the analyst's
technical conceptual schemes' (Jackson and Smith 1984:38).

According to Geertz's hermeneutic approach, the ethnographer's task, and by extension, the task of all those interested in
the constitution of meaning, is the inscription of social discourse
writing down or documenting communicative transactions.
'Ephemeral observations take on new meaning through the very

process of inscription, leading to the production of a text which can then be subjected to examination, revision and interpretation; in other words, hermeneutics.' Rather than as functional activities, social action must be understood as 'an image, a fiction, a model or a metaphor, with "dramatic shape", "metaphoric content" and "social context"' (Geertz 1973 cited in Jackson and Smith 1984: 39). Activities are symbolic as well as functional and must be 'read' as such. They provide, in their organisation of bodies and action, gratuitous and pleasing 'metasocial commentary' for their participants: stories they tell themselves about themselves (Geertz 1973:448; Cohen 1986:10–12).

Geertz's use of the term 'social semiotics' is, however, a loose one. His appropriation of the action of 'reading' to describe the activities of the ethnographer is metaphoric. In the following section, a more rigorous, technically sophisticated use of such terminology will be encountered in the substantial and active field of *semiology* where an entire ontology and epistemology of social action and meaning has been elaborated in linguistics and philosophy, *outside* of the social sciences, to the extent that it has challenged and now begun to displace the dominant positivist bias in social science research.

Returning to the work of Clifford, the problem across the self-proclaimed 'interpretative social sciences' in particular but also for any interpretation of social science data is that

'Translations' of culture, however subtle or inventive in
textual form, take place within relations of 'weak' and 'strong'
languages that govern the international flow of knowledge . . .
still very much a one-way street . . . notions of global
hegemony may miss the reflexive, inventive dimensions of
ethnicity and cultural contact (. . . all narratives of lost
authenticity and vanishing diversity as self-confirming
allegories . . .)

(Clifford and Marcus 1986:22)

He continues,

A major consequence of . . . theoretical movements . . . has
been to dislodge the ground from which persons and groups
securely represent others . . . . We ground things, now, on a
moving earth. There is no longer any place of overview

(mountain top) from which to map human ways of life, no Archimedian point from which to represent the world. Mountains are in constant motion. So are islands: for one cannot occupy, unambiguously, a bounded cultural world from which to journey out and analyze other cultures. Human ways of life increasingly influence, dominate, parody, translate and subvert one another. Cultural analysis is always enmeshed in global movements of difference and power.

(Clifford and Marcus 1986:22)

The question of the meaning itself or *semiosis of the environment*, as opposed to the processes of its perception, has been addressed as the question of *environmental semiotics*.[2] In general, work in this vein has focused on architecture and, more recently, the urban environment. The basis of the field is found in work on the semiology of objects made famous by Barthes's semiological 'readings' of the mythologies of varied objects from the curvaceous lines of the Citroën Diane automobile and the connotations of the Eiffel Tower (1972).[3]

Object semiology has been a focus of interest since the late 1950s following the seminal work of Lévi-Strauss (1958). He suggested that symbolic objects, rituals, and myths could be analysed following the model of the structural linguistics developed by Saussure. The heart of this system is that the meaning of specific signs or objects is dependent on the relation to an entire system of meanings rather than related to their own essence (as criticised above). A single sign or object has no meaning in isolation from the overall system.

Barthes suggested the 'universal semantisation of usage' whereby the use of an object is transformed into a sign for that use (1964:106). Objects acquire symbolic status signifying not only their function but also the context of their use, the social relations through which they are used or operated, and the people who commonly use a given object may come to be associated with it and it with them. The same insight could be applied to a distant place. Particularly beautiful places that people go to for a vacation become signs of the condition which allows one to travel to such a place, 'function signs' (Krampen 1979:6) of leisure. The same place, at one and the same time, can be made to *symbolise* a whole variety of social statuses, personal conditions, and social attitudes.

This 'polysemy' adds a note of ambiguity to the meaning of both words and places which can acquire contrasting connotations. Jerusalem could symbolise both a religious centre of the Judaeo-Christian world and a contested, occupied city. Whereas once such separate meanings would be linked to different viewpoints and different individuals, many people now 'see both sides' of this pair of conflicting images. This is one mark of the equivocality of the age of mass media which some commentators have called 'post-modern': a 'decline of the great narratives' which unified sets of univocal interpretations and images Marxism, Christianity and so on (Lyotard 1980; 1984). But disappointingly for our purposes, these simple insights into place-images are not explored in this literature because research has focused on the process of perception at the point of individual encounters with objects endowed with cultural meanings, rather than considering the symbolism of places. Nonetheless, the notion of the 'semantisation of usage' is important and has a long association with the environment. Krampen (1979) notes that two paradigmatic reductions characterise the variety of approaches to first 'object semiology' and second, attempts to formulate an 'environmental semiology'. On the one hand the reduction of objects to signs, and on the other hand, the reduction of signs to objects. These two poles may be found across both the general work on the semiotics of objects and more specialised work on the semiotics of architecture and the built environment even in pre-semiotic work in the modern theories of aesthetics.

The former semiotic approach may be criticised as being an idealism in its reduction of objects to signs. There is no epistemological origin of meaning, which is reduced to an interpretative process. One can argue, for example, that meaning 'reflects' material reality in answer to the thorny question of how one 'knows' reality. Resnikow (1968) faces this problem by arguing that the solution is in the semantics of any sign, which must be acknowledged as a dialectic of both meaning and sign meaning, neither of which exist independently of the subjective reflection of objective material reality. But this only re-poses the question, this time in terms of the question of representation. The basic problem, as Krampen argues, remains the mentalistic approach where the material status of objects is sacrificed for their symbolic status, existing only in the mind of the user/interpreter which

Krampen sees as a problem for pragmatics (1979:49). No connection is maintained between the mental level of perceived meaningfulness in a setting with the actual performative and functional, pragmatic, characteristics of the environment at hand and one's involvement with it. The result is a reduction to a thorough-going subjectivism of either cognitive maps or utopias.

Turning to the second group of semiological approaches (reduction of signs to objects) we find a risk of falling into an empiricistic materialism by deriving 'meaning from the function of the object, thereby prejudging the extra-semiotic analysis of the historical and humanistic aspects of the problem' (Krampen 1979:20). The development of a semiology of objects within the framework of a general semiology has also been hampered by the difficulties and shortcomings of applying a semiological analysis to objects in general through a 'linguistic analogy'. However, Rossi-Landi (1968; 1972; 1975) suggests that rather than forcing a reduction, considering the *homology* which exists between the production of linguistic and non-linguistic artefacts yields a better, middle-ground, base for theory-building and provides insights into the varying levels of complexity of various types and scales of human artefact. This approach is particularly well suited to objects created with an instrumental purpose in mind. However, landscapes do not result from a unified instrumental action, but reflect different historical uses and projects 'sedimented' in any given site or region. For this reason, while this semiology of objects furnishes precedents (such as the notions of semantisation and trans-functionalisation) semiotics appears as more of a way-station than a terminus in the search for a method by which to approach the problem of the images of places and spaces.

SYNOPSIS

In this survey of literature for precedents to guide the project at hand we have been slowly driven entirely out of the field of geography. In their pursuit of theoretical elegance in the form of a 'Taylorism of perception', the positivist geography of 'mental images' and 'cognitive maps' perpetuate the administrative bias of the social sciences identified by Foucault. They illustrate what Rose has called a modernist Neo-Kantianism (1985) in their methodologism. Implicitly or explicitly, the natural sciences are taken as their model and such social sciences do not question the conditions of their own existence. Like the positivistic research, the phenomenological literature displayed a crude grasp of social-level processes which intercede as mediators of meanings, and assumed a priori meanings and identities in an environment which was argued to be coded and ordered by social mechanisms. The meaning of particular places is a compendium of intersubjective and cultural interpretations over time. Thus, a place might go from being considered a resort to being an industrial centre. Areas of the world go from being considered distant, exotic and sacred to being mere intercontinental junctions for airline travellers where the indigenous, sacred elements have been moved into museums, secularised, or turned into a popular museum.

The importance of language as a medium and mediator by which intersubjective meanings are shared and amended led to an examination of hermeneutic approaches which stress the interpretative element of narratives about, and accounts of, places and regions. In particular, it offered a set of insights by which the 'polyvocality' of place-images – Lowenthal's problem of the multi-coloured subjectivity of ideas about the world – are mediated by normative discourses and power relations. In the chapters that follow, people will be argued to ascribe to particular discourses about places as a mark of their 'insider status' in particular groups and communities. This group affiliation through knowledge of discourses which locate places and areas as particular types of places, with particular relations to other places and people (outsiders) does not restrict the development of personal views of 'the real situation'.

The concept of 'transfunctionalisation' developed in the semiotic literature holds promise. Although it has not been applied to the problem of place-images it was seen to have clear potential for furnishing insights into the manner by which, for example, the resort of Brighton could become a sign of leisure, indolence, and ultimately, illicit sex.

Research on the question of meaning in the environment is characterised over the last thirty years by a steady trend to problematise meaning itself. Both the manner in which we represent this meaning to ourselves in personal 'mental images' and the researchers' representation of people's perceptions as 'cognitive maps' has been called into question as research has become more sophisticated. As Dreyfus and Rabinow have pointed out in a paraphrase of Foucault: 'if the human sciences claim to study human activities, then the human sciences, unlike the natural sciences, must take account of those human activities which make possible their own disciplines' (1982:163).

In general the above approaches involve the reduction of places and spaces first to context-less assemblages of objects and then to a grid of meaning (see for example Pocock's work (1982) on images of Durham cathedral). The object of study, the holistic place or space itself, is destroyed in this Cartesian reduction and fragmentation. While demonstrating something of the mechanics of perception and delineating the most common meanings associated with a particular place or landscape, this does not help one in understanding the manner in which the range of images reflects, and is evidence for, an all-pervasive logic of social spatialisations by which places, views, and scenes are linked to feelings, ideas, and political and cultural ideologies.

The hermeneutic approach substitutes the actor's point of view of the significance of the background practices for an 'objective' grid of the positivist social sciences. This excludes background cultural practices (by which that grid is itself produced by socio-cultural activities) and runs into equally fundamental methodological difficulties. A pure hermeneutics would be inadequate if one is striving for a more broadly based, sociological, explanation. The self-understanding and awareness of social actors leaves much to be desired (as has been pointed out by a generation of Marxian social scientists). 'One cannot suppose that the actors are lucidly or even dimly aware of what their activity means ... that is, how their activity serves to further a complex strategical situation in a given society' (Foucault 1980b:93).

Such a hermeneutic would thus be unable to explain the reasons which people ascribe to collective projects and ideologies. Why do people use stereotyped images of places as a conceptual shorthand and as metaphors to illustrate their arguments? What is this system of place-images which we ascribe to? To develop an understanding of this, we must turn our attention beyond geography and even hermeneutics to locate theorists who might have previously attempted to effect a synthesis between the study of social meaning and geographical perception. The next chapter presents an 'interpretative analytics' which attempts to resolve the methodological problems of trying to theorise cultural constructs from the inside-out, as it were, where the investigator is implicated and ensnared as a bearer of the myths and images that are to be investigated.

NOTES

1. This is not only part of the simplifying logic which accompanies the mind's schematisation of the environment. Rather than being confined to the learning phase when a place is first encountered, it is permanent and universal, with the 'good-figure' tendency increasing with familiarity with the locale and the sophistication of cognitive maps drawn by respondents (see Beazley 1949:549–633; Johns 1965). Perception therefore includes a degree of 'reduction in uncertainty' and the attempted establishment of predictive ability (Gibson 1970).

2. There are few complete monographs and only scattered articles in the field of architectural and environmental semiotics. Krampen (1979) refers his readers to the pioneering efforts of Gamberini, Koenig, and Scalvini, who have written in Italian on the subject, as well as the more recent work of Donald Preziosi, *Architecture, Language and Meaning* (1979) and *The Semiotics of the Built Environment* (1981). The field is developing, however. Nonetheless, the emphasis has been on technical problems of syntax rather than the question of semantics which will be central to this project.

   In English, the major works have also focused on architecture (perhaps due to the opportunities presented by the ongoing methodological vacuum in architectural criticism) as represented by Geoffrey Broadbent's 1981 edited collection *Signs, Symbols and Architecture*. However, after this date work in the field has dried up rapidly, due firstly to the criticism mounted by Marxian social theorists of the semiologists' apolitical focus on the mechanics of meaning rather than the welfare implications of various communications media; and secondly because its highly technical and algebraic discourse (represented by the school led by Greimas 1976) was not well received by the North American social science 'audience' and their publishers who opted instead to focus on the eclectic and iconoclastic research possibilities derived from a vulgarisation of Derrida's (rigourous) methodology of 'deconstructionism'. This term later became almost a slogan for American linguistic pragmatists such as Rorty (1979).

3. The task of semiology has been the investigation of the mechanisms of signs operating in human communication, later generalised to include phenomena transcending the process of intentional communication (generally referred to as 'indices' e.g. fingerprints, tracks). Hence, environmental semiotics is concerned with elucidating the kind of meanings that are connected to a landscape by what kind of mechanisms. How, for example, is meaning 'injected' into or associa-

ted with environments and received or 'decoded' by people. Such a mechanics is intrinsically connected to human activity and thus is not simply a question for philosophy but constitutes one field of research for the 'human sciences'. Ferdinand de Saussure coined the term 'semiology' around the turn of the century to indicate this human science, which he considered as a branch of social psychology. Although there were perhaps hints at the essential features of Saussure's system before him, he is credited with being the first to bring together a non-essentialist semantics in his lectures (compiled by his students as *Cours de linguistique générale*, see Saussure 1971).

Chapter One

ALTERNATIVE GEOGRAPHIES
OF MODERNITY

Do Kepler and Tycho see the same thing in the East at Dawn?
(N.R. Hanson 1958, *Patterns of Discovery*)

Space was understood by Kant to be one dimension of all perception, the other being time (1965; 1968). For Durkheim and Mauss (1963) the division of geographical space into near and far, quadrants and places was one of the first forms of 'primitive classification' underpinning all social division. Whereas most geographers and psychologists have emphasised the individual and subjective nature of spatial images and 'cognitive maps', the focus of attention here is the logic of common spatial perceptions accepted in a culture. This interest directs us away from perception studies of the subjective and idiosyncratic to the social level of collective myth and the culturally-regular/regulated affects accompanying spatial concepts.

Properly social divisions and cultural classifications are often spatialised, that is expressed using spatial metaphors or descriptive spatial divisions. As an ensemble, these are incorporated into 'imaginary geographies'. In these recodings of geographic space, sites become associated with particular values, historical events, and feelings. Often, elements of imaginary geographies are used interchangeably as metaphors for more abstract distinctions. Sites become symbols (of good, evil, or nationalistic events), and in tandem with other sites can be taken up in metaphors to express (gendered) states of mind, of affairs and different value positions (for example 'It will be his *Waterloo*'). Bachelard (1958) and Tuan (1976; 1977) call this 'topophilia': humans' affective ties with their environment which couples sentiment with place. These metaphors are central to the folk wisdom of even this most rationalised

29

.a. California is often referred to as 'Lotus Land', or for Central Canadians we shall see that the North is a 'True North Strong and Free' – not *just* north but a zone of the social imaginary: an unconquerable wilderness and zone of white purity. This tendency to use spatial and geographical metaphors to describe states of mind (Bachelard 1958) is exploited politically and commercially. Phrases such as Winston Churchill's 'Iron Curtain' to describe the division of Europe into Soviet East and capitalist West or 'In deepest, darkest Africa' and 'the Far East' have a potent connotative kick which alludes to the emotional importance of entire systems of spatial images which function as frameworks of cultural order. The spatial is thus an area of intense cultural activity. Thus I will be arguing that the empirical datum of geographical space is mediated by an edifice of social constructions which become guides for action and constraints upon action, not just idiosyncratic or pathological fantasies.[1] In what follows, I will try to clarify the theoretical basis of the case-histories and explain more precisely what spatialisation includes. In the process, four separate 'parentheses' will be opened in which antecedents to this work will be examined for precedents. While these interjections can in no way provide a sufficient introduction to the spatial aspects of the work of Bourdieu, Foucault, Lefebvre, and British Realists such as Andrew Sayer, they are included to 'position' the theory of social spatialisation with respect to structuralist, genealogical, Marxist and realist approaches.

SOCIAL SPATIALISATION

The previous chapter set the stage for a fully *sociological* theory of the space. But as a result of the wide range of conflicting usages of the word, 'space' will be largely avoided as a term, despite its prominence. Here, 'a space' denotes a limited area: a site, zone, or place characterised by specific social activities with a culturally given identity (name) and image. While the acculturated 'social space' that we have been considering is usually described just as 'space', this usage has introduced numerous linguistic difficulties (see Soja 1980; Sack 1980; Lefebvre 1974). As Soja has pointed out, 'space' is a difficult term because of its broad meanings and wide semantic field (1980; see also the earlier and somewhat neglected work of Sorokin 1943; Kolaja 1969). It is also difficult because space is one of the 'unsaid' dimensions of epistemological and ontological structures (Sack 1980) – to question 'space' is to question one of the axes along which reality is conventionally defined. I use the term *social spatialisation* to designate the ongoing social construction of the spatial at the level of the social imaginary (collective mythologies, presuppositions) as well as interventions in the landscape (for example, the built environment). This term allows us to name an object of study which encompasses both the cultural logic of the spatial and its expression and elaboration in language and more concrete actions, constructions and institutional arrangements.

Social spatialisation is thus a rubric under which currently separated objects of investigation will be brought together to demonstrate their inter-connectedness and coordinated nature. This perspective recodes disparate problematics to show that anomalies and paradoxes in social theory that resulted because of numerous dichotomies and dualisms (public–private; base–superstructure; economy–culture) can be made intelligible under a unified framework. Rather than discovering new phenomena, then, what will follow in later chapters will be a *rediscovery* which, it is hoped, will give new vigour to established problematics.

But this project is not a simple structuralist bricolage where details and analogies are disguised as analysis (Schleiser 1988: 144–153). Although the case-histories below appeal to judgements of their intelligibility rather than adequacy, unlike the structuralist project, I am not seeking a coherent and unified structure, nor a timeless structure of the human mind (cf. Lévi-Strauss 1964:18; 1966:346; 1971:571). In the case-histories below, the use which will be made of theoretical constructions like social spatialisation is as heuristic aids in the face of local conditions which diverge from the generalities of grand theory – Marxist, structuralist or anything else – rather than as an authoritative, closed theory of space. Rather than constructing a new discourse about place and space, the interest here is in the pre-constructed cultural discourses about sites. And, beyond an interest in the relations established between sites, we will be assessing how they came into those relationships and under what authority, and by which groups, raising questions of power that lie behind conventions. Because they are contested by a host of minor discourses and spatialisations, the positions and oppositions between sites and regions

31

are neither unequivocal nor universal (contra Lévi-Strauss 1958: 235). To distinguish the project at hand from its structuralist antecedents, I will prefer the looseness of a term like 'formations' rather than 'structures' with all their implied stability, hierarchies and rationality (cf. Lévi-Strauss 1958:303-351).

Bourdieu's Habitus: spatial practices as cultural structures

An illustration of these problems is found in the work of Bourdieu which provides an early example of addressing the spatial as part of a cultural 'structure'. Spatialisation includes elements which are prior to perception (for example the postcard-borne place-myths of Brighton) but it is nonetheless subject to being amended by the uneven experiences of reality (the disappointing experience of the town). John Urry (1982) has referred to this as a 'duality of structure' argument. Besides Bourdieu's theory of *habitus*, another example is Giddens's structure–agency dichotomy (1979). This duality gives rise to problems when Bourdieu tries to describe *habitus* as producing different class patterns of taste and conduct while at the same time arguing that *habitus* is continually reformed and modified by everyday experience.

Bourdieu's work is based on the structuralist postulate of Cassirer (1945) that 'experience is a system' and consequently the 'objective world' is constructed through the imposition of cultural categories on reality. Perception thus takes place through a mediating value-framework which differentiates the facticity of the environment in which one lives (cf. Bourdieu 1968:682–684).

In his well-known *Outline of a Theory of Practice*, Bourdieu argues the necessity of mediating between theory and practice. He calls for a focus on the 'practical logic' or *opus operatum* of the habits and predispositions arising in everyday life rather than the reified abstractions constructed by researchers (1972). People do not simply obey rules in their everyday activities but form habits and acquire views through a complex process of experience and incremental adjustment. With *habitus* Bourdieu explores the area Giddens discusses under the heading of the 'routinisation' of social action. Bourdieu attempts to reject the social science view of people conditioned by determining ideologies and false consciousness, which are in turn determined by an 'economic base'. This classical Marxian formula is transposed to a new position which situates 'ideology' at the level of practices and habitual attitudes as sets of 'embodied ideas'.[2] These are not expressed but are sedimented in the people's 'styles' of getting about their daily lives.

All the actions performed in a space constructed in this way are immediately qualified symbolically and function as so many structural exercises through which is built up practical mastery of the fundamental schemes, which organise . . . practices and representations: going in and coming out, filling and emptying, opening and shutting, going leftwards and going rightwards, going westwards and going eastwards . . . . The mind is a metaphor of the world of objects which is itself but an endless circle of mutually reflecting metaphors. All the symbolic manipulations of body experience, starting with displacements within a mythically structured space, eg. the movements of going in and coming out, tend to impose the *integration* of the body space with cosmic space by grasping in terms of the same concepts (and naturally at the price of great laxity in logic) the relationship between man and the natural world.

> (Bourdieu, 1977:91)

Bourdieu gives the name '*habitus*' to this everyday canon: a 'socially constituted system of cognitive and motivating structures' (Bourdieu and Passeron 1977:76). *Habitus* is the 'deep structure' of personality formed by socialisation but Bourdieu leaves it tantalisingly vague, even while devoting considerable verbiage to definitions of it. This has engendered much criticism and also confusion about his core concepts. Thus he calls it a complex of systems of durable, transposible *dispositions* or 'generative principles' by which improvisations in daily routines are made (Bourdieu 1977:81–82). These 'structured structures . . . principles of the generation and structuring of practices and representations which can be objectively regulated and regular without being . . . the product of obedience to rules' (Bourdieu 1977:72).

One wonders about Bourdieu's redundant terminology of 'structured structures' and whether structures are not *always* both structured and structuring. Indeed, Bourdieu draws attention to the mediating role of such structures which he inserts between the determining, need-driven facts of reality (generally referred to as 'structure' in English debates) and individual actions in his schema. *Habitus* is thus both a postulated (mediating) structure and Bourdieu's solution to the structure-agency tension. However, this introduction of a 'mediating structure' is only one step in a reductio ad infinitum. For Bourdieu is really offering a 'bandage' for the despotic overdeterminism of sociological approaches to the individual. Any number of mediating screens still fails to solve the dilemma of this determinism; fails to deal with the problem of causal determinism.[3]

The strategy-generating principles of the *habitus* as a 'structure of consciousness' (Pitt-Rivers 1971) enable agents to cope with unforeseen and ever-changing situations by providing a panoply of things to say or not to say, things to do or not to do in social situations (Bourdieu and Passeron 1977:76). Bourdieu characterises this as 'invention within limits'. *Habitus* is, then, a set of algorithms (1984:424).

> The schemes of the habitus, the primary forms of
> classification, owe their specific efficacy to the fact that they
> function below the level of consciousness and language,
> beyond the reach of introspective scrutiny or control by the
> will. Orienting practices practically, they embed what some
> would mistakenly call *values* in the most automatic gestures or
> the apparently most insignificant techniques of the body –
> ways of walking or blowing one's nose, ways of eating or
> talking.
>
> (Bourdieu 1984:466)

These algorithms are not internalised in a simple manner; rather, they are continually 'adjusted to the particular conditions in which . . . [they] are constituted' (Bourdieu 1977:95). This internalisation is thus mediated by both the reality of a person's class or ethnic position as well as their subjective expectations. Often 'power relations are perceived not for what they . . . are but in a form which renders them legitimate' (Bourdieu and Passeron 1977:xiii). Drawing now on Weber as well as Marx, this misrecognition (*'méconnaissance'*) contributes to the efficacy of *symbolic* modes of domination. Thus *habitus* is inculcated primarily by early childhood experiences in a family of a particular social class (although no connections are established between childhood experience and class). Yet it is subsequently transformed by

34

experience. Furthermore, expectations are adjusted to match the objective probability of their attainment.[4] This *habitus* is durable but also malleable. It is thus difficult to establish what difference this durability makes, and under what circumstances *habitus* is transformed. To what extent is Bourdieu's class personality stable or plastic? Bourdieu never deals with the question of gender: yet the different stances of men and women in a given situation – the habitual performance of social position which is paradigmatically '*habitus*' – is as clearly defined as the different 'performances' of members of different classes would be. This androgynous aspect of *habitus* makes it appear, however much Bourdieu protests to the contrary, external to the real concerns and dynamics of individuals relating to other individuals of different sexes, ethnic groups, class fractions et cetera. Connell argues that the entire notion of the 'reproduction of social relations' is a chimera whether social relations are recoded as 'learned class habitus' or not: 'We cannot treat social structure as something persisting in its identity behind the backs of mortal people who are inserted into their places by a cosmic cannery called Reproduction' (1983:149).

Bourdieu's best-known illustration of *habitus* is his deconstruction of the spatial arrangements and time-geography of the Kabyle village and house (1971c). Here *habitus* is at its best because the built structure of the houses, the physical layout of the village and patrilineal inheritance of fields provides exactly the durable system of *contexts* which provide cues for action. Rather than a 'cosmic cannery', the mundane environment imposes patterns such as the regular trip to the village well for there is no other source of water. Bourdieu argues that underneath the apparent idiosyncrasy of individual daily routines can be found the regular, common structure of the Kabyle cosmology, which provides a system of categories by which certain activities such as washing, or cooking, appeared appropriate in specific places (Bourdieu 1971c). However, a chicken and egg problem then arises: does the Kabyle cosmology reflect the arrangements of everyday life in the village or vice versa?

Bourdieu argues that daily activities and their placement are related to each other metonymically through their cultural status as manifestations of cosmological myths. Most famously, the Kabyle house is governed by the principle of its being a mirror-image of the Kabyle cosmos. It is thus 'the world reversed', as he calls it. To participate successfully in social encounters and activities in the village it is necessary to internalise these unwritten 'do's and don'ts' in such a way as to be able to improvise appropriate behaviour and a consistent ethics (1977:81). Here, Bourdieu argues that Kabyle cosmology functions as an algorithm for solving the practical problems of everyday social encounters. Yet this gives a somewhat timeless and static picture which is less convincing in his later work on contemporary France (see Garnham and Williams 1980:215). History is flattened into the repetition of the present. Nowhere does Bourdieu examine the process by which *habitus* might change. Which patterns are more durable than others? The village he describes is a kind of assembly-line for living where cosmologies are repeatedly acted out with Taylorian efficiency in every (identical) trip to the village well.

Applied to class societies, *habitus* becomes the embodied essence of class membership (Bourdieu 1984:437). It is the ethos to which all practices are related.

> It is internalised and operationalised by individuals but not to regulate solitary acts but precisely interaction. Thus the habitus is a family, group and especially class phenomenon, a logic derived from a common set of material conditions of existence to regulate the practice of a set of individuals in common response to those conditions.
>
> (Garnham and Williams 1980:213)

Missing, however, from this portrait of the coordination of behaviours is Goffman's (1963; 1973) insights on the symbolic manipulation of space through creating 'staged' 'front spaces' (e.g. the salon, living room, etc.) and relaxed, less-strictly regulated 'back spaces' (e.g. the kitchen or 'family room').

In addition to regulating the tempo and spacing of social intercourse, the dispositions of the habitus are cast as so many marks of social position, and hence of the

> social distance between objective positions, that is, between social persons conjuncturally brought together . . . [thus they are] so many reminders of this distance and of the conduct required in order to 'keep one's distance' or to manipulate it strategically, whether symbolically or actually, to reduce it

(easier for the dominant than for the dominated), increase it, or simply maintain it (by not 'letting oneself go', not 'becoming familiar', in short, 'standing on one's dignity', or on the other hand, refusing to 'take liberties' and 'put oneself forward', in short 'knowing one's place' and staying there).

(Bourdieu 1977:91)

Habitus highlights codes of spatial performance in the context of social situations. As Goffman (1963) argued in his work on private and public behaviour, questions of convention and propriety are regulated through codes. But again, it is difficult to see how it is that in these schemes particular agents may transcend situational frames of meaning and 'resist their subordination' (Jenkins 1982: 273) as they undoubtedly do (otherwise social change and innovation would cease). Like Giddens's work, even though structures are said to be produced in and through the medium of practice, structures are later treated as if dissociated from practice, which is relegated to a different ontological level (see Giddens 1979: 141–145) inaccessible to subsequent practice. Beyond the unresolved problems of causal determinism, *habitus* suffers from the logical problem that it is an argument *post hoc ergo procter hoc* (literally 'after this therefore on account of this') otherwise known as the 'after-so because' fallacy. For example, because food prices in Britain rose after it joined the European Community it does not necessarily follow that membership was the cause of the rise in price. Because *habitus* is postulated to exist, even if the claim remains shadowy, it is then presumed to be the cause of the routines it was proposed to explain. There can be no null hypothesis. Partly because of its vagueness (it would seem to accommodate almost any thought or unconscious habit) it explains every action and begins to appear, willy-nilly, everywhere (see Lash and Urry 1986). As such, it eliminates other possibilities by simply englobing them. *Habitus* is a putative entity endowed with causal powers but it is difficult to prove that it is the cause of anything. The advantage of Bourdieu's conceptualisation of '*habitus*' is that it does have the effect of focusing attention on the moment of mediation between 'ideology' and 'practice', structure and agency. Bourdieu, by holding attention on the moment of mediation itself attempts to put the question of causality in abeyance. However, by his own acceptance of the logic of structural social

37

science, this cannot be prolonged indefinitely. To escape this problem, we must turn to the work of Michel Foucault.

Bourdieu's choice of the term *disposition* (translated as arrangement; placing; frame of mind (as in mental disposition), and aptitude) to describe the link between thought and practice in *habitus* ironically coincides with Foucault's *dispositif* which establishes a similar unity of ideation and action.

> The word disposition seems particularly suited to express what is covered by the concept of habitus (defined as a system of dispositions).... It expresses first the *result of an organising action*, with a meaning close to that of words such as structure; it also designates a way of being, a habitual state (especially of the body) and, in particular, a *predisposition, tendency, propensity* or *inclination*.
>
> (Bourdieu 1984:562, n. 2)

This three-level definition (result of strategic action – habitual arrangement – propensity) will return in the discussion of Foucault's *dispositif*, and Lefebvre's three-part dialectic of spatial action, theories and discourse on space and spaces of representation (see Table 1.1, p.59).

Foucault: Spatialisation as dispositif

In contrast to Bourdieu's study of *habitus*, Foucault's work does not rest upon a causal analysis. He is not interested, for example, in the extent to which political changes or economic processes determine the consciousness of a particular group – 'the horizon and direction of their interest, their system of values, their way of perceiving things, the style of their rationality' (1972:163). The problem is situated differently with an eye to discovering

> far more direct relations than those of causality communicated through the consciousness of the speaking subjects . . . not how political practice has determined the meaning and form of . . . discourse, but how and in what form it [practice] takes part in its [discursive] conditions of emergence, insertion and functioning.
>
> (Foucault 1972:163; see also Cousins and Hussain 1984:106)[5]

Fundamentally, Foucault argues that 'formations cannot be simply displaced, because they are not mere contingencies but have complex conditions of existence' (Major-Poetzl 1983:261).

The project of theorising spatialisation is in many ways akin to Foucault's 'archaeology' of regularities which mark out what he calls a *dispositif*. It reunites previously scattered, marginalised knowledges and trivialised practices to demonstrate that they yield common principles of operation. The test of this spatial 'combinatory' will be if it yields not just a new vantage point but demonstrates the strategic reasons and necessities (in the sense of Hegel's 'necessary illusions') for the fragmentation of the different domains of spatialisation.

Foucault problematises the

> ingrained, unthought distinctions that are often used to set up a 'natural table' of realities. Above all what needs to be questioned is what we may term the 'spatial notion of reality': reality as a well-marked out closed space with an inside and a beyond.
>
> (Cousins and Hussain 1984:261)

Thus, he eschews the conventional distinction between forms of reality, as in 'realty versus fiction', by demonstrating that this assumption rests on an ontology which is itself a discourse. Conceptions of space – which are central to any ontology – are part and parcel of notions of reality. Much more than simply a world view, this sense of space, one's 'spatiality', is a fundamental component of one's relationship to the world. The conventions whereby one separates the real from the unreal, the natural from the supernatural, the reasonable from the insane are expressed through the spatial logic of exclusion and inclusion. The 'real' is further governed by a Cartesian logic of subdivision into ever-smaller units – what Lefebvre calls the fragmentation of the space of the real into homogeneous parcels. Analytical clarity is one result and this permits rational administration of all facets of life.

Spatial control is an essential constituent of modern technologies of discipline and power:

> Discipline proceeds by the organisation of individuals in space, and it therefore requires a specific enclosure of space. In the hospital, the school, or the military field, we find a reliance on an orderly grid. Once established, this grid

permits the sure distribution of the individuals to be disciplined and supervised; this procedure faci iitates the reduction of dangerous multitudes or wandering vagabonds to fixed and docile individuals.

(Dreyfus and Rabinow 1982:154–155)

The human body enters a spatial machinery of power that explores it, breaks it down, and rearranges it (Foucault 1979:137–138), allocating to each person a place, and to each place a person (Foucault 1979:143). In this 'grid' or apparatus, each position or place is coded as a value so that the distribution of functions is transposed into relations fixed in this structured grid. The success of this arrangement thus depends on the coding of this space. In this manner, individuals and values become places and positions in a grid defined by power which are observed and administered with great efficiency.

Foucault has been called a 'cartographer' for good reason. Michel Serres first pointed out his adoption of geometric terminology arguing that this allowed him a unique access to sociopsychological phenomena which operated according to a spatial thematic of inclusion and exclusion (1972:168). Deleuze concludes that:

Foucault's conception of discourse as a fundamental unit in a spatiotemporal field which alters position by crossing thresholds and occupying various levels is a conception very close to the contemporary model of atomic structure . . . which characterises both atoms . . . (a limited variety of distinct formations incorporate more elementary particles) and electrons (mass-energy fields that reach thresholds, occupy specific levels, and interact in complex ways with a number of other fields). . . . *Foucault's entire conceptualisation is spatial in nature* . . . . Although most commentators view this space as flat and immobile . . . in terms of cartography, topography, or geology, a few reviewers recognise that . . . [it] is three-dimensional . . . . Foucault 'has created a new dimension . . . [a] diagonal dimension . . . no longer in a plane but rather in [a] space.

(Deleuze 1970:209 italics added)

By contrast, he was misunderstood by geographers who accused him of giving

> ... a *de facto* privilege to the factor of time, at the cost of nebulous or nomadic spatial demarcations .... This uncertainty about spatialisation contrasts with your profuse use of spatial metaphors – position, displacement, site, field; sometimes geographical metaphors even – territory, domain, soil, horizon, archipelago, geopolitics, region, landscape.
>
> (Foucault 1980a:68)

However, the 'nebulousness' of the 'spatial demarcations' in his narratives is a result of his spatialised discourse and willingness to abandon the discursive priority usually given to time and temporally-rooted conceptualisation. Foucault deals with historical phenomena as parts of fields and constellations of events, rather than clearly demarcated points, nodes, or identities.[6] Later Foucault opts to organise his narratives around exemplary sites (e.g. the Panopticon (1973a) or the Greek polis (1979)).

> Metaphorising the transformations of discourse in a vocabulary of time necessarily leads to the utilisation of the model of individual consciousness with its intrinsic temporality. Endeavouring on the other hand to decipher discourse through the use of spatial, strategic metaphors enables one to grasp precisely the points at which discourses are transformed in, through and on the basis of relations of power.
>
> (Foucault 1980a:69–70)

From 1970, Michel Foucault concentrated on work which was directly related to preparations for his lectures at the Collège de France. He changed his focus from his notion of an 'archaeology' of knowledge (1972)[7] to a 'genealogy' of Reason. Put simply, he moved from a descriptive excavation of discourses and notions of truth to a political reunification of theory with mundane aspects of life. Consequently, he spoke less of a changing *episteme* and more of empirically specifiable discursive *practices* which he characterised as governed by systems of prescriptions that govern exclusions and choices. Foucault describes *discursive practices* as 'characterised by the partitioning of a field of objects, by the definition of a legitimate perspective for the subject of knowledge, and by fixing norms for the elaboration of concepts and theories' (Collège de France 1971:245).

Foucault sought to concentrate his analysis on those cultural practices in which power and knowledge cross, and in which our current understanding of the individual, society, and the human sciences are themselves fabricated: the issues of sexuality, of insanity, illness, and incarceration. The key element common to all of these is that some people or states of mind are excluded and cast out of the realm of civil society. The move from unconscious perceptual structures to concrete power structures broadened Foucault's compass to include the 'non-discursive' or institutional. Broadening the scope of analysis is not as contradictory as some might think. Signs organised in discourses are not disembodied ideas. They exist only in specific material processes

> caught within a network of contextual relations, within a
> definable if exceedingly complex environment, from which
> they are inseparable. They are the stuff of history, of society in
> movement, of conceptual processes in flux, of economic and
> political forces in motion, of developing artistic forms.
>
> (Reiss 1982:10–11)

His method of 'Genealogy', a future-oriented critique, focused on 'the tactics whereby, on the basis of the *descriptions of these local discursivities* [a definition of 'archaeology'], the subjected knowledges which were thus released would be brought into play.' Foucault called it a 'union of erudite knowledge and local memories which allows us to establish a historical knowledge of struggles and to make use of this knowledge tactically today' (Foucault 1980b:85,83, italics added). Major-Poetzl has argued that the political message of Foucault's work is that 'what is variable and subject to the principle of succession is not necessarily transformable within the present conjuncture and generation' except within the context of the future. Yet his genealogy is but one strategy of critique. In order to succeed it has to function like an epistemological tribunal, displaying how disciplines fail to meet their own epistemological requirements. Because genealogy itself refuses epistemology (although this is itself an epistemological 'move') it carries an inherent ambiguity and strategic limitation and cannot displace direct assessments of social science disciplines' theory (Cousins and Hussain 1984: 262–265).

By comparison, then, and in contrast to the various projects which aim to inscribe knowledges in the hierarchical order of power associated with science, a genealogy should be seen as a kind of attempt to emancipate historical knowledges from that subjection, to render them, that is, capable of opposition and of struggle against the coercion of a theoretical, unitary, formal and scientific discourse. It is based on a reactivation of local knowledges – of minor knowledges, as Deleuze might call them – in opposition to the scientific hierarchisation of knowledges and the effects intrinsic to their power: this, then, is the project of these disordered and fragmentary genealogies.

(Foucault 1980b: 86)

The shift to include the non-discursive was signalled by the introduction of the new term *dispositif*. It has been translated as 'apparatus', a word that conveys Foucault's pragmatic concern that concepts be used as tools to aid analysis, not as ends in themselves, and as 'grid of intelligibility'. *Dispositif* is distinguished from *episteme* primarily because it encompasses the non-discursive as well as the discursive. It is resolutely heterogeneous, including 'discourses, institutions, architectural arrangements, regulations, laws, administrative measures, scientific statements, philosophic propositions, morality, philanthropy' (Cooper 1981:194). One recoils from the logical conclusion to this, which Reiss offers as:

such notions as those of truth and valid experiment (in science), of referential language and representation (in all types of discourse), of possessive individualism (in political and economic theory), of contract (in sociopolitical and legal theory), of taste (in aesthetic theory), of common sense and the corresponding notion of concept (in philosophy) are, in fact, hypostatisations of a particular discursive system.

(Reiss 1982:21)

Translations such as 'grid of intelligibility' miss the full sense of 'a disposition' (of power and knowledge) which is central to the punning use that *dispositif* finds in Foucault's rhetoric. An over-emphasis is put on the discursive elements. It is a disposition of rhetorical and ideological 'devices', thus a 'conjunction', an apparatus, an ordering grid, or a plan. But besides this sense of the word, Foucault capitalises on the juridical sense of *dispositif* in French as a legal pronouncement or *judgement*, on its jurisdictional sense of legal purview; and on the military sense of a system of strategic operations. In Foucault's writing, *dispositif* is used in three ways:

1. It denotes a formative act that at any given moment responds to an emergency and so has a dominant strategic function.
2. Jurisdiction. To indicate a mode of conventional relations among elements, that is, a division of labour and meaning and relations between discourses and institutions which actualise them in as political activity.
3. To denote a heterogeneous collection of discourses, institutions, architectural arrangements, rules, legislation, administrative decrees, scientific discussions, philosophical and ethical propositions, philanthropic notions. Thus a *dispositif* is the conceptual and practical line along which apparently unconnected things can all be unified in the mind.

Cooper (1981:72) suggests the example of industrialisation which implied a strategic imperative (1, above) to deal with an unstable and floating population of vagabonds, madmen, and bandits. Little by little this resulted in the *dispositif* – the modern conjunction or disposition of power and knowledge – that controlled madness, mental illness, and delinquency (3, above). Not all of the consequences were intended; there was no implication that the strategy was complete or perfect. Yet once an institution was in place the results of its activity could be bent to conform more or less with the original imperative (2, above; see Foucault 1977). Foucault sought to document the development and contemporary presence of a *dispositif* defined as the conjunction '*Power/Knowledge*' where knowledge is brought into the service of power and conquest: facts are seized and become the basis for the extension of control over reality (for a study of the contrast between the contemporary *dispositif* and historical *dispositives* see Reiss 1982: 1-64).

Foucault defines *dispositif* as the 'strategies of relations of forces supporting types of knowledge and inversely.' He has been criticised, however, for not clearly spelling out the limits of the technique: are there certain necessary components to take into

44

account? Is there a requirement of complexity in this grid? Are there limits to the type of practices that can be analysed?' (Foucault cited in Dreyfus and Rabinow 1982:121). Is this the Eldorado of social theory? It would appear that everything finds its place in the historical *dispositif* which almost amounts to a program of basic principles which, fed into a good computer model of the vagaries of everyday life (including natural catastrophes and frustrations while waiting in queues), would produce a good approximation of individual and group interaction. Change from *dispositif* to *dispositif* is governed by what Foucault speaks of as *discursive ruptures* and Reiss equates this with the Kuhnian view of scientific revolutions which separate periods of conventional 'normal science'. Foucault's problem is one that haunts all totalising discourses (as Foucault's is, even though he claimed immunity from the fallacies of discourses): any view of competition and struggle are occluded except where they are taken to mark schisms or moments of transition. The possibility of competing but co-existing *dispositives* within the same nation-state (for example in countries where there are minority cultures) or between different localities needs to be allowed for. To counterbalance the totalising tendency of this theory, one needs to recognise that there may be schisms or shifts of register internal to a *dispositif* – it is possible to think of a framework which although 'ordered' is not arranged in the manner of a 'natural table' or taxonomy. This might allow a recognition of the suppressed voices (those of women, children, and so on), occluded analyses (such as those of suppressed religions and cultural minorities), competing theories, ironic displacements of norms, folly (for example in a period of carnival like May 1968) within *dispositives*. Such displacements, the 'carnivalising of authority', emerge as central to this thesis in the case-histories of Brighton and Niagara Falls.

While his work provides much material on the nature of *dispositifs* which is relevant to the nature of spatialisation, he does not solve the problem of the formation of individual preferences and decisions. As Cousins and Hussain point out 'the problem does not disappear just because it is "outflanked"' (1984:255). Because he brackets-off the material on which techniques of individualisation work, his theory incorporates an implicit behaviourism where human beings are *merely* 'bodies'. Each body is a *tabula rasa*. Such immanent criticisms reveal that Foucault's work

45

contains as many lacunae as the work of the 'human scientists' and political economists he criticises. At the level of bodies, Lefebvre's phenomenological study will provide a much firmer base for understanding both the spatialised language of psychological discourse on the personality and ego – on the body as a privileged 'space' or 'site' of consciousness as well as the spatial dynamics of self-perception themselves.

THE SOCIAL CONSTRUCTION OF THE SPATIAL

What specifically is included under the title of social spatialisation? Its conventions represent one side of what Anthony Giddens has called the social 'binding of time and space' (1984). This includes, first, the fundamental coordination of perceptions and understandings which allows for the sociality of everyday interaction and the creation of durable social forms and institutions. The coordinating role of social spatialisations represents an often-overlooked part of hegemonic systems of thought and supposition because spatialisation sets in motion more than an imaginary geography. As a fundamental system of spatial divisions (e.g. subject–object, inclusion–exclusion) and distinctions (e.g. near–far, present–absent, civilised–natural) spatialisation provides part of the necessary social coordination of perceptions to ground hegemonic systems of ideology and practice. Foucault argues that such basic 'forms of intuition' are necessarily a priori bases for ideology (1975:10). Spatial suppositions will be argued to ground a cultural edifice of perceptions and prejudices, images of places and regions, and to establish performative codes which relate practices and modes of social interaction to appropriate settings.

Spatialisation manifests itself in conversation topics in that images of places and regions are often cited and commented upon (i.e. discourses on space). It is a means to express ideas – an intellectual shorthand whereby spatial metaphors and place images can convey a complex set of associations without the speaker having to think deeply and to specify exactly which associations or images he or she intends. Sack (1980) argues that the Western three-dimensional conception of the spatial is fundamental to commonsensical, Humean notions of causality through contact. Foucault refers to this as the 'discursive function' of a discourse, in this case the 'discourse of space'.[8] Because people

46

often think laterally, exploiting puns, 'popular etymologies', and suggestive metaphors, discourses on space become influential as discourses of space. That is to say that myths become directive images and 'metaphors we live by' (Lakoff and Johnson 1979). These spatial conceptual forms play a significant part in the rationale by which daily lives are lived and by which decisions, policies and actions are rationalised and legitimised (Lakoff and Johnson 1979).

The manner in which spatialisation is most visible is in spatial practices and in the connotations people associate with places and regions in everyday talk. One notices the spatial metaphors people use, but it is when people attribute certain characteristics to a place and then make a decision – such as whether or not to go there – on this basis that talk becomes deed. As such, there are historical traces of these connotations left. For example, one can trace the rise and fall of a specific conception or *image* of a place partly through the record of the number of people who visited it and a knowledge of what activities people engaged in when they were there. Such *place-images* come about through over-simplification (i.e. reduction to one trait), stereotyping (amplification of one or more traits) and labelling (where a place is deemed to be of a certain nature). Places and spaces are hypostatised from the world of real space relations to the symbolic realm of cultural significations. Traces of these cultural place-images are also left behind in the litter of historical popular cultures: postcards, advertising images, song lyrics and in the settings of novels. These images connected with a place may even come to be held as signifiers of its essential character. Such a label further impacts on material activities and may be clung to despite changes in the 'real' nature of the site.

But, we also organise our lives around spatial routines and around spatial and territorial divisions. These surface as the carriers of central social myths which underwrite ideological divisions between classes, groups and regions. Spaces, fields of homogeneity, are conventionally subdivided into significant nodes and points: places. As Heidegger (1968a:143–162) argued, the concretising, assembling essence of placeness is dialectically linked with space as moments of a 'bringing together' at the same time as they are dissolving into the sea of points which make up a space. A 'bringing together' and the definition of 'placeness' occurs either from remarking on the genus loci of the locale or giving names to places. This process of identification is one essential marker of cultural activity. It forms the basis for the elaboration of spatialisation for it allows the differentiation of both places from space and places from each other (a certain city is identified by the mountain in the middle, and is different from the one with seven hills). The process of identification, division, and differentiation takes on social functions. People are 'placed' according to their putative affiliation with their place of origin; as they say to strangers in Prince Edward Island, Canada, 'Where do you belong?'.

In the old language of commonsense inherited from Bacon and Descartes, 'space' is rendered as a neutral void which contains real objects. In this *abstract spatialisation*, the 'question of space' becomes one of the duality of objects-in-space and their containing void. I have argued that the strong emphasis on the interpretative component of individual understandings of the world implicit in geographic research in this area (Pocock and Hudson 1978) de-emphasises the formative and compelling nature of social spatialisations as part and parcel of social surveillance and 'discipline' (cf. Foucault 1973a).[9] The spatial has also appeared irrelevant to most sociologists, despite the lip service paid to the idea that a society might vary over its various 'locales' (Giddens 1984; for a more focused study see Cooke 1984; for a critique see Duncan 1985). This has occurred partly through the *epistemic* role of spatial understandings which underwrite ideologies by allowing only certain allegorical comparisons and metaphors to appear to be 'rational'. A 'discourse of space' composed of perceptions of place, of the world as a 'space' and of our relationship with it as an external reality is central to everyday conceptions of ourselves and the world we live in. Such conceptions of the spatial character of reality structure the understanding of its other attributes including the types of causal relationships that are countenanced in serious discourses such as that of Western rationality (see Sack 1980).

Realist visions: space as relation

For example, Andrew Sayer has pursued the 'question of space' in the name of finding a Realist solution to the definition of 'space'.

While his work goes a long way toward establishing 'the difference that space makes', posing the problem in this manner is directed by this abstract vision of the spatial and is naturally oriented towards the empiricist's ontological notion of 'space'. As a result, the question of space becomes a question only of *spatial relations* between objects (distances, geometry, the range of effects). Sayer builds his arguments on a limited ontological definition of what has just been argued to be a complex and multi-valent phenomenon of social spatialisation. He challenges the idea that space has an independent existence apart from objects but this conclusion is ultimately insufficient for sociological purposes. However, his argument is worth reviewing if only to contrast the difference in the *sociological* terrain of this book with Sayer's interest in *physical* causality.

Harré had advanced a relative concept in which 'space only exists where it is constituted by matter' (Harré 1971 cited in Sayer 1985:51). But while space is constituted by objects, Harré argued that it is not reducible to them. The Western commonsense position is even more absolute: space is an empty void and phrases such as 'Friction of distance' are a shorthand for 'frictions between particular substances which constitute space'. Sayer argues that the relative position of Harré is untenable because it posits some sort of spatial relations independent of the type of objects involved. He concludes that 'space' is a *contentless abstraction.* 'Matter always necessarily has spatial extension and spatial relations only exist through objects, of whatever kind.' Therefore,

> Since the idea of understanding what happens in the world in abstraction from its content is manifestly absurd, there can be no independent 'science of space' . . . a spatial relation cannot, of itself, be said to have any effects or make any difference. Yet depending on the nature of the constituents, their spatial relations may make a crucial difference, as for example in the case of one's spatial relation with the walls of a prison. So space makes a difference, but only in terms of the particular causal powers and liabilities constituting it. Conversely, what kind of effects are produced by causal mechanisms depends inter alia on the form of the conditions in which they are situated.
>
> (Sayer 1985:52)

This argument achieves its clarity by reducing all aspects of spatial-isation to 'spatial relations' between objects as defined and by classical geometry. We learn nothing about the nature of spatial classification itself, however. The ontic is elided in favour of the ontological. The end result is that a definition is clarified but no insight is achieved into the *sociocultural significance* of changing social spatialisations on, for example, beliefs, forms of expression, and everyday interactions.

As opposed to this reduced-to-the-empirical notion of 'space' as just distance and position a sociological analysis would question this vision as part and parcel of a current social spatialisation. If Sayer laments that 'it is common to separate space and substance and speak of the effects or uses of space – as if it were a thing exist-ing independently of objects' (Sayer 1985:52); this is not a simple category mistake which social scientists are called upon to 'fix' (Sayer 1985:64) but is rather part and parcel of the overarching distinctions of a particular, Western, spatialisation within which research takes place. Such a 'fix' would amount to a complete re-building of day-to-day frameworks of perception. Sayer gives many examples of the difficulties caused by illogical notions of 'space' and these I take to be further indicators of the relative indepen-dence of these 'ideas' or beliefs from empirical conditions.

Lefebvre: dialectics of space

The French philosopher, Henri Lefebvre, has argued that this reductionistic view of spatialisation, which has passed into the discourse of Western social science, conceals from view the frag-mentation of the elements of spatialisation (1974; 1981). A divorce takes place between representations, at the level of the imaginary or mythical, and practices in the interest of founding a socio-technology[10] of control in the service of power. In the common-sensical world that we inherit from the Enlightenment, 'space' has little concreteness: unobservable as such, it is presumed not to exist. However, what exists in the imagination of people and affects their everyday decisions must be considered in social science. As Realists argue for the real existence of 'class', so it might be added that spatialisations exist. For Lefebvre, 'space' is a term which combines land as private property or other systems of territorial-isation, the built environment as 'toolkit' or everyday resource, and the spatial medium of human interaction. This apparent conflation is no mistake, either. It is a rhetorical device which regroups fields of thought and action *artificially* separated at the Enlightenment origins of contemporary thought. The root of Lefebvre's problematic is exactly those semantic games by which spatialisation is blasted apart, split-up into fragments each of which is the cordoned-off area of one or another specialised discipline. It is only the habit of unexamined prejudices which makes the Westerner mistake land and spatiality as separate 'topics' for analysis. Lefebvre argues that all of the spatial phenomena such as 'land', 'territory', 'site', spatial metaphors which are used as a descriptive shorthand, and private property are all part of the same dialectical structure of 'l'espace' or spatialisation. Conventionally, they are held apart through fragmentary discipline-based analyses.

In Lefebvre's view, the modern Western understanding of 'space' is itself a materially produced form, a *concrete abstraction* – in the same sense as Marx's understanding of the commodity. Space is neither a substance nor a 'reality' but only becomes fetishised as such. Like the commodity form which, stripped to its essentials, yields up labour value plus capital, social space as a *form* is a *'concrete abstraction'* of its contents and its production by a *society* (Lefebvre 1981:120–121). Like a work of art, then, it is a material realisation of creative design and labour power. But, the spatial is also a condensation of the social relations of its production.

> In any product, however trivial, the subjective and objective aspects, the activity and the thing, are intimately linked. These are isolated objects that have been separated from Nature . . . . And yet these products still remain objects of Nature . . . . Every product – every object – is therefore turned in one direction towards Nature and in another towards man. It is both concrete and abstract. It is concrete in having a given substance, and still concrete when it becomes part of our activity, by resisting or obeying it, however. It is abstract by virtue of its definite, measurable contours, and also because it can enter into a social existence, be an object amongst other similar objects and become the bearer of a whole series of new relations additional to its substantiality.
>
> (Lefebvre 1939:119 cited in and translated by Gottdiener 1985:129)

The concrete abstraction or *form* is simultaneously (1) a medium of social actions, because it structures them, and (2) a product: that is, both (1) the material ground of labour and (2) the result of the operations and inscriptions of capital in the form of land value and the property regime. Space as form is radically different from Sayer's critique of space as a contingency (Sayer 1985:60). Unlike contentless abstractions, the form has real impacts as the embodiment of constituent elements and processes, even if it is only empirically tangible when 'embodied' as properties, in practices or in objects, hence the difficulty that is encountered in describing it.

This is the starting-point for a unified theory of spatialisation which brings its separated aspects back together. While 'space' might be analysed as land or territory by geographers, private property by jurists, as the built environment by architects and so on; in their place Lefebvre proposes a unifying *threefold* dialectic of space (1981:48–54). He expands this theory on three fronts: (1) spatial practices, (2) discursive representations of space, and (3) what Lefebvre punningly calls spaces of representation – the abstract space of the 'social imaginary'. Although he is unclear about their precise interaction, these summarise well the different aspects of spatialisation which are discussed in this book.

Spatial Practices

This involves the range of activities from individual routines to the creation of zones and regions for specific purposes: a specific range of types of park for recreation; test sites for nuclear weapons; places for this and that; sites for death (graveyards) and remembrance (memorials, battlegrounds, museums, historic walks and tours). Through lived practice, 'space' is re/produced as 'human space'. This practice involves a continual appropriation and re-affirmation of the world as structured according to existing socio-spatial arrangements. This approaches Heidegger's notion of 'dwelling', the practice of being in the world (1968a). These 'social spaces' help to assure the society's continuity in a relatively cohesive fashion and the reproduction of the social relations of production. Such cohesion through space implies, in connection with social practice and the relating of individuals to that space, a certain level of spatial 'competence' and a distinct type of 'spatial performance' by individuals. This, then, consists of the *individual-*

ised performance or enactment of spatialisation by individuals in their daily habits and minute gestures and mannerisms.

Over time, spatial practices, the habitual routines of 'place ballets' are concretised in the built environment and sedimented in the landscape. Giddens refers to this process as the constitution of 'locales' (1984; see also the critique in Duncan 1985) which become resources for social action as contexts: they provide a *mise-en-scène* which suggests the appropriateness of particular actions and, where these are ritualised, particular roles. But, it remains practices which 'articulate' the multitudinous possibilities of any given site. These actions are themselves part of the constitution of the qualitative reality of sites as places where certain events and actions are known and expected to take place. De Certeau amplifies this vision as follows:

> The user of the city takes up fragments . . . to actualise them
> . . . . He dooms certain sites to inertia or to decay, and from others he forms 'rare' ('fortuitous') or illegal spatial 'shapes' . . . the walker, in relation to his position, creates a near and a far, a *here* and a *there* . . . indicative of an actual appropriation of space by an 'I' . . . thereby establishing a conjunctive and disjunctive articulation of places.
> (Barthes cited in De Certeau 1985:130–13)

To take a recent example, a North American shopping mall such as the Eatons Centre in Toronto represents a spatial ensemble which both encourages and requires (for commercial viability) a specific type of 'crowd practice' (Shields 1987). The aggregate, wandering, consumer crowd of *flâneurs* today is both complemented by, and a pre-requisite of, the celebratory and festive galleria-type shopping mall. Though quite different, this type of spatial performance is derived from the less commercialised public behaviour of the 'boulevardier' or '*flâneur*' who strolled the nineteenth-century shopping arcades of Paris (Shields 1987; Benjamin 1973a; Geist 1983) enjoying the crowds. It is thus possible to disrupt the closely woven fabric of social practices and conventions through interventions at the level of spatial practice. Resistance in the form of reterritorialisations of space, abrogations of the private property system (as in squatting, particularly in the context of Third World barrio communities), or denials of pragmatic conventions such as just sitting on the floor rather than using benches (a tactic often used by disenchanted youth) is possible. The resulting counterspaces, even if momentary, present an ever-shifting ground on which power and constraint is exercised by state and society.

Representations of Space

These are the forms of knowledge and hidden ideological content of codes, theories, and the conceptual depictions of space linked to production relations. These are the abstracted *theories and 'philosophies' such as the 'science of planning'* cited by Lefebvre. Taken alone, this 'level' of the dialectic today involves the abstract presentation of the lived experience in space reduced to quantified movements along vectors between x–y coordinates. These discourses are an inner logic of production relations and to the order these impose in their turn.[11] As 'representations' these are central to forms of knowledge and claims of truth made in the social sciences which in turn ground the rational/professional power structure of the capitalist state.

Spaces of Representation

This discursive sphere offers complex re-coded and even de-coded versions of lived spatialisations, veiled criticism of dominant social orders and of the categories of social thought often expressed in aesthetic terms as symbolic resistance. Rather than a representation of space, this facet of Lefebvre's concept of *'l'espace'* is a matter of *functions and effects of a given, often untheorised understanding of space*. This amounts to the effect conceptions of reality have in terms of conditioning discursive possibilities. This is the closest Lefebvre comes to Foucault's interest in the spatial. Lefebvre cites Dada as an example of art which revealed the arbitrariness of the present spatialisation by transgressing the spatial conventions of modes of figuration and representation. Other clandestine and underground spatial practices which suggest and prompt alternative (even, he suggests, revolutionary) restructurings of institutionalised discourses of space and new modes of spatial practice, such as those of squatters, illegal aliens, and Third World slum dwellers.[12] It is on this 'level' that 'space' operates as an overcoding meta-concept which imbues other conceptual categories and symbolic systems with an often unrecognised 'spatial life'. Thus the many spatial metaphors expressing social status ('coming from the "wrong side of town"'); power; time; prestige; order; reason et cetera, catalogued as *Metaphors We Live By* by Lakoff and Johnson (1979).

The example of the West Edmonton Mall which I have discussed at length elsewhere (Shields 1989) shows how these three facets interact. The Mall – the largest in the world and with its indoor 'Fantasyland' the third most popular tourist attraction in North America – expands upon established functions of shopping malls. It promotes a new *representation of space* and encourages the elaboration of the corresponding *spatial practice* of *flânerie* mentioned above by figuratively re-centring the resource periphery city of Edmonton as the centre of civilisation, copying and rebuilding famous sites and pieces of architecture such as the Arc de Triomphe. In so doing it naively but unerringly has become a fantastical magnet for tourist shoppers from as far away as the MidWest and Japan. It creates a new pole of gratification in the geography of sites of consumption. It constructs in a literal sense a '*space of representation*', a privatised public space in which the social imaginary is opened to new visions. That is, the Mall is a type of 'play space' which encourages its users to abandon what we might, for the sake of argument, call the 'modern rational' conception of the world. It plays upon symbolic notions of the spatial. The Mall presents an allegorical rejection of the geographic world of distant centres in which Edmonton is on the periphery. By adopting the Mall's alternative cosmology users can momentarily suspend their hinterland relationship to the difficult capitalist world of distant, abstract powers and indulge in a collective fantasy which produces the illusion of a different logic of space and a different capital logic.

This order is replaced with the Mall's own internal 'hyper-reality' (Jameson 1984; Eco 1985; Gottdiener 1986) where 'everything looks real, and therefore it is real; in any case the fact that it seems real is real, and the thing is real even if, like Alice in Wonderland it never existed.' This is not done with the ethic of 'We are giving you the reproduction so that you will want the original' but rather 'We are giving you the reproduction so you will no longer feel any need for the original' (Eco 1985:16,19). Commercial copies – signs – of authentic experiences of Paris, New Orleans and so on, aspire to supplant their referents. What is being asserted at the West Edmonton Mall is a new, collective sense of place founded on the notion of having transcended the geographical barrier of distance which has so long kept the provincial capital of Edmonton culturally isolated; not only from the rest of Canada but also from the rest of the World. This new 'logic' and the new understanding which goes with it involves a transformation of the spatial indices of location and realty which operate as meta-concepts and imbue conceptual categories and symbolic systems with an often unrecognised 'spatial life'. This dis-placed sense of place also rests on a denial of locality. The Mall has nothing to do with the real setting or history of Edmonton. There are no fake Rockies, no Indians, and no sculpted ranch hands. One hankers after a herd of fibreglass cows being driven down the 'Main Street' of the concourse.

In Lefebvre's analysis, all of the above dimensions can be either ideological or expressed in practice, and may either reinforce or contradict each other in any given site or moment. This 'dialectic of triplicité' is intended to allow the discarding of a dualistic socio-spatial dialectic which tends to degenerate into a debate over the primacy of one or the other of the two terms. Society is already spatial (Sayer 1985). This rhetorical issue is, however, not the sole reason for a three-part structure. While all three 'levels' operate at all times, the varying degrees of repression or domination of one or another 'level' of this dialectic marks out historically specific spatialisations which Lefebvre coordinates with Marxian modes of production. For example, it is by now a commonplace to recognise that Oriental cultures and art forms have long promoted the union of aspects of life which the West divides into different spaces. Tai Chi exercises, for example, promote a union of mind and body which is radically at odds with the Western vision of the body as a 'container' of the ego which is thus 'inside looking out.'

Lefebvre's real object of study is the *process* of the *production* of cultural notions and practices of space (i.e. the process of social spatialisation), not space itself. Linking space and spatiality securely to production is the basis on which Lefebvre argues for the *specificity* of spatialisations according to successive modes of production. Nonetheless, this 'productivism' does not restrain him from arguing strongly for the importance of ideas in determining both 'styles' of production within overall modes of production and in shaping production relations themselves, a classic theme:

No two cultures live conceptually in the same kind of time and space. Space and time, like language itself, are works of art, and like language they help condition and direct practical action. Long before Kant announced that time and space were categories of the mind, long before the mathematicians discovered that there were conceivable and rational forms of space other than the form described by Euclid, mankind at large had acted on this premise.

(Mumford 1934:18)

Nonetheless, it would be a mistake to fetishise 'space' *per se* as a locus of causal relations except where spatialisation has social impacts as an element of belief. Rather than 'a cause' the spatial is *causative*. Spatialisation has a mediating effect because it represents the contingent juxtaposition of social and economic forces, forms of social organisation, and constraints of the natural world and so on. But as a 'cause', in and of itself, it plays no role for it is not a locus of causal forces. Human agents have causal power. As Sayer argues, the spatial has a channelling effect. But, objects may have specific causal forces only because they are divided or aligned in a certain manner; that is, because they are 'spatialised' in a certain arrangement. Spatialisation is 'causative' in the sense that it expresses or channels causation like that class of verbs such as 'persuade' which might express causal relationships in language: someone's words might be 'persuasive' but it is the person who is 'doing' the persuading, not the words themselves (even if one might sometimes say 'That person's words were persuasive.'). Again, spatialisation is not just a matter of Realism's contingent arrangements of objects-in-space, it includes normative perceptions (this should go with that) and designs which pre-exist the actual arrangement of objects.

Of course, what makes spatialisation interesting is that, in spite of the commonsensical veneer of empirical rationality (space is a void), people treat the spatial as charged with emotional content, mythical meanings, community symbolism, and historical significance. It is the latter repressed emotions, not the former rationalism, that one finds built into the framework of intuitions, perceptions and biases which characterise the everyday life (that old Weberian perspective on *Veralltäglichung*) of otherwise rational institutions. One result is the growing professional interest in the sociology of everyday life with its transitory arrangements and fleeting alliances which nonetheless are *the* common elements in any comparative sociology.

In the new language of spatialisations, a new legitimacy is given back to previously separated aspects of culture and politics, environment and economy such as, for example, the complex relations underpinning the conventional separation (in the mind and in reality) of leisure and work (see Gorz 1982). This change may also be found in the spatialised discourse of postmodernists such as Frederic Jameson who, by questioning the status of 'space' and pulling at the threads of the binding garments of the Western spatialisation, acquire a political relevance in fields ranging from neighbourhood interest groups through urban and regional planning and environmental management to geopolitical theory (Jameson 1984). This 'spatial turn' in turn destabilises the parcelisation of contemporary life and throws taken-for-granted categories into the stark relief of arbitrary black–white oppositions. However, the implied political project, which eschews class divisions and national ideology in favour of a radical individualism based on relations of proxemy and locality, has not yet been fully pursued by postmodernists (see B. Anderson 1983; Frampton 1983; Berman 1983).

SOCIAL SPATIALISATIONS AND THE 'SENSE OF PLACE'

As an mnemonic aid, we might now construct a table summarising the similarities and differences between the definitions of Lefebvre's 'dialectic of "space"'; Bourdieu's *habitus*; and Foucault's *dispositif.*

Table 1.1 is only a caricature and some of the comparisons may sit uncomfortably in such simple categories. Yet, caricatures operate by their revelation of seminal characteristics. The table illustrates that each of the three authors aligns their definitions on three 'fronts': (1) conventionally developed Reason, (2) practice or habitual activities, and (3) imagination or creative problem-solving. This is not to say that Bourdieu's 'formative operation' squares exactly with Lefebvre's idea of the science disciplines setting-up the limits of 'reasonable discussion'. Bourdieu's emphasis is on practice, and his comments in the two areas (1 and 3) tend to be corollaries and extensions of his thinking about practices.

Table 1.1 Comparison of Lefebvre's, Bourdieu's, and
Foucault's definitions

Lefebvre *Dialectic of space*	*Bourdieu* *Habitus*	*Foucault* *Dispositif*
1. Representation of Space (formative response to a need)	Organising Action	Strategy
2. Daily Practice	'Habitual State' (Opus operatum)	Jurisdiction
3. Space of Representation (imaginary play disrupting conventional spatial understandings)	Propensity	Legislation (range of judgements seen as appropriate solutions)

Lefebvre is perhaps the most even of the three, but does not develop his arguments on the 'space of representation' along the lines of the social psychology of discourse which is Foucault's emphasis, or, to put it another way, the 'centre of gravity' of his theorising. Foucault refuses to accept any Western ontological discourses: classes, the subject or agent and even social totality are (rightly) metaphysical postulates.[13] Foucault takes up a position 'outside' of the metaphysical tradition, refusing all assumptions. He conducts a rigorous critique of voluntaristic humanisms – theories which locate the subject as source of social relations and fount of their meaningfulness. However, in the manner of Deleuze and Guattari (1976) he also refuses to establish social relations as a totality (although he does analyse the emergence of the concept 'society' (Foucault 1984:241–242)). Thus he leaves no room for a general doctrine of causality, although this does not preclude the examination of the specific effects of empirical practices (Cousins and Hussain 1984:252). This shifts Foucault's concentration away from practice as an encounter with reality where learning and innovation takes place. Instead, he emphasises the legislative and strategic which are at a socio-political level.

At the general level of cultures Michel Foucault once posed this question: 'What if empirical knowledge, at a given time and in a given culture, *did* possess a well-defined regularity? If, in short, the history of non-formal knowledge had itself a system?' (1970b:x). At the level of sites and zones, places and spaces, this question deserves asking again. Social spatialisation has been described as a cultural formation but along with the regularity of a 'system of space' is also marked by schisms, torn by interstices and having fluctuating boundaries – a web of spaces and spacings. The manner in which its presence will be more empirically illustrated is the way that places with particular characteristics become characterised as being appropriate for specific activities. While certain architectonic 'props' may make a particular place better for gymnastics than meditation, beyond this simple notion of appropriateness, places and spaces are actualised and endowed with meaning as certain types of places. In more sociological terms, they are labelled. Partly through ongoing interaction, a site acquires its own history; partly through its relation with other sites, it acquires connotations and symbolic meanings.

To take a well-known example, beaches are one illustration of this phenomenon of spatial assumptions and judgement. Mention 'beach' and people immediately tend to think not just of an empirical datum – a sandy area between water and land caused by deposition, longshore drift, and so on – but also of a particular *kind* of place, peopled by individuals acting in a specific manner and engaging in predictable routines. What's more, these practices (the odd culture of sunbathing, the tradition of sand-castles, and so on) make up a specific ensemble of practices. We learn that bare, carefree and relaxed are not only appropriate but also *natural* attitudes and behaviours for a beach. This naturalness derives from attitudes towards specific spaces such as a beach. Through a process of labelling, sites and zones associated with particular activities become characterised as being appropriate for exactly those types of activities. Other activities are excluded, forced into wilderness or barren spaces 'outside' of civilised realm, or they are associated with their own dichotomous spaces.

The term 'place-images' has already crept into the above discussion. Some definitions are in order. These are the various discrete meanings associated with real places or regions regardless of their character in reality. Images, being partial and often either exaggerated or understated, may be accurate or inaccurate. They result from stereotyping, which over-simplifies groups of places within a region, or from prejudices towards places or their inhabitants. A set of core images forms a widely disseminated and commonly held set of images of a place or space. These form a relatively stable group of ideas in currency, reinforced by their communication value as conventions circulating in a discursive economy. To these, a range of more subtle or modifying connotations can be added. These peripheral images are more ephemeral and transitory. They result from idiosyncratic associations and individual experiences. Generally these find expression in descriptions only where they are set into the terms of more conventional and widely understood core images. Collectively a set of place-images forms a place-myth. Thus, there is both a constancy and a shifting quality to this model of place- or space-myths as the core images change slowly over time, are displaced by radical changes in the nature of a place, and as various images simply lose their connotative power, becoming 'dead metaphors', while others are invented, disseminated, and become accepted in common parlance.

Opposed groups may succeed in generating antithetical place-myths (as opposed to just variations in place-images) reflecting different class experiences or the cultural remembrance of a defeat where conquerors see only glory. One example of this exists between French-speaking Quebecois and English-speaking Canadians' images of the Far North. English-speaking central Canadian intellectuals have constructed an image of the Sub-Arctic as a unterritorialised, undifferentiated, 'unconquerable', zone of purity: a white wilderness. This 'True North Strong and Free' (a line from the national anthem) is presented in the media as a nationalistic myth of a collective patrimony. The North is the soul or psyche of Canada. This space-myth attempts to transcend the East versus West regionalisms that have plagued Canada. The regions are taken up in a spatialisation of Canada in which reality is organised along the lines of geographic metaphors of unity and non-differentiation. The land cannot be divided, territorialised, rendered neutral. Causal power is attributed to the North itself. While this vision has frustrated development and provided overwhelming public support for the non-exploitation of northern resources, the French Canadian, Quebecois vision of 'the North' is almost the antithesis of this vision. The Quebecois North is restricted to northern Quebec – 'Nouveau Québec' – which is presented as an engineering zone rich in resources and hydro-electric potential which are the 'future' of Quebec's development (Hamelin 1980).

Because they engender divergent perceptions, extreme divi-

61

sions would appear to be relatively uncommon within hegemonic nation-states. In general, one expects that class and group-specific place-myths are subsumed into a transcendent spatialisation[14] as they are taken up in hegemonic discourses and re-worked by commercial advertising and propaganda (whether of a class or regional promotional nature) which reinforces certain images just by repeating them and assimilating them to what is considered desirable while discouraging others. While some elements of spatiality – such as gesture, or attitudes about the appropriateness of sites to particular uses – might be correlated with ethnicity, age, gender, and socio-economic classes (Ardener 1983), spatialisation must, to some extent, cross class, ethnic and even 'cultural' lines in the form of basic perceptions and orientations to the world if there is to be the maintenance of a basic sociability between these groups. Spatial divisions such as up and down reflect the human experience of gravity (Needham 1973) and are to some extent rooted in physiology (Shields 1986:35–82), but the interpretations given to them are cultural. A division such as right and left, while reflecting the symmetry of the body must be coordinated amongst people for it to take on a symbolic meaning (Durkheim and Mauss 1963:12). The Western division of here and there or present and absent (Benveniste 1966:I,253) is even more peculiar and culture-specific (although the division of 'this life' and the afterlife, the world and heaven ('above') is more common).[15] At the level of nation-states, a coherent and hegemonic vision of 'the nation' which binds and implicates people with territory and the history of specific regions and localities is a purely social construction.

As an hypothesis which will be further investigated, these ideas could be described in the following manner. Space-myths – aligned and opposed, reinforcing or mutually contradictory – form a mythology or formation of positions which polarises and dichotomises different places and spaces. Place- and space-myths are united into a system by their relative differences from one another even while they achieve their unique identities by being 'set-off' against one another. Even if split by inconsistencies and in continual flux, this formation works as a cosmology: a more emotionally-powerful understanding of the geography of the world than that presented by rational, cartographic techniques and comparative statistics. Through these contrasts of spatialised identity, communities may distinguish themselves from other social collectivities (Cohen 1986; see Chapter Three below). As Benedict Anderson (1983) argues, the success of the nation-state in providing a territorial framework for the elaboration of a distinct spatial 'mythology', thus a distinct social spatialisation, is one key to the successful survival of the state, even where national borders unite different cultures (Lefebvre 1981).

Spatialisation is not proposed as just a cognitive 'structure' but as a set of practical paradigms which does not necessarily have the coherence of an ordered structure. It is a formation more than a framework, a function more than a principle: a *techné*. Such a description moves beyond Bourdieu's relatively static notion of *habitus* as a 'structuring structure' to accommodate the contradictions and schisms apparent in the vignettes above and which will become clearer in the case-histories.

How is it that at least a minimum level of coordination of perception and imagination is maintained and reproduced? Refinements and revisions would be expected where tensions arise when everyday situations can no longer be understood according to the 'old mappings' of reality, as Jameson called them (1984). The result of such anomalies would be hesitation, uncertainty, a vertiginous loss of bearings, and, for some, anguish. The key to the persistence of spatialisation is that it is not proposed as just a cognitive structure which individuals learn. It is a cultural formation embodied not in learned rules but in bodily gestures (*exis*) and trained postures in and toward the world, in sets of practical paradigms and algorithms coordinating group activities and sites ('what to do, when and where'). They need not necessarily have the coherence of structures which are the product of rational thought. It is a social framework more than a mental structure. Whereas Bourdieu conceives of *habitus* as a mediation between ideology and psyche, spatialisation grounds ideology by furnishing the necessary substratum of common perceptions for communication and definitions of the psyche. For Western cultures this is along the lines of a subjective 'I' *inside* a body which circulates in an objective reality *out there* (Foucault 1975:10; Lowe 1982). By contrast, (as noted earlier), the Oriental art form/exercise of Tai Chi is predicated on a relationship of unity between mind and body and a fundamentally different relationship between the individual and group (see also Berque 1982).

Such a description moves beyond Bourdieu's synchronic notion of *habitus* fetishised as a mental 'structuring structure' (1977) borne by individuals. A social formation accommodates the contradictions and schisms apparent in the changing nature of everyday life. Further, while *habitus* is useful in discussions of class and taste, it falters as a theoretical device when one begins to probe the lack of distinctions in fashion and the style of everyday life well prior to the coupling of art, cultural codes, and power (Maffesoli 1988b).

If the element of *habitus*, of a meta-logic guiding practices, is removed from the formation what is left is that which underpins Bourdieu's *habitus* and is its medium, a regime of space. This spatial 'medium' is, unlike *habitus*, necessarily of a cross-class nature. It is one of baselines along which the coordination of classes takes place. Spatialisation founds what Foucault calls 'disciplinary technologies' (1973a) through a coordination of perceptions and understandings of reality. This 'common sense' leads to coordinated problem-definitions whereby social tensions are inscribed in and attributed to be symptoms of grand social problems. For example, Foucault's work deals extensively with the nineteenth-century social reformers' prescription of slum clearance and social control through architecture (of which he argues Bentham's Panopticon was the zenith), and urban design (cf. the partitioning of the city to prevent the spread of contagious disease). Solutions emerge from the definition of problems (Schön 1983), and a seamless discourse of 'common sense' can make alternative definitions of problems or proposed new developments in a region appear ridiculous – a problem faced by all radicals. And by postmodern theorists.

Above, arguments have been presented that spatialisation unifies the discursive (the use of metaphors) and empirical (myths rendered as practice), and indicates their mode of inter-relation (normative codes of spatiality). It also responds to a strategic function which gives it a character of necessity and urgency. This regime of spatiality has the effect of a 'placing' of individuals into social fields, and a 'spacing out' of institutional structures and jurisdictions to constitute a field or ground for the operation of power and the flow of knowledge in regularised, day-to-day situations. The administrative, guiding nature of spatialised discourse about the world is key to the transformation of purely discursive (i.e. ideational, symbolic, and linguistic) 'imaginary geographies' into everyday actions, gestures, crowd-practice, regional identities, the 'imaginary community' (B. Anderson 1983) of the territorial nation-state, and geo-politics. Thus, an overarching order of space, or social spatialisation, is reproduced in concrete forms as a practice *upon* the world. It restates as well as reproduces 'discourses of space' which constitute it. In this manner, spatialisation is theorised to operate as a Foucauldian *dispositif* or formation.

Social formations of this nature cannot be displaced in a simple motion because they are not themselves contingencies but have complex conditions of existence. This accounts for their robust nature and historical continuity. Spatialisation only appears, hypostatised and fetishised, as a 'structure' in a theory inasmuch as it has a relatively robust set of core concepts or foundational metaphors which surface in everyday discourse. These networks of 'mythopoetic' positions in discourse form the support for the rationalisations by which people 'explain away' paradoxes of the way they live and justify styles of activity over other ways of doing the same task. This might be described as a multi-dimensional constellation of relatively durable core concepts with shifting, innovative practices and notions as less durable, perhaps seasonal novae. The entire constellation of a now Western and rapidly emergent Global Spatialisation is split by tensions which rise almost to the status of organising polarities. A multitude of other nodes within this formation may be related in almost infinite combinations through the principle of their relative position within the formation. If it is a creation of imagination and practice, spatialisation as a cultural artefact is inherently unstable because it is always challenged by reality. Contradictions are always being encountered and old notions abandoned; old practices being improved by new ones. This could be thought of as a repository of the habitual 'ways of doing' and 'ways of being' that one lapses into between bouts of individualistic innovation.

NOTES

1. Lowenthal wrote of the problem of generalizing from individual perceptual experience to a wider social universe of shared meanings (Jackson and Smith 1984:21) as the problem of building 'bridges' between 'separate personal worlds of discourse' through common bases of knowledge. 'Despite their congruence with each other and with the world as it is, private milieus [sic] do diverge markedly among

people in different cultures, for individuals within a social group, and for the same person as child and as adult, at various times and places, and in sundry moods' (Lowenthal 1961:251).

Unlike the concern of this thesis, most work in geography has focused on the micro-scale: the 'private milieu' of an individual. Thus the emphasis has been on understanding the perception of the local environment. Basic questions had to be answered: how did environmental cognition take place at all? What elements of the landscape were perceived? And, which of those were the most memorable and would later be used as orienting landmarks? The provision of funding for studies of perception and cognition led to a distinctly psychologistic emphasis with applications in artificial intelligence being the aim of funding bodies. It was established that certain aspects of an environment are commonly prioritized by individuals – for example, Piaget's studies showed infants' innate tendency to fixate on edges and vertical lines. However, this work tells us almost nothing about the symbolic importance of such elements of the landscape. Jackson and Smith have said,

> The subsequent literature concerning environmental perception
> descended rapidly to the empirical analysis of 'mental maps',
> 'cognitive images' and the like, virtually ignoring the
> philosophical insights and challenges . . . an air of predictability
> and resignation has come to characterise the study of 'geographic
> space perception', together with a widespread feeling of
> disillusion: perception studies seem not to have lived up to their
> early promise.
>
> (Jackson and Smith 1984:22)

This work betrays an overwhelming sense of crudity in the conception of society as well as of cognitive process. Pocock and Hudson (1978) note that the same city or suburb may inspire completely different reactions. Yet their subsequent research demonstrates a wide agreement on the emotional affect of particular scenes or environments in which the people interviewed are engaged in the same activity (e.g. the case of tourists looking at the famous view of Durham Cathedral interviewed on Pribend's Bridge: Pocock 1982). My contention that attitudes are not simply equivocal *tout court* but depend on the nature of interaction of the body with the environment steps beyond the boundaries of the existing corpus of research into the social structures of cognition of the environment.

Human geography is therefore an appropriate area of sociologically-informed investigation: a basic premise of this project. Ley speaks of the 'personality of place' being derived from the coherence of 'intersubjective' experience: 'any habitually interacting group of people convey a character to the place they occupy which is immediately apparent to an outsider, though unquestioned and taken-for-granted by habituées' (1977:508). 'Intersubjectivity' refers to the shared character of lived experience and meaning. Merleau-Ponty's theory of the body-subject by which the body 'holds within itself an active, intentional capacity' toward the world (Jackson and Smith 1984:32). This approach rejects both extreme realist and subjectivist views of the world as, on the one hand, either something given, or as potentially available to experience once we get around our blasé attitude which takes the world as objects just 'present-at-hand' (i.e. taken for granted, see p. 60) or, on the other hand, as something wholly constructed by subjects (an extreme solipsism whereby nothing can be said to happen if a subject is not present). Rather Merleau-Ponty's 'philosophy of ambiguity' takes the objects of experience as by nature enigmatic out of which we draw patterns and upon which we impose expectations of consistency. Following this, Seamon conceptualises spatial behaviour in terms of 'time–space routines' and 'place-ballets' which are to be found in the repetitive situations of daily life.

2. The notion of a determining 'base' is still present in a broadened form as Bourdieu argues that these 'embodied ideas' are formed through environmental and social conditioning in given circumstances and situations.

3. Part of the problem is that *habitus* can be argued to be no more than another form of determination in the last instance:

> as a deterministic model it relies upon a simple base-superstructure metaphor inasmuch as the 'objective structures' mediated through the habitus (culture) generate practice. It is correspondingly difficult to imagine a place in Bourdieu's thinking for his own emphasis upon the meaningful practice of social actors in their cultural context.
>
> (Jenkins 1982:272)

This criticism is also made by Garnham and Williams (1980:222).

4. Thus, in one of the most notorious interventions in the history of sociology of education he argued that the tendency for working-class students to drop out of school is the product, not the cause, of the low statistical probability of their academic success (Bourdieu 1971a; 1974; 1977).

5. Foucault says of archaeology that

> If in this analysis . . . [it] suspends . . . a causal analysis, if it wishes to avoid the necessary connection through the speaking subject, it is not in order to guarantee the sovereign, sole independence of discourse; it is in order to discover the domain of existence and functioning of a discursive practice. In other words, . . . it seeks to discover that whole domain of institutions, economic processes and social relations on which a discursive formation can be articulated; it tries to show how the autonomy of discourse and its specificity nevertheless do not give it the status of pure

ideality and total historical independence; what it wishes to uncover is the particular level in which history can give place to definite types of discourse, which have their own type of historicity and which are related to a whole set of various historicities.

(Foucault 1972:164–165)

6. See Heidegger's discussion of the temporal and spatial in the *Appendix on Hegel's Definition of Space* in *Being and Time* (1962).
7. *The Birth of the Clinic* (Foucault 1975) is archaeology,

tied to structural analysis, concerned with spatial relationships and unconscious forms of perception. One has to struggle to orient oneself in time, there are few references to known historical figures or events and the argument proceeds at a high level of abstraction. *Discipline and Punish* by contrast makes explicit references to dates, places, and sources and combines abstract analysis with direct exposition and imagery. Although it too is concerned with spatial relationships, there is a clear narrative line, making this the most readable of Foucault's works.

(Major-Poetzl 1983:202)

8. Reiss argues that,

if a discourse speaks of phenomena it orders them . . . discourse and the material in which it is manifest are never the elements of what might be taken as a neutral mediation . . . even assuming that discourse may, according to its 'class' serve a primary function as mediation of things . . . as opposed to mediation between their enunciators . . . it is not a matter of 'treating discourses as groups of signs (signifying elements referring to the contents of representations) but as' practices that systematically form the objects of which they speak. Of course, discourses are composed of signs: but what they do is more than use these signs to designate things. It is this more that renders them irreducible to the language [langue] and to speech (Foucault 1976:46).

(Reiss 1982:29)

Elaborated discourse therefore always has a 'reference' even if it may only be 'apparent' to a 'reader' accustomed to a different discursive class. Such would necessarily be the case for a discourse whose own elaboration is its references (see Derrida or late Barthes) and because reference is always the creation of discourse, such is always the case. Our Analytico-Referential class of discourse,

assumes an exterior and marks that assumption in its own elaboration . . . this reference is always in some sense grasped by discourse. It is – and I insist on the ambiguity of the word because it enables us to use it of discourse in general – . . . the relation of discourse. This . . . what Foucault calls the more of language, will have to be given a status 'beyond' language which is but one of its possible materials. This relation is the way in which semiotic systems are used, organized (though it goes without saying that such systems can only be studied in that use and organization: they do not preexist).

(Reiss 1982:29)

9. Harvey denounces the phenomenology of human geography as parochial (1973:24) by arguing that it cannot comprehend the objective social forces that lead to the destruction of place. But this 'easy' critique is anticipated in Heidegger's 'phenomenology of being' which rejects the search for a priori foundations of knowledge such as 'objective social forces' for a focus on understanding human existence and experience within the context of a historically constituted social world.

10. 'Sociotechnics' is defined as the study of rational techniques and processes of social change. See Podgorecki (1975).

11. Thus our present discursive practice upon the world, which may be traced back as far as the sixteenth century (Foucault 1973a; Reiss 1982), presumes a schism between interior mind (the terrain of concepts) and exterior reality (the world of objects) and marks out this division in every detail of its elaboration. Reiss says, 'Its exemplary formal statement is cogito ergo sum' (1982:31) and it operates on the basis of, and legitimacy for the notion of a seizure and possession of the external world of phenomena through mediating means or *techné*. This gives rise to a stress upon Reason, a loss of 'enunciative responsibility' whereby the classification and description inherent in language and its tied concepts and definitions is occluded such that the classification appears 'natural'. This practice brings knowledge into the service of power as a descriptive instrument and system. This will be discussed further in the sections on Foucault and the 'thematics' of spatialisation (Chapter 6).

12. These groups fashion a spatial presence and practice outside of the norms of the prevailing (enforced) social spatialisation which, for example in the Third World, often privileges private property systems favouring absentee landlords. Slums, barrios, and favellas are thus seen by Lefebvre as localised 're-appropriations' of space by which certain sites are removed or severed from the governing spatialisation and returned to the realm of 'communitas'. Lefebvre differentiates this 'appropriation' of space from the 'dominated' space of the nation-state, or of the capitalist city. If the latter is the zone of the hegemonic forces of capital, these former sites mark possible, emergent, spatial revolutions. The local and 'punctural' 'détournement' ('diversion' or 'hijacking') of the bourgeois spatial order, as in the tradition of 'occupying' key spatial sites (buildings) as a means of

protest, is similarly an example of the seizure and re-functioning of hegemonic space.

13. To invoke a realm behind objects of discourse, be it things known to experience or objects of an essence, will entail a resort to that ontological category of reality which Foucault wants to jettison . . . a critique founded on the invocation of such a realm would require some general epistemological means for determining knowledge of 'real' things from the knowledge of 'imaginary' things . . . . This [is also] a discourse with general conditions of existence, there are no such general means. Foucault insists on the factitious character of objects of knowledge . . . refuses to use a general category of . . . imaginary things . . . . Foucauldian genealogy cannot be made to stand in for epistemology.

(Dreyfus and Rabinow 1982:261)

14. For example, while George Orwell presents many 'working-class' images of Paris which contrast with the widely known myths of Parisian cultural centrality in his *Down and Out in London and Paris* these do not amount to a separate working-class place-myth of that city (1949).

15. Amongst some cultures, for example, the Ngugu Ymagir aborigines of Australia, the Cambridge linguists Havilland and Levinson have shown that words and concepts describing the relative relations of objects (e.g. the ball is to the left of the child) do not exist. In place of Western relative space (which we presume to be universal and impute to other cultures) absolute spatial systems exist. These require that the language user is oriented (e.g. to cardinal points) at all times and must be able to effect a 'dead reckoning', keeping track of the location of objects as the path to them is described in terms of cardinal directions from the person's actual position (thus, go North to the toy and seven paces West is the child).

PART TWO

Chapter Two

RITUAL PLEASURES OF A SEASIDE RESORT
Liminality, carnivalesque, and dirty weekends

It seems that every review of Brighton, Regency England's south coast 'Capital by the Sea', begins with an obituary to George IV, who as Prince Regent was at least partly responsible for introducing the socialites of his day to the seashore and Brighton to them. Freedom from the constraints of social position (both high and low) developed in the permissive atmosphere of a resort town where people went for their health, for a rest, for entertainment, or merely for a change of scenery. It has been said that from George's first visit 'the amenities of Brighton, including the women he found there and the women he brought, captured his affection and a considerable part of his fortune' (Hern 1967:45 sic). Since his time, Brighton has enjoyed a 'raffish reputation' attracting both those who, with money and time to spare, were in search of glamour, adventure, and excitement; and those who, in a quest for profit by one means or another, were in search of these 'idle rich'. If 'raffish' appears in every description, it captures the contradictions of the place – tawdry and vulgar, yet flashy and rakish. But like the word 'raffish', both the place and the legends are all somehow dated. For most Westerners in the late twentieth century, it is no longer necessary to create marginal zones, such as the seaside was, for reckless enjoyment.

In this chapter an analysis of the cultural positioning of Brighton as a seaside resort is developed to show how its position was constructed within the broader framework of the spatialisation of British culture. As a place Brighton came to be associated with pleasure, with the liminal, and with the carnivalesque (Bakhtin 1984; Stallybrass and White 1986). These concepts are central to developing a coherent vision of Brighton's changing image: from

73

Regency pleasure and healing centre to the gay Victorian resort to 'dirty weekend' destination and Bank Holiday riots on the beach.

We open with a historical review of Brighton which will focus on attitudes to, and literary images of, Brighton as a seaside resort. In particular, the theme of indolence present in both the positive and the critical appraisals of the town will be related to the specific image of Brighton as a 'dirty weekend' destination which developed in the 1920s through the 1930s. This establishes a context for a discussion of the liminal status of the seaside *vis-à-vis* the more closely governed realms of the nation – the productive industrial areas, the 'serious' world of London and the Parliament, or the 'innocent' arcadian spaces of the agricultural counties (see Figure 2.1).

Figure 2.1 Context map of Brighton

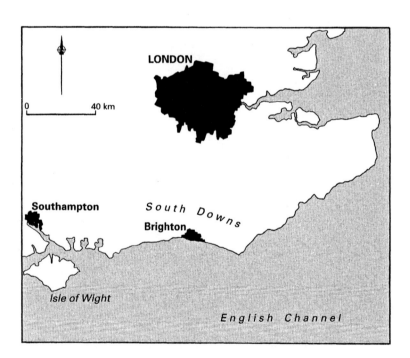

For Western industrial cultures, a beach is more than just a 'thing' or site, and Brighton's beach acquired a particularly well-defined image. It became the locus of an assemblage of practices and of customary norms which, attached to the notion of 'Beach', transformed its nature into a socially defined zone appropriate for specific behaviours and patterns of interaction outside of the norms of everyday behaviour, dress, and activity. 'Beach' became the topos of a set of connected discourses on pleasure and pleasurable activities – discourses and activities without which our entire conception and sense of a beach would be without meaning. It was territorialised as a site fit for leisure, and the story of its transformation over time to support a derivative form of Rabelaisian carnival amounts to a social history of the Beach.

CLINIC BRIGHTON 1730–1820

Then all with ails in heart or lungs,
In liver or in spine,
Rush'd coastwise to be cured like tongues,
By dipping into brine.
(Anon. late 1790s)

In 1783, Brighthelmstone, or 'Brighton' as it was pronounced by the locals (Mawer and Stenton 1930:291), was an impoverished fishing community prone to frequent flooding by the sea.[1] To this fishing village, the Prince Regent, later George IV, was brought for the sea air and for the reputedly restorative powers of sea-bathing, a practice dating from the early 1730s.[2] Spurred on by this royal patronage, by the closing decades of the eighteenth century, sea-water was considered to be as beneficial as the mineral waters that had made Bath and Tunbridge Wells popular Georgian spas. Prescribed by doctors, these dips in the sea were as structured and ritualised as a visit to a doctor's clinic might be today: to bathe or not to bathe, when to bathe and how, were important questions, and sea-bathing was to be undertaken only 'after due preparation and advice' (Gibbon 1923:I,210). For, according to the populariser of sea-water treatments, Dr Russell, although 'Sea-water is imbued with many and great Virtues, the Unskilful may make a very bad Use [sic].' Bathing was an unpleasant medicine taken when the water was coolest – before dawn and preferably in the

75

winter. As a system of ablutions it was preceded by purging with up to twenty-five glasses of sea-water. It was 'taken by doctor's orders and hedged round with a veritable armoury of rules and regulations' (Manning-Sanders 1951:24). Fanny Burney, wishing a swim at Sidmouth in August of 1792, 'having no advice at hand . . . ran no risk' lest the day be too mild and her pores too open.

Nearness to London and its circle of aristocratic patrons was an essential factor in Brighton's rise to fame. Brighton benefited early on from its proximity, acquiring the status of a weekend dormitory town for professionals such as stock-brokers by the 1820s. Through his London practice, Russell proved an influential champion of Brighton as a sea-bathing site. Brighton in the Season, said Thackeray, was 'London *plus* prawns for breakfast and the sea air'. 'A portion of the West End of London *maritimized*' (Granville 1971:565). A second factor in Brighton's expanding reputation was its proximity to the continent. For, bolstered by refugee aristocrats from the French revolution,[3] and from the later wars and revolts which marked the first half of the nineteenth century, the circle of the Prince's friends and hangers-on was to transform the Brighthelmstone summers into a round of social events which rivalled the 'Seasons' at Bath, not to mention those earlier in the century at Versailles. Over thirty years, the Prince Regent was to expand a nondescript local farmhouse into the Royal Pavilion: an Oriental fantasy overlaid with Indian whimsies and imagined-Arabic details dubbed 'the Kremlin' by its critics (Cobbett 1912: I,73). But for observers, Brighton remained 'a place of no trade; of no commerce at all'; with no harbour, 'no place of deposit or of transit for corn or for goods or for cattle' (Cobbett 1912: I,74). The recognised hierarchy of spaces and places descended from London (in particular the aristocratic and parliamentary areas of the city) through the seats of the various duchies and down to the market towns. In this spatialisation, the growth of the seaside resort town figured only as anomalies. Brighton was dismissed in the *Report on the Census of 1851*, along with the seaports and manufacturing centres, as 'of an inferior order', having acquired an 'adventitious but extraordinary importance and magnitude' (cited in Gilbert 1954:10). Nonetheless the town became the fastest growing urban agglomeration in Europe. Brighthelmstone had six streets in 1760, but in 1800 the population was 7,000, double that of 1780, and triple that of 1770 (Gilbert 1939).[4] Brighton displaced both Bath and the other inland British spas, but if Brighton's growth seems inexplicably meteoric, it is because British historians have neglected to figure in the contribution of foreign visitors and migrants who made Brighton a capital of *European* culture, one of the first centres of cultural interchange and cross-fertilisation that was to become a commonplace of modernity.

Encouraged by Dr Russell's medical system of sea-bathing, fashionable invalids in ever-increasing numbers flocked to Brighton. But most – the friends, chaperones, and families of these invalids – were there for the social life, to 'see and be seen'. In the words of Fanny Burney, who visited for the first time in 1779, 'Notwithstanding this is not the season, here are folks enough to fill up time from morning till night' (cited in Manning-Sanders 1951:19). Brighthelmstone acquired an enduring reputation for an unconventional social life complete with a predatory local petit bourgeoisie of landlords and caterers.

Together with the practice of sea-bathing, the social life of 'Brighton' became more elaborate. By the time the Prince Regent arrived it already had its subscription libraries, meeting-rooms, and other diversions. The social activities of the inland spas, of which the seaside resorts were at first off-shoots, were copied. Along with social customs such as a Master of Ceremonies who organized the Season's balls and events; the idea of planned terraces and crescents of town houses built with a continuous palatial façade and promenades were copied from the model of the spas, adding the prefix 'Marine' whenever possible. New Baths built to ease winter bathing reflected Brighton's European flavour in both their names – for example, the German Baths – and their styles (Turkish as well as Roman Baths). The older spas had depended on their mineral springs which were unable to meet the growing numbers as the popularity of medical bathing expanded and the social importance of the Seasons for the fashionable and the marriageable young grew. On the coast, however, capacity was almost unbounded: 'While social life at the spas was necessarily focused on the pumproom and the baths, and there was no satisfactory alternative to living in public, the sea coast was large enough to absorb all comers and social homogeneity mattered less' (Pimlott 1975:55) if only because there was more space for distanciation between groups.

Brighton, free of the 'noxious steams of perspiring trees', with 'bitter sea and glowing light, bright, clear air, dry as fry' (Relhan 1829:3, cited in Manning-Sanders 1951:47), was particularly advertised as a place whose waters were an aid to fecundity. Even the prolific local sheep were tendered as a testimonial to this.[5] Later, a pseudo-scientific theory of ions and ozone in the sea air would be advanced to explain the character of the waters, which, 'to a sweet balsamick, spiritous and sanguinous temperament . . . naturally incites men and women to amorous emotions and titillations' (cited in Manning-Sanders 1951:47). Brighton presented a rare opportunity for the eligible young bourgeois and bourgeoises to meet in a permissive atmosphere and away from home-town gossip. The flirtatious atmosphere of the seafront parade which resulted confirmed Brighton's reputation for loose morals for many commentators (Figure 2.2). The new 'Brighton' included both the best and worst of Disraeli's 'Two Nations' as landless poor were drawn by the possibility of earning wages as servants or beach entertainers (for a detailed history see Stokes 1947). It was the new industrial bourgeoisie, many of whom had bought themselves aristocratic titles, who were to form the enduring market for Brighthelmstone's metamorphosis into a town organised around the servicing of 'pleasure and distraction'.

THE SYSTEM OF PLEASURE

With the arrival of royalty, Brighthelmstone, or rather that event that everyone now called 'Brighton', became 'the centre *luminary* of the system of pleasure: . . . all other places within the *sphere* of its *attraction,* lose their gayest visitants, who fly to that resort: . . . the pretty women, all hasten to see the *Paris* of the day' (*Brighthelmstone Intelligence* 1784:2). The Prince was the central figure at first: he was the 'Paris of the day', not Brighton, and by all accounts there were many women who sought to be his Helen by night. When he withdrew to London, the same paper reported: 'Brighthelmstone . . . [is] a desert.' A Cinderella town. Without the Season's animating crowd of aristocratic 'patients', 'Brighton' ceased to be and reverted to the antediluvian 'Brighthelmstone'. The *Intelligence* complained 'scarce a person of fashion remains; the whole company now consists of antiquated *virgins,* emaciated *beaux,* and wealthy citizens with their wives and daughters.' Even if, later, this class was to transform Brighton into their own 'centre-luminary', their prevalence in the 'off- Season' marked the perennial eclipse of the sense of indolence and dissipation which formed the core of the entire identity of 'Brighton' which had been fabricated on the substratum of the fishing village 'Brighthelmstone'. Many of these community-oriented residents disapproved of the whole goings-on and of the prying local gossip papers:

> The *Brighthelmstone Intelligence* has no novelty to recommend it; merely a repetition of the old story; *morning rides, champagne, dissipation, noise* and *nonsense*: jumble these phrases together, and you have a complete account of all that's passing at *Brighthelmstone.*
>
> (cited in Manning-Sanders 1955:57)

Brighton was popularly know 'for freedom of manners beyond Bath in the old days, and for total dissipation beyond London in new times.' The Prince and his 'glittering' half-court, complete with wealthy, decadent exiles, hangers on and an 'indispensable' *corps d'amour* 'with all the insolence of youth and the haughty indifference of British eighteenth-century upper-class tradition, let loose in a perpetual holiday against a background of bare downs and glittering sea' (Manning-Sanders 1951:55). To this group of visitors, at least, Brighton was 'all beauty, whether as to the streets, the buildings, the carriages, the horses, or the dresses of the people. . . . It is all a scene of evident wealth, of pleasure and of luxury' (Cobbett 1912: I,73).

Through the early 1800s, pleasure moved onto the beach under the guise of 'Doing One Good' (Hern 1967:10). The justification for pleasure was hidden in its medicalisation and was controlled through a complex set of regulating social rituals which governed the social round almost as tightly as the medical beach. Both the social and the medical rituals were presided over by powerful *animateurs* who conducted the ceremonies and acted as intermediary and assistant. In the case of the social functions, this was the 'Master of Ceremonies', who besides planning and presiding arranged all important introductions; while in the case of the bathing rituals it was local 'Dippers' who were responsible for lifting their patients from bathing machines and 'dipping' or plunging them in the water.

Figure 2.2 'Papa sees us bathe', 1856

Source: East Sussex County Library

The mutation of the beach itself into a pleasure zone was accomplished partly through the growing social importance of Brighton as a centre of fashion. Only with the conjunction of a predisposition to actually go to the beach for pleasure – to sit, for a day, in the sun or the wind and turning one's back to the urban comforts beyond the promenade – and the institution of mass holidays could the beach take on its contemporary character as a leisure zone. This 'pleasure beach' simply overtook the naked patients on the 'medical beach' who were mercilessly spied upon from the promenade by the onlookers who gathered to gossip and stare. If it was once a tightly ritualised liminal zone we might hypothesise that it was a combination of the growing sense of spectacle and the growing numbers of people which resulted in its transformation (see Figure 2.3). The seafront parades, crowded with spectators, give a circus atmosphere to the scenes captured in engravings. There was a growing focus on the 'sights' of the naked bathers, who are portrayed as either comic invalids or 'bathing beauties' (see Figure 2.4). The increasing crowds of day-trippers who came not only to Brighton, but also to the purpose-built working-class resorts all around Britain from the 1840s onwards, brought children to the beaches. The encounter of serious-minded invalid-bathers and children splashing along the fore-shore must have been dramatic (see Figure 2.3). The medical order imposed by the Dippers was disrupted with the result that many beaches were partitioned. There was considerable struggle over the parliamentary ban on the Salvation Army's Sabbath music and celebrations on the beach as a 'nuisance' (Walton 1983: 210ff.). This process of invasion and displacement was speeded up only by the decline of the 'working beach': that beach which had seen the launching of generations of fishing boats and the landing of catches from the inshore fishery.

The chief importance of the seaside resorts had always been social – they were 'more fam'd for Pleasure than Cures' with the majority no more than spectators (cited in Pimlott 1975:57; see Figure 2.4). Hence the use of bathing machines, which were really changing-rooms on wheels complete with canopied 'exits' to the water. They were developed to protect bathers' modesty between their state of formal dress and entry into the water (see Figure 2.3). At first bathing was done in the nude; later, woollen swimsuits were adopted. But no matter what the garb, it was by popular convention and moral decree a state of undress and exposure. If there was a dichotomy between the Seasonal 'Brighton' and the locals' Brighthelmstone, there on the seafront was marshalled the elements of the internal dichotomy of 'Brighton': those who came for the Cure and those who came for the Pleasure. Brighton reached its zenith at the Season of 1848–9, when many of the royal and political exiles from European revolutions and wars spent the winter on the south coast (Weiner 1960). These exiles continued to bathe, but they were in no way invalids on a pilgrimage to a Cure. Rather, Brighton had become a full-fledge social centre, a site of repose, retreat from everyday life and leisure. The local historian, Dale, argues that 'it was at this period that Brighton really succeeded Bath as the centre of fashion and the provincial capital of social life' (1947:17).[6] But beyond practical reasons of convenience, location, and political economy, how was it that such a medicalised curative centre could blossom into a social centre? What made a place of cripples and Cures an appropriate basis on which to develop a centre of pleasure? The connection between Cures and the pleasure beach will be argued to be found at the level of the spatialisation of the beach as a liminal zone.

Figure 2.3 Brighton seafront, *c.* 1890

Source: East Sussex County Library

82

Figure 2.4 'Gentlemen! Who pass the morning near the ladies' bathing machines'

Gentlemen! who pass the morning near the Ladies Bathing Machines.

Source: East Sussex County Library

LEISURE SPACES: LIMINALITY AND CARNIVAL

In the work of Victor Turner, 'liminality' is adopted from Van Gennep's pioneering study of *Rites de passage* (1960) to designate moments of discontinuity in the social fabric, in social space, and in history. These moments of 'in between-ness', of a loss of social coordinates, are generally associated with religious experience (cf. Durkheim and Mauss 1963). Classically, liminality occurs when people are in transition from one station of life to another, or from one culturally-defined stage in the life-cycle to another. This also informs pilgrimages where a goal – a sacred site, or indeed a seaside Cure – is ritually presented as a life-changing experience. Liminality represents a liberation from the regimes of normative practices and performance codes of mundane life because of its interstitial nature. As a result, Turner argues,

> action can never be the logical consequence of any grand design. . . . because of the processual structure of social action itself . . . in all ritualized [or systematised] movement there was at least a moment when those being moved in accordance with a cultural script were liberated from normative demands, when they were, indeed, betwixt and between successive lodgements in jural political systems. In this gap between ordered worlds almost anything may happen. . . . That this danger is recognized in all tolerably orderly societies is made evident by the proliferation of taboos that hedge in and constrain those on whom the normative structure loses its grip . . . and by legislation against those who in industrial societies utilize such 'liminoid' genres as literature.
>
> (Turner 1974:13–14)

The liminal status of the eighteenth-century seashore as an ill-defined margin between land and sea fitted well with the medical notion of the 'Cure'. Its shifting nature between high and low tide, and as a consequence the absence of private property, contribute to the unterritorialised status of the beach, unincorporated into the system of controlled, civilised spaces. As a physical threshold, a limen, the beach has been difficult to dominate, providing the basis for its 'outsider' position with regard to areas harnessed for rational production and the possibility of its being appropriated and territorialised as socially marginal. Like other liminal zones, then, Brighton beach provided the setting for a life-changing transition, practically miraculous in nature, which bathers hoped to secure by undertaking the pilgrimage to the seaside and following a prescribed course of 'dippings'.

Beyond the fondness for the beach throughout the early 1800s and onwards, there are many mentions of the Dippers who assisted (or pushed) their charges from the bathing machines. They became famous local figures who, like priests, were mediaries between two worlds, civilised land and the undisciplined waves. They were also technicians of the ritual process: on-site masters of the requirements of the sea-bathing treatment. They judged the waves, the state of their clients, and their daily requirements: bathing at such and such a time or for so long. Many of the bathers could not swim: Dippers, often women, were essential figures of dependable strength and assurance. This might explain the inordinate affection for them. The ritual purging and bathing, the ministrations of the Dipper, and the natural influence of the seashore itself with its salt water, sea air, and 'ozone' were vital ingredients in both the reality and *perception* of a Cure.

The take-over of the aristocratic Brighton Season with the increasing presence of the middle class of 'wealthy citizens' was followed by a boom in popular seaside patronage with the steady growth of the labouring man's family holiday between 1841 and 1930. These day-trippers took advantage of newly opened train lines to enjoy a day at the seaside, often in groups as entire factories shut for a yearly excursion. Seaside resorts such as Brighton gained a real cultural significance for the nation as a whole as old religious feast days were augmented by factory and town holidays and finally by statutory vacations and the Bank Holidays Act of 1871. The railway and pleasure steamer reduced the cost of travel to resorts just as the demand for holidays began to increase due to concern over the health and productivity of the workforce; an increased efficiency in urban factories with a conse-quent demand for a quality workforce and the increased urban-isation of the country added to the pressures for formalised breaks in more rural areas. Thomas Cook's railway excursions ran from the early 1840s onwards. A railway to Brighton was opened in 1841 and this set the destiny of the Brighton as a day-tripper's resort. It was in response to the demands of these working-class families that the seaside land-ladies multiplied and popular cafés and tea rooms, pier-end shows and souvenir shops, rather than pubs or ballrooms, proliferated (Hern 1967:77ff.). Bank Holiday crowds attracted entertainers from the inland fairs which were increas-ingly restricted (Stallybrass and White 1986). London stall-holders introduced what came to be seen as 'typical' seaside food, the Punch and Judy shows and other attractions.[7]

Like the rites of simpler societies, the new holidays marked a collective release from the rationalised regimes of industrial labour. Holidays were thus special and 'extra-ordinary'. This liminal 'time-out' was partly accomplished by a movement out of the neighbourhoods of 'everyday life' to specific resort towns

85

along the English coast and later to specialised holiday camps which were designed to provide a liminal programme more efficiently (Ward and Hardy 1986). The spatial movement concretised the transition from the routinised schedules of workdays to the less routinised, cyclical temporality of annual holidays which accompanied the change of seasons. In this sense, the spatial movement is central to the accomplishment of the temporal shift. Although increasingly ordered and dominated by a rationalised programme, particularly in the schedule of events and entertainments perfected in the holiday camps, for the holiday-makers these days remained outside of the everyday spatialisation. The liminal zones provided a necessary escape from the built-in cues and spatialisation of 'normal', work-a-day life with its eighteenth-century towns and neighbourhoods dominated by their factories.

Mass seaside holidays marked not just a broadening of the social base of the British seaside but a mutation in its nature. What had been the ritualised world of the 'Season' and medicinal sea-bathing became a much looser carnival: the Bank Holiday trip to the seaside was a ritual in name only, for many of the structuring codes of the nineteenth century had been removed. To the horror of many commentators, classes mixed freely in this gay carnival and the beach; the times when one could swim and when one could not, the sort of attire suitable and the spatial division or mixing of the sexes, became nodal issues around which the struggle between personal freedoms and social morality clashed. There were still miraculous sea-water Cure stories in the 1880s but good summer weather was becoming more important (Pimlott 1975:179–80). The bathing machines were too costly and inconvenient so economical families opted for beach tents or toy-villa beach huts; the lower-class day-trippers brought umbrellas for a day on the beach and 'paddled', rolling up pants or daringly holding up dresses to walk along the water's edge, while children changed in the shelter of their mother's skirts (see the *Graphic* 1871 cited in Manning-Sanders 1951:30). There was continuing tension between the still-new re-appropriation of the seaside beaches by the British working classes and restraining Victorian morals. Besides this spatial aspect, the conflict was temporal, from the attempts gradually to extend the number of statutory holidays in the year and the gradual shifting of 'The Season' to the disregard of the **Sabbatarian ban** on bathing or even sitting on the beach on Sundays (Walton 1983:197–207).

Brighton was the first of the seaside resorts to shed its primarily medical orientation in favour of the pleasure beach. It successfully made the transition from patronage to market; from aristocratic seaside spa to mass seaside resort; from eighteenth-century whimsy to the nineteenth-century romanticism of sublime breakers and winter storms, plus the populism of summer sun. Indeed, the stormy seashore suited the emerging Romantic view of the Sublime perfectly. Far from the sort of sunny summer day with a calm sea and throngs on the beach that the day-trippers were to seek, the Brighton seafront of the winter Season was reserved for more adult pleasures. There was a genuine love of feeling that one was standing safely in the teeth of a gale. The Romantic Sublime required that nature display its forces at terrifying, nearly Wagnerian, levels. The daunting force of Nature and a sense of the puniness of human endeavour produced an exhilarating experience. There was a reaction against the ordered, confined, corporatist life of the spas expressed architecturally in Nash's Bath crescents. Each household had been assigned a place within the matrix of the crescent of indistinguishable units. The ruthless uniformity of the crescents functioned in part as a backdrop of univocal order and taste against which the mundane variety of daily life for the aristocracy was played out. By contrast, a fashion for mountain scenery and turbulent seacoasts came into vogue. Brontë displaced Jane Austen; Turner, Constable.

The new appreciation of the sublime was a precondition for the moving of the fashionable Season from August to September and then to October and November to avoid the masses which crowded the beaches and made traditional bathing by means of bathing machines and the 'proper' Victorian enjoyment of the beach nearly impossible. By 1874 Brighton was said to have

ever so many seasons from the time when the first spring
excursionists come down in a wondering phalanx to the
beach; and later still, when trainload after trainload of
holiday-makers . . . [and] family parties determined to have
their full seven hours by the seaside . . . swarm about the
Chain Pier,

(*Brighton Magazine* 1874:289)

until the Season in the late autumn which might last until after Christmas while the fashionable indulged in crashing breakers and gale-force winds and attended the round of social engagements.

> Politics nobody cares about. Spurn a
> Topic whereby all our happiness suffers.
> Dolts in back streets of Brighton return a
> Couple of duffers.
> Fawcett and White in the Westminster Hades
> Strive the reporters' misfortunes to heighten.
> What does it matter? Delicious young ladies
> Winter in Brighton![8]
> (Collins 1868, *Winter in Brighton*)

Well-to-do Victorians – known as 'anti-trippers' (Becker 1884) – had sought quieter, circumspect places offering 'rational recreation and health-giving pleasure' (*Murray's Guide* cited in Manning-Sanders 1951:123). The 'proper' Victorian model of seaside recreation was to reject the socialising of the theatre and the assembly room. Instead, walks on the shore, botany collecting, and sketching (and no swimming on the Sabbath) complemented by comfortable lodgings would suffice to '*wile away* the summer holiday' (*Murray's Guide* cited in Manning-Sanders 1951:123; added emphasis).

In contrast to this refinement, or dullness depending on one's point of view, 'gaiety and dissipation' still pervaded the atmosphere of places such as Margate and Brighton with their 'contaminating atmosphere of excursion trains, rowdyism and uproarious multitudes' (Manning-Sanders 1951:121). Despite Victorian censure, here, it was the 'aliveness' of the place that was the basis of its charm (Becker 1884). Even if fashion did change such that by 1863, men bathing at Brighton for the first time adopted striped French 'caleçons' as bathing costumes in deference to Victorian mores, it was widely held that,

> There remained a flavour of rakishness, of freedom from restraint, of pleasurable excitement, of 'naughtiness' about the exhilarating air of Brighton right through the Nineteenth century. . . . a week-end at Brighton meant something more than a week-end at other resorts.
> (Manning-Sanders 1951:51; see Figures 2.5, 2.6 and 2.7)

Beaches had always been a 'free zone' of sorts by virtue of their status as uncertain land, the surface contours of which might change with every tide. The beach wasn't always a *pleasure zone* but had to be constructed as such, within the system of the social spatialisation. This had required not only changed attitudes, but also institutional changes. A transition accompanied this displacement. The liminal zone controlled by ritual and authoritative intermediaries such as the Dippers was superseded by a still liminal but more chaotic zone secured by the more subtle technologies of manners and modesty. Hence, it would be a mistake to fetishise the chaos of this new beach: in both cases, activities were routinised but under different regimes or sets of codes of social interaction.

Turner points out that the experience of liminality is a socially unifying one. Underscoring the sense of the liminal is the perception of unmediated encounters with other individuals also momentarily stripped of their social status. This experience of equal individuals fosters a sense of *communitas*, 'society experienced or seen as an unstructured or rudimentarily structured and relatively undifferentiated *communitatus*, community or even communion . . . .' (Turner 1979:131). This characteristic is also fundamental to Bakhtin's notion of the Carnivalesque which shares the semantic space of Turner's more analytical use of liminality.

In *Rabelais and his World* (1984), an examination of Rabelais' description of medieval carnival, the Russian literary theorist Mikhail Bakhtin treats carnival as both the 'ritual spectacle' of ecclesiastical processions and displays and as an anti-ritual of festive feasts and celebration. Thus 'a carnival atmosphere reigned on [religious] days when mysteries and *soties* were produced', while insisting that the heart of this classic carnival consisted of

'forms of protocol and ritual based on laughter and
consecrated by tradition . . . which were sharply distinct from
the serious official, ecclesiastical, feudal, and political cult
forms and [ritual] ceremonials. Carnival is a spectacle lived by
people who are all participants, actors, not spectators.
(Bakhtin 1984:7)

Carnival forms 'offered a completely different, non official . . . extra political aspect of the world, of man, and of human relations; they built a second world and a second life outside officialdom' (1984:5–6) in which all people were reduced to the common denominator of participants. This 'world inside out' was often in the form of feasts linked to the cycle of the seasons.

> The lewdness and vulgarity of carnival were directly related to the low degree of control that people had over natural forces and their own emotions. People were openly interdependent upon each other for their bodily sustenance, well-being, recreation, safety and pleasure. We can imagine how populations that could be plunged into crisis by seasonal droughts . . . and other calamities of nature, might take an exaggerated pleasure in their mass leisure forms.
>
> (Rojek 1985:27)

But significantly, if the carnivalesque has been associated with a mode of interaction characteristic of medieval holy days, fairs, and feasts, Bakhtin also finds carnival characterised by the speech and gestures of the marketplace, various forms of free abuse that he called 'Billingsgate', after the old London fish market. Both the work-time relations of the market square and leisure-time social relations provide a context for forms of carnival. The carnivalesque includes a

> temporary suspension, both ideal and real, of hierarchical rank [which] created during carnival time a special type of communication impossible in everyday life. This led to the creation of a special form of marketplace speech and gesture, frank and free, permitting no distance between those who came in contact with each other and liberating them from norms of etiquette and decency imposed at other times. A special carnivalesque, marketplace style of expression.
>
> (Bakhtin 1984:10)

Descended from the Middle Age holy days and feasts, festivals marked a rhythmic cycle of anti-ritual in which social hierarchies, moral codes, and virtues were inverted and mocked. It would, however, be wrong to simply dismiss these as 'safety valves' for developing capitalist societies. The 'social control' argument conceals a conspiracy-thesis regarding capitalism which leads to non-explanation (as there is no political or ideological institution which could not in some way be interpreted as an agency of social control),[9] and reinforces a fallacious notion of society as a closed system, an essentially stable functional totality. Carnival is strongest today in those societies least integrated into the modalities of capitalism (Haiti, for example). Rather, I wish to argue that carnival is the occasion for the enactment of alternative, utopian social arrangements. It was for this reason that Victorian essayists so hotly condemned working-class behaviour on the beach where lewd 'fun' became a threat to not only the social order of classes, but also the discipline which was taken to be synonymous with 'civilisation'.

During the seventeenth and eighteenth centuries a 'process of gradual narrowing down of the spectacle, and carnival forms of folk culture, which became small and trivial' (Bakhtin 1984:33) took place. The state encroached on festive life and turned it into parade, while festivities were brought into the home and privatised. The privileges of the marketplace were restricted.

> Carnival spirit with its freedom, its utopian character oriented toward the future, was gradually transformed into a mere holiday mood. The feast ceased almost entirely to be the people's second life, their temporary renascence and renewal .... but this carnival spirit is indestructible, it continues to fertilize various areas of life and culture.
>
> (Bakhtin 1984:33)

Stallybrass and White (1986) note the manipulation and later villification of carnivalesque modes of social interaction (such as at the feast, fair, theatre) by the emergent eighteenth-century bourgeoisie culminating in Victorian state morality. The separation of the bourgeoisie from the lower classes entailed the repression and individualisation of the carnivalesque. By means of a rigidly enforced set of moral distinctions between 'high' and 'low', the relationship of the middle class to the 'low' and lower classes was transformed from one of inclusion to one of differentiation (Stallybrass and White 1986). However, despite repression and systematic elimination of fairs and fêtes, carnival did not entirely disappear but was merely banished to less 'serious' arenas such as the liminal beach.

Bakhtin's key contribution was his relational approach to the study of high and low cultures and the structural relations between authority and carnival. For example, he notes:

> Earth is an element that devours, swallows up the grave, (the

womb) and at the same time an element of birth, or renascence [sic] (the maternal breasts). Such is the meaning of 'upward' and 'downward' in their cosmic aspect, while in their purely bodily aspect, which is not clearly distinct from the cosmic, the upper part is the face or the head and the lower part is the genital organs, the belly and buttocks. These are absolute not relative topographical connotations.

(Bakhtin 1984:20)

Ivanov argues that Bakhtin anticipated structural anthropology by nearly thirty years. His analysis treats oppositions in a similar manner to that proposed by Lévi-Strauss, seeking links between binary opposites, a process known as *mediation*.

The structural analysis of the ambivalence inherent in the 'marketplace word' and its corresponding imagery led Bakhtin to the conclusion (made independently from and prior to structural mythology) that the 'carnival image strives to embrace and unite in itself both terminal points of the process of becoming or both members of the antithesis: birth–death, youth–age, top–bottom, face–lower bodily stratum, praise–abuse' (Bakhtin). From this standpoint, Bakhtin scrutinized various forms of inverted relations between top and bottom . . . which takes place during carnival.

(Ivanov 1974:335)

The carnivalesque as a ritual inversion of the norms of 'high' culture is underscored by the celebration of the corpulent excesses and flows of the grotesque body and the 'lower bodily strata' as opposed to the controlled, disciplined body of propriety and authority. This 'lowest common denominator' is the opposite of the closure of 'taste' and propriety imposed on the disciplined body. Rather, it is un-closed, full of orifices, in becoming: 'a mobile and hybrid creature, disproportionate, exorbitant, outgrowing all limits, obscenely decentred and off-balance, a figural and symbolic resource for parodic exageration and inversion' (Stallybrass and White 1986:9) brimming over with abundant flows of energy and matter. The grotesque counterpoint to the formal propriety of authority was typical in the contrast between the medieval revels and feasts, on the one hand, and the ecclesiastical processions of the holy days on the other. In the classic case of the medieval carnival, the grotesque provided a metonymic link between the sacred spaces of heaven and the secular places of the world through the principle of degradation, lowering all to the material level of the earth and body, asserting the primacy of life. The 'excessive' grotesque body, a symbol of the irrepressible processes and flow of energies, is associated in Bakhtin's analysis with cosmic, social, topographical, and linguistic elements of the world. It is not a manifestation of rational 'economic man' but of the collective, ancestral body of all people (Bakhtin 1984:19). This recoding or transcoding of not just the grotesque body, but all elements of the 'low' in the carnivalesque leads to the inversion and thence the displacement of high–low divisions. An immediate effect is the destabilisation of official meanings (*langue*) and authoritative discourses which rely on clear oppositions and categorizations. This situation of polysemy, Bakhtin calls *heteroglossia*.

The body exposed in the liminal zone of both the medical and the pleasure beach, common to all, shamefully uncovered and scandalously open to the world is exactly such a grotesque body. It is this body that is celebrated in the thousands of copperplate engravings, cartoons and in the pre-Second World War comic postcards (Figures 2.5 and 2.6). In this corpus, the grotesque body is expressed in stereotypes of fat bathers, holidaying dandies, and buxom ladies. The numerous possible transgressions of the 'classical body' are represented in the cartoons and postcards by the interaction of 'grotesques' with authority figures. Red-faced bobbies, army colonels and majors, or other stiff-collared guardians of public morality and propriety are thoroughly catalogued in this genre, along with drunkards, embarrassed lovers, bathers, and prostitutes. In effect, the comic postcards provide a commercialised form of documentation in which the interconnection of images of Brighton and images of the grotesque, carnivalised body is preserved.

If the mass-holiday seashore ever represented a 'safety valve', site of a capitalistic pseudo-liminality which replaced personal transformation with momentary gratification, it did not last long. The beaches were quickly taken over by the older, and more subversive, tradition of the carnival. While there was a shift from the socially coordinated discipline of the medical beach, the carnivalesque beach was controlled through a mixture of norms of propriety and local by-laws which divided the beaches between different types of user. However, the carnivalesque operated precisely to dissolve the responsible and reasonable individual of Victorian morals into the common member of a mass or community. The carnivalesque zone of the beach liberated subjects from the *micro-powers* encouraging the norms, propriety, and the social dressage of the industrial worker. Amplified by the numbers of Bank Holiday revellers, this instability at the level of the subject was to pose a continuing problem. The debate over morality and dress highlights the operation of the carnivalesque which intervenes on precisely the same discursive level and on the same field as that of the those Foucauldian *micro-powers* which ensure the 'good governance' and commodification of the body. But the carnivalesque operates from the individual to the *socius* to reverse these flows of 'coded power' and erase the inscription of individuals in abstract 'subject positions' such as, for example, their work-functions and titles, or their status as legal citizens as defined by the state. Chris Doran argues that this Foucauldian notion of power as a structuring force is manifest in the classification of people by superficially neutral experts and a supposedly neutral state.

> Terms like 'working class' or other analytic equivalents . . . such as the 'people', have been emptied of their meaning over the last century or so, yet such terms have not disappeared. In fact they probably enjoy almost as much popularity today, as they did in their heyday of the early nineteenth century. The crucial difference today is that now such terms are popular among commentators rather than as terms naturally used by people to describe their own experience. This . . . is . . . the action of contemporary power. It doesn't work to punish bodies, or even to discipline them, it now works to encode them. . . . The amazing power of this codifying power is that it works by reducing anything outside the code to nonsense.
>
> (Doran 1987:4)

Moral codes can be conceived of as a regulating discipline imposed on the body – discursive codes of 'proper' conduct. However, the discursive effects of the carnivalesque have remained untheorised.[10] The explosion of 'excessive' behaviour and social pleasures and leisure forms which is found in the seaside carnival is a mark of *resistant* bodies which at least temporarily escape or exceed moral propriety. Against the restraining empiricism, cerebral rationality, emphasis on control and economy, carnival produces a momentary social space based on the politics of pleasure and physical senses. As a 'ritual of resistance', it is 'of the senses', but it decries good 'sense' (Fiske 1986:75). 'Affective investment . . . outstrips . . . cognitive meanings' (MacLaren 1987: 79). The grotesque carnival bodies on the beach are thus temporarily outside of social norms and embarked on a liminal project, even if they are in sites commercialised and territorialised in such a way as to control or contain any outbreaks of liminality. The foolish, undisciplined body is the most poignant symbol of the carnivalesque – the unclosed body of convexities and orifices, intruding onto and into others' personal space, threatening to transgress and transcend the circumscriptions of the body in the rational categories of Individual, Citizen, Consumer, Worker or Owner. This is the heart of the ecumenicism of Carnival identified by Bakhtin and the source of its power to transcend class divisions.

The lack of sufficient controls (although they had certainly tried: rules, Victorian morals, bathing machines and so on) in the face of the carnival meant that the beach was essentially an open field for social innovation. This re-appropriation and reterritorialisation of the old liminal threshold onto the Other as a social field, the margin of transition between the safety of land and the expanse of the sea, was accomplished through not only the ritual features of liminality. The good-time anarchy of the festival held the old Sublime intimidations of the expansive sea at bay. For some it was more than they could take. Schnyder (1912) documents one local case of hysteria in 'Le cas de Renata', a Freudian study of a young Swiss woman who came to him for treatment for hysteria after a visit to Brighton. Coming from a strict Catholic family of Berne merchants, the sight of promiscuous holidaymakers on the beach provoked deep fears, anorexia, vomiting. Stallybrass and White argue that the case

> reveals both the special phobic power of the carnivalesque . . .
> for the hysteric and at the same time nicely illustrates the way
> in which even the marginalized forms of popular festivity

could suddenly re-emerge in the heart of bourgeois life as the very site of potential neurosis.

(Stallybrass and White 1986:180)

Apart from the social carnival in specific spaces such as the beach, the carnivalesque was repressed in the romantic period into the private terrors exemplified by the Gothic novel and horror film – privatised isolation and neurosis rather than celebration and the insolent play with formal codes.

The crowds at Brighton were far more policed and regulated than the crowds of Bakhtin's ideal-type medieval carnival (through the requirements imposed by the conventions and schedules of railway travel and the commodification of the feast in the food stalls). However, there was a genuine reaching out to embrace the social totality of the *national* holiday. The scene on Brighton beach was no medieval carnival, nor was it simply a space of indivi-dualistic, bourgeois forms of leisure – a word which finds its etymo-logical roots in the fourteenth-century Latin *lésir*, 'to be allowed'. Leisure is not simply the presence of what is pleasurable and the absence of 'unpleasure', nor is it the absence of work (a common usage). Leisure is what is *licensed* (from the same Latin root) as legitimate pleasure within an economy of coded micro-powers. The importance of the medieval carnival is that it was a classic case of an unlicensed celebration of a socially-acknowledged inter-dependence of all people, made especially poignant by the pre-carious circumstances of the Middle Ages (Huizinga 1924:30). The carnivalesque is a form of resistance to coded power which ex-plains both the historical continuity of established leisure forms and persistence of the association between illegitimate pleasure and legitimised leisure. Bourdieu (1984) also notes that a bour-geois economy of the body which imposes a 'critical distance' between reflection and corporeal participation distinguishes middle-class spectacles such as the theatre with its ritualised applause and punctual but discontinuous shouts of 'encore' from more popular events such as the football match with its chanting and pitch invasions.

The sociality of the affective community represents an alter-native set of social ties parallel to the formalised links of class, guild or work-place titles. The realisation, rehearsal, and cele-bration of this same interdependence are at the heart of the scene

96

of holidaying Commoners who shifted aside the weight of moral distinctions of the Sabbath and propriety to practise carnivalesque forms of unlicensed, relativising, minor transgression along with the licensed, commodified, leisure 'attractions' that lined the beach. Particularly through humour, such transgressions deny class barriers founded on moral reasoning. The rowdy fun and mockery of the holiday-makers instigated a heightened level of reciprocity within the crowd from which it was difficult to withdraw and from which no one was exempt. Although not the individualistic, privatised crowd-practice of the late-twentieth-century *mass* (Maffesoli 1988b), these leisure crowds were modern in their size and their opportunities for anonymity. Nonetheless, they were not the threatening and exclusive late-twentieth-century crowds of, say, football revellers or the crowds occasioned by the alien religious days of groups foreign to us. The much-lamented anonymity of these holiday crowds may be seen as more of a metaphor of the carnivalesque loss of identity, the crowd's inclusive, cross-class character, the erosion of bourgeois privacy and marks of a social order founded on distinction. The crowded beaches and promen- ades permitted little privacy, and the masses of bodies swept over social divisions and distinctions like so many sand-castles before the tide.

The mass market success of the comic postcards marks the cross-class appeal of what was described as Brighton's 'aliveness'. Their repertoire of triumphant Privates who flaunt their dates before scandalised Majors and inebriates who present apparently logical excuses for their mishaps to red-faced, overweight bobbies in a parody of Reason includes also many 'pillars of the establishment' who are also accomplices in the fun. In many cards a 'moral figure' – often a woman, a policeman, or army sergeant – presents a caricature of the scandalised busybody. Pursuit of 'The Cure', 'taking the air', or 'the ozone' become codes for flirtation with prostitutes or apparently naive beauties (Figure 2.5). Claims to seriousness are lampooned or mocked by revealing these figures of authority playing on the beach like children, for example. Parsons indulge their desires (through alcohol or indiscrete slips of the tongue), or make ill-advised puns and 'Freudian slips' which hint at a lewd comment. Captions expose the risqué aspects of drawings of mundane encounters, carnivalising the seriousness and formality imposed on everyday life. The captions hint at a carnivalesque parallel-text besides *all* serious discourse. The insistent double coding of a barely-controlled heteroglossia which hints at fundamental social divisions over interpretation and order.

Figure 2.5 'Plenty of ozone', comic postcard

" PLENTY OF OZONE DOWN HERE, OLD MAN."
" YES, BUT NO GOOD TO ME; I'VE GOT THE MISSIS DOWN WITH ME!"

Source: Estate of Donald McGill, East Sussex County Library

Yet, within the carnivalesque one finds a mode of social regulation which tends to moderate the inversions and suspensions of the social order. Why isn't there a permanent, more extreme, carnival? The inversion and mocking of propriety is marked by an instability wherein the normative order is both presented and withdrawn at the same time. While transgressions are allowed, they are restricted to minor transgressions of morbidity, voyeurism, and flirtation with the illicit. In the case of sexual modesty, the comic postcards allude to the same fertile ground of innuendo as the dirty weekend myth. But if they wink at such practices they also exert a kind of governing influence by playing so much on the breaking or bending of taboos. The subject matter is both the carnivalesque transgression of social codes and the embarrassment of being 'caught in the act'. Abashed, red-faced characters – patriarchs, clergymen, and buxom but mature women – appear often. These cards portray the moment when those freed to enjoy the beach catch themselves with a jerk, like a dozing train passenger. They return suddenly to their 'proper' comportment, having transgressed codes of etiquette, carriage, or social position. The cards present a dialectic of impulsive desires and actions which stop short, for one reason or another: discovery, a turn of the tide, vigilant wives or the revealing question of a child-in-tow (Figure 2.6). Such winking at petty scandal and shame-faced embarrassment points to a mode of self-regulation through shame within the carnivalesque which is quite distinct from the operation of justice and moral regulation through guilt which is more characteristic of Western cultures.

Figure 2.6 'Mr Topweight', comic postcard

Source: Estate of Donald McGill, East Sussex County Library

Despite its new-found popularity as a railway terminus resort, turn-of-the-century popular opinion had held that, since the departure of Victoria, Brighton had been in a long decline (see Preston 1928). Even so, Brighton was still the largest seaside resort in 1901 where all classes mixed. Despite large amounts of capital investment most of the developments (Punch and Judy shows, the aquarium, and dancing palaces) looked back to the early nineteenth century not forward (see Pimlott 1975:182). Royal patronage had been a fundamental ingredient in the constitution of the identity of Brighton. It meant an internal inconsistency and frustration in the continuing discourse about Brighton undertaken by such papers as the *Intelligence* and abetted by London journalists who placed it at the centre of the 'system of pleasure'. Even if the town was booming economically, the transition to mass tourist holidays and day-trips was incomplete and the signs of indecision and the decline of the old trade based on the aristocratic Season were palpably evident in the decaying urban environment (see Preston 1928).

However, King Edward chose to visit several times in 1908–9. 'Nothing could exert a finer influence on the fortunes of Brighton. Nothing could be more calculated to bring about an influx of rank and fashion to the town' (*Brighton Herald* 15 February 1908). In 1908 the railway commenced its luxury train service, the *Brighton Belle*, whose scheduled time of 50 minutes from Victoria has never been surpassed to date. The 1909 Easter holiday brought record hotel profits and the crowds in August were the largest ever seen (see Roth 1941:159; Cochran 1945:7).

The hotels became provincial residences for well-known boxers, artists and actresses reaching their zenith in the inter-war years. The Metropole was finished in this period and, as the most modern hotel, together with the West Pier cornered the more 'select' segment of the market (Musgrave 1970:290–1). Brighton hotels provided not only watering-holes but also settings for two generations of British authors:

> The pale sea curdled on the shingle and the green tower of the Metropole looked like dug-up coin verdigrised with age-old mold . . . and a well-known popular author displayed his plump too famous face in the window of the Royal Albion, staring out to sea.
>
> (Greene 1936:173)

Personalities were attracted specifically by Brighton's 'aliveness'; not only an image but also a reality of gay crowds and boisterous fun (see Gilbert 1954:215–216). This period saw the development of new forms of consumption with the extension of mass consumption but also with an increasing sense of relative deprivation. This was partly due to the new visibility of wealth through mass circulation magazines (see Figure 2.7) and radio (see Stevenson and Cook 1979). Brighton boasted its own broadcast hour and resident 'radio organist'. Arnold Bennett's novels *Clayhanger* and *Hilda Lessways* about life in the Staffordshire Potteries were written at the Royal York Hotel and contain several descriptions of Brighton, which provided a thematic contrast with the Potteries which will be taken up in later chapters (Bennett 1910:476; 1911:239).[11]

> The train was in Brighton, sliding over the outskirts of town . . . Hilda saw steep streets of houses that sprawled on the hilly mounds of the great town like ladders: reminiscent of certain streets of her native district, yet quite different, a physiognomy utterly foreign to her. This, then, was Brighton. That which had been a postmark became suddenly a reality, shattering her preconceptions of it, and disappointing her she knew not why.
>
> (Bennett 1911:239)

MODS, ROCKERS AND TURF GANGS: CARNIVALS OF VIOLENCE

Brighton's reputation as a town which accommodated both the wealthy and the poor, both the upright industrial bourgeoisie and the prostitutes and hucksters living by their wits, contributed to a lasting aura of petit-criminality. Inland from the smart Crescents and Parades were narrow terraces where slum-conditions reigned. Some local historians argue that this contrast is a persistent theme in the historiography of Brighton.[12] During the First World War, the impossibility of visiting the Continent had stimulated the Brighton hotel industry. A considerable number of Londoners took refuge from Zeppelin-raids in Brighton and the large Regency houses which had begun to go out of fashion before the war were again easily sold or let (Gilbert 1954:219). But up-turns in the local economy continued to be accompanied by a seedy underside and the striking contrast the poor provided to the very wealthy.

In the inter-war years, Brighton's race-tracks and gambling establishments became the haunt of rival 'turf gangs', who feuded at the race-track and on the front, slashing their victims and enemies with razors. Extortion, loan-sharking, and protection rackets persisted into the 1930s, giving Brighton an unpleasant reputation as a 'nice place to visit' on a day-trip but not a nice environment to live in. It became dangerous to walk on the sea-front with assaults taking place even in broad daylight (*Southern Weekly News* 26 May 1928). These gangs reached their apogee in June 1936 when a gang of thirty men, the 'Hoxton Mob', attacked a bookmaker and his clerk but were detained after a mêlée with the police, who had anticipated violence. Graham Greene's *Brighton Rock* (1936) immortalised this period of gang violence. His Pinkie's gang was an invention and *Brighton Rock* fiction, but it was closely based on the actual reports of track violence. Apart from the slashings, the bizarre 'Trunk Murders' added to Brighton's unsavoury reputation. In one famous case, a man murdered and dismembered his wife, and sent different parts by rail to different destinations as baggage (see Lustgarten 1951:187–238).

But Brighton had long been known as a 'miniature Marseilles' (Lustgarten 1951:188). The Trunk Murders of 1934 were not the first of their kind, the classic case having also taken place in Brighton in 1831 (see Hindley 1875 and Lina Wertmuller's *Seven Beauties* movie version, set in Italy). Lowerson and Howkin's argue that Brighton attracted 'rough cultures', a vertical banding of culture in contrast to the horizontal banding of socio-economic classes (1981:72). However, this poses the problem of why Brighton with its liminal and carnivalesque image attracted these groups. On the one hand, the loosening of restraints on violence is a constitutive part of the carnivalesque, exaggerating violent tendencies that might have emerged anywhere. On the other hand, the scene of relatively wealthy people, with a less cautious hand on their wallets, must have been irresistible to con artists and small-time hucksters. With the structuring elements of everyday life removed or destabilised and the primacy of enjoyment and adventurousness in Brighton, the bases on which judgements could be formed were eroded: people would spend more, more impulsively and take more risk.

The status of Brighton as a liminal zone made any and all rumours of transgression, decadence, crime, and degeneration the basis for sensational newspaper reporting, which formed a staple diet of 'Brighton stories' which have circulated in the British press for almost two centuries. These reports served to restate and confirm the spatialisation of Brighton, on the margins of the orderly sphere of 'good governance' which reigned over other parts of the nation. The 'Brighton Rock' criminal image coexisted with the place-images of decadent, risqué and glamorous Brighton, reinforcing Brighton's liminal place-myth (Figure 2.7).

Figure 2.7 'The million', cartoon, 1920s

Source: East Sussex County Library

The beach fights between groups of 'Mods' and 'Rockers' of the early 1960s are another example of the liminal breakdown of social order (see Figure 2.8). From the late eighteenth century onwards, Brighton had continued to be a destination for anyone searching for escape: a liminal zone and social periphery in a marginal geographic location 'separated-off by the South Downs' (Brighton Tourism Committee 1954:8).[15] Mods (from the bebop term 'Modernists') originated in the suburbs of London. Youth from a largely working-class but white-collar background attempted to abstract themselves from traditional class identities. Upward mobility was indicated with a neat, hip image adopted from the dandyism of black Harlem and European jazz artists. Stylistically the culture of the Mods was largely masculine in its trademarks. These included, for the men, suits with narrow trousers and pointed shoes, anoraks for scootering; and for the women, short hair and a cultivated, dead-pan elegance (Brake 1985:75). Rockers, who eschewed the fashionable snobbery of the Mods (Nuttall 1969:333), presented their alter-ego opposite: class-bound and masculine, low-paid, unskilled manual workers (Barker and Little 1964). Motorcycles became Rockers' symbols of freedom from authority, of mastery and intimidation (Willis 1978), while Mods glamorised accessory-bedecked Italian scooters. Clubs allowed the Mods a glamorous dream world (being in a sense proto-discos) in which class background could be rejected.

The two groups came together on Bank Holidays in the established motoring destination of Brighton (from London, literally the end of the road) with its clubs, glamorous past and reputation for freedom from moral and class restraint. From London, there was no more appropriate Bank Holiday weekend destination, for none of the other seaside resorts in reach of London shared this combination of images. In fact, Mods and Rockers clashed at Brighton on only two occasions (the May and the August Bank Holidays, 1964). In the original news photographs we see scenes of, on the one hand, youths being kicked by assailants, deck chairs been thrown and, on the other hand, grins on the faces of some of the participants in the mêlée (see Figure 2.8). The 'riots' were boisterous and violent but the bitterness one associates with rioting is missing. After the media hysteria, those smiles leave the different impression of a boisterous carnival of violence rather than planned attacks by groups of bitter criminal enemies, or the frustration of disenfranchised ethnic groups or the poor. 'Media coverage of a small amount of damage and violence on British seaside beaches on a rather dismal national holiday led to a situation of deviancy amplification' (Brake 1985:64). Only after the notoriety of being media 'folk devils', was there a conscious embracing of the two deviant roles by large numbers of youth. The 'indiscriminate prosecution, local overreaction and media stereotyping' created a 'moral panic' (Cohen 1972) and implied a type of conspiracy: 'the solidifying of amorphous groups of teenagers into some sort of conspiratorial collectivity, which had no concrete existence' (Brake 1985:64). On Brighton beach, Mods and Rockers became visible and socially identifiable groups. The combination of alcohol, drugs, and the release from the restraints of everyday domestic surroundings combined to make the beach an appropriate and available stage for an explosion of the tensions between the two groups.

Figure 2.8 Beach fights between Mods and Rockers

Source: Brighton and Hove Argus, East Sussex County Library

DIRTY WEEKENDS AND THE CARNIVAL OF SEX

Unreal City
Under the brown fog of a winter noon
Mr. Eugenides, the Smyrna merchant
Unshaven, with a pocket full of currants
C.i.f. London: documents at sight
Asked me in demotic French
To luncheon at the Cannon Street Hotel
Followed by a weekend at the Metropole.
(T.S. Eliot 1922, *The Waste Land:* III, ll.207–214)

The switch to day-trips and holidays with a broad appeal had brought families, not the single and independent few who could afford the services of prostitutes (who would have to wait for the conference trade with its lonely conferencees to expand again).[14] The 'Season' at Brighton, and seaside holidays generally, continued to present opportunities for the young to meet and flirt with a broad variety of other youth away from the constraints of community gossip and in an atmosphere of relaxed parental surveillance.[15] This was heightened by Brighton's exotic and 'continental' reputation – a reputation as an 'unreal' city widespread enough for T.S. Eliot to incorporate a proposition for a dirty weekend at the Metropole Hotel, into his poem *The Waste Land* (1922:III, l.214).

> The seaside holiday had for long been looked upon as an occasion for boy to meet girl . . . . So the precedents existed when the First World War ended and the Boys Came Home. Where precedent was forgotten was the ease with which couples could now pair off, without benefit of chaperon and out of sight of a calculating or a forbidding parental eye. Dance halls showed the way . . . [places] for young middle-class men on holiday to cut a dash and for the girls to have a fling.
>
> (Hern 1967:176)

Despite its prominent image as a place of immorality and indolence, it is very difficult to determine whether or not Brighton's twentieth-century image as a 'dirty weekend destination' was supported by the actual number of divorces that stemmed from adulterous dirty weekends. Records for the Probate and Magistrates Courts and Courts of Assizes are not published in Britain and the original shorthand manuscripts are typically disposed of in an ad hoc manner after fifty years. Neither do law journals routinely publish divorce proceedings unless a point of law has been established. While newspapers generally reported the granting of *decrees nisi* (the nullification of a marriage) the details of the majority of cases are never discussed. Hotel records also prove uninformative sources. Thus, it is impossible to answer whether or not 'dirty weekends' in the 1920s and 1930s – not to mention post-1936 – were just nostalgic re-enactments of the Prince's infidelity. However, as has been argued in the preceding sections, the actual presence or lack of the activity is beside the point: one would not be surprised to find a few cases, but while Brighton enjoyed its 'raffish' reputation, the reality was mostly 'families and a few clergymen'. The question then is about the power of social spatialisation and myths to over-run reality.

Dirty weekends were less spontaneous than one might first expect. They were organised to stage an adulterous affair, as the excuse of infidelity was required for couples seeking a divorce until 1936.

> Divorce . . . still carried a slight social stigma in old-fashioned circles, especially where the woman was the offending party; to oblige their guilty wives, therefore, most men were gentlemanly enough to go through the farce of adultery with a 'woman unkown' and thus give their wives grounds for divorcing them. Divorce lawyers, winking at this collusive irregularity, were usually able to fix the husband up with a professional 'woman unkown' and with chambermaids' evidence at some Brighton hotel.
>
> (Graves and Hodge 1950:109)

The practice of what were really sham 'dirty weekends' was made unnecessary by A.P. Herbert's *Divorce Act 1936*. Herbert, a novelist MP, had made 'dirty weekends' infamous in his book *Holy Deadlock* (1934).

> As a rule, the gentleman takes the lady to a hotel – Brighton or some such place - enters her in the book as his wife – shares a room with her, and sends the bill to his wife. The wife's agents cause inquiries to be made, and eventually they find the chambermaid who brought the guilty couple their morning tea. A single night used to be sufficient, but the President [of the court] has been tightening things up, and we generally advise a good long week-end to-day. What you want to suggest, you see, is that there is a real and continuing attachment, not merely a casual fling or a put-up job. That is why Brighton is good, for all the wild lovers are supposed to go there, though I never saw any one at the Capitol but clergymen and family parties. . . .
> . . . 'do I actually have to – to – you know?'
> 'To sleep with the lady? Technically, no. But you must share the same room and you must be in the same bed in the morning when the tea comes up.'
> 'Good God!' said John. 'What a world!'
>
> (Herbert 1934:31)

The very common-ness of the ploy is fatal to the hopes of the couple for a divorce.

> At the fatal word 'hotel', [the Presiding Magistrate], looked up from the pleadings before him and looked down at Mr. Ransom. . . . 'A hotel? At Brighton? . . . All this seems very familiar, Mr. Ransom. And now you are going to tell me, I suppose, that the respondent and the woman . . . spent two nights at this hotel, and were seen in bed by a chambermaid, and the respondent sent the bill to his wife – and so on?'
>
> (Herbert 1934:99–100)

In the novel the husband hires a 'woman unknown' to take to Brighton where they stay at 'the Capitol', a thinly veiled reference to the paramount dirty weekend hotel – the Metropole. Popularly, the name appears to have become synonymous with the illicit. According to Brightonians, its corridors were reputed to be crowded with private detectives – hired by the co-respondent – who obligingly recorded the damning evidence for the case.

Why was Brighton a good setting for infidelity? Even if we took the novelist at his word that 'all the wild lovers are supposed to go there,' the theory of the carnivalesque provides further insights. Brighton's liminal status pre-dated the re-formalisation of its image in the dirty weekend myth. In the spatialisation of the British Isles, the beach or the seaside provided an appropriate place, because it was a free zone, 'betwixt and between' social codes. It was a zone, even *conducive* (without being determinate) to lapses in normative behaviour. Second, the long association with the carnivalesque had resulted in a reputation for lack of restraint. Actual, as opposed to mythical, dirty weekends appear to be unconventional, but simply functional, ploys within an adverse institutional context which was hostile to divorces. Brighton was convenient to London, with an established reputation for not only frivolity but also continuing defiance of moral standards. Nonetheless, as a new element in the media-borne place-images of Brighton, the real facts of this material practice are relatively marginal and unremembered in a fable that has grown to mythic proportions. The dirty weekend phenomenon exploited the reputation of Brighton as the scene of the carnivalesque lifting of social norms with consequent immorality, violent murder, and general lack of respect for decency. Dirty weekends incorporated the carnivalesque place-myth of Brighton into divorce cases, inflecting them with the emotional overtones of a shocking weekend of debauchery at an infamous Brighton hotel, to over-ride the hesitancy of a conservative judiciary. As a variation on Brighton's association with the liminal, the dirty weekend was designed to change the status of the man involved from that of a 'gentleman' to that of an 'adulterer'. The practice was drawn to Brighton, both extending and confirming the power of the town's place-myth.

Such a practice required both planning and enough money to hire a professional 'woman unknown' and to stage a highly visible weekend in Brighton's nightspots. This economic power had to be flanked by a concern for respectability, particularly that of the wife who became the co-respondent, but who was often the originally guilty party. Such features point to the dirty weekend being a middle-class practice. Those lower down on the socio-economic ladder would not have had the spare money and the wealthy and aristocratic would have maintained marriages for the purposes of maintaining family ties while being able to afford to carry on affairs without fear of being ruined by scandal because they did not depend on personal integrity but their titles. The dirty weekend myth represents a 'packaging' of the older myths of indolence and immorality which were reshaped by a material practice closer to the fantasies of middle-classes bound by Victorian moral sanction and norms which imposed a corset of chastity on marital partners and above all on the order of the family. It continued the liminal/ carnivalesque place-myth of Brighton, providing a poignant example of liminal behaviour aimed at the heart of hegemonic Victorian middle-class values which was exploited by the press and novelists to great effect. So strong was its impact that this material social practice formed Brighton's carnivalesque/liminal *semiosis*, or meaning, into the particular form of the dirty weekend myth, inflecting the place-myth of Brighton to the present day to the extent that hotels run nostalgic 'Dirty Weekend Specials' where couples sign in anonymously as Mr and Mrs Jones.

The Beach remains spatialised as a liminal zone of potential carnival. In the late 1800s and particularly in the twentieth century up until the rise of foreign holidays eclipsed the seaside resorts in the 1950s, the modes of behaviour characteristic of the beach were normalised and generalised to other social fields and spaces – holiday camps, the interiors of clubs and hotels and so on. At

109

Brighton, the 'zone of liminality' itself was dissipated through the town, and the excesses of the holiday-makers were exploited by small-time entrepreneurs, who established clubs, hotels, and even brothels which depended on out-of-town day-trippers attracted by the general liminality of Brighton's place-myth. Hence the appropriateness of Brighton with its freedoms – for the elaboration of modes of marginality from the derelicts and the Mods to punks and homeless youth to Brighton's status in the tabloid press as the 'AIDS Capital of Britain' in the 1980s (although it cannot possibly have more cases than more populous London). Opposed to this, attempts to 'make Brighton respectable' may be seen throughout this century. In the 1950s the *Official Handbook* was purged of its allusions to 'Lovely girls in holiday high spirits' (Brighton Tourism Committee 1953:3 and 1954:2) and photos of 'bathing beauties' were replaced with a safe family sports emphasis (1955 through 1967:6–8) rather than the daily beach-front beauty contests in which women could participate to select a 'Queen of the Day'. The Borough Council had begun to promote the town from the late 1930s, attempting to intervene in the carnivalesque place-myth. The Council advertised using a promotional newsreel, 'Playground of the Kings', which was shown in cinemas in Britain, Canada and the United States. A full-time promotions officer was appointed and official guidebooks or 'handbooks' were published. The *1937–1938 Official Handbook* featured a fictionalised visit by a reluctant couple, 'Northerners by birth and residence, and consequently – like all such – regard the south and all who dwell therein with a kind of indulgent condescension.' Despite their suspicions of Brighton's liminal status, they eventually fall in love with the town – and the guidebook takes every opportunity to stress the literary connections of the town with well-known authors[16] – '"Jane Austen would have felt at home here," said Aunty Penelope. "She would and I did," I said, "A visit to Brighton combines every possibility of earthly happiness," those were her very words' (Brighton Tourism Committee 1937:6).

To summarise, roughly three overlapping phases in the disposition of the beach as a social zone have been distinguished:

- *Phase I* 1800–mid 1840s. The medicalised bathing beach and its attached social promenade. The liminal Brighton of Dr Russell and George IV's seaside was established in relation to what were seen as the staid social arrangements of the Spas and the grimness of London.

• *Phase II* 1850s–1920s: The Brighton beach of the mass seaside day holidays. The carnivalisation of the beach slowly displaced the medicalised, liminal beach and the sublime of the late Victorian middle class. This was complemented by the capitalist reorganisation of liminality by developers, the railway, and the local petit bourgeoisie. With the stress on 'aliveness' and freedom from oppressive codes of conduct, the carnivalesque beach represented the antithesis of the rational productivism of the everyday environment. Regulation was at first achieved by limiting access through the number of holidays but this was superseded by self-regulation through shame, embarrassment, and humour.

• *Phase III* 1920–Present: Dirty weekends and violence as the transgression of social norms supersede the controls of the institutionalised liminal zone of carnival thoughout the town. The images of Brighton as a site of carnival become repackaged in the form of a slowly fading 'dirty weekend' myth.

The position of the beach in the overarching historical social spatialisation has been construed differently over time: reterritorialised from free zone of transition to liminal zone and carnivalesque pleasure zone. Against the theoretical dichotomy which transposes an economistic division of production and consumption into geographical terms, this case-history suggests that such a division is overly-simplistic. In such an approach, for leisure to take place, it is presumed that there must be a separation of the site of work from the site of leisure, raising the problem of the different status of 'production spaces' from 'consumption spaces'. These terms have since been adopted by many urban theorists, most notably David Harvey (1982; see Shields 1989). This enshrines a separation which, in view of many men's use of the home almost solely as an after-work domestic leisure centre, excludes housewives from the analyses of some theorists (including some of those at Birmingham's Centre for Cultural and Community Studies cf. Hobson in Tomlinson 1981:65). Surprisingly, this leads to the conclusion that leisure does not exist for women, rather than to a questioning of this *gendered definition of leisure* and an investigation of women's 'non-work' and perhaps inverted forms of pleasure

111

(for example, the beach-front beauty contests – see *Brighton Herald* 15 August 1938), if it is not to be called leisure. The changing status of the beach, and the furore over the morality and appropriateness of the carnival which erupted at the seaside, open up the question, examined further in the next case, of the relations between genders and with different conventional roles in different periods.

We must take into consideration Bakhtin's contention that the erotic release of carnival is productive in the sense that it re-creates and rejuvenates the psyche. It re-unites the divided parts of the person. Real 'person-work' is thus being done under the guise of leisure on the beach. As the above case-history shows, what divides the beach (pleasure zone) from the factory floor is not a consumption-production divide but a spatial division according to the logic of *rational-libidinal* principles. This is not, then, simply a replacement of the 'hardness' of a geographical site for the intangibilities of 'leisure'. Libidinal energies, as Deleuze and Guattari have argued, are always real and productive (1976). Rational-libidinal divisions have emerged as a primary division of the social spatialisations considered in this case-history and will reappear in the chapters that follow. In an over-arching social spatialisation of Britain, the place-myth of Brighton is located in an imaginary geography *vis-à-vis* the place-myths of other towns and regions which form the contrast which established its reputation as a liminal destination, a social as well as geographical margin, a 'place apart'.

NOTES

1. Defoe said,

> The sea is very unkind to this town and has by its continual encroachments, so gain'd upon them, that in a little time the more they might reasonably expect it would eat up the whole town, about 10 houses having been devoured by the water in a few years past; they are now obliged to get a brief granted them, to beg money all over England, to raise banks against the water; the expense of which. . . . will be eight thousand pounds; which if one were to look on the town, would seem to be more than all the houses in it are worth.
>
> (1724 cited in Manning-Sanders 1951:16)

2. Walton comments:

    > In Lancashire at least, the sea bathing of this time was
    > prophylactic as well as therapeutic in its intent. At various points
    > along the coast, from the Mersey to Morecambe Bay, hundreds of
    > artisans and country people bathed and drank sea water regularly
    > at the August spring tide, which was held to have special powers
    > of purification and regeneration as well as curing all manner of
    > diseases.
    >
    > (1983:10)

3. The census of 1851 groups Brighton together with ten other seaside
    towns. Together with the four inland resorts, such towns had
    experienced a rate of increase in excess of 254 per cent between 1801
    and 1851; higher than London (146 per cent) or the fifty-one
    manufacturing towns (224 per cent) (Census of Great Britain 1851
    1852:xlix 'Population Table I').

4. For example, by 1733 it had become so popular that it was rumoured
    that Walpole proposed to tax sea-bathing:

    > considering the vast consumption of these waters, there is a
    > design laid of excising them next session; and moreover, that as
    > bathing in the sea is become the general practice of both sexes;
    > and as the Kings of England have always been allowed to be
    > masters of the sea, every person so bathing shall be gauged, and
    > pay so much per foot square as their cubical bulk amounts to.
    >
    > (Chesterfield 1773 cited in Pimlott 1975:51)

5. Claims and counter-claims regarding the climate at resorts, and even
    the publication of death-rate of rival resorts, marked the competition
    for, first, Royal patronage, then mass appeal. As one poet satirically
    put it in 1841:

    > If they say that it rains,
    > Or gives rheumatic pains,
    > 'Tis a libel (I'd like to indict one).
    > All the world's in surprise
    > When *any one* dies
    > (Unless he prefers it) – at Brighton.
    > (Anon. 'Arion' in *Blackwood's Magazine* 184:150)

    There were

    > calm waters and health-giving trees, breathing balm and
    > correcting the 'too drying and heating property of the air' (at
    > Bournemouth), or the . . . bracing, nerve-stimulating air (at
    > Scarborough), or relaxing, nerve-soothing air (at Torquay), the
    > 'continual swell and surf of the sea . . . which . . . annoys,
    > frightens and spatters the bathers exceedingly' (on the south

coast, when an east coast resort is being advertised), or the 'million of tons of health-giving salt water that flow daily' past the walls of a hotel on the north Cornwall coast (when this is to be preferred to a milder retreat); the ozone in the mud of a muddy shore or the absence of mud on a sandy one; the life-giving emanations of the iodine in seaweed, or the complete freedom from seaweed's noxious effluvias – each and all can be turned to good account, according to the character of the particular place you wished to extol or condemn.

(Manning-Sanders 1951:48–9)

6. Prince Clement Metternich and King Louis Philippe spent the winter along with the statesmen Brougham, Palmerston, and Aberdeen, as well as the authors Dickens, Macaulay, and Bulwer-Lytton.

7. Even the most localised seaside trades such as selling whelks or Punch and Judy were imported by a London coaster in the former case, and by performers from inland fairs in the case of the latter:

city dwellers at the seaside wanted 'a change of air'. . . . They also want to find . . . [what] they were used to. And what they were used to included stalls or barrows selling gingerbeer, pies, sticky sweets, bowls of soup and jellied eels. Quite often the barrow-boy or portable stall-holder would travel down on the first train along with the earliest of his potential customers.

(Hern 1967:78)

8. James White and Prof. Henry Fawcett were the independent Members of Parliament for Brighton elected in July 1865 and re-elected in November 1868.

9. There is no indication in the phrase of who the agents or instigators of social control may be: no indication of any common mechanism whereby social control is enforced: no constant criterion whereby we may judge whether social control has broken down – certainly not conflict, for this may be ultimately, or even inherently, be a means of reinforcing conformity. Nor finally is there any fixed yardstick whereby we may know when social control has been reimposed. Since capitalism is still with us, we can with impunity suppose, if we wish to, that at any time in the last three hundred years, the mechanisms of social control were operating effectively. If a casual allusion to 'social control' turns out be vacuous, it is equally clear that social control cannot merely be added on to a Marxist interpretation. The phrase social control suggests a static metaphor of equilibrium, which might be disturbed and then reasserted on a new basis. It suggests there-fore three successive states – a prior functioning, a period of breakdown, and a renewed state of functioning. Even stopping at

this point we can see a basic incompatibility with any Marxist interpretation. For if we seriously wish to adopt a Marxist explanation, it is impossible to operate this mechanical separation of periods of control and breakdown. A mode of production is irreducibly a contradictory unity of forces and relations of production. Just as, in order to survive, the relations of production must be continually reproduced so is the contradiction embodied within those relations of production continually reproduced. Contradiction is not episodically, but continually present; the antagonism between the producers of the surplus and the owners and controllers of the means of production extracting the surplus, is a structural and permanent feature. Thus class conflict is a permanent feature, not a sign of breakdown, and the conditions in which class conflict may assume explosive or revolutionary forms bear only the emptiest of resemblances to a crude notion conveyed by the phrase 'breakdown of social control'.

(Stedman-Jones 1981; 164–165)

10. Except in the work of scattered writers such as Sade, Bataille, or Nietzsche who try to formulate Bacchanalian excess (see Maffesoli 1985; MacLaren 1988).
11. In Bennett's novel *Clayhanger* (1910) the whole description of the anticipation of an illicit trip to Brighton (though not actually for a dirty weekend per se) is given dubious overtones:

On the Thursday he had told Maggie, with affected casualness, that on the Friday he might have to go to London, about a new machine. Sheer invention! Fortunately Maggie had been well drilled by her father in the manner proper to women in accepting announcements connected with 'business'. . . . It was a word that ended arguments, or prevented them. . . . At the shop, 'Stifford,' he had said, 'I suppose you don't happen to know a good hotel in Brighton? I might run down there for the week-end if I don't come back to-morrow. But you needn't say anything.'
'No, sir,' Stifford had discreetly concurred in this suggestion. 'They say there's really only one hotel in Brighton, sir – the Royal Sussex. But I've never been there.'
Edwin had replied: 'Not the Metropole, then?' 'Oh no, sir!'

(Bennett 1910:475)

Later, upon his arrival in Brighton, he thinks:

As for Brighton, it corresponded with no dream. It was vaster than any imagining of it. Edwin had only seen the pleasure cities of the poor and of the middling, such as Blackpool and Llandudno. He had not conceived what wealth would do when it

organised itself for the purposes of distraction. . . . Suddenly he
saw Brighton in its autumnal pride, Brighton beginning one of its
fine week-ends, and he had to admit that the number of rich and
idle people in the world surpassed his provincial notions. For
miles westwards and miles eastwards, against a formidable
background of high, yellow and brown architecture, persons the
luxuriousness of any one of whom would have drawn remarks in
Bursley, walked or drove or rode in thronging multitudes. . . .
The air was full of the . . . consciousness of being correct and
successful.

(Bennett 1910:476–477)

12. This argument has been advanced by my colleague at Sussex University, Kevin Meetham.
13. See also the recent movie *Mona Lisa* (1987) where the characters
escape from London gangs to Brighton where they are caught up with
and where a final seduction, betrayal, and show-down takes place.
14. This assertion is based on the author's own personal observation of
the proliferation of 'For a Good Time Call . . . ' messages around the
Brighton Centre and seafront conference hotels and the railway
station in the late 1980s.
15. This continues today. See for example ITV's 1986 TV drama *Seaside*.
The plot turns around the romantic encounter of two young people
during family holidays at a seaside resort in the 1950s and around the
young man's encounters with a youth gang who become his rivals in
romance.
16. A later *Handbook* adds:

In a novel by one of our most interesting recent authors, a man
from the Midlands knows of Brighton as a 'romantic name'. That
is what it had been for Arnold Bennett himself when he lived in
the Potteries. It is a 'romantic name' to people all over the
country. Outside the country too. Its reputation is international.
No one who reads English books can help hearing of it. It has a
secure place in literature.

(Brighton Tourism Committee 1938:12)

Chapter Three

NIAGARA FALLS
Honeymoon capital of the world[1]

Father Hennepin, the first white man to see the Falls at Niagara in 1697, wrote of 'an incredible Cataract or Waterfall, which has no equal', whose waters 'foam and boil in a fearful manner.'

> I wish'd an hundred times that somebody had been with us, who could have describ'd the Wonders of this prodigious frightful Fall, so as to give the Reader a just and natural Idea of it, such as might satisfy him, and create in him an Admiration of this Prodigy of Nature as great as it deserves.
>
> (Hennepin 1698)

Partly because Hennepin's illustrated monograph was so widely distributed, and partly because Hennepin was the first European to have actually seen the Falls,[2] his description became the paradigm for an image of Niagara which dominated the European imagination for a century: a disorganised topography where water pours from different directions over high, claustrophobic cliffs into a gorge set in an otherwise flat landscape (see Figures 3.1 and 3.2).

Progressive changes in the attitude towards Niagara Falls and its images and reputation have taken place as a result of opposed advertising images over more than 200 years. Unlike the case of Brighton, Niagara Falls acquired a reputation through self-promotion rather than notoriety. However, similar questions as in the case of Brighton can be asked about why the Falls were an appropriate site for certain activities and not others. Again, at Niagara these activities were liminoid in nature: for several generations of North Americans and still today for East Asian tourists from Japan, Korea, and China, the Falls formed a true pilgrimage

117

destination as a 'Shrine of Nature' (Figure 3.3). The connotations
of Niagara place-images reveal a transfunctionalisation (Barthes
1972) of Niagara Falls into a signifier of both 'Nature's Goodness',
to borrow the slogan of a breakfast cereal which was promoted
using an image of the Falls, and a signifier of indulgent, even
decadent 'Event Honeymoons'. These often contradictory images
have determined its position, as a real place, within a social spatialisation of places and spaces within the social Imaginary. As noted,
this constellation of meaning-laden geographic sites and spaces is
articulated on the principle of differences. The key to the 'meaning' of Niagara is its distinctness from other places and spaces as a
certain kind of place, territorialised and 'made good' for certain
activities.

How can one introduce this place which today shows the traces
of so many attitudes and activities that it is bewilderingly contradictory? The physical and built environment around Niagara Falls
bears the sedimented traces of the history of visitors, Native and
European, occupants, and the later electrochemical industries
depending on the power of the Falls. Historically, the physical
difficulty in accommodating the Falls and rendering them as a
neutral part of the landscape of everyday life has ensured the
special status of the place. Commentators allowed that it had the
ineffable quality of the extra-ordinary. The engraver Bartlett said
'You may dream of Niagara, but words will never describe it to you'
(1855 cited in Colombo 1974:254; see Figure 3.4). But the
eighteenth- and nineteenth-century myths of the impossibility of
Niagara's representation, of its authentic uniqueness, declined
after Frederick Church's painting, which was hailed as successfully
reproducing it. This 'loss of aura' (Benjamin 1975b) led to a
decline of the liminal status of Niagara as what had become a
privileged honeymoon site, a place for transitions and *rites de
passage* in the life-cycle. If Brighton was 'betwixt and between' the
sublime chaos of the sea and the ordered landscapes of England,
Niagara was consecrated as a place for people who were betwixt
and between one social status and another, passing over all the
taboos separating the lives of the respectable single and the
married. While this attitude (represented today by the Niagara
Parks Commission), which assigns the Falls the status of a shrine or
temple of domesticity, survives in the form of landscape gardening
'cues' and conventions, the loss of aura or authenticity and the

118

twentieth-century overproduction of nuptial clichés have favoured
a more popular, kitsch, and self-consciously ironic reception of the
Falls complemented by the 'eruption' of gratification (Deleuze
and Guattari 1976). Thus the fun-fair 'attractions' and what will be
called the 'Event Honeymoon': no longer a *rite de passage*, merely a
momentary escape into sexual carnival. Not the 'elective re-
centring' (Cohen *et al.* 1987) of the pilgrim/tourist but the carnival of the day-tripper, on the one hand, and the symbolistic
collection of 'points of interest' of the 'post-tourist' on the other
(MacCannell 1976; Urry 1987).[3]

HISTORICAL REACTION TO NIAGARA FALLS

With uproar hideous first the Falls appear
The stunning tumult thundering on the ear.
Above, below, where'er the astonished eye
Turns to behold, new opening wonders lie.
There the broad river, like a lake outspread
The islands, rapids, falls, in grandeur dread
This great o'erwhelming work of awful Time
In all its dread magnificence, sublime.
(Wilson 1818, ll.2059–2062, 2065–2066, 2069–2070)

Reaction to Niagara Falls has always been a matter of superlatives.
Many observers reported themselves lost for words and in awe; they
describe the experience in terms of the natural sublime, awe
verging on terror (Marx 1975). From Hennepin's first report until
the opening of the Erie Canal in 1825, Niagara Falls remained a
remote and exotic wonder which appeared to be destined to defy
all mortal attempts ever to 'conquer her power'.[4] 'Here the consequences of his mightiest efforts have so little influence on the
whole that we are convinced of the majesty of the stream, and that
it will forever scorn the confinements of art' (*Monthly Anthology and
Boston Review* 1806: 457–458). Even when accommodation had
become available at Niagara, travel was difficult and only for the
most adventurous. It involved costly preparations: the requisition-
ing of a ship from Boston, several days' journey, or from Buffalo,
one day's sailing, foodstuffs, pack horses, and native guides.

The difficulty and remoteness of the cataracts enhanced their
liminal status, lying on the far margins of the Known World of the

time. As a site outside of the realm of everyday life, the eighteenth-
and nineteenth-century visions of Niagara Falls give an example of
the symbolic constitution of a sacred place in that environment of
relative placelessness, an undifferentiated expanse of bush, referred to as a wilderness. Within this cultural equivalent of the
biblical desert, Niagara Falls provided a beacon and established
location towards which and from which the traveller could orient
him or herself. The traveller, following a prescribed itinerary and
sequence of resting stations, was, in effect, a pilgrim engaged in
processual ritual of spatial displacement. The goal of Niagara was
compelling enough to transcend the difficulties of the route,
which only added to the value of the pilgrimage and heightened
its potential for self-discovery. These later travellers were explorers, but not at all in the same mode as Hennepin or Champlain.

Figure 3.1 Context map of Niagara Falls

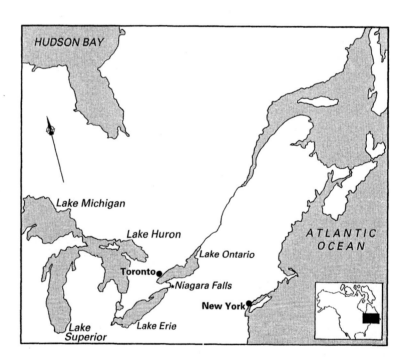

Readily available for wider symbolic appropriation, Niagara became an *axis mundus* tying together heaven and earth: not just a known place in a savage space of the Ontario wilderness but an *existential anchor* providing a sense of security around which the entire world could be figuratively remapped. This remapping and constitution of a sense of 'centredness' is the nub of Heidegger's conceptual and affective sense of 'dwelling' (1968a:149). Hence it is not surprising that reports of Niagara's ineffable spirit conform to Eliade's characterisation of pilgrim shrines as places where 'something of a wholly different order, a reality that does not belong to our world, [was included] in objects that are an integral part of our natural, profane, world' (1959:11). These sites may be heights, sacred mountains, islands, or may lie on topographical boundaries such as that between land and sea, in grottos which penetrate down into the earth. Like Niagara, they are all characterised by their difference from their surroundings. The metaphysical nature of the quest is apparent in the early commentaries and travelogues.

The trip to Niagara, through its social construction as a processual ritual thus substituted a reassuring, sacred spatialisation of the world for rational, modern abstractions of metric distances and senses of 'the world' expressed and imagined as cartographic projections. Space becomes charged with differentials of meaning, with sacred sites such as Niagara consecrated places of power and existential significance. The transposition of one spatial outlook for another is achieved partly through the journey itself which presents a spatial displacement which may become a metaphor for the displacement of one 'space' for another, a religious spatialisation for an abstract, rational spatialisation. Pilgrimage is an existential 'drama' in which information and transformative potentials are 'encoded'. Movement in space and the reorientation of spatialisations around the sacred destination such as a Niagara, Jerusalem, or Mecca, is thus both the context, medium and content of the pilgrimage. Spatial movement both assists and symbolises a movement towards an encounter with the sacred (Turner 1974) and a momentary distancing from the social order and spatialisation of daily life: 'Pilgrims cease to be members of a *perduring* system of social relations . . . and become members of a transient class of initiands and pilgrims, moving *per agros*, through the fields or lands' (Radcliffe-Brown 1957:22 cited in Turner

1979:122). Not only is the pilgrim-traveller spatially itinerant but values and attitudes are susceptible to change with the distance from the strictures and disciplines of everyday life. Turner also notes the role of peripherality in his study of pilgrimage.

> The marked peripherality of pilgrimage shrines, their location outside the main administrative centers of state or church, and, indeed, the temporal structure of the pilgrimage process, beginning in a familiar place, going to a Far Place, and returning to a Familiar Place, theoretically changed relates to . . . *rites de passage*. Van Gennep demonstrated that many types of ritual, notably initiation rites, have three distinguishable stages . . . (1) *separation*, (2) *margin* or *limen*, and (3) *reaggregation*. . . . Van Gennep paid particular attention to the correlation between status movement and spatial position. . . . spatial separation from the familiar and habitual . . . may, in various cultures, have punitive, purificatory, expiatory, cognitive, instructional, therapeutic, transformative, and many other facets, aspects and functions.
>
> (Turner 1974: 195–196)

Like carnival, or liminal initiation rites, pilgrimage operates on the body which is removed from its supporting cocoon of the everyday environment and exposed to both rigours and dangers of an unknown, non-routinised, milieu. In the case of Niagara, this was the New York and Ontario bush or the journey by ship from Boston. Despite the moralising tone of the accounts of this period, it is precisely the non-discursive nature of the Niagara experience which was remarkable. It was encountered by early travellers with few buffering rationalisations which neatly encapsulated the experience and sublimated the roar of the Falls to Reason. Indeed, it appears that the significance of Niagara during this period was that it lay not only outside of the geographic borders of civilisation but also outside of the cognitive borders of Reason. It challenged the secular identity and humanism of the Enlightenment subject of the early eighteenth century. In this respect we may now begin to appreciate the poet's words: *the Falls were hideous, overwhelming.* As Father Hennepin called them: 'prodigious frightful'. This experience was soon to be lost, however, as the Falls became anchored into the defensive alignment of discursive systems of thought and imagery. 'Niagara' no longer referred to itself, the

Figure 3.2 The Falls of Niagara, 1697

Source: Anon. (1697), engraving in Hennepin (1698:24), British Library

cataracts, but became a transfunctionalised signifier of other
things: an advertising logo for breakfast cereals, razor blades, sex,
romance, honeymoons, and spectacle. Peering back in time from
the world of the late twentieth century, the early sublime experience of Niagara is aporetic, a distant, difficult cultural memory.
The multiple, shifting formations of the contemporary, so-called
'postmodern', moment have left us suspicious of metaphysical
referents such as the early Niagara was. It is now more difficult to
ground values, symbols, and identities, yet this once-central icon of
the North American landscape underwent an early and prophetic
loss of aura: comments and complaints about a 'post-modern
condition' in contemporary culture were equally applied to
Niagara Falls from the mid 1800s onward: 'neither transcendental

science nor transcendental religion can be at home in it' (Tyler 1986:135).

In 1825 the completion of the Erie Canal turned the early pilgrim-travellers' self-assured opinion of Niagara's sublime grandeur on its head and proved to be an abrupt turning-point for Niagara. Suddenly it was opened to trade, industry, and tourism on such a scale that it could no longer remain a sacred, separate landscape. Elizabeth McKinsey, in her history of Niagara's iconic character, argues that

> from a national icon, remote and idealistic, Niagara was
> transformed into a fashionable resort, accessible by easy
> transportation. As the middle classes became more affluent
> and travel easier. . . . With them came all the tourist
> accommodations and allurements: hotels, guides hawking
> carriages or oil-cloth clothing, souvenir stands, museums,
> specially-erected vantage points, admission fees, and crowds.
>
> (McKinsey 1985:127)

Niagara was the prime touring destination for the affluent from the late 1820s until the Civil War. This was especially true for the Southern bourgeois who wished to escape the summer heat of their plantations by attending the Niagara 'Season'. Within two years of its opening, an estimated 15,000 people assembled at one time to watch the condemned schooner *Michigan* go over the Falls. These first spectacles were quickly followed by others, including barges of exotic animals, which completed the growing carnival atmosphere of small-time entrepreneurs and hawkers who sought to exploit the moneyed crowds which the Falls attracted. By the late 1840s the Falls were hosting more than 40,000 visitors a year.

Poets had prophesied that a canal would make Niagara a 'most attractive and gratifying object of human curiosity', for which 'No stranger but would make this tour his object, and no traveler of taste would leave it uncelebrated' (Cooper 1810:19, reproduced in New York Historical Society 1974:7). A more accurate forecast came from De Witt Clinton, one of the backers of the Erie Canal. He was awed not by the beauty of the waterfalls, but the sublimity of the *power* captured in them. His emotional reactions, recorded in his diary, were 'interspersed with and subordinated to notions of carding machines, grist and saw mills or comments that Niagara was "the best place in the world for hydraulic works"' (Clinton

1849:129 cited in McKinsey 1985:128). The village on the American bank, previously known simply as Niagara Falls, changed its name to Manchester, an indication of the inhabitants' ambitions to harness more than the fame of Niagara.

As the face of the Falls changed drastically, so did its meaning in the American imagination. And, as the experience became increasingly popular, so did the image. Everyone who could afford it went to Niagara, often as part of the Northern Tour, the American equivalent of the European Grand Tour, which was rapidly institutionalised with the development of the resort hotel and improved transportation in the second quarter of the century. By the latter half of the century average North Americans not only carried a mental picture of the physical scene as one of nature's grandest works, often confirmed or revised by their own experience, but also thought of the Falls more specifically as a fashionable resort or an excellent industrial site. A vast array of popular travelogues, geological speculations, reports of incidents, poetry and song lyrics, and prints of oil paintings both reflected and fuelled their interest. The various aspects of the Falls' liminality, which had formed the foundation of its status as a pilgrimage destination, were gradually broken apart into a liminoid, but not fully liminal, experience. In this new genre of visit to Niagara Falls the Falls as an expression of excessive or useless power was increasingly brought to the fore over the metaphysical aspects of the experience.

McKinsey shows that the 'guidebook writers openly avowed human mastery of the Falls in the canal, in industrial exploitation of its waterpower, in bridges and towers, and even stunts and man-made spectacles.' The effect was to encourage 'a more self-centred, commercial and utilitarian attitude: . . . How can I see it all in the least possible time?' This instrumentalism marked a change which undercut the visitors receptivity to the wonder of the Falls. Oscar Wilde said: 'Niagara Falls is simply a vast unnecessary amount of water going the wrong way and then falling over unnecessary rocks. The wonder would be if the water did not fall' (attributed, news conference, New York 1882 – see Colombo 1974: 632). Yet, visitors continued to measure their experience against their expectation of sublime emotions, blaming themselves for their inability to appreciate the Falls.[5] Largely as a result of this inconsistency between expectation based on image and experience based on reality, visitors 'tended to sentimentalise the experience there, in large part in reaction against the physical changes and consequent undermining of the sublime' (McKinsey 1985: 129–130).

TOURIST RITUALS: 'THE FASHIONABLE, THE OPULENT AND THE LEARNED CONGREGATE HERE'[6]

The sentimental response to the Falls was not a secondary reaction, but a part and parcel of the tourism ritual which, while appearing repetitious and indulging in excesses of commercialism and didactic moralising, aimed to recapture the experience of the natural sublime through a nostalgic melancholy for unadulterated Nature populated only by noble savages. It is useful to recall the fundamentally staged nature of the tourist experience. Tourists generally – and certainly those at Niagara – encounter a package of previously validated and even staged events and artefacts.

> Tourists are rarely left to draw their own conclusions about objects of places before them. Instead, they more often confront a body of public discourse – signs, maps, guides and guide books – that repeatedly mark the boundaries of significance and value at tourist sites.
>
> (Newman 1988:24)

Daniel Boorstein, one of the few writers to try to make sense of the cultural position of North American tourism, has argued that the adventuresome traveller of the nineteenth century was replaced by that more passive, pleasure-seeking twentieth-century tourist: a characteristic figure of the modern age filled with diluted, contrived, prefabricated experiences that transformed travel from an elite form of adventure to a popular act of consumption (Boorstein 1961). However, Niagara illustrates the beginning of this transformation in at least one site in the first half of the *nineteenth* century. By contrast Dean MacCannell in a later study of tourism (1976) argued that tourism is an active response to the difficulties of living in the inauthentic, mass-produced modern world. Where Boorstein suggests that tourists seek contrived experiences, MacCannell argues that contemporary tourists instead search out authenticity – the 'first, original, Niagara Falls amusement' as an advertisement once boasted. Like pilgrims in search of the

'Sacred', MacCannell views modern tourists as making quests in search of 'authentic' experience. These two 'classic' positions address themselves to the case of the contemporary tourist and the nature of mass tourism attractions in this century, setting them off against a putatively different nineteenth-century tourism practice. However, the case of Niagara Falls between 1825 and 1845 suggests that these models reveal more about the 'maturing' of tourism sites rather than the essential character of nineteenth- or twentieth-century tourism. As time passes, a legacy of discourses about a given site – such as the sentimental sublime at Niagara – becomes sedimented in popular imagination and memory. This semiotic excess may then prompt a reactive search for an original experience of a site or artefact.

The sense of loss at Niagara during this time harks back to the natural sublime, ironically also an elaborately constructed discourse. References to the loss of Niagara's aura as a 'temple' or *Shrine of nature* appear often: 'Every place that is sacred is invaded by a glaring hotel, an apple stand, a papermill, or Lady-book and Hiawatha Indians. . . . Turn which way you will at Niagara, you find . . . the money chanters are indeed profaning the great temple' ('Frank Leslie's Illustrated Newspaper' 1856). The French chronicler of post-revolution America, de Tocqueville, had written:

If you wish to see this place in its grandeur, hasten. . . .
Already the forest round about is being cleared. The Romans
are putting steeples on the Pantheon. I don't give the
Americans ten years to establish a saw or flour mill at the base
of the Cataract.

(de Tocqueville 1983:231)

The recoding of the naive and wondering vocabulary of the natural sublime into the sentimental language of the moral sublime not only represents a conceptual change that took place but also mirrors real changes in the repertoire of emotional responses available.[7] The more 'authentic' reactions to the Falls – awe, amazement, vertiginous terror – were overshadowed by the 'proper' responses in terms of moral codes. These were expressed in clichés and catch-phrases. Niagara became more important as a didactic signifier of the benevolence of God, rather than as a reality, an authentic referent. On a material level, there was the emergence of practically-oriented 'how to' guidebooks which, rather than provide descriptions, provided *prescriptions* of how to react in the form of descriptions of others' reactions. Unlike the earlier impressionistic and often exaggerated travelogues, the practical guidebooks emphasised up-to-date accuracy, useful hints for the traveller as opposed to the 'armchair traveller', and a complete and concise recording of all of the various attractions which 'must' be seen. Thus, speaking of the trip behind the cataract of the Horseshoe Falls, one visitor noted 'The trip is decidedly a perilous one, but it is "the thing," and so, to be fashionable, I did it' (Borrett 1865 cited in Dow 1921:I,311). On this level, the Falls became an obstacle course around which the visitor circulated efficiently, fulfilling all the appropriate duties and mouthing the appropriate phrases, very much like a religious service. The conduct of visits to Niagara became *ritualised* and structured in ways which, it was hoped, would re-enhance the moral power of the Falls while conducting the visitor around the popular but vulgar 'tourist traps' and avoiding the industrial developments, warehouses, and mill sites.[8]

> The Americans have disfigured their share of the rapids with mills and manufactories, and horrid red brick houses, and other unacceptable, unseasonable sights and signs of sordid industry. Worse than all is the round tower, which some profane wretch has erected on the Crescent Fall . . . so detestably impudent and mal-a-propos, . . . such a signal yet puny monument of bad taste.
>
> (Jameson 1838 in Dow 1921:I,218)

Ritual at its most effective 'enables us to suspend disbelief in the things that are larger than ourselves, whether they be deities or nature or history' (Turner 1988: 150). On the one hand, the idea of 'improvable nature' resulted in the practical attitudes exemplified in the guidebooks; while on the other, the idea of nature as an object of worship became codified in the sentimental responses of the gift books. With the 'improvement of Niagara Falls, both converged on the same place' at the same time 'glorifying human technological achievement and embracing change, yet honouring the timelessness and power of nature' (McKinsey 1985:132). Both parts of the popular attitude, however, may be seen as parts of a general 'quest for order in American society' (Davison 1933:266).

And, both were essentially anthropocentric and commercial. Some, however, noted the irony of such a disjunction between sublime nature and the commercial encampment focused on exploitation which had bloomed around it. So it is that ironic and witty poems and sketches appear for the first time in the second quarter of the nineteenth century.

Figure 3.3 The Season at Niagara Falls Photographing Visitors, 1877

Source: J.W. Champney (1877), engraving in *Harper's Weekly* (18 Aug. 1877: 644–645), British Library

The Falls became a backdrop to people: the photos place the tourist at the centre of interest and the Falls themselves become either mostly cropped out or relegated into the out-of-focus background. A record of the experience and the possession of a surrogate Niagara in the form of photographs and engraved souvenirs became an important *de rigueur* aspect of any visit. The photography trade boomed as evidenced in the many popular engravings of couples being photographed in front of the Falls (see Figures 3.3 and 3.5). Until recently, Niagara was the site of the greatest annual sales of photographic film, as witnessed by the towers sponsored by film companies (Minolta and Kodak) which now overlook the Falls.

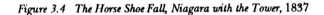

Figure 3.4   The Horse Shoe Fall, Niagara with the Tower, 1837

Source: W.H. Bartlett (1837), engraving in Willis (1840),
British Library

Not surprisingly, the urge to challenge and control that inspired the bridge and tower engineers (see Figure 3.4) soon captured the imagination of popular writers and sensationalistic performers. The result was a transformation of Niagara from primarily a sublime natural prodigy into a spectacle itself, and into a site for other public spectacles. The first organised by promoters to entertain and attract paying visitors was in 1827 when the *Michigan*, a condemned ship loaded with circus animals, was set adrift to go over the Falls where it broke up. Similarly Sam Patch, a daredevil, dived 'over the Falls', actually 85 feet into the pool at the base, survived, and immortalised himself by competing with the Falls and arrogating its esteem to himself: 'Niagara's roar was fairly beat' (Mackenzie cited in Greenhill and Mahoney 1969:82). 'Because he challenged Niagara gratuitously, simply for the sake of the challenge, Sam Patch was applauded above and beyond others who performed feats of strength or courage there' (Rourke 1959: 74 cited in McKinsey 1985:150). The metaphoric human conquest was made complete in the spectacles of the daredevils who tested themselves against the dangers of the Falls.[9]

The guidebooks hint at a sense of deliberately staged spectacle run for the viewer, whereby bridges are 'calculated to alarm the traveller for his safety', and boat rides through the eddies 'calculated to impress a stranger with an idea that a passage in the ferry is hazardous'. The word 'spectacle' emerges in the guidebooks denoting the attraction of great crowds. In these popular images, the emphasis was less on the sublime emotion than on the egocentric consumerism of the spectators. McKinsey concludes this also: 'the language of the guidebooks suggests Niagara stages its shows and exhibits its wonders as if it were a theatrical review' (McKinsey 1985:150).[10]

Given the widening gulf between the commercialised spectacles and the legendary sublime sentiments expressed by the first visitors, the experience of the sublime became increasingly inaccessible. McKinsey argues that due to this incongruity, the human throngs felt mocked and unable to bridge the gap between expectation and reality, between the Falls themselves and the spectacles surrounding them. In literature, but also in visitors' responses in *The Table Rock Album*, an anthology of comments written on the spot, this dichotomy is reconciled with humour (McKinsey 1985: Ch.6).[11] However, the original, sublime experience of the Falls was as constructed as any other. Its reification in the guidebooks as the 'proper' experience of Niagara is an example of the authoritative, and somewhat intimidating effect of discourses which enshrine artefacts and dictate their 'proper' experience. What was reconciled through the humour was perhaps not so much the incongruous reality but the impossibility of the discourse of the guidebooks: their lofty and moralising tone was reversed in jokes which were carnivalising repudiations of discursive authority.

If the guidebooks imposed an official and legitimate way of experiencing the Falls on people by categorising that experience in certain ways, this is carnivalised, inverted, and rendered trivial through the humorous comments visitors have left. Humour becomes a way of reasserting personal control (see also Barry 1978:22–23). This has been advanced as an explanation for the carnivalesque attractions. Perhaps they are really distractions, psychic defences which bolster the aloof ego against the huge scale of the Falls which has then been bolstered by its discursive construction as an overwhelming spectacle:

> Standing in the throng of people on the pavement, immediately above the white uproar of the cataract, one can't help wondering, in fact, if there isn't some therapeutic or self-defensive intention in all the rubbish with which the spectacle has been surrounded. What else could one do with it? In making such a stupendous gesture, Nature embarrasses us. . . . We are not explorers, we are not believers . . . we are not 19th-century romantics, we are just tourists.
>
> (Jacobson 1971:39)

Artists in the later part of the nineteenth century such as Hawthorne, Cole, and Church had devoted themselves to rediscovering and reclaiming this power of the sublime (see McKinsey 1985: Chs.8–10). These efforts culminated in Frederick Church's painting, which rendered the view, dramatically sighting almost at water level along the curving lip of the Horseshoe Falls. It was exhibited at the Paris Universal Exhibition of 1867 and hailed as a triumph for its focused treatment of water at the moment it began to fall. This was taken as a closing of a chapter on the sublime reception of the Falls. As one critic put it, people were 'for the first time, satisfied that even this awful reality is not beyond the range of human imitation.'[12] Here lay the Falls' fascination at that time: not their dimensions, measurement or the grandeur of the scene from a commanding distance (see Figure 3.2), but the giddy impression of vertigo which could be gained by watching the water from up close at Table Rock and from the Tower as it plunged over the precipice (see Figure 3.4). Perhaps ironically, it seemed that it was now only a matter of going in person to see whether Nature could compare with Art (Curtis 1852:175). The success and acceptance of Church's rendition vitiated the appeal of Niagara Falls for younger artists. It was no longer regarded as one of the supreme subjects which defied attempts to capture its meaning, it was just 'one artistic opportunity among countless others' (McKinsey 1985:251).

The tourists continued to come, of course, but what remained to be exclaimed at was the prodigious 'waste' of power at Niagara. By 1895 a state-licensed power corporation was formed to generate electricity, using the newly perfected technology of dynamos, and transmit it to Buffalo in the first electrical utility system. This pioneer development transformed Niagara Falls, which quickly became a locus of energy-intensive heavy industry. As H.G. Wells put it

The dynamos and galleries of the Niagara Falls Power Company impressed me far more profoundly than the Cave of the Winds [behind the American Falls]; they are indeed, to my mind, greater and more beautiful than the accidental eddying of air beside a downpour. They are will made visible, thought translated into easy and commanding things.
(H.G. Wells 1906 *The Future in America* quoted in Conrad 1980:25)

This loss of what Benjamin referred to as 'aura' – defined as the critical distance, uniqueness and durability of high culture works of art and sacred sites (1975b:225) – may be traced to Niagara's increasingly accessible location, the clash of opposed advertising images and tourist reports of Niagara which combined to carnivalise it and to impose many different interpretations on it, turning into a logo, as on packages of Nabisco's 'Shredded Wheat' brand of cereal, a backdrop, or advertising 'gimmick' and the metaphoric 'defeat' of its ineffability through increasingly accurate and convincing paintings, as well as the stunts of conquest which have already been mentioned. The Falls became the subject of minute mapping projects and geological profiles which were also vulgarised and published in popular magazines. Lash (1987) argues that such a demise of aura, that 'strange weave of space and time' (Benjamin 1975a:250), is essential to the cross-fertilisation where high becomes 'vulgarised' as low culture and vice versa. In

Weberian terms, the obliteration of aura brings about the demise of the bourgeois distinctions between the moral, aesthetic, and the rational with, as Benjamin predicted, political implications (1975b). The carnivalesque inversion of the Falls' sublimity is one means of accomplishing this 'vulgarisation'. Not surprisingly, the outcry from the bourgeois side of this equation gathered momentum with each souvenir stand and fun-fair attraction that was erected. But the growing number of petit-entrepreneurs, although certainly predatory opportunists, proved to be able to mount a lasting discourse which casts Niagara as a day-trippers' carnival paradise, thus leavening the moral and sentimental discourse which cloaked the Falls.

The same period had also seen the creation of state-run Parks on either side of the Falls to protect them from rampant 'greed, bad taste and exploitation'. In 1873, a Board of Inquiry reported to the Canadian government that

> The difficulty of escape from the organised band of cabmen, fancy and variety store keepers, guides, sight showers, picture takers, oil clothes furnishers, conductors under what is alleged to be the sheet of water, hotel keepers and runners, all working to plunder . . . has been so great as to elicit comments of travellers and the criticisms of the public press throughout the civilised world.
>
> (Wood 1873:6)

A provincial park was established in 1886 upon the recommendation of an Ontario Commission which concluded by arguing that 'Free enjoyment of these noblest works of nature is now felt to be one of man's most precious privileges, not to be abridged by private rights or greed for gain' (see Commissioners for Niagara Falls Park 1886). On the New York side, James C. Carter dedicated the American reserve 'to declare that the awful symbol of Infinite Power, in whose dread presence we stand, these visions of Infinite Beauty here unfolded to the eye are not a property but a shrine', to which society must, in an allusion to the New Testament expulsion of the moneychangers from the temple,

> confess the duty of guardianship imposed by her empire over the place; that she marks out the boundaries of the sanctuary,

expels from the interior all ordinary human pursuits and claims, so that visitors and pilgrims from near and far may come hither, and be permitted to behold, to love, to worship, to adore.

(Gardner quoted in Greenhill and Mahoney 1969:115)

At the time, many felt that the move was too late. The old, absolute Niagara had been lost. In this statement, the movement from a view of Niagara as an expression of God to an emphasis on Niagara as Nature's shrine is encapsulated. At this point the way was open for a transformation of the symbolism of Niagara from the domain of the expression of an absolute and powerful holiness to a more dispersed sense of a natural wonder, a great spectacle. Mark Twain parodied the move by producing a fictional account of a week in the life of Adam and Eve in the Garden of Eden, relocated in time and space to the Niagara State Park.

After the Civil War, Niagara Falls was no longer quite fashionable. It was overtaken by Saratoga Springs and Newport News on the coast. McKinsey assembles the evidence that the prodigious spectacle of Niagara had both ceased to impress in the way that it once had and that its 'meaning', its intrinsic sense was no longer a supposedly intrinsic characteristic but simply a projection of the viewers' own minds. As one of H.G. Wells's characters in a science fiction novel set at Niagara Falls (1908:308) puts it ' . . . silly great catarac'. There ain't no sense in it, fallin' and fallin'.'

McKinsey notes that in literary descriptions such as those of Walt Whitman and Emerson the cataracts appear as only visual experiences, like a silent movie with no sense of three-dimensional tactility. The power, the roar is gone (1985:274). H.G. Wells's characters see the Falls only for their hydroelectric potential; they have no other sense. Howells (1808), in his influential book *Their Wedding Journey*, suggests that 'any meaning earlier visitors might have found in the cataract was simply a creation of their own fancy' (see McKinsey 1985:270–275). The Falls themselves mean and symbolise nothing, which then makes them available for meaning almost anything to anybody. In such a cacophony, any one meaning appears arbitrary. Thus, while North American tourists continue to travel to Niagara Falls in our century, a picture of the Falls or the word 'Niagara' is as likely to connote breakfast cereal, laundry soap, or Gillette razors as it is likely to raise a mental picture of a natural spectacle. These are deconstructed as fragmentary and illusive 'moments' of meaning in Butor's novel *6,810,000 litres d'eau par seconde* (1965) where the 'spirit', the 'aura', of Niagara evaporates completely.

Table 3.1 Chronology of the development of Niagara Falls

1697	Father Hennepin, first white man to see Niagara
1803	Jerome Bonaparte, the brother of Napoleon I, goes to Niagara Falls as part of a Northern Tour with his bride of one year. Pre-1825 Niagara Falls is an ideal, isolated, natural pilgrimage shrine visited by the wealthy few. Niagara Falls became a place where the eligible young could meet a wide variety of potential partners.
1825	Opening of the Erie Canal opens the way for mass tourism. Within five years it becomes a popular site for stops on Bridal Tours and an integrated part of the 'Northern Tour'.
1827	First mass spectacle draws an audience of more than 40,000. Niagara Falls acquires the reputation and physical infrastructure of a popular tourist resort.
1834	The appearance of practically oriented guidebooks marks the emergence of the notion of the need for human 'improvement' of the natural spectacle. Niagara Falls New York changes its name to Manchester signalling its ambitions to exploit the water power potential of the Falls.
1840	The notion of 'Honey-Lunacy' is institutionalised in the practice of Honeymoons. This is dissimulated in popular songs and in magazine accounts. A pseudo-scientific theory emerges to explain the 'romantic effect' of the Falls on susceptible young couples.
1850	The commercial huckstering around the Falls reaches extremes with William Forsythe's fence through which one had to pay to view the Falls. Authors record their disappointment at the trivialising surroundings compared with their idealised expectations.
1887	Founding of the Niagara Parks Commission to 'preserve' the sacred site in the face of heavy industrialisation of the area.
1920	Niagara Falls Honeymoons reach the point of being a clichéd 'done thing'.
1930	Majority of visitors aren't honeymooners.
1950	Ontario Hydro provincial Rationalised Grid homogenises electricity prices. Niagara Falls loses its status as a privileged site for cheap power for industry.
1952	Marilyn Monroe, Joseph Cotton in *Niagara*.
1961	Marineland begins the latest phase of secondary 'attractions' which supplant the Falls themselves.
1970	Niagara Falls area in decline. Emergence of prostitution as a major social problem and industry.
1980	First academic studies of Niagara Falls since the 1920s begin to proliferate.

HONEY LUNACY: PRACTICE AND IMAGE

The precise origin of the honeymoon reputation of Niagara Falls is difficult to discover. Popularly, Jerome Bonaparte, the younger brother of Napoleon, and his bride, Elizabeth Patterson of Baltimore, supposedly spent a 'honeymoon' there in 1803. But this is more likely a late nineteenth-century construction of their intentions in terms of more modern practices. They actually spent the weeks following their wedding on 24 December at her father's estate in Maryland and went to Niagara only in the following summer of 1804 with 'a party' of travellers,[13] as part of a Northern Tour as was popular amongst members of the American bourgeoisie of the time. Akin to the European 'Grand Tour', this would also have included Quebec City and Boston. Other early honeymoons such as that of Theodosia, the daughter of the art patron Aaron Burr,[14] similarly appear to be summer visits to the North to escape the Southern heat. Few outside the wealthy leisure class could afford to undertake such (frontier) travel. Popular bridal trips planned around places required safe mass transportation and organised accommodation: in other words, a tourist industry.

It has been suggested that the custom of elopement had some influence on the honeymoon becoming a private trip to a particular place. Originally elopement was a permanent escape. Later, it became a more temporary removal; a spatial practice establishing de facto independence and expressing family differentiation through spatial removal. 'As early as 1830, the Lake Drummond Hotel, on the Virginia–North Carolina border, was known as an "establishment . . . in a superior degree calculated to render facilities for matrimonial and dualistic engagements"' (Rogerson 1946:9). The American tradition had been to take a 'Bridal Tour' or 'nuptial tour' visiting relatives and friends who had not attended the wedding. This social duty often included time spent at the home of the bride's family. The couple was always accompanied by cousins or other relatives. Because historians have projected present-day notions of the honeymoon back onto these past practices many early journeys have been mislabelled and the motivation for early nineteenth-century visits to the Falls misconstrued.

Thus for example, in the early 1840s Sir James Edward Alexander recorded encountering a 'marriage party' which included 'about a score of blithe folk' (Williams 1947:154 cited in McKinsey 1985: 306, nn. 4,6) and in 1845 'a bridegroom, a young and blooming bride, and two other ladies' are noted amongst the fellow passengers on the Lake Ontario steamer bound for Niagara by an anonymous author.[15] Ellen Rothman noted in her study of nineteenth-century American courtship that private honeymoons of the romantic variety were not taken until mid-century while the family-oriented Bridal Tour, even if sometimes renamed 'honeymoon', continued until the 1880s (see Figure 3.5). Only by the late 1830s and 1840s did the middle classes become prosperous enough and sufficiently freed from the daily duties of agriculture so that they could afford the fares and time off for extended journeys, following the influence of the British upper classes who began to take wedding trips early in the century.[16] Nonetheless, McKinsey finds references that would support the beginning of the romantic Niagara honeymoon in the late 1830s. The diarist Caroline Gilman noted 'a young married couple, who had come to pay true homage to nature, by consecrating their new happiness at this shrine' (1838:115 cited in McKinsey 1985:179) and in 'A Letter from the Falls of Niagara' in Littel's *Spirit of the Magazines* (1839) mentions that,

> At the present genial season this beautiful spot is a favorite resort of lately married pairs. I have counted several cooing couples, both Canadian and American, fulfilling the fleeting period of their honey-lunacy at the great staring 'Pavilion'.
> (cited in Williams 1947:153–154)

Another indicator is the 'Song of the Year' of 1841 'Niagara Falls'. Predating Church's artistic conquest of the Falls by sixteen years, it is unequivocal about the aura of romance which supposedly wrapped Niagara:

> Oh the lovers come a thousand miles,
> They leave their home and mother;
> Yet when they reach Niagara Falls
> They only see each other.
>
> See Niagara's water rolling
> See the misty spray
> See the happy lovers strolling
> It's everybody's wedding day.

To see the Falls they took a ride
On the steamship 'Maid O' the Mist';
She forgot the Falls she was so busy
Being hugged and kissed.

See the mighty river rushing
'Tween its rocky walls
See the happy lovers strolling
By our Niagara Falls.

He said 'Is oo my darling?'
He said 'Whose darling is oo?'
He said 'Is oo my baby?'
And she always answered 'Goo-goo-goo.'[17]

One modern critic suggests that this song helped institutionalise the custom. It 'proved so popular that it is believed to have initiated the vogue for honeymooners' going to Niagara Falls' (Ewen 1966:282). In any case it shows that at least the notion of 'leaving home and mother' (rather than taking the bridegroom back to the family home) had entered popular parlance. The majority of references to Niagara Falls in connection with honeymoons are from the latter half of the century when it was firmly established in popular song and magazines. 'Everyone' went to Niagara and one bride remarked in 1873 that 'the conventional bridal tour to that delectable place is considered as much a part of the mortant [sic] even as a ring, orange blossoms, etc' (quoted in Rothman 1984:175).

EXPLANATIONS OF THE NIAGARA FALLS HONEYMOON

Researchers have puzzled over the reason for Niagara Falls' attraction as a honeymoon site. One answer is to simply say that it was (and for many still is, judging by the honeymoon figures)[18] one place young people wanted to visit not only because it was the custom but also because it represented the trip of a lifetime. As McKinsey points out, however,

> this argument seems less satisfactory the later we date the widespread acceptance of the custom, for . . . general public interest in the Falls diminished drastically after the Civil War,

as refined travelers went more and more to Newport or Long
Branch or Europe, and the truly adventurous trekked farther
westward. Yet its popularity as a honeymoon spot soared,
perhaps because it was the cheaper and more familiar
alternative.

(McKinsey 1985:182)

Yet this too begs the question as well as ignoring the expansion of
the North American tourism market. Although there are few available figures, through the last two decades of the nineteenth
century many more people could afford a 'once in a lifetime trip'
to Niagara, if not further afield. The broadening class patronage at
Niagara assisted the development of the more popular entertainments and the 'vulgar' attractions which appealed to sentiment, to
whimsy and the freedom of the escape from community surveillance.

A number of writers have volunteered journalistic responses
which adopt either the theme of the appropriateness of waterfalls
to nuptial consecration or argue for an essentialistic attractiveness.
For example, an 1893 souvenir book suggested that the Falls
'distracts . . . [honeymooners'] attention gently from one another,
which is a kindness, and when they speak together it prevents alien
ears from overhearing what they say' (Martin 1893:276). And more
recently 'For some reason Niagara Falls has always been a favourite
haven for honeymooners possibly because people are so busy looking at the waterfalls that they have little time to gape at those who
are obviously newly married' (Catton 1964:42). Another writer
comments,

> No one knows why or when the tradition of honeymooning at
> Niagara Falls began or why it should persist. The most
> plausible surmise is that . . . it seemed an ideal place for
> embarrassed newlyweds to lose themselves among great
> quantities of souls who were not only total strangers to them,
> but to one another as well, a crowd of individuals, a lonely
> crowd.

(Braider undated:255)

The cataracts themselves were considered by some in the late
1800s to have an instructive moral value. The Falls could give a
young couple

so many useful points for the shaping of their future destinies! It teaches them to let things slide when opposition will do no good. It stands to them for the restless stream of life which sweeps all over its falls first or last, so that it pays us to float tranquilly while we may and not mar so brief a passage with altercation. The individuality of so impetuous a flood can hardly fail to make its impression on them, suggesting that every individuality, even that of the married woman, has a right to its own development, and comes swifter and safer to a tranquil haven if left reasonably free to follow out its natural course.

(Martin 1893:276)

Yet despite this sermonising there is little evidence that the didactic significance of the Falls was widely appreciated or particularly significant. The theme is not taken up in more serious discourse and it strikes one as whimsical: were honeymooners sent to Niagara Falls for its moral overtones and didactic virtues? Likely not.

Another explanation was 'the ions electrically charged atoms in the air. Positive ions, such as those produced by desert winds cause irritability and depression. Negative ions cheer you up, invigorate you, and start you thinking about sex. . . . Happy negative ions are produced by falling water.' Niagara Falls would be the ultimate source of negative 'sexy' ions (Donaldson 1979:227–228). This resort to biology and electrical engineering is as unconvincing as it is appealing: it certainly isn't a universal effect. While a conclusive answer may never be possible the cultural associations of waterfalls in general and Niagara Falls in particular suggest an analysis with more explanatory power.

THE NORTH AMERICAN GEOMANCY OF WATERFALLS

Falls have been primary tourist attractions for a thousand years . . . as fundamental to the wonder of nature. . . . Falls belong to a category which includes fire, clouds and even trees tossing in the wind.

(Shepard 1967:254)

Early on, Niagara Falls was associated with romance. In his novel *The Spy*, James Fenimore Cooper has a young lieutenant assert his masculinity by declaring his insulation from any feelings of awe: 'Oh the falls! they are a thing to be looked at on a moonshiny night, by your Aunt Sarah and that gay old bachelor, Colonel Singleton; but a fellow like myself never shows any surprise' (1821: 347). And even after the building of the Erie Canal, Goat Island, between the two Falls, continued to be described in the 1836 edition of Horatio Parsons' guidebook as a particularly romantic spot: 'It was poetry indeed; it was one of those bright and verdant oases sometimes met with in the journey of life' (Parsons 1836:35).

Figure 3.5 Their Bridal Tour at Niagara Falls, 1888

Source: C.S. Reinhart (1888), engraving in *Harper's Weekly* (29 Sept. 1888: 732), British Library

Underlying this romantic myth is perhaps a wider practice, not of honeymooning but of courting. Because there was a 'Season' at Niagara Falls, a time in the summer during which the fashionable regularly visited each year, Niagara Falls provided a site where the eligible young, often from geographically isolated and socially insular homes, had the possibility of meeting a more suitable partner than would be available in either the small frontier towns or the distant plantations of the South. Pictures depict couples strolling beside the Falls but this gives no clue as to whether they were courting or honeymooning (compare the background couple and the foreground couple in Figure 3.5). Indeed, all the emphasis on romance seems more appropriate to courting than honeymooning. In 1850 George Francis Train pursued one young 'lady of fashion' whom he met on the railroad car from Syracuse. By the time they arrived at Niagara they were acquainted and two days later they were engaged (Severance undated:35). Even today, Niagara Falls is a popular spot for weddings away from home.

In Western cultural traditions, waterfalls have a longstanding association with passion and obsession; specifically, motifs of passionate love and the suicide of the distraught. Thus, traditionally, iconologies have portrayed passion and often sin in settings dominated by waterfalls.[19] Such scenes were also a staple of the Gothic novel (see McKinsey 1985:184). Waterfalls have often been associated with the biblical Fall of Adam and Eve, which was also a sexual initiation. In the nineteenth century, the Falls served as a sentimental metaphor for 'falling in love'. Like the water at the crest of the Falls, passion is seen as irresistible. In this century, Marilyn Monroe was cast as an adulterous and 'over-sexed' newlywed in a film about a honeymoon couple, where discord and uncontrolled passion leads to death, called *Niagara*. A poster portrays a fantasy of Monroe lying across the Falls while the water flows over the curves of her body: '*Marilyn Monroe and Niagara* a raging torrent of emotion that even nature can't control!' (Henry Hathaway, Director, Twentieth Century Fox Corporation 1952). The curve of her hips becomes a metonymy of the curve of the lip of the Horseshoe Falls while the 'raging torrent' of water suggests the danger of passion to domestic harmony. The Canadian novelist Tom Marshall remembers this in *Voices on the Brink*:

> A publicity poster for the film depicts her lying on her side atop the curved Canadian horseshoe falls. Her flesh is spilling out at us like water, like milk struck from a magic rock, inviting, uncontainable. She is a goddess here too. She is

queen of sexual magic, that pagan torrent. Red lips, a red
dress. Puritan America's doomed sacrificial Aphrodite laid on
cold Canada.

(Marshall 1988:27)

But, in this film, at the same time as continuing to function as an
icon for passion for one character, a salesman with his wife on a
deferred honeymoon, is oblivious to the romance his wife would
like him to find at Niagara. For him, Niagara Falls means
'Shredded Wheat', the American cereal which has always included
a vignette of the Falls on its packaging. He is a 'Shredded Wheat'
salesman intent on mixing business into pleasure (visiting with
other salesmen and so on) with near fatal results.[20] Niagara figures
in many other films, for example in the self-parodying movie
Superman II, Lois Lane tries to tempt the leotarded hero at
Niagara.

In native legend, the Falls was inhabited by a Manitto (a mortal
spirit-being) who kidnaps a young bride who must then be re-
captured by her true lover before she is sent over the Falls by the
Manitto in order to unite her with himself. Although one must add
a note of caution to assimilating native legend to European
cultural predispositions, this has been interpreted as a 'parable of
the dangers of sexual passion and of exploitation by those with evil
intent and power, [in which] the young couple must undergo a
trial and overcome such temptation' (McKinsey 1985:184). In
another legend, a tragically frustrated 'Romeo and Juliet' style pair
are united only after their death to live as spirit-lovers in the lunar
bow as the moon shines on the mist at night (see Canfield
1902:47–50, 200–201). There is a tradition of suicide at Niagara
which competes with its honeymoon tradition. This is strong
enough for the Chief of Police to have commented recently that
Niagara suicides are seldom a spur-of-the-moment decision. 'We
get people coming from as far away as Pennsylvania. They drive all
that time thinking about it. It's not spontaneous. I think Niagara
Falls has the reputation of a place where there's just no turning
back.' Many take their shoes off before they jump (cited in
Leighton 1984:90).

In the nineteenth century Niagara, like many romanticised
objects, came to be associated with the theme of death. Apart from
such parables of passion, the Falls present a Janus-faced set of

metaphors of masculinity and femininity. The relative stress on either side of this male–female continuum changes over history. Early descriptions that stressed the power and might of the Falls resort to masculine metaphors. Yet in the sentimental period, the literature resorts to portraying Niagara as a feminine object, as not the ultimate creation of God but as a goddess, as not awesome but calm and majestic, as not violent but beautiful (see Note 3). Drawing on earlier mythologies and iconographies, the Earth-mother is the source of all fertility and creativity (see Neumann 1955).[21] Water and waterfalls represent her creative power. Often, a nude woman is posed in the water itself.

The key to the iconography of Niagara is to be found in both the equivocal nature of the various images and descriptions and the possibility of seeing in it a unity of male and female principles. Thus one nineteenth-century writer comments of the Native legends 'The mixed character of the Niagara would have troubled these old Godmakers; for it would have demanded a union of grace and beauty more than masculine, and of force and dignity more than feminine, as a true symbol of its varied qualities' ('Cousin George' 1846:28). McKinsey agrees, noting that 'Such a union of male and female in a domestic image of Niagara must have been essential to its suitability as a honeymoon haven . . . a ritual of domestication and integration into the family circle.' It was transformed from a wild and untamed wilderness into a sentimentalised version 'available for honeymooners, compatible for women and for couples, whose sphere was by definition domestic' (1985:188). The human mastery of the Falls through exploits, commercialisation, and industrial exploitation leaves to Niagara not the connotations of dangerous power but of controlled natural energy subordinated to human purposes which are morally sanctioned. This is accompanied by the metaphor of the mastery of sexual passion in the name of controlled domestic order. The union of the couple, their establishment as a new household and taboos surrounding sex and marriage are mediated in the rituals of the honeymoon.

Having concluded a historical examination of the progressively changing image of Niagara Falls and its historically changing status as a honeymoon resort, a resort of 'lately married pairs', it is time to ask if, beyond a simple iconography or geomancy of waterfalls, there is a social logic to the predominance at any one time in history of a given image of Niagara. In particular, is its equivocal status simply a result of the binary structure of meanings associated with waterfalls? Unlike other, more literary analyses (McKinsey 1985; McGreevy 1985), this question is central to this project. Why, for example, when strong vested interests were involved did no one image of Niagara prevail? Unlike Brighton, for example, Niagara's popular image was due not to reputation but to advertisement and promotion. Even by the mid 1800s, the media discourse of more often than not impressionistic and slanted journalistic accounts and early photographs had become a major source of knowledge about the world.

An ideal-typical typology of three basic images of Niagara may be drawn from the literature, much of which might be regarded as the work of 'local boosters' (Suttles 1985) who, such as the hoteliers who produced guidebooks, wished to promote Niagara Falls as a tourist destination which would attract a certain type of clientele preferably to the promoter's particular business. First there is the 'Shrine of Nature' image, the transformations of which McKinsey treats in her analysis of the Sublime. This is fundamental to the other two. This includes the 'Honeymoon Haven' images of romance under the stars with the cascading water pouring gently over the rim of the cataract by the light of the moon. Second is the 'Industrial Powerhouse' image as propounded by Clifton and other developers who wished to exploit Niagara's power. Third is the 'Attractions and Spectacle' image of the carnival and the prodigious and ongoing Event of the felt weight of millions of litres of falling water.

With each image a specific set of local interests is associated. With the first, the hoteliers and 'conservers' including the Parks Commission bureaucracy. With the second, the local industrial managers and bourgeoisie. With the third, the petit bourgeois entrepreneurs and self-made hucksters and entertainment operators. With each discourse, then, a specific faction, a coalition of classes and class fractions around a common interest is implicated. Each faction has promoted its own, historically-specific, visions of the Falls over and against the discourses of the other factions. Some produced brochures as in the case of the Parks Commission, others relied on billboards and other media channels. Each group has 'cast' the Falls as a different character in their narratives. Indeed, they are all what might be called 'parasitic' internal ggrowth coalitions who exploit the natural site and boost the particular images associated with their services. No single faction dominates but each has left an imprint. While the Falls are surrounded by landscaped parkland with a promenade where the speed of the many cars and coaches is limited, the Ferris wheel of the Clifton Hill amusements area can be seen above the trees. Meanwhile, with its infamous 'Love Canal' waste dump and draining dead Lake Erie, Niagara suffers seriously from the pollution of industrial toxins: standing in the spray leaves brown stains on one's clothes. A powerplant stands just below the Horseshoe Falls which have been called 'The polluted falls: tainted wonder of the world' (Marshall 1988:83). The three images can be summarised in the schema shown in Table 3.2.

Table 3.2 Class coalitions and images

Image	Faction	Major institutions
Romantic	Public Sector	Niagara Parks Commission
Natural Shrine	Bureaucracy	Hoteliers Tourist Board
Industrial Powerhouse	Local Manufacturers	Niagara Power Corp Chamber of Commerce
Spectacular Event/Carnival	Petit Bourgeoisie Entrepreneurs	Clifton Hill Owners Assoc. Hoteliers Tourist Board

Given the contradictory, polyvocal nature of the resulting discourse about Niagara Falls no single image has predominated, contributing to the loss of aura. Appropriated into this heteroglossia of competing discourses, Niagara Falls has lost not only its auratic authenticity but also its semiotic identity. The Grand Canyon presents a comparative example of a feature of the natural landscape which has become a tourism site. Walker Percy has argued that the contemporary tourist cannot experience the Grand Canyon in the same manner as its European 'discoverer', Garcia Lopez de Cardenas, because they do not confront the Canyon directly:

It is almost impossible because the Grand Canyon, the thing as it is, has been appropriated by the symbolic complex which

147

has already been formed in the sightseer's mind. Seeing the canyon under approved circumstances [from the appointed viewing sites, according to the approved interpretative plaques and so on] is seeing the symbolic complex head on.

(Percy 1977 cited in Newman 1988:24)

Mark Newman elaborates on this comment to note that the Canyon is ultimately a piece of evidence, no longer of itself, but of the discursive complex which establishes the canyon as an ideal landscape of the American West.

Percy's modern tourist is satisfied with the 'real' canyon to the extent that it measures up to preconceived ideas about it that are present in the symbolic rendering of the Grand Canyon made by mass media, postcards, and other images of the canyon that circulate in the culture . . . it is not that some authentic or essential, pure object exists beneath or behind the discourse that encloses it. Rather, the choice of a specific interpretation . . . of the Grand Canyon . . . eclipses other possibilities of interpretation and of perhaps discovering those things in another way.

(Newman 1988:24)

By comparison to the more univocal discourse of the Grand Canyon, one or more aspects of Niagara Falls stand ready to exhibit a blatant non-conformism to any given interpretative discourse. Tourist expectations are doomed to be disappointed, especially if one is in search of Niagara, the 'Shrine of Nature'. Niagara the Carnival is a great deal more resilient. This is likely to continue into the future given the tourism planning of the Niagara Falls Parks Commission which continues to ignore the carnival-esque sideshow which has succeeded in limiting any appreciation of Niagara as a 'Shrine of Nature' to within the realm of the ironic.

LIMINALITY, *RITES DE PASSAGE*, AND TOURISM

This section returns to synthesise the various strands of the above analyses of honeymoons, liminality, and carnival. We have noted that to the metaphors of passionate union and domesticity was linked the empirical practice of the honeymoon, a nuptial period during which the marriage should be consummated and a time free from the everyday realities of the relationship enjoyed. Psychologically, this period might have once served to ensure the bonding of a couple who might not know each other intimately. Contrary to the undercurrent of McKinsey's study, the change from chaperoned 'wedding tour' to intimate and romantic honeymoon in the nineteenth century marks out not only an increasingly autonomous position of the nuclear family from the extended family of relatives and 'in-laws' but also the increasingly 'Victorian' morality. Journalists have claimed that by the end of the century, it appears that many North American married couples who could afford it no longer slept together in fear of temptation. This is difficult to substantiate and one suspects that only lip-service might have been paid to the medical and marriage manuals that recommended this practice (the only evidence by which to correlate this claim); however, sexual matters would be an increasingly taboo subject. Because of this it would become easy for hotel clerks to spot the honeymooners because they would be amongst the exceptions to the rule, asking for a double bed rather than the room with separate beds preferred by the more tight-laced and established couples (see Callwood and Frayne 1950). In the productive regime of family-based sexuality (Foucault 1979) sex was repressed except for productive copulation. Honeymoons would become an embarrassing and possibly difficult trial for naive couples.

The honeymoon served as a period of adjustment to the transformation of status. It stands as both a *rite de passage* and as an event in its own terms marking the transformation to marriage. In the nineteenth century, travellers expected Niagara Falls to be fabulous; a place where the limits of ordinary experience were transcended. Even if they had been warned about its honky-tonk reality, their voyage was a ritual of anticipative excitement. Nathaniel Hawthorne wrote of going 'haunted with a vision of foam and fury, and dizzy cliffs, and an ocean tumbling down out of the sky.' The trip to Niagara Falls was analogous to a medieval pilgrimage. Like their medieval counterparts, the pilgrims to Niagara anticipated a difficult and possibly dangerous passage which would be rewarded at the end by their arrival at a shrine or place where their world achieved a connection with a timeless essence. One booster, George Carlisle, said in an 1850 lecture:

'Living at Niagara was not like ordinary life. The whole of existence there has a dreamy but not frivolous impress; you feel that you are not in the common world, but in its sublimest temple.' In this sense, Niagara Falls was, at least in myth, a sacred expression of the dynamism and powerful unity of nature. 'Nature's loudest voice speaking to the soul through the medium of those ever rushing waters the holy place of the earth!' (from *The Table Rock Album*, cited in Dow 1921:I,120).

As argued in the previous chapter, in such pilgrimages people do step outside of their everyday world into an experience of liminality in which the conventions and codes of normal social experience are reversed (Turner 1973). In 'primitive' societies, just as at Niagara, rituals of manhood, womanhood, and other transitions in the life-cycle involve liminality. Like Turner's pilgrims, travellers to Niagara and particularly (1) the eligible young hoping to meet possible partners and (2) honeymooners were in an ideal liminal zone where the strict social conventions of the class-conscious New World bourgeois were relaxed under the exigencies of travel and of relative anonymity and freedom from community scrutiny. Honeymooners, furthermore, were engaged in a specifically Western *rite de passage* but, unlike more traditional *rites de passage*, it is conducted 'on autopilot' so to speak. The rituals, especially the 'wedding night', having been established allowed the couple to be sent off alone. This is one example where setting is one important factor structuring (though not determining) action. Thus there is an important qualitative difference in the social context of the brand of liminality with which we are concerned here. Turner has argued that there is also a '*rite de passage*, even an initiatory, ritual, character about pilgrimage.' Like the initiates in Van Gennep's primitive societies, pilgrims and travellers also withdraw temporarily from the usual structures of their society into the special world of traveller. Patrick McGreevy has described the honeymoon as 'a hiatus between two portions of life, a temporal no-man's land' (1985:32). The two poles of the structure of liminality in pilgrimage and *rites de passage* are the 'familiar' or 'everyday' and the 'remote' or 'ideal'. As one of William Dean Howells characters in his influential Niagara novel *Our Wedding Journey* says 'I think with tenderness of all the lives that have opened so fairly there. . . . Elsewhere there are carking cares of business and of fashion, there are age, and sorrow, and heartbreak; but here only youth, faith, rapture' (1808 cited in McKinsey 1985:272).

In this meta-structure of social conventions, Niagara Falls, spatialised as an exotic pilgrimage destination, was also ideally suited for *rites de passage* and doubly so if they concerned passion: the honeymoon and the suicide. But today, however, it would appear that the honeymoon has been emptied of its symbolic, liminal, status as a socially-constituted limbo from which two persons re-emerge as a couple. Emptied of meaning, it is like a sign which refers to nothing, is meaningless. The only possibility is that it may refer back to itself, to honeymoons in self-conscious irony. Niagara Falls, construed in such different ways that it is no longer clear quite what 'Niagara' refers to, a signifier emptied of significance, is linked to a ritual without social meaning. Having become the ultimate, meaningless, nuptial cliché the honeymoon could only become either an Event or a cover for some other activity, such as tourism. This is the model of doubly ironic Niagara Falls honeymoon today where two distinct markets have emerged. The first is the 'Event Honeymoon' which is stagnant (*Financial Post* 1 September 1962).[22] These are centred around a 'blue-collar market' (Niagara Falls Tourism and Convention Bureau 1949–86) of honeymooners interested in the spectacular and the carnival atmosphere of what are locally known as the 'attractions' of Clifton Hill (see Figure 3.6); 'MarineLand' with its kissing sea lions; helicopter rides; Ripley's 'Believe it or Not' Museum featuring Elvis Presley's last pink Cadillac and so on (see *Financial Post* 23 November 1957:9; see above pp. 89–99).[23] As noted in the case of Brighton beach, this capitalist derivative of the carnival free-for-all is characterised by its anti-ritualistic style, the manner in which all social roles are levelled in activities in which the participants are involved on an equal basis as consumers of gratification and momentary abandon, or even as sight-seers.

> Sometimes I imagine myself . . . . When there was only forest and sky and cliff and river . . . .
> When there were no wax museums, and there was no giant Ferris wheel turning and turning like a reminder of the cyclical futility of industrial history.
> Now the cars stream along the parkway in the summer dusk.
> A gleaming stream of metal-clad humanity. . . . By day they

seek out the rainbow, by night the artificial, garish colored lights projected on the falls. This is pure Hollywood even without Monroe. A stimulus to 'love', whether in a cave, a car, or a pink motel. This is the city of cut-rate dreams. A tawdry slut made up to take advantage of the glamorous kindness of twilight.

(Marshall 1988:29)

Bakhtin's medieval carnival is a spectacle lived by people who are all participants, actors, not spectators (1984:7). Unlike this 'pure' carnivalesque, the Event Honeymoon is composed of a commercialised residuum of rituals (see Table 3.3). Nonetheless, all carnival forms, even if reduced to the status of mass holidays 'offer a completely different, non-official . . . extra political aspect of the world, of man, and of human relations; they [build] a second world and a second life outside officialdom' (Bakhtin 1984:5–6). The inverted world of the carnival momentarily legitimises heterodox, scorned cultural styles and activities. Hence, humour and kitsch 'anti-style' are harnessed in this suspension of the realm of the 'proper'. These enter into a 'dialogue' with official culture with the result that an arena of heteroglossia and a plurality of choices between official and unofficial, 'proper' and 'kitsch' is opened up (Figure 3.7). The official attractions centring on the beauty of the Falls are ironic remnants which provide the basis on which the carnivalesque operates. Foucault once referred to this sort of counterspace as a 'heterotopia'. These are

real places . . . which are something like counter-sites, a kind of effectively enacted utopia in which . . . all the other real sites . . . within a culture, are simultaneous represented, contested and inverted . . . privileged or sacred or forbidden places, reserved for individuals who are . . . in a state of crisis . . . these crisis heterotopias are persistently disappearing, though a few remnants can still be found. For example, the boarding school . . . military service . . . the 'honeymoon trip'. . . . The young woman's deflowering could take place 'nowhere' and at the moment of its occurrence, the train or honeymoon hotel was indeed the place of this nowhere, this heterotopia without geographical markers.

(Foucault 1986:24–25)

An Event Honeymoon is expected to be a ludic explosion: a high of repressed sexual energy. The Niagara Falls hotels' numerous 'honeymoon suites' are stages set with every possible artifice of the sexual carnival popularised in the pictorial features of soft core pornographic magazines. There is an emphasis on props: Jacuzzis, or whirlpool baths are one commonplace usually red and heart-shaped, 'just for two'. Euphemistically known as 'luv tubs', they are figurative, commodified embodiments of North American sexual fantasies. An adjunct of this market is the 'second honeymoon' which couples may take as a holiday, a re-dedication of their marriage, or as a nostalgic return to their youth. To accommodate this more easy-going group, hotels have changed to more neutral colour schemes: the days of the red 'luv tub' may be limited.

Figure 3.6 Map of Niagara Falls and Clifton Hill

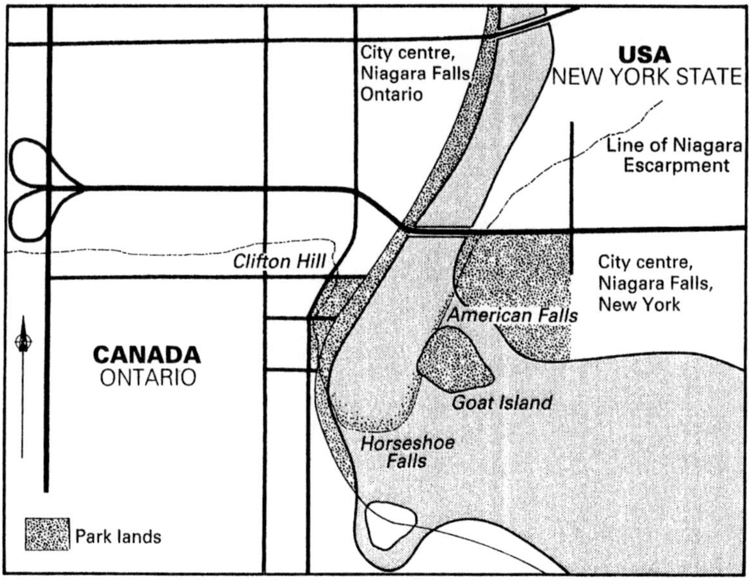

Uncomfortably accommodated along with the Event Honey-moon is a growing second market based around overseas tourists such as young Japanese on 'Honeymoon Tours'. The incongruity

Figure 3.7 Mugs: souvenirs of the carnivalesque

of the spectacle-oriented world of Clifton Hill and the sober land-scape of the Parks reflect this clash of opposed cultural discourses which appropriate the Falls in quite different ways. For the Japanese, honeymoons have been one of the few excuses (along with funerals) for which time off could be taken from work. They come for a glimpse of what they describe as 'Grand Nature', the opposite of civilisation and including a synthesis of natural ele-ments (flowing water, vegetation, rock), the sites of which are 'collected' for their symbolic value in Japanese society. Typically a tour would include the Rocky Mountains, the Prairies, Niagara and Prince Edward Island's nostalgic *Anne of Green Gables* house which commemorates a loosely autobiographical story of a young girl growing up on a turn-of-the-century Canadian farm which is highly popular in the West and in Japan (Montgomery 1942). This 'Grand Nature' is not a contemporary version of the older Sublime 'quest for meaning' at Niagara nor an attempt to 'recentre the world' around elective centres in a radically 'decentred' world (Cohen *et al.* 1987:320). But Niagara Falls' suitability for the fulfilment of this sort of role, its 'fit' into the mythopoetic position established for it by Japanese cultural discourse, has diminished considerably since the early 1800s due simply to the domination of Niagara by technology, its practical overpowering by hucksters, industrial development and the urban sprawl which surrounds it. This is exacerbated by the only half-hearted response of the Niagara tourism industry which has kept one eye fixed upon a romanticised image of Niagara as a honeymoon site. These oppositions can best be summarised in a table (see Table 3.3).

Table 3.3 Contrasts between Niagara Falls' tourism markets

Event honeymoon	*Honeymoon tourism*
– Spectacle.	– Nature, magnificent scenes.
– Attractions.	– Wonder and awe.
– Diversion.	
– Local or provincial visitors driving from within 300 miles.	– Long distance, often foreign travellers on package air tours or travelling.
– Independently by bus.	
– Blue collar but extravagant demanding plush, overtly luxurious decor. Luv Tubs. Theme restaurants.	– High-end of tourist market seeking interesting theme accommodation. Elegance. High quality cuisine.
– Short Honeymoon break.	– Honeymoon tour (several destinations).

CONCLUSION

Niagara Falls, it would appear, is ripe for a redevelopment and a revival which might mediate the incongruous juxtaposition of the 'attractions' of Clifton Hill and the Niagara Parks Commission system which attempts to preserve an administrative version of nature as a setting for the now polluted Falls themselves. The deadlocked discourses of opposing interests have prevented a more unified development either in the direction of a Shrine through its separation from the urban property system as a

155

National Park; or in the direction of a re-integration of Niagara Falls and its parks with the urban environment which surrounds it. These historical notes trace the development of Niagara Falls as a site territorialised as a certain *kind* of place within both successive and overlapping spatialisations. Today, one finds a multi-layered history of practices and built environments organised around the changing mytho-poetic position of Niagara Falls in the social spatialisations of eighteenth-century Europeans, nineteenth- and twentieth-century North Americans, and, recently, Japanese. Niagara Falls has changed from being a remote, exotic Shrine, an icon of the sublime, through being a concretisation of moral values, to a liminal site of *rites de passage* and, lately, a confused site of spectacle and consumption. In this set of cultural formations, the place has been brought together with myths of the wilderness; with religion, discourses on domestic conduct; with processual rituals built around the *rites de passage* of first, pilgrimages, and later, newly-weds; with the promotional discourses of commodities and of tourism. Postmodern from before the invention of the term, Niagara has been assimilated into a European tradition of sites of passion dating from the Middle Ages and it has appeared both as a high cultural Shrine and figured in popular culture on cereal packaging as well as alongside Marilyn Monroe and other paragons of sexuality and commerce in Hollywood movies. Out of this, the most enduring and resilient territorialisation of Niagara Falls has been as a site of the carnivalesque, a landscape of kitsch and popular parodies of dominant aesthetic and moral judgement which is kept at bay only by the narrow girdle of parkland which surrounds the Falls themselves.

Operating in the marchlands between human geography and conventional sociology or anthropology allows us to expose one final significance of the Event Honeymoon, the compulsive buying of kitsch anti-style souvenirs and taking of personal photographs highlights the enormous expenditure of personal energies on the creation of meanings and interpretations for Niagara Falls. Paradoxically, however, these are centred around the individual in the form of elaborate, documentary biographies, rather than social discourses. Moreover, the body itself – displayed, mocked, posed against landmarks, embraced in groups – becomes a central vehicle for this process of resistance and self-composition. In times, such as the interwar years, or the present 'postmodern' conjuncture, when foundational narratives lose their trustworthy status as guidelines for living, the turn to individualism becomes particularly important. It is at such *mass* tourism sites that one finds people engaged in the struggle to have *individual selves* by situating themselves in both regular and ironic relationships with spectacles of society and of nature, documenting for themselves a biography which reflexively establishes a coherent relationship between themselves and the world, and which elaborates on the position of individuals within a spatialisation of their social and geographical world.

NOTES

1. This promotional slogan emerged around the turn of the century and has been adopted in most of the advertising literature associated with Niagara Falls. Many postcards, for example, bear this slogan as their title on the message side, followed by a description of the scene which is actually shown.
2. For example, the first reference to Oniugaahra (pronounced as 'Nee-uh-gar-uh' at the time) appears in a 1641 letter from the Jesuit Jerome Lalement (McKinsey 1985:8). Champlain notes its reported existence in his *Voyages* of 1604.
3. Symbolist in the sense of the collection of experiences for their status-value as symbolic capital. See Bourdieu 1981.
4. The use of the feminine to describe Niagara, its personalisation as a female figure provides the ground against which the figure of the language of masculine domination, conquest, possession, rape, and taming to a 'domestic' state is cast in bold relief. Specifically, this included the feminisation of the Falls, which takes on not the supposedly masculine attributes of power and violence but of gentle quietness, of the majestic, softened by the beautiful – calm, gentle, tranquil, exceeding loveliness. Here its power is not really felt. The sentimental was specifically associated with 'scribbling women' and one male visitor believed that it could be appreciated only in the company of women. Thus Walter Henry remarked, 'I have visited . . . Niagara four times, and on three of these occasions in company with ladies – for the view of anything grand or sublime in nature or art is not worth two pence . . . unembellished by the sex. . . . One of the ladies alluded to, of a refined mind and ingenuous nature, after gazing for the first time, with a long and fixed expression, on the sublime object before her, looked for an instant in my face and burst into tears.' (*Events of a Military Life* (London 1843) cited in Dow 1921:I,186–187). Only in the presence of women – 'the register of man's capacity for personal experience' could men show emotion (Henry 1843 cited in Dow 1921, 1.187). See A. Douglas, 1977:48, 102.

The Feminization of American Culture (New York: Knopf) and also N. Cott, 1977. *The Bonds of Womanhood: 'Woman's Sphere' in New England, 1780–1835* (New Haven, Conn.: Yale University Press).

5. 'I am metamorphosed: I am translated; I am an ass's head, a clod, a wooden spoon, a fat weed growing on Lethe's brink, a stock, a stone, a petrification. For have I not seen Niagara, the wonder of wonders, and felt – no words can tell what disappointment.' (Anna Jameson, 1838. *Winter Studies and Summer Rambles* I:83).
6. From Horatio Parsons, 1836. *The Book of Niagara Falls.*
7. On emotional repertoires see M. Maffesoli, 1988. *Le Temps du tribus* (Paris: Meridiens Klincksieck).
8. The guidebooks were to be consulted, not read. Various points of interest are extolled as to their virtues, not for the purpose of impressing the visitor with their collective sublimity, but rather with a view to recommending the best and most convenient vantage points: 'a judicious routine of observation . . . without loss of time or unnecessary toil' (McKinsey 1985:134) as if to sell a package deal. Local boosterism ensured a lively competition between Niagara Falls and the emergent resorts at Newport and Saratoga. Even local proprietors published competing guidebooks designed to extend their trade by extolling the advantages to their particular hotel – either within minutes' walk to the Falls or, alternately, removed from the crowds. While the sublime is mentioned it appears more and more as just a bid in an advertising war of competing claims. In her analysis, McKinsey notes that a dispassionate, more objective tone replaces the affective and emotional language of the earlier travelogues. If the guidebooks elaborate on sublime emotions at all 'they invariably quote from earlier well-known travel accounts rather than write new descriptions. Like the accommodations they advertise, they seem to want to be elegant and fashionable instead of enthusiastic or personal' (McKinsey 1985:134).

In these books, industrial developments and 'improvements' to the local area often provide the main focus of attention. The canal itself is often the centre of attention becoming a new 'Eighth Wonder of the World' which demonstrates man's growing conquest over nature. This illustrates what Leo Marx has called the 'technological sublime' which emerges at this time where the machine and technology supplant nature as the mainspring of sublime inspiration.
9. One, Blondin, walked across the gorge below the Falls on a tight-rope in 1859. Subsequently he made the walk with many variations including wearing buckets on his feet and carrying his agent across on his back while blindfolded. This culminated in a command performance for the Prince of Wales (later Edward VII) at night in 1860 in a scheme which involved lighting up the entire Falls with over 200 searchlights. The human conquest was complete when Anna Edson Taylor went over the Horseshoe Falls in a barrel in 1901 and survived.
10. McKinsey also presents evidence that while promoters and daredevils transformed the cataract into a theatrical event, others appropriated

Niagara for use in the theatre itself. Dioramas, scale models, and sound-and-light panoramas proliferated at carnivals in Europe and in the United States: 'All this "selling" of the Falls elsewhere was of a piece of what had happened to Niagara itself – it had become an object not of awe but of curiosity, a setting for worship not of nature but of humans and their industry, a spectacle to be "consumed" in comfort, fashion, and probably haste' (McKinsey 1985:153).

11. For example, one address by 'Niagara' to its visitors who are 'welcome to my banks but cautioned against liquidation':

> I'm proof against malignant shafts;
> Am ready still to honor drafts
> Have a large capital afloat,
> More current than a U.S. note!
> (Anon. 1828 in *The Table Rock Album* 1848:28–29)

12. See *New York Daily Times* 'Notes on the West' in *The Crayon* 6 (July 1859) 221–222.
13. Reported by W.T.R. Saffell (1873:92–93) in *The Bonaparte-Patterson Marriage* (Philadelphia: Safell) who quotes an unnamed New York newspaper notice 9 July 1804.
14. This visit by his patron's daughter is reported to have inspired the paintings of Niagara Falls by the American artist John Vanderlyn. See K.C. Lindsay (1970:56) *The Works of John Vanderlyn* (Binghampton, NY: State University of New York Art Gallery).
15. 'Two Days at Niagara' in *Southern Literary Messenger* 11 (December 1845) 726, cited in J.H. Franklin (1976:15) *A Southern Odyssey: Travellers in the Antebellum North* (Baton Rouge: Louisiana State University Press).
16. One early example was Charles Dickens, who journeyed to Gravesend. See A.J. Phillip (1912) *Dickens' Honeymoon and Where He Spent it* (London: Chapman & Hall).
17. Lyrics from F. Luther (1942:108) *Americans and their Songs* (New York: Harper).
18. Park Traffic Count and Honeymoon Certificates (Annual Figures)

Year	Car traffic*	Honeymoons/yr
1954	1 821 808	
1956	2 174 570	5 679
1957	1 844 660	6 626
1958	1 813 966	5 736
1959	1 863 940	5 922
1960	1 913 371	5 654
1961	2 109 448	5 620
1962	2 391 847	6 841
1963	2 796 239	6 968

(cont'd)

Year	Car traffic [*]	Honeymoons/yr
1964	2 859 824	6 194
1965	2 702 575	6 780
1966	3 097 576	7 471
1967	3 090 707	8 635
1968	3 210 339	11 591
1969	3 368 439	10 771
1970	3 535 407	11 483
1971	3 360 876	11 253
1972	3 385 319	13 064
1973	3 287 770	15 410
1974	3 287 770	13 298
1975	3 198 905	13 191
1976	3 228 098	11 851
1977	5 155 317	12 199
1978	4 767 476	11 517
1979	5 263 695	12 845
1980	3 442 784	12 286
1981	3 615 227	13 478
1982	3 378 953	13 641
1983	3 241 029	15 020
1984	3 826 300	11 534
1985	3 787 038	12 172
1986	3 684 566	10 826

[*] Traffic count of cars entering Niagara Falls Promenade.
[**] Total number of honeymoons from commencement of figures, 19 June 1949–31 December 1955.

19. For a historical discussion of the fascination with death that characterised the age of romanticism see Ariès 1974; Levin 1970; Rowell 1974; Thompson 1974. For one poet, the brink of the Falls symbolised death –

That mysterious line
That separates eternity from time
(Liston 1843 cited in McGreevy 1987:49)

– for others the Falls simply served as an icon for speculative descriptions of heaven or hell.

20. Marilyn Monroe, cast as a honeymooning newly-wed with a depressed husband sickened by her sensuality, plans to have a boyfriend kill her husband at the Falls. Caught up in this scheme on the account of a double-booked hotel room, another hapless couple – a blithe 'Shredded Wheat' cereal salesman and his wife – are on a long-deferred honeymoon-for-her/business-trip-for-him. All plans fail, the now-neurotic husband kills his assailant, the boyfriend, and goes after his wife, played by Monroe. By coincidence, only the two wives realise that the neurotic husband is still alive, but of course, the salesman

ignores his wife, intent on everyone going fishing with a senior salesman. The neurotic husband kills his wife, Monroe, and steals a fishing boat with (coincidentally) the salesman's wife on board. The boat runs out of gas and drifts towards the Falls. At this point, both wives might be said to have become the 'victims of passion' – one is dead, the other apparently soon to be, perhaps because of her salesman-husband's blithe ignorance of her desires. Read another way, both estranged characters, the neurotic husband and the salesman's wife, are 'in the same boat', *prisoners* of their frustrated passion. The suspense concludes with the neurotic helping the salesman's wife out onto a rock above the Falls (from which she is rescued) just before the boat goes over the edge of the cataract. The Falls provide both a setting for romance within the dominant patriarchal paradigm and for passion which disturbs this 'balance'. The Falls then become the site of a judgement where the 'good' (i.e. 'normal') ultimately survive and the delinquent perish.

A recent novel by Tom Marshall (1988) set at the time of the filming of *Niagara, Voices on the Brink* (Toronto: Macmillan) provides an anthology of images of Niagara Falls.

21. See, for example, Francis Whetley's 'Girls Bathing by a Waterfall' (1783) (Collection of Mr and Mrs Paul Mellon illustrated in the 1963 exhibition catalogue *Painting in England, 1700–1850* Richmond, Virginia: Virginia Museum of Fine Arts p. 205) or J.M.W. Turner's 'The Fall of the Clyde' (1801) (illustrated in C. White, 1977. *English Landscape, 1630–1850* (New Haven: Yale Centre for British Art) Plate 118) or the various waterfall pictures of Louis Eilshemius in the early twentieth century (P.J. Karlstrom, 1978. *Louis Michel Eilshemius* (New York: Abrams) Ch. 5).

22. The information on 'Event Honeymoons' is based on summary figures of the Niagara Falls Honeymoon Register 1949–1986 kept by the Niagara Falls Tourism and Convention Bureau and on an interview with Mrs Stella Howlett of the Bureau. Ms Rosanna Schincariol, Group Sales Director of the Travel Lodge 'Coral Inn' at Niagara Falls, was kind enough to show me round their honeymoon suites and provided rough data on Japanese tours and the problem of the decline of the 'Event Honeymoon'.

23. This emerges in the types of souvenirs sold. Apart from the typical mug with a printed message, are the mugs in the shape of women's breasts with a slightly risqué message; towels showing a newly-wed couple, wife on the phone, husband urinating in the bathroom with the caption 'We're at Niagara, Mom . . . Can't you hear the Falls?', or an ashtray in the shape of a foot with the message 'We got a kick out of Niagara Falls CANADA' [sic] and various printed satin pillows and lingerie. The *Financial Post* reported in 1987 that this 'frog and bust business' was in a boom phase (12 July, 1987:3).

Chapter Four

THE TRUE NORTH STRONG
AND FREE

O Canada! Our home and native land!
True patriot love in all thy sons command.
With glowing hearts we see thee rise,
The True North strong and free!
From far and wide, O Canada,
  we stand on guard for thee.
God keep our land, glorious and free
O Canada, we stand on guard for thee,
O Canada, we stand on guard for thee.

(Calixa Lavallée, *Oh Canada*) [1]

In earlier chapters, the position of spatial beliefs, theories, and practices within the matrix of culture was formulated in terms of place-images and myths. The influence of these myths on the development of particular places was discussed in the context of situating places with respect to each other within social spatial-isations. This was a matter not only of mytho-poetic positions but also of complex relationships with the empirical geography of places and spaces and to have tangible effects as 'causative' formations.

Space-myths present another level and scale for investigation. They approach the status of 'mythologies' because they marshal so many place-images and myths. This chapter turns to North America, and particularly southern, central Canadian myths of the Arctic and Sub-Arctic. It will be argued that the space-myth which will be called the myth of the 'True North Strong and Free' has been appropriated as one symbol of specific Canadian national-istic discourse which, although not completely hegemonic, attempts to reconcile regional viewpoints. This myth resides within an oppositional spatialisation whereby Southerners construe the North as a counter-balance to the civilised world of the Southern cities yet the core of their own, personal, Canadian identity. The historian Hayden White has called this 'the technique of ostensive self-definition by negation'. He provides the archetypal opposition of civilised and wild noting that historical discussions of wildness always serve the agenda of reinforcing a priori notions of civilisation in different historical moments.

> In times of sociocultural stress, when the need for positive self-definition asserts itself but no compelling criterion of self-identification appears, it is always possible to say something like: 'I may not know the precise content of my own felt humanity, but I am most certainly not like that,' and simply point to something in the landscape that is manifestly different from oneself. . . . It appears as a kind of reflex action in conflicts between nations, classes and political parties. . . . If we do not know what we think 'civilisation' is, we can always find an example of what it is not. . . . Similarly, in the past, when men were uncertain as to the precise quality of their sensed humanity, they appealed to the concept of wildness to designate an area of subhumanity that was characterized by everything they hoped they were not.
>
> (White 1978:151–152)

In this light, the 'True North Strong and Free' is a perverse case of building a cultural identity from both sides of the equation civilised–uncivilised or culture–nature: of defining a dichotomy and then reappropriating elements which are often rejected because the dualism becomes associated, metaphorically, with other black and white categories such as good–bad. This 'True North' is a masculine-gendered, liminal zone of *rites de passage* and re-creative freedom and escape. It is a resource and economic hinterland which is simultaneously incorporated in a social spatial-isation as a mythic heartland. I shall argue that such a dualism provides a foundation for Canadian nationalists because it provides the possibility of setting a 'Canadian nature' (The 'True North') off against 'American mass culture' entirely originating, or so we are asked to believe, south of the border. The mass culture

163

of southern Canadian cities is fantasised away as a minor exception. The Canadian dualism of north and south appears also in Australia, where Stratton has argued that Southern Australia discursively defines itself as 'civilised' in relation to its Northern Territory, which is 'constructed as the site of the Other, of that which has been repressed in the south's production of the real' (Stratton 1989:38).

'The True North Strong and Free', a phrase from the English version of the Canadian national anthem, summarises many aspects of southern central Canadian myths of the North: truth or honesty to an autochthonous spirit of the land, a 'strength' that defies human incursion, and freedom from conquest by those with imperial ambitions. The notions around the imaginary geography of this 'True North Strong and Free' provide an example of the discursive power in spatialisation, especially when it involves nationalistic 'representations of space'. The concepts harnessed to the physical datum of the 'North' – truth, purity, freedom, power – serve in the establishment of a particular 'social spatialisation' as an order of the world and cosmos; a specification of priorities and threats, friends and foes, and helps to reinforce the cultural solidarity of individuals and communities. There are, of course, competing spatial mythologies, but the 'True North Strong and Free' has a striking prominence amongst English-speaking, central, southern Canadians and in the dominant political rhetoric this majority generates.

IMAGES AND REALITIES

Robert Service spoke of the 'Spell of the Yukon.' Many others have written volumes on the north's effects on human intruders, particularly whites. All agree that the Canadian north exerts a powerful influence on those who inhabit, explore, or contemplate its vast reaches. To many, the region assumes almost mystical proportions, growing beyond its political status or geography to become a state of mind. . . . Many, shackled by the distances and the sameness of its horizons, are overwhelmed by the minuteness of their human intrusion.

(Coates 1985:16)

There are several common definitions of the Canadian North. Perhaps the most widely known equates the North with the Northwest Territories and the Yukon, an administrative definition which may be attributed to the Federal Government. This definition masks another. For most English-speaking Canadians the 'North' is not just a factual geographical region but also an imaginary zone: a frontier, a wilderness, an empty 'space' which, seen from southern Canada is white, blank. Or at least this is what we are told by essayists and writers, and what we will see Canadians are taught in school. The ideological 'True North' is an empty page onto which can be projected images of the essence of 'Canadian-ness' and also images to define one's urban existence against. For this reason, definitions of the North oscillate between the poles of frozen wilderness hinterland and hotly-defended cultural heartland. But this must not be mistaken for equivocation. The North is less a real region signified by a name and more a name, a signifier, with a historically-variable, socially-defined content. An 'official', social mythology appears to overlie the palimpsest of personal images and experiences: subscription to this social mythology will be seen to define central Canadian identity.

Even as 'objectively' presented on Mercator projection maps, the North is a zone of indeterminacy, fading away from the crisply drawn line of the 49th parallel and breaking up into the myriad fragments of the islands of the Northern archipelago. Summer nights are as bright as day, and in winter ice sheets blur the distinctions of land and sea. Much to the frustration of Northerners, the North has been defined solely in terms of Southern interests. It is a resource-rich hinterland, but there is a sense that development must be limited: the cultural heartland must be preserved. 'The presence of a North in man is even more critical than the presence of men in the North' (Warwick 1968:47). This has furnished the basis for paternalistic policies on Northern development and the 'civilising' of the Inuit (Milne *et al.* 1982) with little power exercised by Northern inhabitants. The Territories lack any power or self-government in the way that Provinces (with as few as Prince Edward Island's 128,000 inhabitants: Statistics Canada 1985) have – control over energy and resources, judiciary, health, education, housing and land use policies, taxation powers, constitutional veto, and the use of coordinated inter-provincial pressure on the Federal Government.

The 'North' is not limited to the two Territories. Commonly in Canadian texts one finds introductory comments which stress this:

> we define the North in its broadest sense. Rather than restricting it geographically to the Northwest Territories and the Yukon, we consider the North as a territorially shifting entity and an imaginative construct. . . . the historic North moves southward as one moves backward in time . . . the North . . . shifts through time and place. When the fur traders of the North-West Company assembled their great brigades with their long Montreal canoes to voyage into the interior, the *pays d'en haut*,[2] or north country, began just above the Lachine [rapids at Montreal]. Thus we include not only the region north of latitude 60, but also the northern portions of most of the provinces, and some areas even farther south . . . for instance . . . in the 1830s . . . present-day Muskoka, Haliburton, and Algonquin Park – hardly part of the North of the 1980s.
>
> (Hodgins and Hobbs 1985:3)

But even expanded in this manner, Northern residents comprise less than 2 per cent of the total Canadian population of 26.5 million,[3] making them doubly marginalised: first in the sense of geographical isolation, second in the sense of lacking in power over local developments.

With this problem of definition goes an academic geography debate over the southern boundary of this half-real, half-imaginary 'North'. What factors determine 'nordicity' (Hamelin 1980)? As the novelist Margaret Atwood has commented, 'Where you cross the border from here to there is a matter of opinion. Is it the first gift shop shaped like a wigwam? The first town that proclaims itself the "Gateway to the North"?' (1987:141). Writing in a popular Canadian magazine she presents one southern Canadian view of the North.

> It is not only a place but a direction, and as such its location is relative: to the Mexicans, the United States is North. . . . Wherever it is for us [Canadians], there's a lot of it. You stand in Windsor and imagine a line going north, all the way to the pole. . . . That's the sort of map we grew up with, at the front

of the classroom in Mercator projection, which made it look even bigger than it was, all that pink stretching on forever with cities sprinkled along the bottom edge. It's not only geographical space, it's space related to body image. When we face south, as we often do, our conscious mind may be directed down there, towards crowds, bright lights, some Hollywood version of fame and fortune, but the north is at the back of our minds, always. There's something, not someone, looking over our shoulders; there's a chill at the nape of the neck. The north focuses our anxieties. Turning to face north, face *the north*, we enter our own unconscious. Always in retrospect, the journey north has the quality of a dream.

(Atwood 1987:143, italics added)

This is a good beginning. Atwood's popularity and central position in what the critics call 'Canadian literature' contributes a certain authority to her observations. But, it is difficult to abandon the suspicious stance of the social scientist so easily. Does this novelist *speak for* the 'average' Canadian, or is there a hint of the prescriptive in Atwood's rhetoric: 'true' Canadians remember the North? Does she not also *speak to* Canadians? To what extent is she engaged in *shaping* public perception as opposed to accurately *echoing* it? Most Canadians rarely if ever visit the far North (Government of the Northwest Territories 1987). That is, despite publicly expressed sentiments, people's actions correspond to some other pattern of understandings. Largely, experience of the North is only through secondary images and narratives, such as Atwood's would be for most readers, and television news clips.[4] The 1936 comment of the popular essayist, Stephen Leacock, is still true: 'I never have gone to the James Bay; I never go to it; I never shall. But somehow I'd feel lonely without it' (1957:212).

NORDICITY

The Canadian geographer Louis-Edmond Hamelin has considered the geographical extent of the North and the question of Canadian nordicity, or 'northern-ness', methodically and at length (1977; 1980). He argues for a more disaggregated view of the

167

North which would reflect the divisions of experience, geography, development, and administration of the nor h. Based on a measure of six environmental and four cultur: l criteria of the nordicity[5] of Canadian towns he differentiates four zones (see Figure 4.1). Assigning a maximum of 100 points to each criterion makes for a theoretical 1,000 points on this scale at the North Pole. 'Base Canada' is what most Northerners would call 'Southern Canada'. A minimum of 200 points is required to qualify as falling within the North. Edmonton, Canada's northernmost large city and provincial capital, scores 135 and is, therefore, not 'Northern'.[6] For Hamelin, this roughly reflects the popular perception of that city. However, Hamelin's choice of 200 out of 1,000 as the significant statistical dividing point is less easily justified. The appeal to popular perception is indicative of a tautological circle in all of these studies: starting out from commonsensical intuition, statistics are gathered and then interpreted in the light of commonsense. Thus ennobled by the clothes of empiricism, commonsense is represented as scientific conclusions. A decade after his original publication, academics and Edmontonians hail themselves and examine the city as a 'Liveable Winter City': being 'in the North' has begun to acquire more cachet than it once had and popular perception continues to change, making it an unstable basis on which to justify measures of 'nordicity'.

The first Northern zone Hamelin calls the 'Middle North': the northern areas of the ten provinces, Labrador, and much of the Yukon where road access is possible. All of these areas are at roughly the same level of economic development in terms of physical infrastructure. Yet, because Hamelin aggregates his measures of perception with environmental data such as climate and development, this classification masks the different popular perception of the Yukon which lies 'North of 60' degrees latitude – a phrase used by the federal bureaucracy partly because it distinguishes the Territories, which are federally administered from the capital, Ottawa, from the various Northern administrative spaces of the provincial governments. Thus, it has been widely disseminated and popularised through Federal-Government-funded documentary films, educational videos, and magazines.[7] 'North of 60' is somehow 'really North' as opposed to the northern no man's lands of the provinces.

Figure 4.1 Map of the extent of the Canadian 'North'

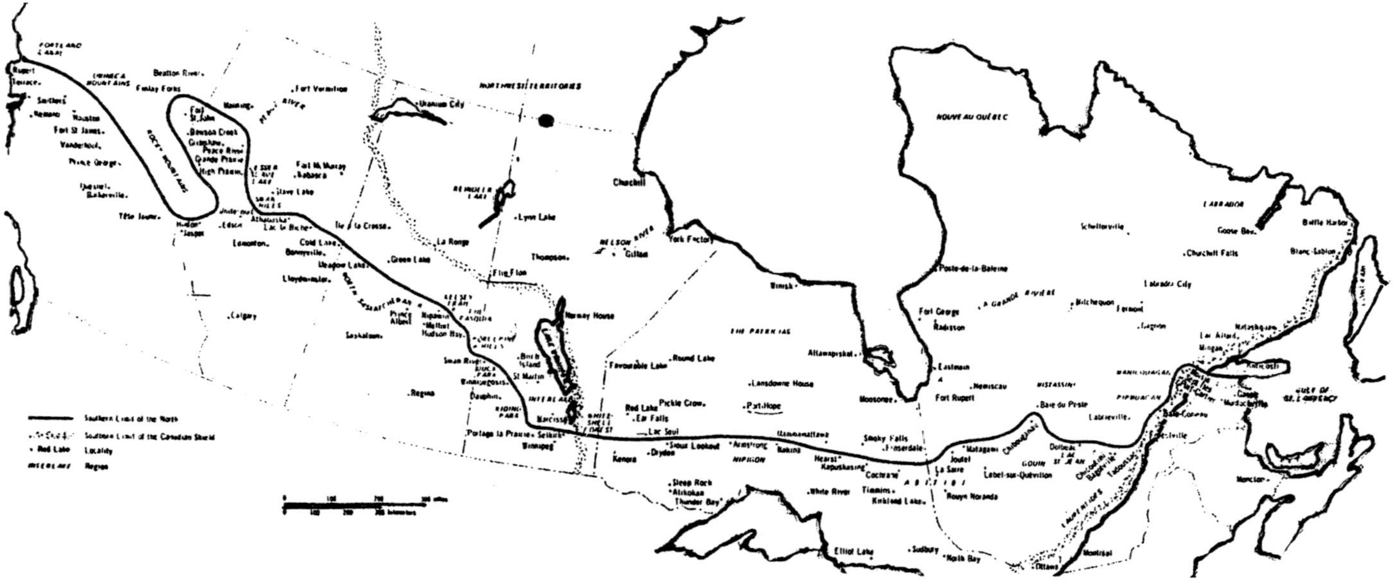

Source: Adapted from Hamelin (1980)

Beyond the Middle North lies what Hamelin calls the 'Far North' (500–800 points) and the 'Extreme North' (800 points or more). These take in most of the Arctic archipelago, much of the Northwest Territories[8] and northern Quebec (known as Nouveau Québec). Indeed, most of these two zones might be thought of as the 'Far North' in the popular imagination – an inhospitable land of ice and snow populated by Musk Oxen and the occasional Inuit hunter or oil drilling platform.

Using Hamelin's definition of a gradated northern-ness underlines the extension of the geographical North beyond the political North of the two Territories north of 60 degrees. Every province except the Maritime provinces of New Brunswick, Prince Edward Island, and Nova Scotia includes a significant amount of 'northern' land. By Hamelin's method, this ranges from 77 per cent of Newfoundland (i.e. Labrador) and 70 per cent of Québec down to 31 per cent of British Columbia. Speaking for most geographers, William Wonders has commented,

> a multiplicity of criteria for varying types gives a much better 'total impact' of northern conditions in the aggregate. It includes marine areas as well as land, represents year-round conditions and is not just seasonal, enables useful comparisons to be made, can provide for differences over time, and is relatively simple to use. Whether the best criteria have been selected, or whether the correct ratio of environmental/cultural is involved, may be argued. Important variations within one criterion often do not emerge.
>
> (Wonders 1984:227)

But Hodgins and Hobbs, echoing Atwood's sentiment above, suggest that Hamelin's index should be expanded with a psychological component.

> North . . . is a state of mind as well as certain material conditions. Central to this revised notion of *nordicity* is the concept of wilderness. Indeed, as wilderness has shrunk and remoteness declined over time, so too have Canada's various Norths. The North is not a frontier. It is the wilderness beyond the interrupted agrarian frontier and the urban islands of mid-Canada. The North is not found along a line. It is a space with depth . . . .
>
> (Hodgins and Hobbs 1985:1–2)

Indeed, the exact location of any southern boundary of the North is highly debatable. Hamelin's method of scoring places still involves a considerable amount of personal judgement. This leaves a certain latitude for idiosyncratic assessments. Nonetheless, his definitions have been accepted as one helpful attempt at systematically defining the North according to the empiricistic criteria of geography. As such, they provide not so much a yardstick by which to measure northern-ness as an indicator of one profession's fascination with organising and recoding popular perceptions in the discourse of empirical rationalism and an indicator of the seriousness with which the entire northern-ness issue is treated.

More important is Hamelin's motivation. Hamelin is reacting to the plethora of stereotypes and lack of meaningful order amongst the different regions of the Canadian North. This he has referred to as the 'gap between perceptions and reality,' of transplanted southern administrators' attitudes who thereby adopt the wrong means to deal with northern problems (Hamelin 1984:172,173). But we must ask why is it necessary to define the *limits* of the North? The debate revolves partly around entitlements to tax exemptions and 'isolation allowances' although northern-ness is not the primary criterion, only a corollary. The main standard of 'isolation' is distance from major cities. It is futile to draw further lines across the maps of the continent: '60 degrees north' is at least a memorable phrase.

When discussing images, it is not enough to simply conclude that southern images of the North are inaccurate, or that they 'lag behind' in recognizing the modernisation of Northern communities. Hamelin's work and its stated motivation is, in its own way, an indicator of the fecundity of the North as a source of images despite its harsh infertility. Such images are by their very nature un-rationalised: fiats of the imagination. The implication of geographers, 'culture theorists' and some noted Canadian intellectuals and authors in the elaboration of an image of the North without regard to its socio-political implications and economic impacts, as will be argued below, puts them in an uncomfortable position indeed. However, the generalised disinterestedness of social scientists to 'lift the lid' on the spatialisation of the Canadian nation state through such space-myths as the 'True North Strong and Free' is perhaps even more serious.

It is popularly recognized that across the diverse regions of

Canada, the North provides a important source of readily understood metaphors, jokes, images, and allegorical narratives. The
trivialisation of once serious sayings and political rhetoric about
the North (see below) and the entry of many metaphors into
the realm of cliché is partial evidence of this diffusion and also of
the appropriation of official metaphors mobilised to support
government ambitions for the North as a resource hinterland into
less consensual, polyvocal, vocabulary of popular discourses. For
Canadians, these are the easy to identify with, but over-idealised
claims that Canadians make about themselves, those explanations
one learns to give to foreigners or hears the Prime Minister giving
on the evening news. Canadian comedy teams such as SCTV's
popular 'Bob and Doug Mackenzie' lampoon myths of the North
by appearing as two beer-drinking bumpkins in red-checked
'lumberjack shirts' and wearing toques (knitted hats) who reduce
all contemporary issues to the sardonic one-liner 'the Great White
North, eh' (Knelman 1983:28).[9] As Cook (1984:17) notes, they re-
mind one that the rhetorically 'clean psychic atmosphere' (Harris
1926:86) of the great, white 'True North Strong and Free' has long
since been polluted by beer cans and garbage (see Salutin 1981:
28–29). More importantly, such trivialising jokes point to and
make fun of the Canadian obsession with that 'state of mind', the
'chill at the nape of the neck' that Atwood alludes to, the 'True
North Strong and Free'. Such popular appropriations satirise the
moralistic and authoritarian nature of 'serious' discourses. While
it is held out as extra-ordinary space, beyond the daily itineraries
of most Canadians, it has also entered the realm of the commonplace and the banal as a set of slogans.

A BRIEF HISTORY OF NORTHERN IMAGES

European images of the Canadian North begin in the reports of
the first explorers and missionaries who reported on their journeys. Inadequate space means that only a few examples will be
presented. A full treatment would run to encyclopaedic length
(Hamelin 1980:31).[10] Samuel Hearne, an English explorer who
travelled across the Barren Lands[11] west of Hudson Bay to the
Arctic Ocean in the late eighteenth century, saw little beauty in the
environment he struggled through.

In my opinion, there cannot exist a stronger proof that
mankind was not created to enjoy happiness in this world,
than the conduct of the miserable beings who inhabit this
wretched part of it.

(Hearne 1795:81)

The Barren Lands present a treeless barrier of almost a thousand
miles of peat bog, tundra, and innumerable lakes and ponds where
water lies on the surface above an impermeable membrane of
permafrost.

Lakes, lakes, lakes innumerable. Some seem interlocking,
some do not. This is all a crazy jigsaw puzzle of sand and
water, dry potholes, coulees, kettle holes. God help the man
who gets off the route in this country! Nothing – nothing to
go by, just up and down, around sandhills and dry washes,
and thousands and thousands of caribou trails.

(Downes 1943:136)

By contrast, there was another assessment of the aesthetic value of
this landscape, which is found in the response of Saltatha, a Yellow
Knife Indian, to a missionary priest of the late nineteenth century
who had offered the biblical description of heaven:

My father, you have spoken well; you have told me that
heaven is very beautiful; tell me now one thing more. Is it
more beautiful than the country of the muskox in summer,
when sometimes the mist blows over the lakes, and sometimes
the water is blue, and the loons cry very often?

(Saltatha, reported in Warburton Pike 1892:302)

These two points of view betray two different cultures,[12] but also
express a contemporary tension in Canadian attitudes toward the
North. The North is treated as a paradise which has temporarily
lost its charm (Hamelin 1984:167). On the one hand, starkly
beautiful; on the other, inhospitable – such beauty as is only to be
experienced with the comfort of the best survival equipment. This
ambivalence continues to be in evidence, as shown (despite the
limitations as noted in Chapter 2) in research on contemporary
locational preferences of single Southern Canadian under-
graduate university students (Whitney 1984). This group has
almost no first-hand experience of the North yet a large and recent

experience of educational films and media portraits of the North. Echoing their sentiment (Vancouver is the preferred location for undergraduates, no matter where their origin, but see also Gould and White's (1974) study of adolescents in central Canada), Luste says, 'One could argue that this dichotomy of love and fear for our wilderness surroundings is still with us: that it is the heart of the Canadian psyche' (1985:40). If only because the South is the land of daily life, for most the North is the land of the extraordinary, a land of dreams and *rites de passage* (James 1985:11), unsuited to civilised life. But if this 'True North' is a liminal zone, it is different from the type encountered at Brighton and Niagara because it has historically been the space of pilgrimages – to the Pacific, to the Orient, to the Pole, and so on. It has been the space of the pilgrimage moment of 'between-ness', of travelling and of the quest, between home and goal.

Thompson's chronicle (1962) reflects this ambivalence and presents further evidence of the historical existence of this attitude. Crossing the continental divide on 10 January 1811, Thompson recorded the mixed feelings of himself and his men:

> The view now before us was an ascent of deep snow, in all appearance to the height of land between the Atlantic and Pacific Oceans. It was to me a most exhilarating sight, but to my uneducated men a dreadful sight. They had no scientific object in view, their feelings were of the place they were [in]. Our guide Thomas told us that, although we could barely find wood to make a fire, we must now provide wood to pass the following night on the height of the defile we were in, and which we had to follow.
>
> My men were the most hardy that could be picked out of a hundred brave hardy men, but the scene of desolation before us was dreadful, and I knew it. A heavy gale of wind, much more a mountain storm, would have buried us beneath it, but thank God the weather was fine. We had to cut wood such as it was, and each took a little on his sled. Yet such was the despondency of the men, aided by the coward Du Nord, sitting down at every half mile, that when night came we had only wood to make a bottom, and on this lay [the] wherewith to make a small fire, which soon burnt out, and in this exposed situation we passed the rest of a long night without

fire, and part of my men had strong feelings of personal insecurity.

(Thompson 1971:282–283)

In his voyages Thompson encountered many places which defied his European experience of proportioned landscape gardens:

... we were now on the banks of the Manito Lake, all around which, as far as the eye could see, were bold shores, the land rising several hundred feet in bold swells, all crowned with Forests of Pines; in the Lake were several fine Isles of a rude conical form, equally well clothed with Woods. I was highly pleased with this grand scenery; but soon found the apparent fine forests to be an illusion, they were only dwarf Pines growing on the rocks; and held together by their roots being twisted with each other. On our route, seeing a fine Isle, which appeared a perfect cone of about sixty feet in height, apparently remarkably well wooded to the very top of the cone; I went to it, my companions [native guides] saying it was lost time; on landing, we walked through the apparent fine forest, with our heads clear above all the trees, the tallest only came to our chins; while we were thus amusing ourselves, the Wind arose and detained us until near sunset ...

(Thompson 1962:111–112)

Over the next two centuries, the search for the Northwest Passage led to incredible feats of human endurance which seized the imagination of people around the world. In 1817, the British Admiralty, idle after Waterloo, offered twenty thousand pounds to the discoverer of the Northwest Passage. In 1819–20, Sir William Parry penetrated to within 250 miles of the Beaufort. However, it was the ambitious and well-outfitted 1845 expedition under the experienced Sir John Franklin which raised most interest and popularised the hostile image of the North. When this expedition was lost without a trace further awards were offered to the discoverer of the sensationalistic fate of the members. Thirty-eight different expeditions produced little hard evidence except the 1854 paper on native reports by Dr John Rae of the Hudson's Bay Company (see Rae 1855:246; see also Rich 1953:265, 276–277). The news that the company had resorted to cannibalism in their last days raised a storm of controversy and challenged the values of

Victorians. An Arctic which had broken the discipline of Her Majesty's Royal Navy amounted to the ultimate test of civilisation as well as skill (Dickens was moved to defend the expedition members' honour in his *Household Words* 5 February 1855; see Roberts 1980:70; see also Dickens's play on the subject *The Frozen Deep*).

Further muddying the waters is a multitude of half-truths which have entered the space-myth of the 'True North Strong and Free'. 'Tall tales' such as Robert Service's poem 'The Shooting of Dan McGrew' have become as much part of the image of the North as the cold. Yet, what purports to be an account of a true figure and an actual Klondike saloon brawl was written ten years after the boom years of the Klondike Gold Rush days it supposedly reports and in the face of residents' protests about its inaccuracy (Hamelin 1980:29). In films, the removal of the roofs of igloos to permit the filming of life inside necessitated the inhabitants' being fully clothed in the sub-zero temperatures, introducing the idea that igloos are uncomfortable and cold habitations (Hamelin 1980:24; see also note 8). Negative images of the North are also conveyed in many supposedly purely factual works by the use of meaningless clichés. Climatological surveys have called the North a 'Land without Summer' (Estienne and Godard cited in Hamelin 1980:28). As Stefansson pointed out with resignation, 'man finds it easier to change the face of nature rather than to change his own mind' (1945:96).

Another important ingredient in Canadian thoughts about the North has been Canada's contested claim to it. The 'northern rhetoric' of successive governments and the media has echoed with nationalism if only because the North has posed a set of de facto nationalistic issues for Canadians. The consolidation of Confederation involved the acquisition of Rupert's Land from the Hudson's Bay Company. With the emergence of economic potential in the high Arctic, the question of sovereignty was posed by the British government in London in 1874. The British were reluctant to over-extend themselves in the Arctic at a time when they had demanding territorial concerns in Africa and Asia. But, if they renounced the region it was likely that the Americans, who had purchased Alaska from the Czar in 1867, would claim it. Unlikely to receive imperial military support, the Canadian government was reluctant to act and attempted to smother the problem. American graphite and mica mining interests commenced operation on Baffin Island in 1877 and the Canadian government of John A. MacDonald was forced by London to acknowledge a transfer of territorial responsibility to the Dominion of Canada. This was completed in 1880 with MacDonald emphasising that the annexation of North was a necessary resource-rich foundation of the country's future (House of Commons *Debates* V: 5 May 1878: 2,390–2,391). While optimism was expressed by Senate select committees, little attempt was made to establish an effective government presence in the North.[15] It was contested ground, jealously guarded, if with trepidation. It was felt that great mineral deposits lay waiting for exploitation in the North and that there could even be serious agriculture in the Mackenzie Valley all the way up to the Arctic Ocean – a piece of incredible optimism (House of Commons *Debates* 1 May 1902:3,951–3,978; 30 September 1903:12,819 and Senate of Canada 1888:10–15).

Concerns about the sovereignty of the Yukon emerged during the migrations of the Klondike Gold Rush in the late 1890s. There were also worries over American whaling in the Beaufort Sea. Parliamentary debates of 1901–03 attest to Canadian fears that the United States might purchase Greenland and then annex the entire Arctic to link Greenland with Alaska in a repetition of the American seizure of territory in the Spanish American war. There was concern that overt or bold Canadian moves might provoke 'official' American concern where little existed at the time (House of Commons *Debates* 1 May 1902:3,951–61,78; 30 September 1903: 12,819). Yet, newspapers announced that any 'purchaser of Greenland must be prepared to defend his purchase by force of arms' (*Quebec Chronicle* cited in Hopkins 1904:389). The few Canadian expeditions that did travel north were supported with rhetoric rather than funds. Partly because the territory remained unmapped, the entire wedge-shaped sector from Greenland in the East to the line of 141 degrees longitude was claimed.[14] Today, although the Canadian government has established a tangible presence and enforces marine pollution measures, this claim, never recognised by the United States, has remained a source of irritation into the present day with incursions by the icebreaking oil tanker *Manhattan* (1969) and the American Coast Guard icebreaker *Polar Sea* (1985). Nonetheless, it is accepted political policy that,

one of the few shared and deeply felt beliefs in Ottawa is that
Canadian sovereignty in the North is non-negotiable. The
political cost of retreating publicly ... is perceived by both
senior officials and the leaders of all political parties as
intolerable and a certain defeat for any government in office.

(Doxman 1976:34)

The sensationalistic nature of the North and the fate of many of its
explorers have long been presented in schools in a manner
designed to encourage patriotic responses. Educational series
such as the Ryerson Historical Readers were built around easily
assimilated historical figures. Explorers such as Franklin and
Hearne have been appropriated as heroes, 'Argonauts of the
North' (Service 1911:34) in the struggle of man against nature.
Page notes

> The exploration of the Canadian Arctic was an example of
> those stern Victorian qualities and values on which the
> Empire had been built. As one school text put it: 'It is as
> though one listens to the muffled heart-beats of a nation and
> an empire. And it is fitting that here the name of Franklin
> should be preserved, for the qualities of body, heart, and
> mind which made Britain great among nations there is no
> nobler embodiment'.
>
> (Long undated:2 cited in Page 1986:6)[15]

This combination of nationalism and patriotism weights the
images and myths of the 'North' with an almost over-political
importance.

Canadians also inherited the notion that being a northern
nation not only endowed them with a tradition but also guaran-
teed their racial supremacy: '... bracing northern winters ...
preserve us from the effeminacy which naturally steals over the
most vigorous races when long under the relaxing influence of
tropical or even generally mild and genial skies' (Toronto *Globe* 2
April, 1869). This 'cold-weather determinism' (Page 1986:6) reinforced a sense of northern, imperial, destiny for Canada and
movements grew up around this racialist notion (Berger 1966:
4–5). This view was revived several times, given impetus by racial
Darwinism (e.g. Dinbaldo 1978). Others worried that such a

robust Northern image might discourage prospective immigrants
(House of Commons *Debates* 30 September 1903:12,816–12,819).

O, we are the men of the Northern Zone;
Shall a bit be placed in our mouth?
if ever a Northman lost his throne
Did the conqueror come from the South?
Nay, nay – and the answer blent
In chorus is southward sent:
'Since when has a Southerner placed his heel
On the men of the Northern zone?'
  (R.K. Kernighan 1896 'Men of the Northern Zone'
  cited in Hamilton and Shields 1979:629)

The greatest publicist of some of these ideas was the explorer
Vilhjalmur Stefansson. In his book *The Northward Course of Empire*
(1923),[16] and lectures he argued that the centres of the great
empires had moved progressively northward over history. As
England succeeded the Roman Empire, so Canada would succeed
England. This tone continued in government publications even
until the late 1950s: 'It is a curious fact that civilization has been
expanding northward ever since the dawn of history . . . converg-
ing from both sides of the world toward a common centre. That
centre is the arctic' (Department of Northern Affairs and Natural
Resources 1958:35).

Successive Prime Ministers used the North as a rallying call for
nationalistic trade policies and to spur on private enterprise.
Prime Minister Diefenbaker used a development-oriented version
of the 'Northern Vision' to appeal to the nationalist sentiment of
the late 1950s. He urged the development of the North through
government provision of the infrastructure for development. A
'Roads to Resources' programme of transport subsidies was
designed to encourage investment. Northern development would
give a 'sense of national purpose', 'safeguard independence' and
restore 'unity'. It was even to provide the stimulus for a new,
pioneering, 'national soul' (Diefenbaker, Speech, 12 February
1958).

However, the general pattern of development of the North has
been in the form of stops and starts. Billion-dollar mega-projects
surge forward which see the construction of massive resource

extraction facilities or hydroelectric power projects and the attendant infrastructure of roads and towns. In between there is little activity or incentive for small-scale economic expansion, partly because economies of scale are needed to overcome transportation and labour costs. This economic history betrays a pattern of investment which does not conform to the above idealism. For example, although they packed his lectures, few people bought Stefansson's book (see Note 18). The periods of greatest development of the North have been during the 1898–9 Klondike Gold Rush in the Yukon and during the Second World War when American fears of a Japanese invasion of Alaska prompted them to build the Alaska Highway through the Yukon, to encourage the Canadian government to establish a series of airstrips and begin development of the Northern Oilfields in the Mackenzie basin. In the immediate post-war era another slump in Northern activity occurred, despite the attempts of Stefansson to popularise the notion that the North was 'Canada's destiny'.

Between 1968 and 1971, Toronto entrepreneurs promoted the notion of 'Mid-Canada Development' meaning the development of resource extraction projects in Hamelin's Middle North. But on the whole, little resulted from these efforts which were mostly confined to publicity announcements. Few got rich during the Klondike Gold Rush and this pattern continued. Many saw their hopes of quick profits dashed in the years since. The expansion of nickel and copper mining in the Sudbury area took place only years after the discovery of copper ores during extension of the Trans-Canada road network north of lake Superior.

The space-myth of the 'True North Strong and Free' with all that implies has real impacts on economic fortunes and tangible effects on the shape and pace of regional development. The discovery of oil and natural gas in the Beaufort has proved far more difficult to exploit than anticipated. Billions have been lost in petroleum ventures and more wasted in schemes to encourage development by allowing companies and individuals to deduct exploration costs. First, with the 1968 discovery of the largest gas fields in North America a proposal was made by twenty-seven major oil companies to build a 48-foot-high pressure pipeline from Prudhoe Bay, Alaska, to Calgary, Alberta thence branching to California and the American Mid-West. It was to be the largest project ever financed by private capital. However, the Berger Inquiry into the impacts of the proposal became a media extravaganza, where development-oriented corporations clashed head on with a coalition of Natives and local residents, environmentalists and the southern public who described the development as the exploitation of Canada's soul. The widely televised Berger Inquiry revealed deep-seated romantic myths which Southern intervenors defended before the commission. Anti-development forces succeeded in mobilising Canadians' images of the North and to invoke a latent nationalistic mythology contra the multinational corporate plans. The historic importance of the North for the Canadian imagination was misunderstood or at least neglected by these sponsors (Page 1986:2). As a result, the proposal was first delayed by a moratorium on development for ten years, then defeated by economics as the collapse of the world oil price made the risky and difficult extraction of Arctic oil and gas uneconomic. The rhetoric of purity figures in similar emotional outcries have erupted, with good reason, over American requests for the diversion of Canadian rivers to supply fresh-water to the drought-prone western states and over plans for a continental economic common market which will come into effect in the late 1990s. Recent applications to consider building a pipeline south to United States markets have reopened this debate.

This historical survey reveals three main stances toward the North that were prominent among southern Canadians: (1) the idolisation of the North as a wilderness zone of purity, an unstained (*purus*) cultural 'heartland'; (2) the North as a resource frontier offering riches to developers; (3) ignorance founded on its irrelevance to everyday life. The rhetorical stress on the first, the periodic bouts of the second, and the individual practice of the third produces a difficult picture. These stances have coexisted for many years in complex and shifting formations of inconsistent practices and prejudices, institutional policies and individual behaviour. This complexity is either denied or treated as equivocation (e.g. between (2) and (3)) in the works reviewed up to this point and below. The following sections will go beyond these to propose a more adequate 'reading' based on the thesis developed in earlier chapters and sections that the North participates in some sort of spatialisation which grounds national ideologies.

THE NATIONALISTIC 'TRADITION' OF IMAGES

It has been said that power, that empire came from the
north. Northern people have always stood for courage and
unconquerability. They have the muscle, the wholesomeness
of life, the strength of will.

(Lord Strathcona in a letter to William Garson
cited in Willson 1915:601)

Since the 1970s, a public revival of elements of Northern myths as
part of a nationalistic ideology – the one, true, *Canadian* vision of
the North – has become apparent. In this case spatialisation takes
an unusually prominent position, appearing explicitly in ideology.
One important figure in this nationalistic vision of the North has
been the historian W.L. Morton. In his *The Canadian Identity*
(1961) he argues that the topography of the 'grim Precambrian
horseshoe' of the Canadian Shield (which includes the Barrens,
for example) is central to 'all understanding of Canada'. In contrast to the United States, this cultural heartland of Canada is a
forbidding wilderness. It was traversed by (male) fur traders,
lumberjacks, prospectors, and miners who 'wrested from it the
staples by which Canada has lived', but they had always to return
to their home bases (women and families) in the St Lawrence
valley, or in the prairies, for that was where their food came from.
Morton claims that 'this alternate penetration of the wilderness
and return to civilization is the basic rhythm of Canadian life'
(Morton 1961:5), thus enshrining (despite its entirely past nature)
a gendered opposition of nature versus civilisation as the enduring
rule of Canadian daily life. His work marks the transformation of
the earlier climatic determinism into a geographic determinism
where power becomes vested in the land rather than the weather.
In this manner, Southern Canadians have integrated something of
the traditional native understandings of *genus loci* – the spirit of
places – into their own mythology. This vision systematises the
treatment of the North as an icon and zone of purity and develops
an ordering narrative of everyday life in Canada which relates
habits and opinions of an idealised 'typical Canadian' to the
presence of this 'True North'. One corollary, however, is that
development becomes fraught with all the problems of the viol-
ation of this purity, the sacrilege of plundering the 'heart' of the
Canadian nation.

Morton argues that 'The ultimate and the comprehensive meaning of Canadian history is to be found where there has been no Canadian history: in the North' (1970:40). But such a displacement of meaning and sense – of the so-called 'motor of history' – to the barely inhabited North obscures some of the fundamental socio-political ingredients which have shaped the progress of Canada as a national society. There is place for neither domestic politics nor the trans-national economics of the historical staples trades (first in furs, later in wheat and minerals) which have shaped Canadian settlement and class patterns, nor does it offer any historical logic for some of the great social struggles such as the Suffragettes and the workers' movements. Landscape becomes the 'heart' of Canada rather than individuals. It is difficult to see how such a vision of the North, an obsessive paranoia at the back of Canadians' imagination, could be credited as *the* unequivocal 'meaning' of Canadian history.

This environmentalism also figures in the work of other influential Canadian scholars such as the political economist Harold Innis[17] and the historian Donald Creighton whose work through the 1960s laid the historical bases for the elaboration of a nationalistic ideology. Their tendency to introduce the North as a causal factor, as opposed to the argument that it has merely 'causative' status as an element of social spatialisation, is found in the work of the well-known literary critic Northrop Frye, Professor Emeritus of English at the University of Toronto, who has argued that European settlers saw nature in Canada as a hostile Leviathan (1977:24–25). 'Fear of nature' is an important ingredient in this 'tradition' of reporting on the Canadian character (see also Atwood 1979; Moss 1973). This view, based largely on an interpretation of Canadian literature, is crystallised by a so-called 'garrison mentality'. Historically, in many Canadian novels, the protagonists encounter a rapacious, masculine-gendered, natural environment which leads them to retreat into the safety of their frontier garrisons.[18] Thus, there is a tradition of Canadian anti-heroes: passive, poetic, and sexually ambivalent male protagonist-victims. It also often finds expression in a version of Turner's frontier thesis: whereas the American western frontier represented, 'the *limit of knowledge* or the limit of control. . . . A northern frontier, in contrast, denotes *the limits of endurance*. . . . While the western frontier is simply a culturally defined interface, the northern frontier is an existential one' (McGregor 1985:59).

Two problems arise with this statement which characterises all these works. First, the frontier is said to 'denote' rather than 'connote' or 'represent' a limit. That is, the 'frontier' is accorded the status of a real, physical, object, rather than a feature of a historical spatialisation of Canada which exists *grace à* the imaginative capacities of people. Also, the problem of meaning is reduced to mimesis: rather than being a *metaphor* for limits, the frontier is treated as denotative signifier (as, for example, in the case of the word 'Tree' when used to indicate a real tree). Here is one manifestation of a particular spatialisation which takes a region as a symbol for mental and social states and then attributes causal power to the region itself (as opposed to, for example, the influence on development of distance from markets). Cook says, 'it is the fashion in which . . . geography has been interpreted that provides each of these two nations [the United States and Canada] with a culture' (1984:11). Frye comments, 'The countries men live in feed their minds as much as their bodies: the bodily food they provide is absorbed in farms and cities; the mental religion and the arts. In all countries this process of material and imaginative *digestion* goes on' (1971:199). Second, limits of existence or physical 'endurance' are implied to be consonant with 'existential' limits. The subtle and unexamined rhetorical gloss from 'existence' to 'existential' has gross implications for such analyses.

More than any other critic, McGregor has attempted to weld this 'tradition' into a unified mythology by attempting to isolate the principal structure or structures informing the 'Canadian cultural consciousness' (1985) by studying Canadian cultural productions such as literary texts, poetry, graphic art and so on. McGregor deals with these as indicators of a Canadian 'Langscape', or the social 'process of mythicising nature by converting it into a set of iconic images to reflect the Canadian's experience of and accommodation, even complicity with this environment . . . having a determinative effect on Canada's cultural history' (Ferres 1986:372). Descriptions of landscape are thus a code or codified linguistic construct for McGregor. But, reading and interpretation is not recognised as problematic, as an act which sets up representations of the world with political overtones. The problem of diverse interpretations is not dealt with.[19] She argues to have found this structuring principle in the containment imagery, boxed experience and figure-to-ground or inside-to-outside organisation of space in Canadian art. A fear of the wilderness is bred in the northern frontier experience. Borrowing the title of the first Canadian novel (*Wacousta*, written in 1832) by John Richardson (1964), this is labelled as the 'Wacousta syndrome'.[20] According to this thesis, the hallmark of the Canadian *Weltanschauung* is a negative response to nature exemplified by Richardson's *Wacousta* with its powerful evocation of terror aroused by the 'hostile wilderness' which has historically back-dropped the Canadian sense of self (McGregor 1985:26).

> When the eye turned woodward it fell heavily and without interest upon a dim and dusky point known to enter upon savage scenes and unexplored countries, whereas whenever it reposed upon the lake it was with an eagerness and energy that embraced the most vivid recollections of the past, and led the imagination buoyantly over every well remembered scene that had previously been traversed, and which must be traversed again before the land of the European could be pressed once more. The forests, in a word, formed the gloomy and impenetrable walls of a prison house and the bright lake that lay before it the only portal through which happiness and liberty could again be secured.
>
> (Richardson 1964:159)

One result of this treatment of spatiality is that McGregor is led to propound an ideology of eighteenth-century rationalisms: that the physical world is supported by a transcendent order. 'Truths', as the American Declaration of Independence reported, can be held to 'be self-evident', experience is knowable, controllable, and real. Human nature is assumed to be uniform and unchanging, writing in the royal 'We' as if there were only one unanimous humankind for her to speak for (Davey 1986:41).

McGregor's text is only the most recent manifestation of a Richardson revival started by James Reaney (1979) in the early 1970s.[21] Some critics have suggested that this genre of 'Canadian identity quest' books (e.g. Atwood 1979; Moss 1973) is motivated in part by the weight of overbearing American myths of origin and transcendent national identity from which they take their approach. Davey continues,

The most professedly nationalistic of our recent cultural
books appear American in their fundamental assumptions:
that a culture must have a unitary, monolithic identity, and
that this identity is to be found in that culture's earliest
moments, the experiences of its settlers or its time of
revolution.

(Davey 1986:40)

These assumptions are not specifically 'American' but they do
contrast with the strong assertion of regional identities (Elkins and
Simeon 1980) and ethnic communalism in Canada. This partly
explains why so little comment has been registered at the extent to
which literary texts have been read from a slanted 'Canadian an-
gle' and the degree to which evidence has been abused to support
the argument.

This almost complicitous silence must be contrasted with the
alternate vision which argues that, 'Canadians exhibit a curious
lack of faith in the land that supposedly informs their character,
demonstrating a continuing fear of frozen isolation that has
shaped the pattern of development' (Coates 1985:13). The ambivalence of this third stance (above) manifests itself in a general
ignorance of the factual North. The 'Real North', as opposed to
the imagined 'True North', has had no continuity in southern
minds:

Neglect . . . has characterised southern response to the
Canadian North. . . . Were it not for . . . short interludes when
northern resources seemed of immediate benefit to the south,
the region would have almost no place in the national
consciousness. This sporadic attention, which had wide-
ranging implications for the evolution of the northern
colonies, rests on simple foundations. Despite pious claims to
their special status as citizens of a 'Northern Nation,' the
Canadian people have shied away from their northlands. . . .
visionaries, more romantics than pragmatists, remain
propagators of an ideal that Canadians pay homage to, then
consciously reject.

(Coates 1985:12)

Many of the nineteenth-century literary works cited by critics who
adopt the Nationalist stance were originally aimed at an American

audience even further removed from the realities of the North. Publishers favoured popularistic works which tended to confirm and validate rather than challenge the beliefs of the majority (Kline 1970). Thus, William Shields has suggested that it is difficult to cleanly separate Canadian and American literature in the late 1800s. Canadian authors often submitted to the priorities of American editors. The prevalent American view of the North at that time was also

> rather ambivalent. While often deeply moved by the immensity and primitive grandeur of the barren Arctic islands and the 'trackless' forests of the northern interior, . . . observers were at the same time given to dwelling upon the North's unforgiving character. The region, in many instances, was ascribed a basic sentience; it was transformed into a malevolent, brooding force possessed of a multitude of wiles and powers that it frequently utilised to discomfit or destroy the unwary. Man . . . assumed the role of interloper; it became his task to conquer the North or, at the very least, to prevent it from conquering him.
>
> (Wm. Shields 1982:18)

The negative aspects of the climate were stressed partly for the purpose of exciting readers. 'With this prime consideration in mind, many writers set about embellishing their travelogues, popular histories, or works of fiction with sensationalised accounts of the perils that could be encountered . . . . Small wonder, then, that so many of the works dealing with northern Canada were set in winter' (Wm. Shields 1982:19).

> . . . the picture of the Northland presented to the . . . public during this period oft times bore little relation to objective reality. . . . On occasion even the most . . . intellectual of . . . journals . . . presented ideas for public consumption that bordered on the fantastical. This tendency reached its apogee in the early twentieth century with the writings of men like James Oliver Curwood (1913), Jack London, and, to a lesser extent, Robert Service (1907). These authors refined existing notions about the North in such a manner that they created a mythical realm. The North to them became, in many ways, a screen upon which they could project their own personal

visions of an idealised human environment, an environment
of a kind which the forces of progress and civilization seemed
to have forever destroyed.

(Wm. Shields 1982:4)

Another source of Northern images which has mediated Southern
Canadians' conception of the North has been the Hollywood film
industry portrait of the North.[22] This 'Hollywood' Vision of the
North' with its freezing igloo-dwellers was characterised by a
number of recurring themes which included a fascination with the
Northern landscape and climate to which was later added a notion
of the North as a font of spirituality and moral regeneration; the
'comically subhuman Inuit, Indians and Métis'; the 'cruelly poor
but virile trapper'; the commercial empire of the Hudson's Bay
posts and the institutional framework of the Northwest Mounted
Police; and the 'abused yet heroic northern woman' (Wm. Shields
1982:106–108).

Hearing and reading about the exploits of Northern explorers
was a romantic hobby which allowed a sense of involvement in
their tribulations but within the safety of home. It was an escape
from the difficulties of day-to-day life into a deterritorialised and
unpopulated realm. Also, it must be noted that this 'True North'
is a peculiarly masculine realm in which stories locate feats of virile
endurance. The work of Service and London offers an escape from
the domesticated world into an imaginary space where trappers,
prospectors, and rebels pit their will against the climatic odds.
Stephen Leacock, one of Canada's most popular essayists ever,
made this point in his Introduction to Stefansson's *Unsolved Mysteries of the Arctic* (1938).

Arctic exploration, in so far as it can be carried out from an
armchair before a winter fire, has long been for me a pursuit
that verges on a passion. . . . Let the hour be as late as it likes,
let the snow beat at the window as it will, let the trees outside
groan and creak with the frost. I can stand it. With the help
perhaps of an odd glass of hot toddy kept warm on the
hearth, I can face any arctic winter that ever was. No igloo was
ever snugger than my study-library on the Côte des Neiges
road, with a volume of arctic adventure to centre its warmth
and comfort.

(Leacock 1938:7)

In yet another interpretation, Cook argues that Canadians lagged behind their southern neighbours in coming to terms with their North American environment. Catherine Parr Traill, a Canadian settler who, unlike her American contemporaries Emerson or Thoreau, for example, found nothing in the landscape to inspire her.

> As to ghosts or spirits they appear totally banished. . . . This is too matter-of-fact a country for such supernaturals to visit. Here there are no historical associations, no legendary tales of those that come before us. Fancy would starve for marvellous food to keep her alive in the backwoods.
>
> (Parr Traill 1836:153)

But even she admitted that there was another source of least 'amusement and interest'. 'If its [Canada's] volume of history is yet blank, that of Nature is open, and eloquently marked by the finger of God' (1836:155 cited in Cook 1984:15). Goldwin Smith (1971) argued that Canada was in reality a fully North American nation by the 1880s and it would be only a matter of time before she accepted the destiny of geography and merged with the United States.[23] The British institutions were only a shallow veneer.

Cook does acknowledge that, 'If Americans during the Nineteenth century "imaginatively digested" North America, Canadians were certainly beginning the same process' (Cook 1984:17). As Canada became more urbanised the old view faded. The urban culture of the Southern Canadian seems in many respects to have been very similar and closely linked as an adjunct market (at least in terms of cultural consumption) to the eastern United States. The coincidence of urbanisation and a pantheistic nostalgia, followed later by a Darwinist vision of the 'battlefield' of nature, correspond to a growing isolation from the countryside on the part of the population and changes in the practices and order of the social spatialisation. One cannot over-simplify this transition, but it would appear that by 1900 Canadian literary artists were as much in demand in the United States as American artists. A good example is Robert Service, one of the best known of Canadian poets, who provides one of the clearest poetic statements of the social Darwinism which Cook argues was characteristic of the American idea of nature (Cosgrove 1982; Cook 1984:17) in his 'Spell of the Yukon'

This is the law of the Yukon, that only
the Strong shall thrive;
That surely the Weak shall perish, and
only the Fit survive.
(Service 1911:18)[24]

After the First World War, there was a distinct discovery of nature
and the North in particular and a rejection of European viewpoints which regarded the wilderness with aversion as 'totally
inappropriate to the expression of the character, the power and
clarity and rugged elemental beauty of Canada' (Harris 1948:29).
Particularly for the artists of the Group of Seven, the North was
seen as a 'living whiteness', of 'loneliness and replenishment...
resignations and release ... cleansing rhythms' (Harris 1926:
85–86). This theosophical North (Lacombe 1982) had a spiritual
value as a source of culture. It was a liminal zone, roughly equivalent to the biblical desert, where redemption was achieved through
struggle and communion with the elements.

Urbanisation emerges as an important factor affecting Canadians' leisure patterns and hence the beginnings of the development of the North as a recreational area. This development
from old frontier to weekend or yearly holiday zone preserved the
North's status as an extra-ordinary region out of the patterns of
quotidian working life in the cities. Hodgins and Hobbs argue that
changing images of the North and different motivations for
tourism there are reflected in the fluctuations in the popularity of
wilderness canoeing and other such recreational activities (1985).
These amount to a quest for certain essential experiences which
are held to encapsulate a spirit of the North which is describable
only by contrast with the experience of the metropolis (1985:3–4).
This 'True North' is constructed in opposition to the urban
experience. Hodgins and Hobbs' study argues that the early adventurers before the First World War came from abroad with the
intention of exploring a far-off exotic region which they could
later expect to write about in profitable and popular travelogues.
'The Thelon and the Porcupine [rivers] in Canada's far Northwest
were, in their minds, similar to the Khyber Pass in India's
Northwest Frontier or the Upper Nile of Uganda in "darkest
Africa"' (1985:39). After the Second World War, while the market
for colourful wilderness travelogues collapsed, the numbers of

Northern adventurers increased and came increasingly from North American metropolitan centres reflecting the expansion of leisure time and the diffusion of economic wealth. Despite the tendency for the old exoticism of underdevelopment and isolation to remain as a 'frozen vision' in mass media images, the experience of at least the Near North – the rocky and coniferous lake lands of the Canadian Shield – expanded across all classes through the activities of youth clubs (Scouting movement, YM/YWCA, Boys and Girls Clubs), the accessibility of wilderness areas made possible by the motorcar and the popularity of camping.

'Somehow the wilderness, made experiential by the canoe and the snowshoe, became and remains . . . an ironic but essential part of Canada's urban-centred way of life. . . . Urbanism, even metropolitanism, and wilderness travel expanded together.' The canoe trip became a personal test, the canoe, 'a vehicle for exploring the landscape of the mind' (Hodgins and Hobbs 1985:4–5). James (1985) argues that this paradigm follows the 'monomyth' of the composite hero:

A hero sets out from the world of common day into a region of supernatural wonder: fabulous forces are there encountered and a decisive victory is won: the hero comes back from this mysterious adventure with the power to bestow boons on his fellow man.

(Campbell 1956:30 cited in James 1985:9–10)

This echoes through the poetry of Service also which can be interpreted as stressing the dangers of the Arctic in order to set the scene for manly bravado and allusions to escape from social codes which pervades his works.

'North' is a place of recreative freedom which in turn poses a threat to the ordered structures of the European psyche. Location is not so important as the idea that the frontier holds a redemptive disorder for highly ordered societies (see Morton 1971). But, in the extreme, '"chaos" might be utterly destructive, or might leave at best only a lame handful of survivors' (Moss 1974:7–8). Thus the 'True North' is cast as a projection of repressed unconscious tensions which can be resolved only by a person undergoing a symbolic death and re-creation of him- or herself (for an extreme example, see Kroetsch 1966) in a liminoid *rite de passage*. This

191

image in particular coincides with the private practice of recreational tourism interspersed by periods of apparent neglect in the everyday life of urbanised central Canadians (making up 75.7 per cent of the total Canadian population, 86.3 per cent of the population of Ontario, the most 'central Canadian' of the provinces: Statistics Canada 1985:39). This practice transforms the 'True North' from being merely an icon (as in the case of Niagara Falls) into a setting incorporated into social rituals.

With such contradictory claims made about the North, one must be careful about accepting any one of them. They all have weaknesses and tend to stretch the available evidence to fit the purposes being advanced. One might expect at least some figures on urbanisation to be advanced (and they would be highly schematic) to support the above theory about the North as a leisure space, yet even if one could do so, comparable, historical recreation statistics would be hard to generate. Despite these difficulties, one finds Canadian intellectuals and social scientists dwelling on this question of the 'Canadian Identity', and also asserting their views on radio and television – in effect campaigning to establish a hegemonic status for their views – brings this case-history to new pastures. This partly explains the wide dissemination of 'Wacousta revival' which originated from Toronto-area intellectuals with peerless access to the national radio and television broadcasting system, the CBC, through the Toronto production studios.[25] What is doubly intriguing is the lack of alternate, perhaps more subtle, views in public discussions. Thus several questions arise about the 'nationalistic' tradition of Northern space-myths and the role of central Canadian ideologues. To what extent, and why, is the exposition of this particular myth an appealing and beneficial activity for those writers involved? Why has it received such a ready and uncritical reception in the media, the public, and the government? The discourse of the 'True North' is difficult to escape. When talking about the factual conditions of either the Northern spaces of Canada or about Canadian nationalism, it becomes clear that a spatialisation of the North and, indeed, of Canada as a whole, as the 'True North Strong and Free' founds both the metaphors *and* is built into the commonsensical, apparently empirical, classifications through which one might describe reality. One finds this spatialisation re-stated in a hundred slightly different ways in newspapers, statistical reports, and yearbooks:

> Developed or not, the North remains all important to the Canadians' self-image. It makes their country the second largest on earth. . . . Above all, its brooding physical presence over the land is a warning that Canadians have not yet conquered their universe.
>
> (Government of Canada 1963:ii; 1968:i)

The 'True North' remains the stock-in-trade of not only government-sponsored coffee-table books and tourism advertisements but also news reports and documentaries. Hamelin suggests:

> Nordicity poses the problem of Canada itself, or to give a provincial example, the problem of Quebec with respect to Ungava. Can 'Base Canada,' in its own southern fashion, continue to seduce the immensity of the North? Is it an exaggeration to suggest that one of the major problems of the North is the South? Or will the North, over the long haul, be able to surrender to its southern fringe enough of its identifying elements to create a true Canadianity? Or, if North and South are truly different, will the North succeed in evolving according to political models that are foreign to it?
>
> (Hamelin 1979:xii)

There is a certain sense of guilt in the face of an exploited internal colony (Hechter 1975). Canadians are reluctant imperialists. It comes as little surprise that the 'True North' myth also disguises the realities of the exploitation of the North for Southern profit (Coates 1985). A hypothesis for further research would be that such a spatialisation, which a Marxist would label as a *phantasmagoria*, appears to be an essential, if neurotic, part of a nation split by deep heartland–hinterland inequalities (in democratic control, provision of social services, average income and so on – see p. 166 and Berger 1977; Coates 1985; Page 1986). If 'the region has had difficulty shedding its singular image [wherein it is seen as a single landscape of]. . . . The solitary Inuit crossing an unbroken icy expanse, the light grey haze of the winter sky all but indistinguishable from the snow-covered land and sea', it is because of the *importance* of this belief to Southern Canadians. What is being discussed, after all, is the *Southern image* of the North, something that Northerners, lacking in media access, economic power, and without political control, are unable to change. As Coates continues, it seems that even with developments such as, 'oil exploration rigs on artificial islands . . . their perpendicular girders only reinforce the horizontal nature of the environment' (1985:15–16) – in the eyes of Southerners. The 'True North Strong and Free' provides an example of a great national foundation myth.

This 'True North Strong and Free' is archetypally an unconquerable wilderness devoid of 'places' in the sense of centres of habitation; the last reserve of a theosophical vision of Nature which must be preserved, not developed (see for example Wadland 1985: Drew 1973). If it must be encroached upon, this should be 'temporary' in the form of 'men-only' style work-camps: it is as if it was a zone which was hostile to domestic order.[26] It is as if living in the North has some feared impact on the structure of society and the family: an 'etching process' on human relations. The range of images available gives no hint of the existence of kitchen sinks beyond the urban and agricultural regions of Southern Canada.

To the extent that the 'True North Strong and Free' is a region of the 'Other', it is the 'pole' in the Southern Canadian popular imagination to which everything that presents a contrast with 'civilisation' and its values can be assimilated. This includes native mythologies such as the Cree Windigo myth,[27] reported sitings of creatures such as the reputed Sasquatch and fearsome animals such as Grizzlies or Wolverines. This reinforces the argument that the North is a liminal zone where 'civilised' social norms are suspended on the lines of *rites de passage* (see Chapter 2).

It is mockery to speak of the Arctic as the land of the Esquimaux, for nowhere on earth is man less sovereign . . . . Nature is indeed beautiful in her northern strongholds, but her beauty shows only its terrible aspects, its dread grandure [sic]. The face of the mighty mother does not soften into a smile for the feebleness of her youngest-born offspring . . .
(*Catholic World* 1865:708)

These apparently inescapable myths circulate in literary and media channels side by side with self-consciously factual accounts. Where

THE TRUE NORTH STRONG AND FREE

there are attempts to present Northern conditions and life accurately, for example in National Film Board documentaries, the wildness of the region – its autochthonous 'indigenous spirit' – is always contrasted with development reports which appear as figures on the common-sense ground of the mythified North. No one is surprised when these grand schemes run into trouble (for example, see the extensive coverage given to Beaufort Sea oil and gas developments in the 1970s and to the (abandoned) Athabaska Tar Sands oil extraction project). This contributes to what American commentators have called Canadians' fatalistic character. However, those that succeed fall from the pages of newspapers and disappear from television reports (there has been little detailed coverage in the English-language press of the James Bay hydro-electric power developments, and none of several Northern mines e.g. Coppermine and Nanasivik). Behind the superficial oscillation of (public) homage and (private) ignorance is not merely a paranoid 'fear of nature' (McGregor 1984) but the construction of the 'North' as a zone of Otherness so alien that it cannot even be thought without beginning to criticise the fundamentals of Canadian nationalism. The 'True North' – reality mediated by imagination – has come to be constituted as a space with a romantic image in the context of regional inequalities which have become more visible through news coverage of northern development in the late 1970s (i.e. the Berger Inquiry 1977). The recreational use of the North mediates repressed reality of the 'Real North' and the mythology of the 'True North' in the structure of ritualistic trips to summer cottages, and (still largely men's) fishing, hunting, and canoeing trips. Much could be said of the *rites de passage* of adolescent Boy Scouts and rituals of reconfirmation for greying sport-fishermen. But, the political importance of this critique is the effect this space-myth and related social spatialisation has of masking and even of promoting regional exploitation, the enforced genocidal poverty of northern inhabitants (significantly, mostly native Indians, Inuit, and Métis), the national unity of a federal state and cultural hegemony of central Canadian ideologues as opposed to the continentalistic culture of the United States. The seductiveness of this myth helps one understand why the very inegalitarian 'mapping' of the Canadian nation attracts very little head-on critique from social scientists.

A systematic constellation of meanings is at once the orbit and limit of possible interpretations which can be put on the North as a myth without challenging the set of inter-related assumptions about the character of places and their suitability for specific activities. As has been argued in previous chapters, while we can disagree on the applicability of possibly idiosyncratic images we are governed by limits of an overall, naturalised (i.e. become what is understood as 'natural') discourse on the North which both constitutes and organises the space, and implicitly positions us with respect to it. A personal 'Canadian identity' is partially constituted through ascription into the mythology of the 'True North Strong and Free'. But public acceptance of this myth as part of a nationalistic ideology is often contradicted by private neglect of its premises. The 'True North Strong and Free' mythology bursts out of its repressed status in jokes and clichés of Canadianness which are met with embarrassed laughter. Hence, the mismatch between public rhetoric, even if it is hotly defended, and private investment decisions. This is but one local effect of a discourse of space or better, of a 'spacing', which organises reality as *geographical*, coherent in three dimensions, and *rationalises* knowledge of the world. The mythological space of the 'True North Strong and Free' is not a closed region but is organised in respect to and, indeed, penetrates to the centre of Canadian society in much the same manner that Solzhenitsyn said that the Gulag Archipelago haunted the streets of Moscow and the minds of Russians:

> And the Kolyma was the greatest and most famous island, the pole of ferocity of that amazing country of Gulag which, though scattered in an Archipelago geographically, was, in the psychological sense, fused into a continent – an almost invisible, almost imperceptible country inhabited by the 'zek' people. And this Archipelago criss-crossed and patterned that other country within which it was located, like a gigantic patchwork, cutting into its cities, hovering over its streets.
>
> (Solzhenitsyn 1977:1)

The nationalistic 'tradition' expresses a Canadian social spatialisation which relies on the privileged territorial space of the North for differentiating and 'grounding' a cultural identity opposed to the continentalism projected by the United States. In this latter spatial order, Canada is merely an accident of historical stubbornness and refusal to accept the distinctiveness of North America from Europe. If the reality of the Canadian North, the 'Real North', is one of an internal colony (Hechter 1975), of a zone of systematic exploitation (of mineral wealth, of populations) and under-development, this is swept under the carpet by the force of a view of the 'True North' which is comparable to an idyllic seventeenth-century vision of the pastoral countryside which neglects to notice the impoverished and demoralised peasant population.

Dorfman and Mattelart argue that each great urban civilisation creates its own pastoral myth, and extra-social Eden, chaste and pure, where,

> The only relation the centre (adult–city folk–bourgeoisie)
> manages to establish with the periphery (child–noble
> savage/worker/peasant) is touristic and sensationalist. . . .
> The innocence of this marginal sector is what guarantees the
> Duckburger his touristic salvation . . . his childish rejuven-
> ation. The primitive infrastructure offered by the Third World
> Countries [or, as will be seen in the case of *Nationwide* (see
> Chapter 5), 'The Countryside'] becomes the nostalgic echo of
> a lost primitivism, a world of purity . . . reduced to a picture
> postcard to be enjoyed by a service-oriented world.
> (Dorfman and Mattelart 1975:96)

This circulation of notions, the mythology of the 'True North Strong and Free', as part of the social spatialisation of the Canadian nation serves to gloss over more than North–South disparities. It also provides a unifying sense that all those, whether living in the East or West, are Canadians by virtue of the patrimony of the North.

> Now the North, which is common to both East and West is a
> natural bridge to unite the two divisions. I look to the North
> as one of the great unifying factors in the future of the
> Dominion.
> (Lord Tweedsmuir, Notes for Mackenzie King's speeches in
> Britain, Summer 1937, cited in Hamilton and Shields
> 1979:629)

It opposes the different regional interests with a strong emotional argument. Central to this counterpoint of interests, is the Federal

Government policy of 'developing the north for the benefit of all Canadians' (i.e. as a resource-rich colony). The Northern Territories are prevented from attaining provincial status despite popular demand. This would mean relinquishing Southern control over development and resources and involve sacrificing the 'for the benefit of all' policy. Nor is this only a question of power and economics. The literal re-territorialisation of the North, the re-drawing of maps, would make the North suddenly *someone's*, a place where people dwelt and appropriated the land as their own. It would no longer be an 'empty space' but a territorialised place, a place of communities, a landscape made meaningful by personal biographies, and acknowledged as such. This is nearly unimaginable in the terms of the current notions of purity and inviolability. The discursive economy of the 'True North' coincides neatly with a set of non-discursive practices, namely, the institutions of Canadian federalism and the recreational practices of summer tourists who indulge in a type of *rite de passage* which re-confirms their self-image as 'Canadian'. The 'True North' is a common reference 'point' marking an invisible national community of the initiated (B. Anderson 1983). It is the common appeal to and self-inscription – the 'writing-in' – of the North into a territorial heritage that constitutes the Vancouverite and the Newfoundlander as Canadian. This is further to say, that the 'True North Strong and Free' is an essential and determining component of the view which imaginatively repositions Canada as a 'Northern nation' with more in common with Norway, for example, than with the United States. It is on this basis that Canadians often set out their differences from the United States.[28]

CONCLUSION

We have covered a cross-section of 'readings' of the Canadian North: 'objective' interpretations which delimit its boundaries as in the case of Hamelin's work, and more 'subjective' or culturally-oriented work which classifies its themes and occurrence. The implications and effects of the space-myth of the 'True North Strong and Free', of which it is both a cause and a part, have not been widely recognised.

The various images circulating around the 'True North Strong and Free' constitute a system of signification, a discursive representation which requires analysis *in toto*. Yet this mythological discourse is only a part and hint of an overall spatialisation: a modern *geomancy*. In this system, places or regions mean something only in relation to other places as a constellation of meanings, that is, the North makes sense only with reference to other regions: the 'urban jungle', the southern agricultural fringe, or the commodified consumer landscape of Toronto's suburban strip developments. The images are oriented towards each other in a mutually supporting dialogical exchange (Bakhtin 1984: 10–12).

The importance of the 'True North Strong and Free' mythology is in its paradoxical reinforcement of a sense of Canadian identity while disguising the simultaneous exploitation and under-development of the North. This takes place through its presence as a community 'yarn', a national mythology as well as its role in underpinning the institutional arrangement of the Canadian state. This is, however, at some cost to those inhabitants of the region. The manner in which the North is used metaphorically in narratives and texts to convey abstract ideas or metonymically appropriated for its nationalistic connotations quite apart from direct presentations of 'The North' *per se* reveals the importance of spatialisation as a cognitive tool. A 'True North' rises out of the datum of the 'Real North'. The North becomes 'the North in men': a sort of essentialistic human nature revealed by ritualistic journeys, *rites de passage*, and re-confirmation in a landscape empty of human traces.

But, the 'True North' is more than just a myth or a story. It motivates, and is articulated with a set of active practices which are both institutional and personal. It is, in view of people's personal neglect of it (despite the jokes and embarrassed clichés), a mythology which is first of all practised, and only second consciously contemplated. As a result, the 'True North Strong and Free' has empirical effects on patterns of development, economic impacts on its inhabitants, political implications for the nation-state and cultural impacts on Canadian citizens.

NOTES

1. Canadian National Anthem, official English versio i. Tune by Calixa Lavallée, lyrics by Adolphe-Basile Routhier as the Québecois 'Chante Nationale'. English translation by Robert Stanley Weir, a Toronto school teacher, approved 1967. *O Canada* was first commissioned by Theodore Robitaille, lieutenant-governor of Quebec, for a banquet in Quebec City on 24 June 1880. The French lyrics were written by Sir Adolphe-Basile Routhier, a prominent Quebec City lawyer and writer, in the form of a poem, which was set to music by Calixa Lavallée. Parliament refused to accept the English words of *O Canada*, only the melody was accepted, in 1967. The principal objection was the lack of any mention of God. In 1972, a revised version of the lyrics was considered, finally being accepted in the National Anthem Act, 27 June 1980. The phrases 'True North' and 'White North' (see Note 9, below) also appear in Tennyson's *Idylls of the King* (1873) in direct reference to Canada: and in the epigraph Tennyson wrote for Franklin's monu- ment in Westminster Abbey (1847), respectively.
2. This translates literally as the Maritime-Canadian colloquialism, derived from Arcadian French, of 'up-country' to refer to the interior of New Brunswick upstream from the coastal settlements.
3. The 1983 population estimate for the Yukon and Northwest Territories was 22,000 and 48,000 respectively. This comprises 0.28 per cent of the total Canadian population (Statistics Canada 1985:51 Table 2.1). However, to this one must add, as a minimum, those living in the Northern towns of the ten provinces. Using Hamelin's place-name index of Northern towns (see Figure 4.1) and a Canadian Gazetteer (which includes only towns over 5,000 population) the following table results:

Happy Valley-Goose Bay, Nfld.	7,103
Labrador City, Nfld.	11,538
Flin Flon Man.	7,894
Thompson Man.	14,288
Fort McMurray, Alta.	31,000
Total	71,823

(Statistics Canada 1985)

This brings the population to 141,763 or 0.57 per cent of the total population. Even including smaller towns and the few rural inhabitants, this suggests that the total population of the North would amount to no more than 1 per cent or 2 per cent of the total population.
4. Precise tourism or migration statistics are unavailable, but given the extremely low population and the low level of physical infrastructure (there are no paved roads north of 60 degrees latitude, for example) it would be impossible for more than a tiny minority to visit the North

in any one year. Even with the boom in the oil economy in the mid to late 1970s, no more than 500,000 migrant workers in total would have visited even the northern areas of the provinces from 1975 to 1980. Tourism data from the Division of Tourism and Parks, Dept of Economic Development and Tourism, Government of the Northwest Territories (abbreviated GNWT) puts annual summer visits at approximately 52,000, who have above average incomes above C$34,500 (about £18,000). Tourists engaged in camping or motoring mostly come from the Western provinces, California and Sport Fishermen who come from Ontario and the states bordering on the Great Lakes. Source: *Tourism Facts* (GNWT 1987).

5. Hamelin's scale is based on the factors of climate, geography, vegetation, remoteness, economic activity, and population density.
6. A 'really Northern' city would be one like Yellowknife where permafrost means that municipal services are delivered above ground in insulated, corrugated aluminum 'runs' which connect every house in a network which, standing 2 to 3 feet off the ground on its insulated posts, runs over the landscape like a creeping vine. The futuristic urbanists of the 1970s, Archigram, couldn't have dreamt of anything more bizarre to most eyes.
7. For example, Robert Flaherty's documentary about an Inuit hunter, *Nanook of the North* (National Film Board of Canada 1920) became well known, world-wide. In order to produce the film, new hunting rules for the shooting of walrus were laid down by Flaherty: the natives would wait for the walrus to approach relatively close, in order to give the camera crew the opportunity to film close-up shots of the animal. Igloos also had to be partially deconstructed in order to allow enough light for filming and to permit good camera angles (see R. Griffith, 1953. *The World of Robert Flaherty* (Toronto: McClelland & Stewart)).

Another important source was American films – the Hollywood view of the North (see Note 22, below) – and Canadian television serials. One such series which gained popularity and is even shown in re-runs today for its clichéd humour value is Republic Pictures' 1953 *Canadian Mounties vs. Atomic Invaders* (F. Adreon, dir.): 'A band of foreign agents who are engineering a mysterious operation in the frozen regions of Canada are the subject of a widespread search by the Canadian Mounted Police . . . ' (see K. Weiss and E. Goodgold, 1972. *To be Continued . . .* (Toronto: Schuster)).

8. Today, the Northwest Territories are more 'North' than 'West' due to the successive carving off of segments of the original Northwest Territories to make new provinces or add to the size of the older provinces. The Yukon became a separate territory in 1898 at the time of the Klondike Gold Rush. In 1870, Manitoba was first created as a province encompassing the area around present-day Winnipeg, being added to in 1881 and 1912. Alberta and Saskatchewan were formed as provinces in 1905. Northern Ontario and Nouveau Québec were ceded to Ontario and Quebec in 1912.
9. *The Great White North* was originally the title of a nationalistic, and

rather bombastic, book written about polar exploration (White 1910).
See Note 1, above.

10. Some of the most accurate and intimate descriptions are to be found
in the writings of the Hudson Bay Co. explorer David Thompson
(1770–1875) who mapped much of Northwestern Canada in his
travels from 1798–1812 (see David Thompson (1962), *David
Thompson's Narrative*) and in the works of Knud Rasmussen, the part-
Inuit and native-speaker of Inuktituk who pioneered ethnography in
North America with his studies from 1902 until the mid 1920s. In
particular, his reports of his meeting the Padlermiut, the Willow-Folk,
a tribe of the Caribou Inuit are landmark sources (Rasmussen 1927).

11. The term 'Barren Lands' originates in Hearne's narrative. See Hearne
1795. See also Maclaren 1977.

12. This divergence in response partly reflects the mismatch between the
environment within which Hearne and other English explorers found
themselves and their contemporary standards of landscape beauty as
crystallised in the English landscape garden. An analysis of their
narratives reveals a clear consciousness of these standards and careful
attempts to contrast the Canadian landscape with the norms of the
eighteenth-century English country garden. See Maclaren 1977.

13. See Senate of Canada *Report of the Select Committee Appointed to Inquire
into the Resources of the Great Mackenzie Basin* Ottawa 1888:10–15. There
was claimed to be several hundred thousand acres suitable for
potatoes, barley, and wheat cultivation – a claim which still seems
incredible today given the short growing season.

14. The sector theory is generally dated to the motion by Sen. Poirier of
20 February 1907. See Senate *Debates* 1906–1907:271. See also, House
of Commons *Debates* 1 May 1902:3,951–61,78; 30 September
1903:12,819).

15. This idea can be traced back to Thomas D'Arcy McGee, Lord Monck
and Alexander Morris, the author and negotiator of *The Treaties of
Canada with the Indians of Manitoba and the North-West Territories* (1880).
Morris talked of 'a new nationality', a phrase which later became a
catch-phrase, in his 1858 lectures in Montreal later published as *The
Hudson's Bay and Pacific Territories* (Mercantile Library Assoc. of
Montreal (Winter) 1858).

16. Stefansson adapted the phrase 'Westward the course of empire takes
its way' from Bishop Berkeley's verse 'On the prospect of Planting Arts
and Learning in America' (1752) for the title and theme of his book.
Stefansson notes in his autobiography that *The Northward Course of
Empire* (1923) sold only 200 copies in Canada, but 20,000 in Russian
translation.

17. Harold Innis (1894–1952), Professor of Political Economy at the
University of Toronto, was an influential figure in pressing for the
establishment of the first geography department in Canada at
Toronto. For Innis, geography was an important element in his career
strategy (Sanderson 1982; Dunbar 1985). His interest in the staples

trade and export patterns led him to propound what has been called the Laurentian hypothesis along with Creighton. That is, that much of Canadian history is explained by the nature and location of the St Lawrence River which represented a 'highway' to the heart of the continent. This contrasts with the barrier to westward expansion posed by the Appalachian Mountains in the case of the young United States. It might also be contrasted to the Québecois perception of the St Lawrence which included the added dimension of the river as 'mainstreet': the main communications route between the various seigneuries along the shore (for this insight I am indebted to the participants in the seminar on the 'Laurentian Hypothesis Revisited' held at the Canadian Association of Geographers meetings, Hamilton, Ont., June 1987). This hypothesis was also suggested by the British geographer Marion Newbigin in her book on Canada (1927) which emphasised the importance of the St Lawrence and the lands of its drainage basin (Winks 1966:80).

18. On gendered spaces see also Carolyn Andrews and Beth Moore Milroy eds. 1988. *Life Spaces: Gender, Household, Employment* (Vancouver: University of British Columbia Press) and Sophie Watson 1989. 'Gilding the smokestacks: the symbolic representations of deindustrialised regions' (copies available from University of Bristol, Dept. of Social Policy).

19. Worse, she exhibits in her interpretations (which she sees as non-problematic: meaning lies indelibly in texts, not in the reader's response to it, a highly dubious assumption) a naive faith in transcendence, in the existence of some immutable realm of being and value beyond materiality, that gives to the latter stability and knowability. This naive belief that mimesis is possible, that there is a natural correlation between signifier and signified, that genre mixing ('genre confusion') in Canadian writing shows an unwillingness to face 'facts'; that Canadian books don't represent satisfactorily the reality to which they are applied. What reality? For McGregor, all authors or artists ever born on Canadian soil reproduce this typological Canadian complex centring around the fear of nature. This even includes authors such as Saul Bellow (generally considered a member of the New York School of Jewish Writers) who lived in Montreal for the first six months of his life. Montreal Jewish author, Québecois playwright, or Winnipeg Ukrainian artist are all homogeneously Canadian.

She proceeds by attempting to establish 'the norm of American practice' and then applies this to Canada, which is continually said by McGregor to 'lack', to have 'missed out', to be 'captive', to show 'inability' and 'failure', to be 'flawed', 'incapable', and 'inadequate'. She repeatedly and approvingly points to the Stateside myths of America as paradise-regained, the American as the New Adam, and to 'the aggressive, wilful humanistic confidence with which these myths have endowed American life' (Davey 1986).

20. See also, for example, M. Northey, 1976. *The Haunted Wilderness* esp. the chapter on 'Canadian Prototype: *Wacousta*' and see R. Matthews, 1978. *Canadian Literature*, which uses the notion of *Wacousta* as a structuring theme, for example see Ch.1 'The Wacousta Factor'.
21. Atwood (1973) is perhaps the best known proponent of this view. She makes the 'sweeping generalization' that the 'single unifying and informing symbol at the core of Canadian literature, English and French is Survival, la Survivance' (Atwood 1973:32). Thus, 'Our stories are likely to be tales not of those who make it but of those who made it back from the awful experience – the North, the snowstorm, the sinking ship – that killed everyone else. The survivor has no triumph or victory but the fact of his survival . . . ' (Atwood 1973:33). But, writing in the mode of critic, Atwood deals in descriptions more than with explanations of the origins of this mindset. She suggests that our colonial mentality is in part responsible for our victim-mentality, but she does not explain why (Moss 1974:2). Thus, Canadian protagonists are, in Atwood's scheme, less victors than victims of a country they somewhat pretentiously call their own.
22. Berton argues that:

> The only consistent impression of us that outsiders have received in this century has come from the motion picture. Books, newspapers, magazines, radio, and television have scarcely any impact beyond our own borders. It is the movies that have projected our image to the world and also, to a considerable extent, to our selves. And by the 'movies' I don't mean the earnest and often brilliant documentaries of the National Film Board. I mean the commercial pictures that Hollywood made, scores of which are still being seen on smaller screens.
>
> (Berton 1975:12)

While American feature films have certainly had a formative role in shaping both American and Canadian perceptions, nonetheless, Berton errs by attributing an 'unduly minor significance to the possible impact of the written word upon such views during the pre-celluloid era.' For example, William Shields (1982:2) concurs that, 'in the fifteen years following the turn of the century, Canada became a favourite setting for . . . popular fiction which had a broad-based appeal south of the border.'
23. Smith's book (1971) is the original denunciation of formation of Canada through the National Policy protective tariffs and the transcontinental railway. Written in the pessimistic period of the 1880s when these policies had failed to generate sustained prosperity and integrate the regions. Separatist emotions ran high in Nova Scotia, Quebec, and the West. 'Thousands of young Canadians left for the United States; one of the familiar figures in the popular novels of the

day was the youth who goes to the States, succeeds, and returns to marry the girl he left behind' (Berger 1971:vi).

24. Jack London wrote in a 1903 story 'The White Silence':

> Nature has many tricks wherewith she convinces man of his finity
> . . . but the most tremendous, the most stupefying of all, is the
> passive phase of the White Silence . . . the slightest whisper seems
> sacrilege, and man becomes timid . . . he trembles at his audacity,
> realizes that his is maggot life, nothing more.
>
> (London 1977:72)

25. By virtue of their presence in and around Toronto and central southern Ontario, this group of writers, including Berton, McGregor, Frye, Morton, Berger, and so on have peerless access to the nationally-aired morning 'chat shows' which have provided a vehicle for the wide dissemination of their ideas. Nor do they function as cautious academics, but speak as intellectuals about their work which they 'boost' without reservation. These radio and television interviews are partly arranged by publishers to launch books to the Canadian public. One of the best examples is Gaile McGregor's appearance on 'Peter Gzoski's *Morningside*' (the CBC's three-hour flagship Monday–Friday morning programme which has a broad 'up market' national audience) 16 January 1985.

26. This has also had other specific impacts which demand a full-scale study in their own right. While the pace of Northern development follows a thoroughly capitalist logic, the 'style' of development and change in the North has, by the logic of purity encapsulated by the mythology of the 'True North', helped to maintain the separation of the North from the inhabited lands of Canada. Partly on the basis of the antithesis of civilisation versus nature that is set up, work-camps provisioned from Edmonton, Winnipeg, or Montreal have been favoured rather than more economic, permanent towns which might act as 'growth poles', such as Churchill, Manitoba. This returns to my argument that the North is treated as if it is an improper place for families, for civilisation.

27. The Windigo Myth appears in several variants amongst the Cree tribes in the Northern areas of the provinces. According to the Mistassini Cree, 'Windigo' is a bush spirit which may 'possess' an individual making them uncommunicative, withdrawn, and morose. According to legend (and practice) in the context of extended-family hunting groups, possessed individuals must be ritually killed otherwise they will become violent and murder-off the entire group.

28. This has begun to change since the 1981 constitution came into effect and made some of the social values explicit. These contrast with those given primacy in American constitutional and legal practice and might include an emphasis on community solidarity over individual freedom (good government over individual rights), equity over

equality, and the provision of a 'welfare net' as opposed to the neo-liberal social values of individual independence in the United States.

Chapter Five

THE NORTH–SOUTH DIVIDE IN ENGLAND

Like the Canadian North, the 'North' of England is not a precisely defined and mapped out jurisdiction with clear borders. It is said by many to extend as far south as the Cheshire border, including Manchester, and by a few to include even the Midlands – everything 'North of Watford' (see Figure 5.1).[1] This 'North', which is seen as an undifferentiated unity no more diverse than the motorway signs to 'The North',[2] provides a second example of a representation of a region as a pastoral foil to other, collectively romanticised images of London and the South of England. Unlike the Canadian 'True North', however, the images of the British North, if produced in the cultural hub of London, are also re-worked, accepted, or rejected by Northerners for their own, internal, reasons. A spatial mythology surrounding the British North is dialogically interwoven with other spatial mythologies and their attendant practices which collectively comprise the formation of attitudes, institutionalised arrangements, and practices we have been calling social spatialisation.

Environmental perception research over the past two decades has it that the characteristics of the North of England have emerged as a historical product of 'established [and largely southern] intellectual and literary channels', which 'for the past hundred and fifty years have projected a consistent image of "the north" in sharp contrast, overt or implied, to that of the south, so that the country has come to be seen in this way' (Pocock and Hudson 1978:111–112). The contemporary dichotomous North and South view came into focus with nineteenth-century literary works which responded to the rapid industrialisation of the North (and the emergence of an urbanised industrial elite which challenged the social status of the landed aristocracy largely centred in the Home Counties around London). More recently, the space and places of the North have been an important theme in British realist cinema of the late 1950s and 1960s. This tradition of what were called 'Kitchen Sink' films included *Room at the Top* (Jack Clayton, dir., 1958), *Saturday Night and Sunday Morning* (Karel Reisz, dir., 1960) and *A Taste of Honey* (Tony Richardson, dir., 1961). Along with on-going television serials such as *Coronation Street*, and the North–South Divide rhetoric in the 'quality dailies' of the mid 1980s, this provides a diverse set of related cases which will be examined to build a multi-faceted picture of this 'imaginary geography'. In the case of the work in the area of environmental perception, 'images' have not always been linked to institutional policies and personal practices which make up the banal fabric of the experience of 'difference' between regions which stabilises and reinforces the various discourses organising images of the north. A number of analyses of such cultural productions as the space-myth of 'the North' have been made but attention has largely been directed towards class analysis; few pause to take their often striking spatial insights seriously. What is also needed is a second reading which also pays attention to the cross-class consistencies of this space-myth, and, indeed, of the social spatialisation of the nation.

NORTH AND SOUTH: A LITERARY HISTORY

Nineteenth-century industrialisation reinforced and added to more traditional North–South contrasts. 'Regional' novelists and poets and travellers projected aspects of what is widely accepted to be a consistent and *singular* image of the North as the 'Land of the Working Class' (Laing 1986).[3] Both the region and this economic group – the 'Northern Working Class' – acquired a spurious, homogenised identity despite both being gross generalisations.

> The environment now considered characteristic of the North had become increasing [sic] apparent in the second quarter of the last century . . . bringing with it a shift in the centre of gravity from south to north. A new class of merchants and manufacturers arose, together with a new, much larger class of industrial workers. The poor working and living conditions

of the latter, emphasised by the very scale, concentration and novelty of the developments, soon attracted the attention of social commentators, some of whom saw the novel as an effective form of didactic fiction to arouse the social conscience.

(Pocock 1978:3)

Figure 5.1 Map of the extent of the British 'North'

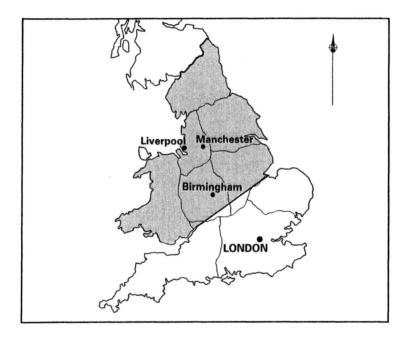

Tillotson (1954:120) cites Disraeli, for example, who, with his trilogy of political novels in the 1840s, commented that fiction 'offered the best chance of influencing opinion'. Pocock and Hudson, who have done extensive research on Northern images (1978), suggest that this literary media became the most important factor in setting the modern notion of the 'North' into the popular imagination. For example, Disraeli's (1845) *Sybil: The Two Nations* (1904) contrasts life of the rich in London with that of the poor in the mines of Mowbray, Lancashire and in the metal-working district of Woodgate (Birmingham). Mrs Gaskell's (1848) *Mary Barton: A Tale of Manchester Life* (1976) and (1855) *North and South* (1973) emphasises the regional contrast of the North with the South. Her heroine lives an idyllic life in a South England village 'sleeping in the warm light of the pure sun' until her father abruptly resigns from the church and transports his family to Milton (Manchester) in the pseudonymic county of 'Darkshire' to become private tutor to a mill owner. She wonders 'what in the world do manufacturers want with the classics, or literature, or the accomplishments of a gentleman?' She has 'almost a detestation for all she had ever heard of the North of England, the manufacturers, the people, the wild and bleak country' (Gaskell 1973: 39). In the novel, these fears are confirmed as they reach the fictional Milton:

> For several miles before they reached Milton, they saw a deep lead-coloured cloud hanging over the horizon. . . . Nearer the town the air had a faint taste and smell of smoke. Quickly they were whirled over long, straight, hopeless streets of regularly-built houses, all small and of brick. Here and there a great oblong many-windowed factory stood up, like a hen among her chickens, puffing out black 'unparliamentary' smoke and sufficiently accounting for the cloud which Margaret had taken to be rain.
>
> (Gaskell 1973:59)

Dickens's (1854) description of Coketown (Preston, Lancashire) in *Hard Times* (1966) is similar. It became the stereotype of the nineteenth-century Northern manufacturing town:

> It was a town of red brick, or of brick that would have been red if the smoke and ashes had allowed it; but as matters stood it was a town of unnatural red and black like the painted face of a savage. It was a town of machinery and tall chimneys, out of which interminable serpents of smoke trailed themselves for ever and ever, and never got uncoiled. It had a black canal in it, and a river that ran purple with ill-smelling dye, and vast piles of buildings full of windows where there was a rattling and trembling all day long. . . . You saw nothing in Coketown but what was severely workful. . . . The jail might have been the infirmary, the infirmary might

have been the jail, the town-hall might have been either, or both, or anything else.

(Dickens 1966:17)

Although London's East End became by the end of the century the country's largest centre of urban poverty (see Whipple 1966:324), the stereotypical contrast of London as the centre of wealth and civilisation versus the primitive and bleakly functional North was firmly established and reinforced in literary circles at least until Booth's survey of poverty in London at the turn of the century. There is much evidence to suggest that social displacement and hardship were more serious in the more hierarchical social conditions of the agrarian South than in the North where new working patterns and work relations were being pioneered (Savage 1988:101–102). The consolidation of a literary tradition which foregrounded both industrial conditions of the North and its 'wild hills' did much to obliterate the realities of the condition of the industrial and agricultural working classes in London and the South from our current historical imagination. This space-myth of Northern Britain underlies popular notions of a 'North–South Divide'.

The Northern space-myth may be found in the work of other major novelists down to the present day. The Potteries area of Nottinghamshire in Arnold Bennett's (1917) *Anna of the Five Towns* is an area 'long given up to unredeemed ugliness . . . somber, hardfeatured, uncouth' a 'great smoke-grit amphitheatre' (1917: 25). D.H. Lawrence's native mining areas of the Nottinghamshire–Derbyshire border are marred by urbanisation: 'red-brick rapidly spreading, like a skin disease' (1915:345 cited in Pocock and Hudson 1978:114). Lawrence carries this further in *Lady Chatterley's Lover* where the industrialism of the coal field environment is absorbed by the personalities of the inhabitants (1929:180) but, to be fair, there is a sense of beauty in the mining landscape which Lawrence expresses in his 1930 essay 'Nottingham and the mining countryside'.

To me as a child and a young man, it was still the old England of the forest and the agricultural past. . . . The mines in a sense were an accident in the landscape, and Robin Hood and his merry men were not very far away. . . . So that life was a curious cross between industrialism, and the old agricultural England, Shakespeare, and Milton, and Fielding, and George Eliot.

(Lawrence 1977:613–616)

A 'Cult of Northern-ness', a kind of snobbishness by which Northerners regard anyone to the South as in some way compromised, has helped to engender and enforce the North–South antithesis. The Northerner is thus warm-hearted and hardworking; in contrast the Southerner is seen as snobbish, soft, and lazy (Orwell 1959:112). Of course, by an inversion of these same attributes, the Southerner sees himself as civilised and living by intelligence rather than brawn, in contrast to the nosey, dogged, aggressive Northerners. The 'North's' image of itself was as a place where wealth was created, and the South as a place where it was squandered. Pocock and Hudson, amongst other researchers, note that this view, quoted by Orwell (1937), is found frequently in Northern literature from the middle of the last century, when Brighton was usually chosen as the epitome of southern dissipation. 'All is loss at Brighton . . . Middlesbrough . . . [is] an addition to the riches of the world' (Praed 1863:4 cited in Pocock and Hudson 1978:115).

In his 1937 book, *The Road to Wigan Pier* (1959), Orwell gives an extensive treatment of the North–South divide theme, drawing the 'line a little north of Birmingham to demarcate the beginning of the "real ugliness of industrialisation," an environment to which northerners were conditioned and, therefore, no longer aware' (Pocock and Hudson 1978:115). As a Southerner, however, Orwell asserts that he is

conscious, quite apart from the unfamiliar scenery, of
entering a strange country. This is partly because of certain
real differences which do exist, but still more because of the
north-south antithesis which has been rubbed into us for such
a long time past.

(Orwell 1959:106—107)

It is significant that Orwell identifies not some journalist's sensitivity but his 'Southern-ness' as the source of his exceptional perceptiveness: his clear-sighted perception of the 'real ugliness' is contrasted with the inhabitants' 'conditioning' which causes their

212

inability to see 'clearly'. What is at issue here is beyond a question of perspicacity. In Orwell's text the *authority* to pronounce upon the 'real' character of the British North is implicitly based on being not just a foreigner seeing the landscape with new eyes but a foreigner from 'the South'. Significantly, being from the North would not give one the same sort of authority to pronounce upon the character of the South. The South is always left implicit, defined only by its being implicitly different from the description of the North being given, or undefined.

These literary works form a tradition in the same sense that the nationalistic work on the Canadian North is identifiable. They take pains to separate themselves off from works promoting other views, and the tradition is internally consistent. These books all ascribe to a vision of the North as an industrial 'Land of the Working Class' with wild hinterlands such as the moors.

> Lesser publications merely reinforce the contrast in less eloquent terms. For the popular reader . . . Morton's *In Search of England* [1934] naturally spends little time in 'Industrial England' compared with 'beautiful Old England'; the transition at the Cheshire–Lancashire border is described in terms . . . reminiscent of Mrs. Gaskell. For the more socially motivated, *Britain and the Beast* (1938) with its chapter on the North-East headed 'Hills and Hells' (Sharp 1938:141–59), or *The Town that was Murdered* (Wilkinson 1939) were instances of crossing t's and dotting i's of a pattern by now well established.
>
> (Pocock and Hudson 1978:116)

Using such historical sources, researchers on environmental perception, such as Pocock and Hudson, have provided a description of Northern images and contrast these with Northern realities to establish their mythical nature as 'misconceived stereotypes' (Pocock and Hudson 1978). They present evidence of recent policy bias against the North by Southern politicians and industrialists but do little to establish the tangible socio-economic impacts of such space-myths in the past, nor do they follow the genealogy of the space-myth to its origins apart from hypothesising that it was an amplification of some 'natural bias' of Southerners. Was the divide which marks off the North so clearly in the novels

cited above simply a nineteenth-century invention? An archaeology of the Northern space-myth is beyond the scope of this work
but it is sorely needed if we are to understand the conditions in
which it originated and the scope of its effects. The previous cases
have provided ample evidence of the interaction of space- and
place-myths with the economic well-being of regions and places.

It is surprising that this has not been more directly addressed
through an examination of inherited, pre-nineteenth-century
images and myths (e.g. the eighteenth-century travelogues of
Johnson and Cobbett 1912) which, together with the industrial
developments, formed the base from which the Dickensian
descriptions and images were elaborated. The industrialisation of
the North saw the emergence of a powerful, urbanised, industrial
bourgeoisie who aspired to the cultural legitimacy of the
established aristocracy. Tutors, artists, and scholars from the
genteel South and in particular London were imported to the
households of the new Northern bourgeoisie. One might hypothesise that the social relations of these new patrons, their work
relations with labourers, and what were at that time anomalous
ambitions – 'what in the world do manufacturers want with the
classics, or literature, or the accomplishments of a gentleman?'
(Gaskell 1973:59) – presented a series of new urban forms (see
Dennis 1984:200–249) and political challenges to the landed aristocracy which were not clearly resolved until the closing decades of
the century. The 'severely workful' character of the industrial
cities' and suburbs' conformism to the logic of social relations of
industrial production; the threat of contagion brought on by over-
crowding; and the fear of the poor produced an aversion to the city
(Williams 1973). But these problems characterised Southern as
much as Northern cities (Kirk 1984).

An industrial society ordered according to the new relations of
production and commercial exchange was established unevenly,
being at first more typical of the North than the South. This
uneven geography, the perceptions of social anomalies, the threat
of class rebellion, the debasement of living conditions, the political
challenge of the rising middle classes are reflected in the language
used to describe the North: a language which constituted a spatial
discourse which privileged the centre, London, and sought to
re-establish the North as not only an economic but also a cultural
periphery around this core (Laing 1986). Geographically, the

spatialisation of England is constructed around London with peripheral regions taking different mytho-poetic positions irrespective of their detailed realities – the hellish industrial North, for example, or the pastoral South. A gradation from South to North marks an additional shading of supposedly decreasing cultural 'sophistication' with the North being associated with the strenuous 'outdoors' and the South with refinement to the point of indolence.

Figure 5.2 Realist 'grit' in *Saturday Night and Sunday Morning*

Source: Samuel Goldwin Co.

THE 'NORTH' IN BRITISH REALIST CINEMA

The next section focuses on the iconography of the Northern landscape in the so-called 'Kitchen Sink' cycle of British films from

1958 to 1963 and its continuation in the televisual conventions of Granada Television's soap opera, *Coronation Street.*[4] The late 1950s films revived the realism of the 1930s documentary film movement around figures such as Grierson. They were called 'Kitchen Sink' films because of their supposed lack of self-conscious aesthetic stylisation and their supposed truth to the daily life of 'ordinary people' (see Figure 5.2).[5] But Walter Lassally, the cinematographer of *A Taste of Honey*, once commented:

> the remarkable thing about *The Loneliness of the Long Distance Runner* and *A Taste of Honey* et cetera is not that they treat working class people, working class problems, but that they have a very poetic view of them. It's not at all a strictly realistic view. It's very much a romantic view, and that's what attracted me to them, I think.
>
> (Lassally cited in White 1974:61,62)

Even though most of these films concerned the Midlands, often being shot on location in Birmingham, they portray the 'Land of the British Working Class', that region 'North of Watford' which bleeds into the North proper and has irrevocably altered the images of the North which is seen as a single, undifferentiated landscape. The image of the British 'North', then, projected directly through apparently documentary film images of Northern towns and landscapes, of the working class, and of social conditions in the North, is particularly powerful. And this, not only in an aesthetic sense: these films also used landscape and *mise-en-scène* to establish an air of authenticity (see Figures 5.3 and 5.4).

Andrew Higson has argued that the background and surroundings are not just a neutral cinematographic *space* implied by camera movements and angles but is presented with cues that they are to be read as a real and authentic *place* – the North: 'place becomes a signifier of character, a metaphor for the state of mind of the protagonists, in the well-worn naturalist tradition' (Higson 1984:3). Krish (1963:14) identifies what he calls 'That Long Shot of Our Town from That Hill' as one iconographic cliché of this set of films. This is typically a panoramic view over a town, sometimes with a contrasting foreground object (statue, window sill, parapet, or railing), blurred by industrial smoke, with the camera focused on the far horizon, past the town itself (see Figure 5.3).[6]

Figure 5.3 'That long shot of our town from that hill': the example in
A Kind of Loving

Source: Samuel Goldwin Co.

While establishing the general space of action, such shots
render Northern towns as spectacular but emptied, distant and
alien townscapes in which landmarks are blurred.[7] These are like
the commanding panoramas of a general's view over a field of
battle: the audience is given a view from a position of spatial power
and authority. Such shots are not subordinated to the narrative by
being simply a site of action (Bordwell and Thompson 1976:42)
but become a sort of visual spectacle themselves. These descriptive
shots exist in a tension with the narrative sequence whereby the
spectator is interested to know what happens next and is instead
presented with a pause in the narrative movement of the film. In
his iconographic analysis of these films, Higson has argued that
this tension is

217

intensified by the moral demand that the spectator *investigate* the image. . . . This moral obligation depends upon an empiricist ontology of the photographic image inscribed in the Griersonian discourse of the documentary ideal. This ideal institutes a particular mode of looking as observation, a belief that we can *see the real,* in images which document the social condition of the people who inhabit the landscape. It institutes at the same time a particular status of the image as denotative, as referential. . . . Place becomes a 'sign of reality'.

(Higson 1984:9)

This effect is reinforced by the shots being on the screen long enough for one to notice a certain amount of movement, to note that these are spaces of industrial labour: landscapes transformed by a history of capitalist development (for example, see Figure 5.4). Power transmission pylons, gas works, and old industrial buildings frame every moment of leisure in these movies. The image of the North as the 'Land of the Working Class' established in the literary tradition is thus echoed with inflections of a new romanticism of the urban-industrial environment. But the cinematic conventions are less subtle after only twenty-five to thirty years. Far from being 'realist', these shots are entirely selective and *conventionalistic* in that they do not challenge commonsensical, 'folksy', categorisations of the region, thereby framing and presenting a one-sided vision of the 'North'. The North is in a sense as disordered as a kitchen sink full of dirty dishes; a place where purified, monological narratives are challenged by the dialogical displacements of codes and recombinations which position actions in improper settings (romantic encounters in a gas-works – Figure 5.4). The Northern Working Class is an invention cast as the foreign 'Other' of the socially constructed orderliness of the British nation centred around London. Class imagery again collapses into spatial imagery. But at the same time, this Other is reappropriated into a cultural framework in which it is allocated a subsidiary position. The plots, camera angles, *mise-en-scène,* and the audience's omniscient view all contribute to a reappropriation which betrays the presence of an ordering authority which is not included in the film but is at all times behind the camera. The powerful position of the directors is glossed over by the films' realism. But the apparent 'naturalness' of the views presented in the films and the distanced treatment of the Northern working class as a homogeneous 'Other' suggests the presence of a broader framework than merely being the idiosyncratic vision of an individual. The naturalness and 'transparency' of these shots is the sign of an external, London-centred, political authority and economic power which is in turn legitimised in the films.

Figure 5.4 A Taste of Honey: the landscape of industrial capital

Source: Weintraub Entertainment

Higson and others have argued that these films' claims to authenticity, underpinned by 'real' on-location landscapes, were legitimised by critics. Not only could an audience enjoy these film, but also some could gain a vicarious, even voyeuristic, view into the landscape, culture, and personal life of the Northern working class which was authorised and legitimised under the banner of socially-conscious realist film-making. The audience's omniscient position, which has the advantage of the visual mastery of the narrative provided by the camera, is also a sort of class position of paternalism whereby the characters, marked as working class, are portrayed as victims. This identification – this *interpellation* – with the camera as the point of a 'sure and centrally embracing view' (Heath 1981:30) encourages an identification with a monocentric position outside and above the city and landscapes (Higson 1984:18). In the films, 'That Long Shot' establishes the privileged position of the audience's vantage point – a vantage point which allows an organizing, uncluttered overview: 'Space [is] set out as spectacle for the eye of the spectator. Eye and knowledge come together; subject, object, and the distance of the steady observation that allows the one to master the other' (Heath 1981:30). Such a viewpoint allows one not just to see but a tantalising moment of mastery.[8] In this moment one is in the presence of a monological, South-centred narrative which asserts the symbolic and empirical identity of the North in terms of the space-myth we have already encountered. Higson puts this in class terms, but this assessment carries the implication that realist films were seen only by bourgeois audiences:

> That Long Shot is a betrayal of authorship (and a betrayal of
> the class position of that authority as outside the city and the
> consciousness of its inhabitants). The distance in That Long
> Shot, between the vantage-point of the subject and its
> ostensible object, the city, is at the same time a representation
> of the distance between the classes. From the class outside the
> city [the audience], the city is unknowable, impenetrable. But
> in constructing the shot as spectacular, the distance is
> disavowed; the impenetrability of the real living city is
> transformed into a surface, a representation, an image which
> does not need to be penetrated, but which can be gazed at
> precisely as an image: the fascinated, fetishistic gaze.
>
> (Higson 1984:21)

This is the gaze from the position of an outsider. But the 'class outside' is not a conventional social class but a 'spatial class', so to speak. Higson's categorisation of the audience as bourgeois and the characters as working class seems overly-simplified to be convincing. The gaze of the (at least momentary) outsider is a 'south-centred gaze': a gaze from that privileged position in which the South has been placed with respect to the North. The monological position of the omniscient view brings order into a cluttered, 'gritty' kitchen sink world of contrasting, heterogeneous things and voices.

In these films, centring the spectator's attention is an individual character – often a single figure in the landscape – who develops morally through the course of the film according to stereotyped 'universal' human values of bourgeois subjectivity and humanism. This easy identification with the characters at a personal level affirms the 'oneness' of all people – of the *British people* – reinforcing a sense of solidarity, and the feeling that one understands the problems of other people from different class backgrounds and other, distant, places. It collapses the distance between the viewers' position and the symbolic 'North' of the film screen. But there is also a clear appeal to people to share, *on the basis of their own experiences of increasing post-war affluence*, in the characters' traumatic experiences of leaving their homes and communities to go out into the world (usually to London) and the subsequent problems which come with success and affluence. Even though there is no record of the reception of the films by class, a cathartic release built upon this more authentic identification is plausible, even if some look on (or, rather, down) patronisingly (Higson 1984:10).

The films also present an opportunity to re-tell the old myths about the North. The rehearsal of images suggests that re-telling these stories or 'yarns' (e.g. about the industrial hells of the North) allows a vicarious experience of re-affirmation of a mythological component of the reality shared by British spectators who are 'in the know'. Anthony Cohen suggests that such 'group stories' or 'yarns' further the symbolic construction of community by differentiating insiders (those who are in the know) from outsiders who do not share the knowledge of the myth of the North which would lead to a film being understood quite differently by the knowing insiders. In this process, a knowing audience's membership in a 'community of belief' (see Cohen 1986:7) is re-confirmed. This can be applied to the re-confirmation of membership in, and the existence of, a national 'invisible community' (B. Anderson 1983).

Nationalism, always a myth of space to begin with, locates people in a space. It constructs a relation of identity between them and that space. In this case, the mechanism (undoubtedly one of many) of shared 'yarns' and myths reinforces a process of spatialising people, placing them as citizens within communities and a nation-territory. This is mirrored by the symbolism of the myth which takes up a space and identifies it with a particular group of people, the Working Class. On one side, people are united with a space (England); on the other side, a space (the North of England) is united with people, territorialised as the 'Land of the Working Class' as the land of the true British. In this manner, the stage is set for a series of ideological cues, interpellations, and discourses which manipulate metaphors of the people and the land.

Echoes of this notion of 'symbolic community' can be found in other cultural criticism such as the work of Barthes (1972). Brunsdon and Morley's 1978 study of the BBC's regional news television programme, *Nationwide*, reveals a similar process of re-affirmation. Their study was a landmark in television criticism, but they did not synthesise their insights nor pay specific attention to the spatial character of much of the material they examined, despite their conclusion that

> the social structure of the nation is denied; spatial difference
> replaces social structure and the nation is seen to be
> composed not of social units in any relation of exploitation or
> antagonism but of geographical units often reduced to
> regional stereotypes of 'characters'.
>
> (Brunsdon and Morley 1978:87)

THE NORTH IN *CORONATION STREET*

> A fascinating freemasonry, a volume of unwritten rules.
> These are the driving forces behind life in a working class
> street in the north of England. The purpose of 'Florizel
> Street' is to examine a community of this nature, and to
> entertain.
>
> (From the Granada Television Memo proposing
> what was to become *Coronation Street*)

A message similar to that delivered by the realist films of the 1950s may be found in the Granada Television serial *Coronation Street*. While many media critics have produced 'readings' of this serial, the spatial-temporal underpinning of the Northern and daily-life character of the series has been neglected in favour of comments on the working class character of the shows.[9] Against the simple reading of *Coronation Street* as the last preserve of the working-class community, I will argue that the series is rather a *class-denying* celebration of an organic community struggling against outsider bureaucracies.

Coronation Street, and particularly its famous opening shot amongst the chimney pots of terrace houses, needs little introduction for most British or even foreign television viewers.[10] For the former it is widely held to represent 'the life of the northern working class', the last redoubt of the working-class community; for the latter, *Coronation Street* represents the industrial face of England. Its location is far more implicit but, generally speaking, it is difficult to be British and not know that *Coronation Street* is shot in Manchester and represents Salford just to the West. It has been called a Dickensian 'folk opera in praise of . . . the "ordinary" people of Britain' (Granada, 1985:94) which has portrayed the on-going life of a Northern, British working-class community for over twenty-five years maintaining consistently high ratings all along. A discourse of authenticity figures highly in *Coronation Street*, which adopts the same realist strategies as films like *A Taste of Honey* considered earlier as well as reproducing a street- and roof-scape reminiscent of a late-nineteenth-century working-class area. The effort at authenticity is considerable. One learns from the studio that the stage-set street was built flanking a real cobbled street 'which is still visible in the derelict railway marshalling yard' out of old Salford bricks, 'knitted with mortar mixed with paint to give the brickwork a pre-war drabness' and 'reclaimed roofing slates'. 'The finished set [included] . . . the Viaduct and a section of Rosamund Street, . . . and the added realism of Manchester's pudding-bag clouds floating low overhead' (Granada 1985:16). The dialectic between the stage-set reality of this street and the accuracy of authentic detail sets up a network of effects and tensions.

We might ask why *Coronation Street* is set where it is. Considering the initial regional audience of the series' producers a theme of Northern organic communities struggling against the

223

institutional social powers-that-be (represented by 'outsiders' speaking Standard English, i.e. from the South, especially London) makes good economic and programming sense. This correlates with other analysts' observations who have pointed out:

> Granada Television . . . has established its own regional identity through its network and local output. Its reputation for reflecting its regional base is due in part to the realism of *Coronation Street* . . . which also achieved large audiences in Granada's franchise area and consequent high advertising revenue expectations; it almost invariably tops the ratings in the Northwest.
>
> (Paterson and Stewart 1980:55)

Despite its working-class image the characters and activities portrayed do in fact cross the conventional working–middle–upper class lines. Not only are some characters managers of, for example, the factory where many of the women characters work, but also there are factory owners. As Richard Paterson and John Stewart have remarked, this

> plurality of 'ideologies' is dependent in large part on the serial's . . . origin . . . as a community tale. . . . After twenty years refracting social change through a basic set of characters represented as living in a 'working class' community in northern England, its initial pluralism has multiplied and intensified, concretising a mythic reality that at times reverberates with the divisions of British society. This accumulation is still underpinned, however, by the nostalgic notion of 'community' that was dominant in representations of British working-class life in the late 1950s.
>
> (Paterson and Stewart 1980:98)

The source of both this nostalgic representation of working-class life and this reading of the series as 'working class' is to be found in the post-war vision pre-eminently expressed in Hoggart's *The Uses of Literacy* (1957). It materialises in the series as an emphasis on common sense, the absence of work and politics, the stress on women and the strength of women, and the perspective of nostalgia (Dyer 1980:4). Using Mary Douglas's (1982) distinction of social arrangements by grid (based on status, wealth, etc.) and group (based on locality, interest, etc.), there is a generalised absence of grid distinctions such as socio-economic class in favour of group affinities based on the proximity of the *Street*. Class is subsumed under a commonsensical 'us–them' orientation which sees 'outsiders' (always threatening or 'dangerous' in the sense of disturbing the status quo on the programme) as more politically problematic than the cross-class relations within the neighbourhood community of the *Street*. M. Maffesoli refers to this as the 'tribal spirit' of the various forms of *sociality*, or the sensual ethos of modern life as opposed to more common stress on *social structure* so beloved of sociology (cf. the so-called structure-agency debate of Giddens (1984) and others).

> If meaning is given back to the *quartier*, to neighbourly practices and to the affectual . . . it is first of all because they permit networks of relationships. Proxemy . . . sends one back to the very bottom of a succession of 'we's' who constitute the substance of any 'sociability.' . . . the constitution of micro-groups, of the tribes that punctuate spatiality, starts in the feeling of *belonging*, as a function of a specific ethics, and within the framework of a communication *network*.
> . . . a 'multitude of villages' . . . criss-cross one another. . . . The city object is a succession of territories where people, in a more or less nonsystematic manner, take root . . . a *cosa mentale*, a symbolic territory – whatever its type, it is just as real.
> [Furthermore] . . . .the tribalism under consideration here may be completely ephemeral: it organises itself as the occasions present themselves . . . [through, e.g. Minitel], sports, friendships, sexual liaisons, religious groups, or others, tribes are formed. [And] . . . even though these tribes are stamped with the seal of a seasonal quality, and with a tragic dimension, they control the mechanism of belonging.
> (Maffesoli 1988b:39)

The street becomes a symbol and icon of community, of belonging. Indeed, more than twenty-five years later, the community of the show has expanded beyond the naive limits of the physical street itself. The abnegation on the part of the characters in favour of their community underwrites a conservative doctrine of mutuality and strength through collective solidarity. *Coronation Street* is clearly not simply a realist evocation of a way of life but also a prescriptive utopian fantasy. The common-sense focus of *Coronation*

Street is the meat of the expression of a nostalgia for an insular world of certainties. No awareness, for example, of meta-personal problems (such as nuclear waste disposal, Chernobyl, etc.) is betrayed in this contracted vision of the world 'beyond'. But this utopian aspect is equivocal: in distinction to most modern utopias which depend on 'progress' to accomplish the utopian project of reaching some pre-set social state, this sort of social progress has been edited out of the *Coronation Street* script. Hence its strange stasis in a curious 'childhood' state of pre-adult, pre-awareness, innocence. If the programme asserts a utopian 'image of how life should be' it also withdraws, erases, it. Partly this is demanded because, instead of the linear, social, temporality of utopian ideologies, the series proceeds wholly on the temporality of individual life-cycles, opposed to the temporality of social institutions which are independent of individual lifetimes. As opposed to utopian, it is edenic. And, it is significant that this British Eden is located in that imaginary space called 'the North' which, as we have seen, has less to do with the north than with the *nation*. The communion of classes in the programmes, if uncomfortable, reaffirms the idea of a basic oneness and a belief in the importance of a shared ethos of 'Britishness' under attack by bureaucratic authority and elitist officials.

This becomes clearer when the temporal aspect of the series is considered. The characters, living in a shared temporality of the pace of their individual lives, deal with various problems raised by social institutions (banks, the bureaucracy of the welfare state) and individuals who are committed to them (white-collar workers, bureaucrats, tax collectors, clerks). In a way, topics such as threatened demolition of the street in a slum clearance programme make *Coronation Street* into a sort of TV serialisation of a Jane Jacobs-style hidden urban community (cf. Jacobs 1961).

This sub-theme shouldn't be overstated – the essence of the action is to be found in the never-ending sequence of deaths, romances, and ironic mis-understandings. However, based on a survey of the summary plot outlines for the first twenty-five years, there is a clear case for arguing that the surface drama is often built upon and driven by the obligations and the almost coerced, often resented, responsibilities placed on the characters by the social institutions which form the off-stage context of the *Street*. There are, for example, conflicts over job promotion and transfer;[11] conflicts with school examining boards,[12] and more importantly with the police,[13] social workers,[14] health inspectors,[15] and above all the Local Authority bureaucracy.[16] Less prominent are disputes with the Inland Revenue (February 1969), various consuls (August 1967) and embassy officials (November 1971), with marriage bureaux (December 1967), money lenders,[17] and with churches urging temperance.[18] By contrast, in the first twenty years, racism and the question of immigrants appeared clearly only once (December 1962).

In line with conflicts over the tempo of life (bio-social time vs. calendar-legal time) there are spatialised conflicts. Social institutions and their representatives are 'outsiders' who are distinguished spatially from the central characters of the *Street*. *Coronation Street* is not primarily about working-class community but about the assault upon the individual by institutions which are wholly other – most fundamentally they operate in a different temporal and spatial mode. *Coronation Street* represents this social David and Goliath drama where 'the common folk' win by their ingenuity and neighbourly solidarity. Through their sociability they preserve a neighbourhood oasis in a land of rampant bureaucracy and institutionalised social structures. Where academic analyses of the series emphasise the elements and representations of social structure (class, institutions, etc.) this reading has foregrounded the programme's presentation of sociality and the important role this old Weberian notion of 'emotional community' plays in the show's appeal and apparent naturalness. In addition, not only is the community's vision of the world limited but also their spatial practice is largely confined to the street-set. These two components comprise the *contracted spatialisation* of *Coronation Street*. Whereas in the films, one looked from the outside-in, in *Coronation Street*, one looks from the inside-out.

The image of the North projected in *Coronation Street* is one of a traditional region populated by close-knit working-class communities oriented and revolving around neighbourhood relations and the local pub. The built environment of the street is one of the monotonous streets of bay villas of the twentieth-century working class. The characters are well accommodated by British standards, having left the 'two-up, two-down' terraces of their parents' generation. While the characters do live in the 'bounded milieu' of a restrictive spatialisation, it is the built environment of everyone's past. The programme 'speaks to its audience' and asserts its relevance to their lives not only on the plane of nostalgia for a common 'memory-fetish' but also on the plane of the on-going present life of the viewers. Part of the success of *Coronation Street* then is to be found in the fact that it avoids presenting a community of a minority occupational group such as miners or textile workers. Instead the characters are involved in a range of occupations typical of the 'working class'. However, they largely work in a homogeneous set of occupations with a large overlap between the occupational friendships of, for example, women's work outside the home and community, 'street-based' life. The 'community of women' is paramount in the constitution of social life in the programmes, giving the street a female-gendered, domestic feel which is inset within an implicitly male-gender space. For British viewers this world, innocent of the hypercapitalist penetration of a market logic to all facets of daily life, is 'the North'.

This regional image presented is of a female-gendered domestic place within a masculine-gendered space but it is non-religious. There are no church-based community ties to distract from the supremacy of the *Street*, and, there are no churches to link, even symbolically, the characters and their world with any extended community 'outside' of the restricted world of the street. Strikingly, the mass media and television (while the de facto targets of the polemic which *Coronation Street* advances and the explicit target of Hogarth's work) are absent. The programme opposes by denying the importance of such aspects of modern life to the daily life of the individual which it reconstructs in a zone uncontaminated by the mass media or advertising. There are no 'Sundays' or daily tabloids to distract from the street focus. In place of the national, 'imagined community' (B. Anderson 1983) defined by a national media, a local community, defined by gossip is paramount. This contributes to the edenic, 'out of time' quality of the series.

The characters are anti-heroes. They do not stand out, but are rather typical, their strength lies in their community – *The Street*. They struggle to remain where they are and the episodes of the programme document over and over the pains of breaking away of leaving to seek careers, educations, or to accompany husbands to jobs in London or the south. Thus the characters again and again pose the same question: 'What will we do now that x is gone?'. The programme elevates Northern concerns of both men and women to a central position. The programme constitutes a laboratory in which fictional alternative solutions and strategic stalemates may be tested for their effectiveness as means to slow the onset of social change, cope with economic restructuring and the attendant erosion of the social fabric.

THE 'NORTH' OF ENGLAND

To summarise, the above studies demonstrate that since the nineteenth century a relatively coherent and continuous image of the 'North' of England divided off from the South has persisted. Other studies could also be cited to further establish this set of images (for example, Parkinson's (1967) study of the North in British satire). A nostalgic discourse of tradition valorises the North as the homeland of a traditional British Working Class and the culture associated with it – ferrets, pigeon racing, mines and mills, fish and chips, regional accents and football – as well as organic communities. It is also the locus for industrial images of the UK: coal-mining, bleak urban landscapes, and windswept countryside (e.g. the Yorkshire Dales). More recently it is 'Fourth Division England' (*Guardian*, 2, 9, 16, 23 March 1988) with the connotation of having failed, 'down and out' communities. Its rougher pleasures of the outdoors contrast with the more refined pleasures of the high-culture of London and its commuter belt.

The North of England acquired its image as an industrial area populated by rough working classes at the end of the eighteenth century. The presence of water power and deposits of coal and iron led to the development of first a resource economy. Later, with the expansion of manufacturing enterprises producing goods for British colonies, the availability of water power for mills resulted in the expansion of a secondary economic base. Together with the proletarianisation of an agrarian peasant class, immense changes took place in both the spatial and socio-economic morphology of this area. This contrasted with the agricultural basis of the Southern 'home counties', and the emergence of financial capital in London. The landscape of the 'North' became populated by mills with their adjoining villages and company towns; the 'South' (an equally imaginary region) retained a pastoral landscape to which the aristocracy of the London-based court escaped. Whereas this 'Southern pastoral' represented, through trans-functionalisation – all the pleasures of their country estates, the landscape of Northern industry represented the social challenges of the nineteenth-century industrial bourgeoisie and the problems of a changing economic base. This change had its attendant social impacts as chronicled by Engels: the concentration of the landless, disenfranchised poor into industrial slums. This change in social composition altered the face of the eighteenth-century city mor- phology just as dramatically as the landscape of towns grouped around coal mines and mills was to alter the countryside. Thus the image of the 'North' has become closely related to images of the British industrial working class.

As the paradigmatic industrial heartland, the North continues to overshadow the contemporary centre of gravity of British industry: the Midlands, South-east, and the Heathrow–Bristol stretch of the M4 motorway corridor. This will be argued to remain true despite the decline of Northern industries. The clearance of old factory sites and diversification of single industry towns has removed many of the old red-brick industrial buildings but the infrastructure of the towns, their siting at good mill sites, the provision of pubs and working men's clubs, the terraces of cramped housing climbing the hillside – all reflect the social relations of the old industrial arrangements. Only here and there a new bright-painted school or the metallic shed of light industry marks new growth. The past hangs over these towns like factory smoke must once have. The old images have budged only little compared with the affluent reality of areas of Tyneside, for example. Cities such as Bradford have even capitalised on their industrial image by re-presenting themselves as industrial heritage museums (Urry 1990). As the land of the working class the reality of working-class London as the largest concentration of those low down on the socio-economic ladder is suppressed. In all cases, the image of the North is firmly in orbit around the cultural hub and pinnacle of London where the images are purveyed and enunciated in the London-based national press (Laing 1986; see also Pocock and Hudson 1978:111–112; Raleigh 1968:290–328; Leclaire 1954). The North is the pole against which the civilisation of the South has been compared according to the following oppositions:

'North'		'South'
Peripheral region	–	Centre, hub
Working class	–	Economic, political elites
Bleak countryside	–	Tamed landscape
Industry, factories	–	Stockbroking, management
Rugged leisure pursuits (football, dale walking)	–	High culture (opera, ballet)
Wet and cold climate	–	Warmer climate
Gemeinschaft	–	*Gesellschaft*
Sociality, emotional community	–	Social structure, institutions

The media sources for the 'North versus South' theme re-present the articulated and accepted system of values of society -- articulated on the whole by the privileged, maybe, but received by another privileged group, who have included political, social, and economic decision-makers besides being disseminated widely through the channels of formal education such as English literature and poetry.

Thus while there are changes from a perception of the 'North' as an homogeneously uncultured industrial hell to a more differentiated perception where the Lake District emerges as a leisure zone, the model of oppositions proposed above continues – one does not go to the 'North' for high culture but for hiking, fishing, or for the British version of 'unspoiled nature'.

> The important landscape is the one in the mind, the imagined one, and consequently in any contest between reality and fiction, the latter is likely to win (Prince 1973:17). Besides, for those who subscribe to the view that 'seeing is believing', the stereotype image of the north is still very much alive on television screens through working-class plays, serials and period revivals.
>
> (Pocock and Hudson 1978:119)

THE 'NORTH–SOUTH DIVIDE' RHETORIC OF THE 1980s

The notion of an imaginary North set apart from but firmly linked

231

with the South of England is still alive in the 1980s. It remains a persistent sub-theme which re-emerges onto the centre stage of public debate from time to time. Generally, it doe: so by appearing in comments made in the print and broadcast media. It either serves as a metaphor for other social divisions ('Southern' political and economic elites versus 'Northern' working class), or part of a counterfactual argument where folk 'common sense' stereotypes are 'discovered' to be true despite their over-generalisation, or it serves as a rhetorical device for orienting an audience 'in the know' about myths of the British 'North' to the context of an argument. As such, it is a real factor which shapes these debates, not only inflecting them with a mythical element of imagery but also distorting the debate by introducing inaccurate stereotypes or deflecting the debate into the cul-de-sac of 'Two Nations' clichés. Consider the following statement from *The Economist*:

> Britain is split by a North–South Divide running from Bristol to the Wash. The victims of decaying smokestack industry live in the North, the beneficiaries of new high-tech, finance, scientific and service industries, plus London's cultural and political elite, are in the South. Cross the Divide, going north, and visibly the cars get fewer, the clothes shabbier, the people chattier.
>
> (7 February 1987)

Many of the components of this claim are, if not false then misleading (fewer cars, for example)[19] and subjective (the people wear shabby clothes). It reiterates both the demarcation of the 'Divide' (Bristol to the Wash) and the package of images which make up the myth of 'The North'. These images include: the industrial character of the 'North'; the 'chattiness' of the 'victims' who are not beneficiaries of recent technical advances but live in the conditions of an earlier age, and a general atmosphere of shabbiness and unkempt functionality. Beyond introducing the 'factual content' of the article which is the problem of industrial restructuring and decaying 'smokestack industries', the readership is reminded of the social fantasy or myth of the industrial 'North'. This 'fantasy content' appears to have seized the imagination of the author who rhetorically piles up images of daily life (ordinariness, once again) – cars, clothes, and chattiness (gossipy friendliness) – to draw a vivid picture. The painterly effect must have been dramatic for *The Economist*'s international readership, many of whom have never had any direct experience of the North of England or the Midlands, nor, for many, even secondary experience through televised images or movies. Unfortunately one can only speculate about the economic impacts of such examples of negative imagery. But it would be too crude a project to just try to track the impact of news articles, just as it would be naive to attribute to them the status of causal agents. Rather, they are manifestations, symptoms, of a more embracing set of predispositions: a *dispositif* which includes the coding of spaces and places, that is a particular spatialisation.

Despite the industrial decline of the North, the depopulation of the working classes of many Northern cities, the clearance of old factory sites for huge shopping centres such as the Metrocentre in Gateshead, Tyneside, or industrial museums such as in Bradford, the stereotyped notions of the 'North' have been reshuffled into the recently popular rhetoric of a 'North–South Divide'. The above quotation is an example of the renaissance of this old phrase which dates from Gaskell and Disraeli through Priestley's 'Journey through Britain' (1934). According to this 'imaginary geography', the economic life and social conditions of the country are seen to be fundamentally different north of Birmingham (or even north of London) compared with the 'South of England'. This section examines the imaginary 'divide' itself, as opposed to the earlier sections which dealt primarily with images of the North. The basis for this study is a comprehensive scanning of the British 'quality dailies': *Guardian, The Times, Financial Times, Daily Telegraph,* and *The Independent* over three years, plus a key-phrase search of a sample of 'hard news' articles from these papers between 1986 and 1987 held on the *Tex Line* database for the phrases 'North–South', 'North and South', 'North–South Divide', 'North South Divide' and 'Two Nations'. A search was also made for articles containing the three keywords 'North', 'South' and 'Divide' in relation to the British North. After excluding many unrelated articles, this yielded an additional set of articles which, although they did not use the phrase itself, discussed the issue in terms of, for example, a 'division between the North and South' (*Financial Times* Friday 6 December 1985:9). The frequency of the mention of these phrases is given in tabular form in Note 22 and as a table (Table 5.1). Bearing in mind the somewhat artificial nature of this restricted quantitative sample, the comprehensive scan was added to pick up letters to the editor and 'life-style' articles which might otherwise have been neglected. While it is possible to generalise to other media from this limited sample, I will confine myself to claims about the print media.

This rhetoric is taken as an indicator of a particular social spatialisation. The use of such language, what we might call a *discourse of status distinction by division*, is a barometer of the fluctuating emergence and submergence of the myth of a 'North–South Divide' into consciousness. That is, the extent to which it becomes explicit and recognised by social agents, as opposed to being either implicit or repressed (as in the Canadian case). This myth becomes an organising concept by which the taxonomy of everyday distinctions and divisions becomes a conscious factor in personal and policy decision-making.

Relatively few mentions of the above phrases occur in 1984 and 1985. Even where there is talk of a 'divided nation' it is in terms of the social division of rich and poor, not the geographic division of different regions. For example, when Neil Kinnock made his New Year's speech he argued that 'under Mrs. Thatcher . . . we have seen another . . . year of division' (cited in *Financial Times* 31 December 1985:6). Similarly, articles on regional inequalities in a *Financial Times* survey 'Investing in Britain' do not mention any sort of divide, division, or 'gap' (19 November 1986:7–15). From June 1984 to June 1985 there are only ten references to a 'North–South Divide'. Occasional allusions to the growing regional economic divisions in Britain are made in 1985 (especially in the *Financial Times* where the notion occurs eight times in the sense of a 'growing gap' between the North-East and North-West and the South-East and Greater London). Typically, this follows the release of annual regional employment figures in December or January. The phrase 'North–South Divide' and the accompanying rhetoric of 'gaps', 'splits', and 'divisions' become more common in the spring and summer of 1986 and then take off across most of the papers in early 1987 after the release of regional unemployment figures for the last quarter of 1986.[21]

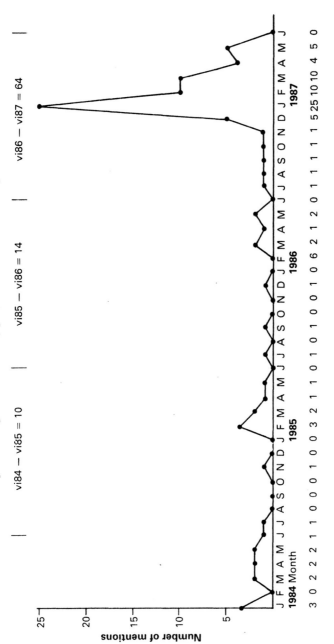

Table 5.1 Graph showing mentions of key phrases in the *Tex Line* sample, 1985–87

vi84 — vi85 = 10   vi85 — vi86 = 14   vi86 — vi87 = 64

vi84 — vi85 = 10

Table 5.2 United Kingdom regional contrasts

Areas	1 Job losses June 79–83	2ᵃ Job losses June 83–86	3ᵇ Work-force	4ᶜ Likelihood of becoming/ceasing Unemp. %	5ᵈ Likelihood of becoming/ceasing Unemp. %	6ᵉ QOL	7ᶠ House price rise
North-West	–374	–41	452.0	5.6	28	+2.9	n. av.
North	–191	+20	237.7	6.8	29	+11.0	7
Yorkshire & Humberside	–240	+5	305.8	5.7	32	+6.3	6
Sub total	–805	–16	995.5	6.03*	29.6*	+6.7	6.5
E. Midlands	–132	+91	202.2	5.0	34	+1.7	15
W. Midlands	–298	+78	349.7	4.8	27	+1.5	13
'North' sub total	–1,235	+153	1,547.4	5.58*	30*	+6.5	10.25
South-West	–84	+54	204.7	5.5	40	–8.6	29
South-East	–391	+269	782.3	4.5	38	–10.4	37
E. Anglia	–15	+74	81.3	5.1	42	+0.1	30
'South' sub total	–490	+397	1,068.3	5.03*	40*	–6.3	32
UK avg.	–2,071	+500	3,271.2**	n. av.	n. av.	n. av.	n. av.

* Averaged figures.
** Totals.

Notes to columns
a   Figures in 1,000s.
b   1985 figures (from 1 April 1983, the figures reflect the effects of the provisions in the 1983 Budget for some men aged 60 and over who no longer have to register at an unemployment office).
c   The inflow to unemployment expressed as a percentage of the average number of employees in employment plus the unemployed for the year to October 1985 (*Regional Trends* 23: 101).
d   The outflow from unemployment expressed as a percentage of the average number unemployed over the quarters (*Regional Trends* 23:101).
e   Quality of Life, expressed as what one can buy with an average local salary from Reward Group Survey.
f   The rate of rise of house prices (£/day) is disaggregated for comparison. Figures for the 1st half of 1988 (from Reward Group Regional Cost of Living Report 1988, cited in *Guardian* 22 March 1988:4). Greater London QOL = –25.0; House price rise = +67.

Source: Social Trends 21, *Regional Trends* 23.

As Table 5.2 indicates, there is more than a grain of truth in the notion. Statistically, there is a slightly higher chance of becoming unemployed and, once out of work, it is more difficult to find work in the 'North' (Northerners have only an average likelihood of ceasing to be unemployed of 30 per cent as against 40 per cent for Southerners). The myth of a 'Divide' and the resurgence of this rhetoric is associated with statistical indicators of geographical inequality. The point is not to deny this close liaison, but to note that (1) these factual differences are augmented by imaginary elements and (2) people do not bother to re-examine these conflated elements when making decisions to act in one way or another. Even if one asked people it would be difficult to prompt them to separate these elements without asking them to re-analyse their understanding of the character of the 'North'. The result would bear as much relationship to everyday life as a laboratory maze to city streets.

As to the empirically specifiable differences, some quantitative figures are available. First, rising Southern house prices made it more difficult to move from North to South – one employer called it an 'exclusion zone south of Watford' (*Observer* 6 September 1987:19). One newspaper announced that three luxury houses could be bought in the 'North' for the price of one economy-sized house in the South (*Today* 4 February 1987 – see Table 5.2, Col.7). Second, in the North there was a concentration of localities suffering from industrial restructuring while Southern localities had suffered earlier and were at that time benefiting from the shift in economic importance from manufacturing and 'smokestack industries' to services (see the discussion by Minford in *Daily Telegraph* 26 January 1987:20). A report of the Low Pay Unit noted that low wages in the North were combining with high unemployment rates to 'produce two nations in the United Kingdom' (cited in *Financial Times* 14 March 1986:9). Thus readers were informed:

> the apparently stark north–south contrast arises because the south, after suffering 30% of the earlier job cuts (which was not far out of line with its relative share of the population) then went on to win a quite disproportionate 78% slice of the last three years' gains.

But this article goes on to say 'What is perfectly clear though, is that this relative good fortune has not been evenly spread, even in the south . . . ', reporting that while eighteen of the twenty poorest places in the country had 'hitched their former prosperity to either steel, mining or some form of shipping, and although most of the victims are in the north, the complete list includes Penzance, Deal . . . '(*Sunday Times* 11 January 1987:25). In an editorial, it argued:

> The 'North–South Divide' is the fashionable phrase now tripping off the tongues and typewriters of politicians and pundits to describe Britain's uneven spread of prosperity. Like most such generalisations it obscures more than it illumines. . . .
> The real economic inequality in Britain is not the glib north–south divide but a rather more complicated division. Decaying Britain is to [be] found in one-industry towns and decaying inner cities, booming Britain in the pleasant market towns and suburban countryside and in those towns and cities which could attract the new service and high-tech industries. . . .
> It is true that more of the decay can be found in the north and more of the boom in the south, which leads people to think that Britain's 'two nations' are geographical. But boom and decay can be found in nearly all Britain's regions . . .
> (*Sunday Times* 11 January 1987:26)

This more balanced view came at the end of a running debate (see the listing in Note 21) where the notion of a 'Divide' was quickly 'hyped up' in the British press taking on all the components of the great traditional theme of the Dickensian 'North'. To the empirical differences were added the traditional images which make up the mythology of the North. The detail of the econometric reports was recast along the lines of the old narratives which represent a storehouse of traditional images, called forth from time to time for rhetorical effect. In response to this rhetoric, academics appeared with political pundits on current affairs programmes, letters were written to editors, and questions asked in the British House of Commons (see Note 21). While the agenda was clearly set by the print media, television exposés and documentaries provided visual evidence of the closure of Northern factories, and of graffiti-covered walls of 'unemployment blackspots'.

Comments such as

> More and more people are aghast at the growing divisions
> which besmirch our country. The North–South Divide creeps
> ever lower down the country. The unemployment and factory
> closures are going down past Luton and the North–South
> barrier will soon start at Potters Bar.
>
> (*Guardian* 15 February 1986)

are typical. The sense of a creeping southward glaciation of England appeared rampant through the winter of 1986–87 in particular:

> Almost everyone recognizes that there is a serious division in
> the country between the North, including the Midlands, and
> all the great cities, and the Southeast. However, few remedies
> are being proposed. Indeed, there is a widespread sense of
> fatalism that industrial decline is irreversible, and that to do
> anything about it would require additional public money
> which is simply not available.
>
> (*Guardian* 24 March 1987:12)

It is important to go beyond a mere count of the number of mentions of these phrases which mark out, for the purposes of this study, the 'North–South Divide' rhetoric. While the 'North–South Divide' was rediscovered by the media with much fanfare, very quickly much of the commentary (since January 1987) focused on portraying the 'North–South Divide' as a caricature which was either untrue – 'look at comfortable Didsbury, on the fringes of Manchester, or Bearsden, in Glasgow, or the handsome Hallam district of Sheffield, all three visibly oozing money' (*The Economist* 4 April 1987) – or as not the central 'divide' that debate should be focused around. Contrast the following, concluding, statement with the introductory statement (above), both from the same issue of *The Economist*:

> There is an east–west [divide]: in Scotland oil and finance
> flourish in the east, engineering stumbles in the west;
> Lancashire is cut from neighbouring Yorkshire by history,
> cricket and the Pennine mountains; farther South, the Welsh
> are poorer even than northern England or Scotland . . .
> elsewhere the contrasts between country life and that of

hustling multiracial cities far outweigh any between North
and South.

(The Economist 7 February 1987)

Such a quotation which discovers geographical divisions of social
conditions at every hand echoes the report on the 'East–West
Divide' in *Regional Trends* 20 (1985; see *The Times* 22 May 1985).
Clearly this geographic metaphor was attractive even to academics.
While, as a rhetorical device, the 'North–South Divide' provided
an apt description of the pattern of 'patchy' post-1982 economic
recovery which was led by the South-East, it overwhelmed the
factual content of the debate, reflecting divisions which articles
argued 'existed more in British minds than reality'(see *Financial
Times* 19 November 1986; *The Economist* 7 February 1987). For
example, comparing Reward Group's 'quality of life' index by
urban centres reveals that the North ranks highest when average
regional salary is cross-tabulated against regional cost of living with
the South-East and Greater London at the bottom of a 'league
table' of regions (see Table 5.2, Col. 6).

To return to the *Sunday Times*:

> Britain, when it comes to prosperity, is an increasingly divided
> nation. But despite last week's widely-publicised job-loss
> statistics, the main split is not geographical but social. There
> is no neat Severn–Wash line separating the haves and
> have-nots. . . . The poor . . . are certainly concentrated in the
> old, one-industry towns and decaying inner cities of the north.
> But they represent an equally intractable and numerically
> even larger problem in the boroughs at the heart of London.

(Sunday Times 11 January 1987:25)

Thus there were continual *rhetorical* assertions of the inappro-
priateness of the notion 'North–South Divide' but always with a
knowing wink at the mythology of the 'North' – an 'odd impre-
cision' (*The Economist* 21 February 1987). The traditional mythology of the 'North' is re-circulated and re-cycled in a modified but
fundamentally unchallenged manner, re-confirming the position
of the 'North' in the national discourse on the British regions even
while providing evidence of its non-conformity to the stereotypes
of that discourse. Rather than changing the mythology, the old
notions were amended according to the above dichotomous

model with the addition of 'depression' and 'unemployment' to the left (North) side of the equation and 'recovery', 'growth', and 'employment' to the right (South) side of the table of oppositions in the preceding section.

Only *The Times* refrained from using the terms in the database sample for 1986 and 1987. Mostly, debate on the topic of the 'Divide' appeared in the *Guardian*, followed by the *Financial Times* and the newer colour tabloid paper *Today*. Notions of the country reverting to the 'Two Nations' of Dickens's *Hard Times* – a rich 'South' and a poor 'North' – provided a calculated political (spatial-) myth for the opposition parties and was most debated in the progressively-oriented press such as the *Guardian* and the liberal *The Independent*. The conservative-oriented press (*The Times, Daily Telegraph*) suppressed the phrase, while the business press, *The Economist* and *Financial Times* equivocated between using the phrase evocatively and debunking it as a product of imagination and over-exaggeration. The official government response was both to deny that it existed while proposing solutions (*Financial Times* 21 January 1987). Mr Peter Walker, the Energy Secretary, argued that the government would act to prevent Britain becoming 'a divided nation' (*Financial Times* 27 January 1987:3; *Guardian* 27 January 1987:1). Mr Nicholas Ridley MP was appointed as unofficial Minister for the North and promised the setting up of Development Corporations for areas with the highest unemployment. The opposition argued that it was Mr Ridley's fault to begin with:

He has created the most dangerous confrontation between the prosperous South and the impoverished North ever perpetrated in my time in political life. It cannot be right that the knights of the shires with all their southern prosperity should gain at the expense of those of us from the Midlands and the North.

(*The Times* 10 December 1986:4)

The political value of this rhetoric was underlined by the Conservative government's release of figures designed to dispel the myth (see *The Independent* 18 December 1986:5). Mrs Thatcher denounced the cliché saying, 'I don't think there is anything like the North–South Divide that some people like to think . . . ' (cited in *The Times* 12 December 1986:2). But, it proved more robust than a slogan which might be dispelled with a few facts (*Observer* 6

September 1987:19). The government argued that 'there has not been a substantial widening of the economic gap between North and South under Mrs Margaret Thatcher' (cited in *Financial Times* 6 December 1986:9).

The limit of the political value of this rhetoric was reached when Northerners began to object to the one-sided portrayal of the North as a 'wasteland'. As the *Guardian* argued, even in the middle of the fray, in January 1986:

> The British media have recently wallowed in the North–South Divide. Excessively so. Most television commercials are shown – and presumably sell – without change, even of accent, nationwide. More than in other big western countries, the capital's newspapers are seen as the national press. In few other countries can a would-be politician from outside so easily win local acceptance.
>
> (*Guardian* 16 January 1986)

A later series of articles in 1987 was greeted with one letter to the editor which complained, 'We hear enough of the North–South divide. Your article did nothing to dispel this myth or emphasise the positive regeneration now taking place in our town . . .' (*Guardian* 2 March 1988:12).

Since this time, the geographer Doreen Massey has also noted the increased importance of the 'North–South Divide' in the political vocabulary and that 'some elements are being re-worked' (1988:12). While she does not reach a firm conclusion, her comments suggest that this is taking place as a result of a London middle-class 'colonisation' of first the South and more recently the North (although she really means the Midlands) as part of an pattern of avoiding 'blighted areas' and of status declaration by selecting genteel, rural environments redolent of social privilege. Their strength in the labour market has led to the supplementing of wage differentials (such as the 'London allowance') by differentials in housing costs as they compete to live in desirably 'rural' areas. These differentials have contributed to a reorganisation of inequality along geographical lines. The 'South' (whose exact location or extent is never specified) is a 'commuterland' which has been colonised by middle-class migrants, seeking to distance themselves from poverty and dereliction, and

seeking out the image of a gentrified existence in this
manicured, supposedly-rural setting, amid all the imagery of a
socially-settled village past in a landscape of church spires and
cricket pitches which has so often been held up to typify
'England'. Thus they establish their claim to have 'arrived'.

(Massey 1988:13)

This coincides with the thesis of a discourse of status distinction by
spatial division advanced above. Government spokesmen, treating
areas as if they were subjects in their own right, just as seen above,
use this genteel, yet entrepreneurial and individualistic, representation of the south in polemical condemnations of the north which
is portrayed as a labour-voting, unionised and Luddite Land of the
Working Class. 'If only other areas could act like this [i.e. like the
South] they too could have jobs' (Massey 1988:13). But this image
is not borne out by the voting patterns of the 1987 elections (see
Savage 1987).

The image of the north seems to have been reworked a bit of
late. There is less mention of the satanic mills. More the talk
(in the south) of how *wonderful* the countryside is, and the
quality of life . . . and of how low house prices are. . . . it is an
extension northwards of the search for rurality . . . it is not
about economic development at all. Commuterland is
spreading. . . . Much of the current reconstruction of the
image of the north is about turning some of its more rural
areas into overspill dormitories for people whose jobs remain
in the south.

(Massey 1988:17)

The industrial areas of the North are excluded from this migration, being defined as problem areas: 'inner cities', suffering from
industrial decline or 'planning blight', in need of a cure.

The movement North thus coincides with a change of emphasis
between the various images of the North seen earlier which
amounts to a re-configuration of the myths of both the South and
of the North. This takes place both in terms of discourse such as
the political polemics of the 'North–South Divide' and of practices
such as the 'search for rurality' and policies (the use of representations of a prosperous South as a model for Northern reconstruction).

Massey, who has done much work on this 'regional question' (1978), does not comment on the international factors affecting such a 'geographical division of inequality'. She is not helped in fending off a critique based on this omission, as advanced by Läpple (1985), by her topical resort to such notions as the 'North–South Divide' which, as noted above, carries with it a set of 'problem definitions' and images (ranging from Dickensian to pastoral). These suggest an unexamined definition of two historically static 'regions' as entities which are more or less coherent in terms of social relations, and imply a sub-national level of analysis suited to a sub-national problem (see Massey 1978:106). Analysis which begins laden with such preconceptions – or should it not be *predispositions* – produces results strictly in accordance with the *dispositif*, the spatialisation, implied. In containing commonsensical definitions of the problem and thus implying solutions, such a spatialisation forms both the cradle and the coffin of any such study.

This has been shown to be a common problem in the discussions of social and geographical inequality by the print media. In our 'What the Papers Say' review we can see the rise and fall of the popularity of the rhetoric of a 'North–South Divide' as a mnemonic device which captures reader's attention and explains unemployment figures by reminding them of a piece of old common-sense wisdom. It served to resurrect the scandal of the nineteenth-century working conditions in the minds of voters and was exploited by the left in political debates, something which contributed to its popularity. It provides an example of the same genre of 'yarns' or group 'story-telling' that was evidenced in *Coronation Street*. The emotive rhetoric became so powerful as to 'run away with the debate' requiring later, corrective commentaries. This provides further support for the argument advanced in the first chapter that spatialisation is of central importance and is a 'causative' factor which has specifiable impacts on conceptual thinking and, over time, on economic development. On the one hand, it functions as a culture-specific 'conceptual shorthand' allowing diverse differences to be assembled under the banner of a 'North–South Divide'. On the other hand, it has the effect of skewing the debate towards the connotative elements of historical narratives on the 'North–South Divide' like the nineteenth-century literature on the North and South.

CONCLUSION

This diverse review shows the persistence of a space-myth of the British North over time which emerges in a consistent form across different debates and in different narratives. This mythological North includes geographical areas as far south as the Midlands. It persists even in a relatively compact, clearly bounded and apparently homogeneous, island country. It subsumes in one set of myths the contradictory images of the pastoral myth of the land of tradition, the myth of the nineteenth-century industrial blight, and the myth of the 'Land of the Working Class'. All of these are marshalled to form a foil for the myths and images built up around London and the South as the cultural, spiritual and political heartland of the nation. This repeats the thematics of the Canadian 'True North Strong and Free' but with the important difference that the mythology of the British North has been appropriated and re-worked in indigenous narratives, which have made this mythical 'North' into their own regional identity, and have cherished the images first propounded in the literature of (southern-based) writers in the nineteenth century. This is aided by the fact that the myths were not simple fictions but related in a complex manner with tangible conditions. In many cases, the images accentuated those conditions; in others, the images became self-fulfilling prophecies which were incorporated into the logic of concrete arrangements of space (e.g. architecture and urban plans) over time. The myth of the British North is much more than a simple space-myth, for it is also the myth of the Land of the Working Class, and indeed stands in as a symbol of the common unity of the British 'folk'. The myth of the British North is an important element of a social spatialisation and cultural discourses which locate the British industrial working class both spatially and hierarchically *vis-à-vis* the spaces and positions of other classes and groups: in particular, to London, the centre of authority and finance, and to the pastoral South of the gentry.

NOTES

1. This is the oldest motorway service station, which is actually at Watford Gap, a fair distance from Watford itself, on the North London Orbital road which has passed into cliché. See, as an example of a journalistic

245

account, Byron Rogers, 1986. 'What a Relief! It's Watford Gap' in the *Observer Magazine*, p.24.

2. The signs appear on the M25 London orbital motorway near East Grinstead, for example. The use of the slogan 'The North' implies almost some homogeneous entity or place, rather than a heterogeneous space. I am indebted to Marie Brisson for pointing out that there are no signs saying 'The West' in Canada, for as it is simply a relative space (one can ask the question how far West?) it is meaningless as a destination. Rather it is a direction, instead of going to 'The West' one goes 'Out West' to a specific place or region, for example Calgary or Alberta.

3. See also Nicholls and Armstrong 1976:130. In their study, *Workers Divided* they found foremen in a northern 'Chemco' plant 'given to use any of the terms "the North", "the working class", or "the past" as a shorthand for the others [the workers].'

4. This study is not intended to present a comprehensive survey of contemporary British cinema, but rather a contemporary case which serves as background material for the following section on the 'North–South Divide' rhetoric in the national press during the 1980s. See Chapter Five for a defence of this 'case-history' method.

5. Higson's analysis (1984) of this point is very perceptive. On the one hand the films are clearly fictional and employ similar narrative techniques as those of the classic realist films of the Hollywood studios. The visible is taken to be a revelation of the truth. 'The real is not articulated, it is'. In a 'suspension of disbelief', attention is shifted from the production of representations of reality, to the content which is presented. On the other hand there is also a claim for a surface realism, 'an iconography which authentically reproduces the visual and aural surfaces of the "British way of life"'. This, however, involves the fetishisation of certain details which become icons, and as such, a spectacle of the real, rather than incorporated into the narrative (Higson 1984:4). In conjunction with a claim to moral realism, for film critics in the 1960s, this separated the British 'quality film' from Hollywood dramas when used. That is, there was a moral commitment to a social formation and the dignity of the working man. However, Higson points out that this truth to ordinary life involves a 'construction of the social in terms of "universal human values"', or bourgeois family and emotional norms which are imposed on the working-class characters. 'A concern for personal relations and human values invests the landscape with a greater sense of moral urgency and a more compelling sense of human sympathy, while the real historical landscape, local and concrete, legitimates and authenticates this moral universe' (Higson 1984:4–5) which is focused on the figure in the landscape (see Figure 5.4). Visual beauty is thus problematic given this 'sociological' rhetoric of social responsibility and factual accuracy as moral truth. It can only be resolved by making the ordinary strange, poetic.

6. These include the view from the bus stop outside Joe Lampton's

lodgings in *Room at the Top*, the view from the parapet outside Notting-ham Castle in the Sunday morning section of *Saturday Night, Sunday Morning*, the view from the hilltop park in *A Kind of Loving*, the view from the kitchen window of the flat rented by Jo's mother in *A Taste of Honey*, and the view from above the quarry where Colin and his friends go in *The Loneliness of the Long Distance Runner*.

7. At around this time, Raymond Williams was writing his book *The Country and the City*, and it is not surprising to find this distinction figures highly in the narrative design of all of these films. The cities are seen as peopled by 'masses', faceless crowds, and these films take the upward class mobility of the working-class male youth (which is articulated as sexual mobility and generational differences from their parents' values) and their attempts to create a more individuated identity as their main social theme. Higson argues that the protag-onists of these movies are metaphorically imprisoned in the mass society of the squalid city and long for the individualistic freedom they see in the open countryside:' . . . the landscapes do not so much refer to real places outside the text as produce meaning at the level of representation, in terms of a system of differences: urban/rural, imprisonment/escape, the mass/the individual, social structure/ bohemian fantasy, deferral of pleasure/wish fulfillment, the everyday/ romance' (Higson 1984:11). The countryside becomes a signifier of pleasure and gratification.

8. This argument could be further developed by referring to the Lacan-ian thesis of an essentially violent 'phallic gaze' (see Jardine 1985).

9. More recently it has been suggested to me that *EastEnders*, a soap opera set in the working-class areas of London's docklands, could be contrasted with *Coronation Street* to isolate the specifically Northern elements of the latter.

10. *Coronation Street* is the most popular English language television series. It is shown in fourteen countries and still regularly breaks audience rating records after twenty-five years and has produced record sales to foreign networks and distributors for its producers, Granada Tele-vision.

11. For example, beginning in June 1963 there are a number of such incidents: Dennis's wedding night (May 1968); Brian to work in Qatar (January 1982); Brian decides not to go back because of 'heart strings' attachments (July 1982).

12. For example, Ena terrorises college selection board (August 1970).

13. For example, selling drink after hours (November 1964); trading without a licence (June 1966); raid on betting house (February 1967); police disciplinary review of Cyril Turpin who saves Betty (May 1970); Renee reported for Sunday trading (June 1976); TV detector vans (February 1976).

14. Beginning for example in April 1966 and continuing, for example: hospital self-discharge by Ena (May 1966); hospitalisation ultimatum for Stan Ogden (July 1969); hospital for trip accident (October 1969).

15. Beginning in September 1966 with a food poisoning incident; then

when, for example, health inspectors fumigate Dan and Hilda's for mice (April 1973).

16. For example: demolition rumours (March 1961); demolition of Ena's, the Mission, and Raincoat factory (January 1968); slum clearance programme (March 1968); threat to rename street (May 1962); rents raised (March 1963); eviction/bailiffs (April 1963); with respect to Len from November 1966 on; allocation of a maisonette to Ken Barlow (June 1968); Ena's sit-in protest against demolition of the Pensioners' Club-room to make way for a car park (April 1969); lack of support for demonstration against building the Warehouse (March 1971); work at the community centre/warehouse (April 1971); lack of planning permission (May 1972); social security benefit stopped; woman at 19 Inkerman St (December 1972); demolition plans for the street by the 'London Development Co.' (January 1974); Minnie's pension might have been reduced but Albert breaks off his engagement (February 1974); council withdraw offer of employment to Stan and Hilda because of their record with the Health Dept (August 1974); rate payers association formed (May 1975); rent withheld in protest (August 1975); Stan forced to change house number back to 13 by council (February 1977); and Fred Gee asked to leave the Centre because he is rude to the public (November 1981).

17. For example, May 1968 and again, Hilda a bad credit risk (May 1982).

18. For example: first in September 1961; later, a 'naive' vicar believes 'Street's materialistic values outweigh its spiritual ones' (March 1969); another vicar refuses to baptise Tracey for Deirdre (April 1977).

19. Statistics in *Regional Trends* shows that there are fewer cars per capita in the North but the trend is towards greater regional equality in cars and, indeed, in all consumer durables. Porsche UK noted in their 1986 annual report that they sold 47 per cent of their cars in their Northern sales regions (cited in *Sunday Times* 11 January 1987:25).

20. Research for this section was carried out by means of a computer-based content-analysis on the British 'serious press'. The following table summarises the number of articles and letters in the sample concerning British regional issues in which the phrase 'North–South Divide' was used from January 1984 to June 1987.

Newspaper	June 84–June 85	June 85–June 86	June 86–June 87
The Economist	0	0	4
Guardian	0	8	29
Daily Telegraph	1	0	7
The Times	3	0	7
Financial Times	7	8	15
Totals	11	16	62

21. Table of frequency of mentions of 'North–South Divide' rhetoric between 1984 and mid 1987:

Table of frequency

Newspaper	Date: page(s)	Notes
Yorkshire Post	1 Dec. 86: 3	
Observer	24 Mar. 85: 2	
British Business	14 Feb. 86: 20–21	
Daily Telegraph	22 Feb. 85: 1 EEC	
	28 Aug. 86	
	13 Dec. 86: 2	
	14 Jan. 87	
	26 Jan. 87: 20	Prof. P. Minford: 'The main reason for the disparity between growth rates and unemployment levels in the north and south of Britain is the shift in demand away from traditional manufacturing (sited predominantly in the north) towards the services...'
	20 Feb. 87: 4	Health divide
	24 Mar. 87	
	13 Apr. 87	
Guardian	25 Sep. 85	
	11 Feb. 86	
	15 Feb. 86	
	22 Feb. 86	
	24 Mar. 86: 5	
	11 Apr. 86: 21	Liverpool
	3 May 86	Football and the N/S divide
	30 May 86	
	27 Sep. 86	Great Divide . . . living in the N/S
	8 Oct. 86	
	13 Dec. 86: 2	
	2 Jan. 87	Energy Sec. warning of N/S divide
	8 Jan. 87	The other Thatcher nation
	8 Jan. 87	Starker N/S divide job figs
	10 Jan. 87	Kinnock warning
	15 Jan. 87	Frontiers: forces that divide a nation: N/S gap
	15 Jan. 87	Development grants delayed
	16 Jan. 87	N/S gap may swallow Tories
	21 Jan. 87:3	N/S divide in TV
	21 Jan. 87	Thatcher rejects N/S divide
	23 Jan. 87	Liverpool bishops
	24 Jan. 87	Church and N/S divide (Grassroots)
	29 Jan. 87	Two nations gap widens
	3 Feb. 87: 1, 26	Runcie vs. Lord Young
	13 Feb. 87: 4	
	24 Feb. 87	N/S divide house prices
	25 Feb. 87: 17	House prices
	26 Feb. 87	Chambers of Commerce reject N/S divide
	6 Mar. 87	
	10 Mar. 87	New approach to regions
	13 Mar. 87	

(cont'd)

Table of frequency

Newspaper	Date: page(s)	Notes
	14 Mar. 87	House prices
	24 Mar. 87	
	25 Mar. 87: 17	Quality of Life Survey
	28 Mar. 87	Etonians all agog at the other England
	7 Apr. 87	North refutes recovery claim
	6 May 87	
Financial Weekly	11 Dec. 86: 20–27	
	14 Dec. 86	
	26 Mar. 87: 41	
Financial Times	11 Jan. 84: 13–18	
	12 Jan. 84: 6	
	25 Jan. 84: 6	
	8 Mar. 84: 31–34	Warrington and Runcorn
	21 Mar. 84: 15–19	Merseyside survey
	28 Apr. 84: 4	Regional labour disparities
	28 Apr. 84: 21–24	Lancashire survey
	5 Nov. 84:1, 32	Regional Development survey EEC
	22 Feb. 85:6	
	14 Mar. 85	
	17 Apr. 85: 9	
	17 Jul. 85	
	7 Feb. 86: 14	Problems of NW and NE
	21 Feb. 86	
	17 Mar. 86	
	31 Jul. 86	Exodus: *Regional Trends* 21
	19 Nov. 86	Political market: N/S divide
	2 Jan. 87	
	8 Jan. 87	South better-off in jobs
	9 Jan. 87	Minister's response on job divide
	15 Jan. 87	Letters to editor
	15 Jan. 87	Grant delay
	19 Jan. 87: 4	Dept of Employment figures
	20 Jan. 87	SE gaining jobs disproportionately
	21 Jan. 87: 10	K. Clarke denies N/S divide
	28 Jan. 87: 8	Heseltine comments
	29 Jan. 87	*Social Trends* report
	3 Feb. 87: 4	Runcie vs. Lord Young
	31 Mar. 87: 14	A number of divisions exist within British society which have probably increased since 1979 . . . the most serious of these exist in the minds of the British people. The prime example . . . is the north–south divide regarding wealth and job prospects. While divisions do undeniably exist, and have worsened as unemployment totals have risen . . . they are not as simple as often portrayed. Pockets of poverty exist in areas of the south while some in the north prosper.

(cont'd.)

Table of frequency

Newspaper	Date: page(s)	Notes
		... After-tax earnings for the lowest decile of earners ... grew by 2.9% in real terms between April 79 and 86, while for the highest decile they grew by 21%.
The Times	7 Apr. 87 10 Jul. 87	

PART THREE

Chapter Six

SYNTHESIS AND IMPLICATIONS

The case-histories reveal a common set of spatial themes and practices across four localities that diverge in their histories, cultures, and geographical sizes and locations. They demonstrate the empirical unity of what was theorised as social spatialisation – a social construction of the spatial and its imposition and enactment in the real topography of the world. It would be possible to multiply the examples that support this argument, but the cases presented here are sufficient to establish the point as a basis on which further research will proceed. I have attempted to show that social spatialisation, which was introduced as a 'ungraspable' and ineffable cultural formation, can be rendered visible and specified not just through theory but across various empirical case-histories.

The reader will recall that after a synthetic review of elements of the work of Lefebvre, Bourdieu and Foucault, an anthropologically consistent terminology of 'images', 'myths', and 'mythologies' was introduced. Drawing on their work, which although dissimilar, converged on the cultural importance of spatial concepts and their linked practices, the spatial was theorised as a social construct. Anthropological work on liminality, carnival, and the social construction of community provided a number of 'bridges' by which belief (about places and spatiality) has been correlated with ritual and spatial practice. Incorporating belief, theory, and action, this *dispositif,* always in flux yet forming a coherent whole, was termed social spatialisation.

As a cultural formation, spatialisation has been explored through the framework of place- and space-images. The case-histories have attempted to expose the articulation of space-images and myths with each other such that they derive their

255

meaning from their relative difference. This formation was portrayed as a 'constellation' of myths and images. Even when the
characteristics of a place change so radically that one would expect
a change in the place-myth, this does not always take place. The
explanation for this has been argued to be that changes necessitate
not just an adjustment of the myth, 'cleaning out' the inappropriate images and installing new ones, but a restructuring of the
entire mythology and the development of new metaphors by which
ideology is presented. Changing the relative position of one place-
myth *vis-à-vis* other place-myths affects all of their meanings.
Hence the conservative robustness of place-images. As 'guiding
metaphors' these were argued to provide a set of rules of conduct
and procedure – for practices of space and regimes of thought.

SYNTHESIS

Each case leaves its own legacy. A short reprise and synthesis will
set the stage for new departures. In the case of Brighton, the dirty
weekend reputation of the town presents a curious 'packaging', a
carnivalesque recoding of an older, liminal place-myth. The 'dirty
weekend' can be made intelligible when seen as an anomalous set
of core images in the place-myth of Brighton's status as a 'free-
zone' for social innovation on the levels of norms and practices.
The dirty weekend was once a practice within a specific institutional conjuncture which survived beyond the reform of those
institutions to become an myth anchoring the town's carnivalesque reputation. It is a manifest example of the independence of
myth from economic and institutional bases. Because the myth
survives it helps maintain the tourism reputation of the town. Built
on the substratum of Brighthelmstone, the quiet fishing village
within reach of London, Brighton was, as much as anything,
discursively invented by the late-eighteenth-century scandal sheets
even while it was elaborated as a practice, as the 'centre of the
system of pleasure' by the Prince Regent and his circle. But as a
geographic and liminal margin, Brighton also presents a historical
progression from the beach as a 'free zone' through a liminal
space administered by medical ritual into a dispersed site of
carnival. The re-territorialisation of the beach from the 'working
beach' of Brighthelmstone's fishing economy through the liminal
zone of Cures and medical ritual, to a site of the carnivalesque, the

grotesque body, and anti-authoritarian rituals of resistance reflect changes in the wider social spatialisation wherein people were 'placed' with respect to power or came together for leisure on the margins of the British state. The Brighton case-history demonstrated the discursive power of the 'labelling' of places which translated into real impacts in the form of the attraction of great crowds and the development of the town as a seaside resort.

In the case-history of Niagara Falls, competing images disseminated by opposed local interests have produced an equivocal place-myth which has contained opposed 'core images' since the early nineteenth century when industrialisation began to compete with the Falls' status as a tourism destination. Tension between Niagara's liminal, pilgrimage status as a 'Shrine of Nature' and the exploitation of the raw power of Niagara led to disappointed expectations and a sentimentalisation of tourists' experience. In its status as a Shrine, as a kind of existential anchor or *axis mundus* it has suffered a progressive loss of aura coming to be more and more dominated by a kitsch aesthetic which parodies the moralising tone of Niagara's boosters and a carnival environment of 'attractions' which contrast with the 'parkified' area maintained by the Niagara Parks Commission bureaucracy and the industrial areas that begin a few blocks from the Falls. Niagara was commodified as a promotional image. The collision of images, myths, and spatialisations of the Falls is further heightened by the collapse of Niagara as a destination for honeymoon *rites de passage* into the blue-collar North American 'Event Honeymoon'. This contrasts strongly with the bus-loads of Japanese 'Honeymoon Tourists' for whom Niagara Falls is touted as condensing elements of 'Grand Nature' (moving water, rock, trees, sky) on a par with the Rocky Mountains.

The contemporary tension between Niagara Falls' spatialisation as part of Japanese high culture and North American low culture illustrates the conflicts that arise when the contemporary, over-dimensionally extended, spatialisations and cultures collide. The coincidence of the Falls, a Disneylandesque Carnival, sexual innuendo and grave Love Canal pollution from its industrial past, makes Niagara a condensation of the North American condition. As such it also presents a neat summary of those elements of contemporary culture which are usually dubbed 'postmodern'. However, at Niagara, they go back more than a hundred years. The

trouble staking out a clear identity which would be attractive to
tourists derives from Niagara's equivocal status and lack of differentiation of its place-myth from other mytho-poetic positions
within at least two social spatialisations - that of the dominant
cultures of North America and Japan.

In what emerges as characteristic for Western spatial cultures,
the Central Canadians' 'True North Strong and Free' mythology
forms part of an oppositional spatialisation which (unlike the
Japanese, above, who include 'Grand Nature' within the aesthetic
of high culture) insists upon distinguishing 'civilisation' by separating it as different from wild 'nature'. As an important source of
metaphors and images, the 'True North' has been taken up in a
nationalistic discourse from even before the time of Confederation. The 'True North' has been suggested as the ideal form or
'affect' (in the sense of the emotion associated with a concept) of
the concept of a Canadian nation. The 'True North' space-myth
functions as a unifying 'national myth' because it provides the
groundwork for a nationalistic and anti-continentalist discourse. It
suggests that Canadians are both united by the patrimony of the
North and derive some hidden part of their subjective identity
from it. It thereby identifies Canadians and forms part of a cultural
survival strategy played out on a metaphysical level against the
continentalism of American culture industries – even if (especially
southern urban) Canadians and Americans share the same material culture, their mental cultures are thus said to be different. The
'True North' is a core space-myth in a spatialisation which helps to
assemble cognitively regions, peoples (indigenous natives, immigrants and colonials) and topography, 'placing' them in the
unitary geo-institutional framework of the nation-state in which
specific relationships between them are, if not preordained, then
implied by this cultural formation.

Implicated with this is another set of tensions and guilty
ambitions toward the 'internal colony' of the northern territories.
The North, posited as the 'motor of Canadian history' by some
central Canadian intellectuals, resolves this 'guilty conscience' by
obscuring processes of exploitation driven by southern commercial ambitions. It removes people and politics from the centre
stage of responsibility for forming their own history. A previously
unanalysed northern 'geographic determinism' was found at the
heart of the work of the founders of Canadian political economy

(Innis), Canadian literary criticism (Frye), and Canadian history (Creighton). Not as a geographic determinism, but as the 'national illusion', this spatialisation is one of the key explanatory elements in understanding Canadian development policies toward the North and also in explaining the individual's ambivalence toward the North as more than its hinterland/pure white wilderness image.

The various discourses on the theme of a 'True North' have been long neglected partly because, while strongly represented in the discursive arenas of political rhetoric and newspaper editorials, it appears less baldly in the realm of everyday practice and individual pursuits. In the case material, however, the 'True North' emerges as an internalised groundwork for recreational arrangements and masculine-gendered wilderness rituals of revitalisation. To use an architectural metaphor, the 'True North Strong and Free' is first and foremost this sort of 'formwork' within which the 'concrete' of daily practices and habits is cast. Once established, the formwork is removed to expose the cast concrete walls, floors and thresholds of this metaphoric structure of everyday life. So too, the 'True North' is not consciously articulated but is an a priori 'formwork' which informs both individual and institutional practices.

Like the 'True North Strong and Free', the British debate over 'The North–South Divide' and unequal regional divisions presents a tendency to attribute causal power to space itself, again demonstrating the process of fetishisation and hypostatisation central to the common-sense vision of the spatial common across Western social spatialisations. The 'North' appears as a foil for the centre and hub of the culture in London. Spatialisation is exemplified as a causative cultural formation, a concrete abstract, *more* than a 'contingent effect' or contentless abstraction to be ignored but less than a causal force. The spatial must be treated as a concrete abstraction – the transposition of concepts and belief onto the canvas of real divisions, movements and physical constructions. The North–South opposition of Northern 'Land of the Working Class' to Southern 'High Culture' was paired with the Natural–Civilised opposition noted in the case of the Canadian North. This has been perpetuated over the years despite the industrialised state of much of what falls under the spell of the imaginary map of 'the North'.

The 'North–South Divide' mythology reveals a spatial encoding
of a set of non-spatial myths about the British folk and about
traditional culture which amount to a set of shared narratives of
national origin which reinforce a sense of 'unity in diversity' at the
same time as propounding a nostalgia for the past, for a state of
childhood innocence and, in its extreme, a contracted spatialisation (as observed in *Coronation Street*).

THEMES OF DISTINCTION-BY-DIVISION AND COMMUNITY IDENTITY

The method used here and the focus on the spatial has not
flattened out issues and problematics but has revealed both new
detail and new linkages. Chaotic collisions of, for example, the
beach-front carnival of rowdy Mods and Rockers with the more
'traditional' seaside Bank Holiday activities have been shown to be
consistent conjunctures of the positioning of Brighton-the-
carnivalesque within the overall division of the ludic and rational
in the British spatialisation (Chapter Two). The objective has not
been to displace problematics such as class or gender but to show
how a *spatial problematic* might transcode other processes to reveal
the intersection of, for example, class coalitions and place-myths in
the case of Niagara Falls (Chapter Three) without presupposing
that such a process operates everywhere else.

As a whole, the case-histories suggest the paradigmatic tension
of divisions between the rational and the erotic, of what is
considered 'civilised' and what is considered 'uncivilised'. This
opposition takes the following form:

Rational	–	Ludic
Civilised	–	Nature
Centre	–	Periphery
Social Order	–	Carnivalesque
Mundane	–	Liminal

The case-histories reveal the distinction of civility from barbarity
taking the form of spatial divisions which embody and illustrate
the opposition of these two mytho-poetic positions. Within the
formation of spatialisations both imply the presence of their opposite. A geographic division both metaphorically expresses social
divisions as well as making the difference tangible. Not only are

places recognised by their relative difference from each other, but also spatial metaphors and spatialised contrasts are used to differentiate a wide range of social phenomena. The case-histories of spaces (Chapters Four and Five) support the original hypothesis that imaginary divisions became causative sources of further divisions because they are institutionalised or rendered as a natural division. In this process of misrecognition, the geographic distinction becomes a new origin for further distinctions, and more importantly economic divisions and social segregations. Spatialisation thus plays an important role in social causality and should be incorporated into social science discussions of cause and effect. Social spatialisation is a 'concrete abstraction' rather than being merely 'contingent' as argued by Sayer (1985), but it is not 'causal' as suggested in the dialectical position of Lefebvre (1974) and Soja (1980). Images and myths were found to have a complex, historically-changing relationship with empirical facts and practices. In some cases images preserved past practices, in other cases they followed changing 'realities' strictly. Rather than a strictly dialectical swing of causalities between 'society' on the one hand and 'the spatial' on the other, in. the case-histories thesis and antithesis (e.g. ancient spatial arrangements which defied contemporary trends and material influences) coexisted in a tension which defied the label 'synthesis'. Spatialisations thus have a degree of 'robustness', despite internal schisms and margins of opposition, which allow them to be treated as social facts. They have empirical impacts by being enacted – becoming the prejudices of people making decisions.

Across all four case-histories, spatial divisions of the liminal, natural, or the ludic from the rational and civilised were found. These divisions appeared both empirically as in the liminal and ludic practices of medical rituals and holiday traditions as well as in the images and myths of marginal places and spaces. A culture in which such a spatial expression of conceptual divisions is deployed offers back to its members and participants a tangible reaffirmation of these abstract oppositions in their everyday lives. As a cultural tension incorporated into territorial division and spatial practices down to the minutiae of bodily gesture and 'crowd practice', the spatialisation of such tensions becomes a form of 'embodied memory' by which bodies are tutored in the correct performance of roles and routines.

In only some cases and only for specific individuals who take up a privileged role, for example, that of 'tourist', does this division also take on the form so highly stressed by Lefebvre (1974) and in political economy in general of production and consumption as follows:

Production	–	Consumption
(work)	–	(play)
(rational)	–	(ludic)

This binary pair of production and consumption characterises the whole course of political economy where it becomes the founding and then organising dualism which is applied universally to distinguish all facets of life. In his decision to seek a primarily Marxian analysis of the spatial form, using the model of the commodity form, this separation is cast into the precepts of Lefebvre's work on 'space'. Its helpfulness is no longer clear, however, for it forces analyses of, for example, leisure activities into the strait-jacket of consumption, making it difficult to understand the *exchanges* between producers and consumers and the productive nature of ludic activities.

The second important thematic which has emerged is the tendency of space-myths to become what might be called 'yarns'. In the case-histories, myths and images function as insider stories and hence as part of symbolic constructions of community despite the polyvocality of the images at the level of individual experience. Core images consistently reappear in different accounts. Over time they change more slowly than peripheral, more idiosyncratic images, partly because they anchor entire clusters of images which are used to describe the experience of places. The knowledge of these group myths marks 'insiders' who are members of a community. In the case of the 'True North' and of the 'North–South Divide' space-myths these 'yarns' reaffirmed the national 'invisible community' concerned. The inconsistency encountered between the public myth of the Canadian 'True North' and private practices (investment in the North is not forthcoming; many individuals construe the public, nationalistic myth as the basis for periodic *rites de passage*, but ignore the North at other times) supports Cohen's (1986) thesis of the symbolic construction of community identity through myths and group stories. As a relatively-hegemonic discourse, acknowledged even in the face of evidence or personal experience to the contrary, these myths cross divisions of grid and group so emphasised in the 'mental maps' literature of geography. Such consistencies at the social level go a long way to giving a sense of order in the face of the chaos of competing, personal-level 'cognitive maps'. In some cases the myth was accepted as a basis for action, in other cases personal experience was prioritised.

This again supports the argument that a *social* level of 'imaginary geographies' surpasses the polyphony of individual differences. People transcend and suppress their own experience in order to identify with broader social groups. And, not only do people seek to identify with their own circle ('group') or their class ('grid') but also they seek to affirm community, regional, and national identities and coalitions. Spatialisation enters into and under- scores the perceived unity of social groups, communities, and nations. This has important implications and warrants more sustained consideration by the social sciences than can be given here. But having seen Foucault's rejection of the concept of 'society' or 'community' as sociological presumptions, we can now point to social and community identities that are created as the sum of an open set of individual meanings and experiences. While not necessarily consensual, they are normative and, as has been shown, have empirically specifiable effects. If people are willing to act in terms of an imaginary community, to enact and actualise such cultural identities, then we may conclude that a term such as 'society' does have a real meaning and is empirically 'real' as a causative formation. This counter-argument to Foucault's cautious rejection of social totality cannot be pursued here. But, developed, it would represent an important revision of both his method and claims.

Within the interstices of spatial identities such as 'The North' or 'The South', a host of both tensions and common elements establish a heavily-textured and detailed network of contrasting meanings within the case-histories. In the case of Brighton's 'dirty weekend' myth, older liminal and carnivalesque traditions of seaside revels were recoded in a quite different but still carnivalised format of staged adultery. These anomalies, contradictions and recodings scar any simplistic structural vision of social spatialisations. Thus, we need to move beyond a view of spatialisation which posits a set of cognitive algorithms one might resort to when, for example, choosing a vacation destination. Myths are actualised, acted out in space, as both ritual and as spatial practices such as the renascent crowd behaviour of flânerie noted in the vignette of the shopping mall (see pp. 53, 55–56). Anthropologists have long privileged ritual as a bearer of mythological symbolism. But there have been few studies of 'daily life' except in the French literature (Lefebvre, de Certeau, Maffesoli, and Bourdieu have all been cited). The tendency to seek order and consistency between thought and action leads to everyday practices and spatial routines which both coincide with people's thinking on what is deemed a 'natural' way of perceiving and proceeding and what types of behaviour and comportment are considered 'civilised'. The rituals of honeymoon travel, and of dirty weekends demonstrates also the tendency of activity to form a context for thought and discourse, as was suggested by Giddens and as argued by Bourdieu in his study of the Berber House (1971c, 1977, pp. 35–36).

Throughout, spatialisation has been characterised as a generalised process of comparative distinctions and relative differences between socially constructed mytho-poetic positions. Spatialisation spreads out to incorporate a broad variety of oppositions, becoming one 'template' or die for the conceptualisation of difference. While it may be theorised, and appears in linguistic concepts and metaphors, spatialisation is not a primarily conceptual or logical process. By arguing that it is as much internalised through the 'embodied' memory of habit, gesture, and spatial practice, the theory of social spatialisation embraces both the discursive and empirical forming the groundwork on which ideology may be elaborated. In social spatialisation, cosmology is extended to the physical sites and spaces of the world which is populated by the mind with places and inhabitants which express the *nature* of each given area. As the Greeks looked at the stars and saw constellations which outlined mythical figures on the inside surface of a dome (as opposed to near and far galaxies and stars), so people today might look at a map of the world and see similar, non-empirical, gestalt constellations of good places and bad places. *Real spaces are hypostatised into the symbolic realm of imaginary space relations.* The world is cognitively territorialised so that on the datum of physical geographic knowledge, the world is recoded as a set of spaces and places which are infinitely shaded with connotative characteristics and emotive associations.

The resulting formation – half topology, half metaphor – is inscribed as an emotive ordering or *coded geography*. It is enacted in ritual, as gesture, and encoded in further guiding metaphors which define our relationship to the world. Beyond a set of mistaken stereotypes and faulty logic as argued in the environmental perception literature, rather than being relegated to the status of the pathological, spatialisation must be seen as an essential ingredient in the process of dwelling in the world. They are exactly that mental and social 'cognitive mapping', the disruption of which Jameson (1984) identifies as the key experience of postmodernity. We may now say that he is calling for a new social spatialisation, a complex and risky undertaking and one which is not at the level of individuals but undertaken incrementally by groups. Postmodernity's iconoclasm may just be that, then, the wilful play with different elements of 'traditional' cultural formations in search of new relationships between – and thus re-valuations of – these mytho-poetic elements and positions that they may better correspond to and guide everyday life in the contemporary moment.

Having synthesised this 'plateau' of observations and conclusions, the preceding chapters and comments indicate that it is indeed a fertile plain for hypothesis and further investigation. It is now possible to look to the horizons and to note some implications which might begin to 'set the ball moving again'. Rather than conclusions then, what follows are programmatic notes which will be followed up in a subsequent volume. It would be impossible to define the full range of implications; however, three areas are clearly affected by these conclusions on social spatialisation: (1) conceptions of the human subject; (2) debates over 'agency and structure', and (3) debates over the importance of the spatial to social theory. These in fact suggest each other in a progression of questions from those concerning subjectivity (1) to the powers of that subject with respect to the 'social order' (2) and finally to questions concerning that order itself (3).

IMPLICATIONS

Bodies in space: individuum or personae?

The question of the subject continues to pose problems for the human sciences. The case-histories suggest that it is impossible to talk about the self except in relational terms such as 'here' and 'there', or 'inside' and 'beside', even when that self is, our culture assures us, whole and sufficient (for an introduction see Silverman 1983:154). The recognition of and reflection upon our 'selves' entails the loss of the supposed perfect fullness of self-absorption and sufficiency. We speak of 'standing outside' of ourselves, for example, and debate whether or not we 'see ourselves the way others see us'. This finds inevitable expression in a sense of lack, loss, and consequently, desire, as in the psychoanalytic paradigms of Lacan and Freud.

Humanism posits a spatialised view of the self as an ego which is 'inside' a self-sufficient body-container and an objective 'real world' which is 'outside'. This representation of the relationship of the self to the body and to its milieu is but one of a series of spatial divisions imposed on the person which found a later series of oppositions between the private and public realms, between the civilised and the natural, and between 'in'siders and 'out'siders. Lacan and Freud both suggest that the 'subject' is an imaginary signifier of the individual. It is a virtual image, like an image in a mirror. The mirror image provides a coherence and unity which the subject in fact does not have. This mirror image is invested-in as an identity which the subject takes as his or her own. This fantasy is part of the project of individuation and the construction of a cohesive biography which then grounds agents' voluntaristic explanations of their actions.

Foucault's rejection of the humanist subject was noted in Chapter One as an attempt to bypass ontological discourses which postulate social or psychological identities: these included classes, communities and societies as well as the subject. In the preceding section, I argued that a seminal objection to his approach may be raised on the basis that individual agents have been shown to actualise the images and myths of a *dispositif* such as social spatialisation. Despite their metaphysical nature, individuals act out the myths of self and community identity. He dismisses all such social fictions. His ontological manoeuvre is all the more outrageous because, by dismissing the general category of imaginary things, the synthetic descriptions of abstract 'social facts' around which individuals and groups organise ritual and action are transformed into meaningless babble. The advancement of critical understanding is blocked and ultimately our own self-understanding is impeded. However, Foucault's critique of voluntarism and his rejection of both the subject and social totality did allow him to redescribe the individual–society relation in terms of an open field of flows and powers. The two are brought into a new relationship rather than being cast as opposed poles as under humanism. This allows an unimpeded discussion of how and in what form practical agency takes part in shaping its own structural conditions of emergence, insertion, and functioning. In such an approach, there is no way that structures could be seen as directly caused by an agency of which they are simply the expression (i.e. voluntarism). The implication of the case-histories is that this works in the reverse direction also: the subject should not be seen as simply the expression of structures. If only because Foucault eliminates the elements on which individuation operates, this reversal is difficult for him.

Baudrillard (1982; 1983) encounters this difficulty also, arguing that subjects have arrived at the point of being mere expressions of the maelstorm of media messages in which they find themselves. Kroker and Cook (1988:26) argue: 'Under the sign of invasion, the body becomes the virtual text of particle physics.' That is, whereas classical physics elaborated a discourse on 'real' bodies based on their empirical mass; quantum physics eclipses the object-as-mass to focus on the object-as-energy. In terms of persons' bodies, they can also be treated as no longer material entities but, like atomic nucleii,

> an infinitely permeable and spatialised field whose
> boundaries are freely pierced . . . in the microphysics of
> power. Once the veil of materiality/subjectivity has been
> transgressed (and abandoned), then the body as something
> real vanishes into the spectre of hyperrealism. Now, it is the
> postmodern body as space, linked together by force fields and
> capable of being represented finally only as a fractal entity.
> The postmodern self, then, as a fractal subject – a minute
> temporal ordering midst the chaotic entropy of a
> contemporary culture.
>
> (Kroker and Cook 1988:v)

In this Nietzschean position, the self is an empty sign: colonised from within by humanistic techniques for immunity and differentiation while seduced from without by fashion and media images.

> Spread out over a topographic field, the imploded self is energized creating the movement over a power grid where *all* ontologies are merely the sites of local 'catastrophes'. Neither self nor other but, rather, a quasi object/subject picks up cultural characteristics as it shuttles from node to node. [For this body without any subjective presence,] each movement across the power field *tattoos* the body until it represents a *cartography* of the field itself.
>
> (Serres 1982 cited in Kroker and Cook 1988:26, added emphasis)

The sovereign individual of the nineteenth century appears to have been displaced and certainly the relationship between the individual and society is undergoing radical change. However, the post-structuralist position does not well explain the continuing ideology of individualism and privatism in Western culture, nor does it help understand the rituals of individuation and identi-fication with groups that have appeared throughout the case-histories. Is it possible to perceive an identity to this 'fragmented subject' which supports positive human companionship as reciprocity rather than the radical isolation which follows from the deterministic position of post-structuralists such as Foucault, Baudrillard, or Kroker? That is to say that we need to comprehend both the radical fluidity of identities in contemporary culture as well as the evident creativity of actors encountered here – Niagara honeymooners, recreational canoeists in the Canadian 'North', bathers on Brighton Beach, all those 'insiders' subscribing to nationalistic myths of identity.

What is required is at least a partial inversion of the flow of forces that Foucault describes. In this vision, which has its roots in Lefebvre's work (1981: Ch.3), the individual subject is cast as a crossroads of flows of information and internally-generated de-sires. But, as a unique node, the person retains elements of each current or flow and also struggles to redirect them as opposed to being trampled underfoot or overwhelmed by them as in Fou-cault's description. Without necessarily achieving the closure of the classic individuum, the body extends itself in its milieu – physically through the use of tools, sensorially with devices to receive information and so on – while this same body is penetrated by the environment through its pores and senses. Similarly the subject is elaborated in the environment, emotions, and memories becoming tied to and even metonymies of places and their characteristic smells and sounds. Private places such as homes and bedrooms become encrusted with souvenirs to the point of becoming an extension of the memory. The bricolage of memorabilia, being so many reminders of the self, is supporting evidence in the narration of a coherent personal biography. But this need not be a linear unified narrative but may be divided into phases and alternate identities. Rather than the individual who presents a uniform identity over time, for certain social groups this may take the form of a *persona* possessing multiple, mask-like identities (a *dramatis persona*) realised in different situations while remaining non-committal and 'cool' to any one identity. Subjectivity in the ironic mode. The 'subject' is now staged as a self-conscious spectacle of tactile surfaces and masks, rejecting attempts to stereotype and specify its identity, defying any hermeneutics of depth which attempts to locate the 'real' subject (Maffesoli 1988b). Such a persona still has allegiances at least temporarily and energy to invest in scenes where identities can be realised. It is also not just a body being acted upon, but a fractured/multiple agent which is possibly contradictory but always actualising and deforming structural codes; hence elaborating a performance supported by social rituals and exchanges which confirm different personae. One colloquial saying speaks of a person 'wearing different hats' in different situations; swapping roles, flipping between masks and groups rather than carrying out only one social function.

A great deal more could be said about this inversion which looks beyond the spatial categorisation of the subject as a unified whole. However, because agents formulate stratagems in the context of their self-images, their masks, the investigation of this subject as a system of formal representation cannot be rejected completely. Rather than adopting the metaphor of the body as a container of the subject, body and environment have been transcoded through the different spatial metaphor of a set of *fields*. Rather than focusing on the unitary, empirical body of humanism, it is necessary to go beyond merely noting the dispersion of the *individuum* to focusing on the *identity-effects* of the fragmented subject as a more abstract, probabilistic *dramatis persona,* a multiple agent. While this blurs Cartesian distinctions, it allows relationships between the subject and the 'objective' world 'outside' to be reconnected and theoretically taken into account. Rather than replacing the Cartesian, inside–outside paradigm it offers to extend the vision of the subject by re-posing the question of the subject in intra- and inter-relational terms.

Structures and agents

The 'structure–agency debate' has been alluded to in several parts of this book – the debate over the role of individual's freedoms as agents contra structuralist determinations which is by now famous. There has been a renewed emphasis on the role of creative action and individual initiative creating new social arrangements against structural determinants of action. Urry (1982) has pointed to one class of attempts to mediate between structure and agency which includes the work of Giddens, Bhaskar, Bourdieu, and Touraine. As discussed on pp. 32–33, these authors propose versions of a 'duality of structure' argument; namely, that structure is both medium and outcome of the activities whereby actors knowledgeably reproduce social life in the course of daily social encounters. They have however been criticised for advancing a weak theory of creative action which is unsatisfactorily linked to a strong theory of dominating social structures (Storper 1985). I have also argued that some of Bourdieu's formulations merely propose mediating 'structures' which defer an inevitable determination of the individual by his or her social structure.

Giddens's work has been particularly concerned with attempting to theorise structure and agency with respect to his theory of 'time-space distanciation'. Elsewhere (Shields 1986), I have argued that he does not make explicit why structure and practice should be recast in these terms. Also the debate becomes muddied when, on the one hand, he argues that 'social structures' are nothing but the contingent and fleeting effect of routinised, 'systems' of individuals' social practices; and then on the other hand, he advances a behaviourist model of subjective action (Jensen-Butler 1981). This is imported into his work through the use of Hagerstrand's chronogeography (Giddens 1984:116-117).

Structural changes resulting from human agency collapse into the results of unintended consequences of routine activity. Giddens's work has been praised as opening a route out of the dilemmas of post-structuralist social theory. However, it maintains the traditional theoretical positions of the autonomous subject confronting a constraining environment. Having 'embedded' this distinction within his theoretical arrangements, it becomes more and more difficult for him to specify the interaction and mutual self-implication of these two poles (agency and structure). Along with 'Subject and Object', 'Structure and Agency' is thus one of a series of suspicious dualisms which have been identified in previous chapters as contiguous with a dominant Western spatialisation characterised by binary divisions (civilised–natural; rational–ludic, etc.). It carries with it the inherent tendency to imply a voluntaristic view of the human subject. Against this tendency, a great deal of work then has to be put into shoring up a non-voluntarist human 'agent' and in defining exactly what the powers of that agent are. While raising questions about the character of the two pole positions, the division is rarely questioned. The 'Structure–Agency' appellation legitimises their division, *keeps them apart*, and makes their interaction a difficult topic. In effect, a no man's land between the two positions is smuggled into the argument. A basic spatial metaphor of distinction-through-division elides the necessity of the two terms to each other's existence. The argument in preceding sections has been that such a division depends on a spatial logic of division. This noted, one question-mark arising is the suggestion that the division of Structure versus Agency is not critically useful but reproduces an alienation of the two from each other. The structure–agency dichotomy reproduces the venerable bourgeois individual-versus-society trope. Structuralist thought, with its founding distinction between *langue* and *parole,* traces a similar path which ends up only with the monadic ego facing an alienated system of signification.

A different solution to this problem framed as a dilemma would again be the installation of a different spatial paradigm in which the subject was treated as a node in a field rather than 'inside' and containing body. Social structures would not exist unless they have been created, and cannot continue to exist unless they are actualised, or put into *practice.* Similarly, this actualisation takes place in large part due to the internalisation of codes and performative

271

norms on the part of agents. If anywhere, the real 'structure' or 'system' is within the position of 'agent' or 'subject'.

> The individual, even in his/her dreams, is permeated by the social; indeed, one develops individuality not against but through the social. The process of constructing the self . . . involves the hearing and assimilating of the words and discourses of others . . . all processed dialogically so that the words in a sense become half 'one's own words'.
>
> (Stam 1988:119)

But the position of 'the subject' cannot be dismissed merely because it is an imaginary representation, and is not a firm basis for theory. It shares the difficulties which characterise 'structure' in social theory but people do act on the basis of this humanistic construct. A great many structured narratives of social order and practical traditions intersect in the individual with regimes of need, desire, and values as well as judgement of risk and opportunity. These may be remembered in fragments; routinised as what I earlier called 'embodied memory', or codified as theoretical knowledge and practical directives. I agree with Giddens's (1984) suggestion that structures are not objective independent social forces and have only a 'virtual existence' – much like the mirror image of the Lacanian subject. This imaginary identity glosses over the instabilities and disjunctions within a social group. Thus, in the foregoing chapters it was argued that the knowledge of key 'yarns' which reinforce or express this identity could be the mark of a person's insider status and could strengthen their sense of belonging to a community. Bakhtin adopts a similar position in which the individual self-awareness of the subject is permanently decentered because meaning, signification and 'signs can only arise on inter-individual territory' (Bakhtin 1981:345) requiring a socially-constructed and linguistically-competent speaker and addressee. Bakhtin (1973) posits consciousness as a socio-ideological fact rather than the product of a self-generating ego because self-consciousness must always be constructed in a socially-generated semiotic medium, whether this is 'inner speech' or verbal communication with others. Stam notes:

> A self is constituted by acquiring the ambient languages and discourses of its world. The self, in this sense, is a kind of

hybrid sum of institutional and discursive practices bearing on family, class, gender, race, generation and locale. Ideological development is generated by an intense and open struggle within us for hegemony amongst the various available verbal and ideological points of view.

(Stam 1988:120)

He then cites Bakhtin, who continues 'consciousness awakens to independent ideological life precisely in the world of alien discourses surrounding it, and from which it cannot initially separate itself' (1981:345).

While the 'structure–agency debate' has served to map out the contrasts and contiguities of the two terms, ultimately the terms of the debate will have to be changed if we are to advance beyond the dilemmas of this 'chicken and egg' formulation. One interesting problem is the interaction the forces and powers that these two representations stand in for. A second problem, which we have only partially explored, is their constitution and legitimation as a duality through a 'spacing out' of their constitutive elements. This spatialisation makes it at first difficult to imagine the rapprochement between the two terms or theoretical positions suggested here despite the new spatialisation proposed above.

Therefore, I am suggesting that analysis go beyond dualisms which impose a binary split on our conception of social problematics to a relational exercise where we explore humanism's 'internal' structuration of the agent as well as the agent's relation to so-called 'external' structures (institutional codes of conduct, physical, myth and belief etc.). Social spatialisation involves the construction and legitimation of relationships between a series of elements rather than just structure and agent. To simply list these, they are:

1. Between Subjects and Bodies to form an imaginary unified 'self' maintained by repression. To draw a metaphor from computing, spatialisation provides a process which 'boots' the subject, forming a coherent subjectivity upon which culture may be inscribed and on which ideology operates.
2. Between Subjects and other Subjects as a basic form of sociability.
3. Between Subjects and Social Institutions maintained partly by representations of the spatial.

273

4. Between Subjects and Groups in the sense of the relations between the individuum and totality.
5. Between Subjects and the World, or 'reality' through a discourse on possibility, which Lefebvre called the 'space of representation'.

Modernity was marked by a dialectic in which the individual had to find a place within mass societies which has previously been characterised primarily by competing classes: As Baudelaire put it,

> For the perfect *flâneur*, for the passionate spectator, it is an immense joy to set up house in the heart of the multitude, amid the ebb and flow of movement, in the midst of the fugitive and the infinite. *To be away from home and yet to feel oneself everywhere at home; to see the world, to be at the centre of the world, and yet to remain hidden from the world.*
>
> (Baudelaire 1964:9)

There is a similar loss of identity – a simultaneous centrality and marginality – in the postmodern moment. But by contrast, the secure identity of the individual in the postmodernity is less clear. The individual is less a sovereign *individuum* and more a collection of masks, images, or *personae* under which it can no longer be taken for granted that a simple actor exists. In one case we find the individual revelling in the loss of their self in the modern crowd of others; in the other, the individual plays with the possibility of submergence in the crowd of *themselves*. This in part involves a new spatialisation of the individual from being simply a body which 'contains' an ego or 'I' to a body which 'supports' multiple 'guises' (Maffesoli 1988b).

Social theory and the domain of space

Culture is both regionalised and, as Williams (1981) has shown, is an unclear abstraction, a 'whisp of nothingness', until actualised in a particular site and situation. Therefore, the spatial – both as sites and as social visions of the world – is a crucial ingredient to any study of culture and social action. Space forms a '*regime of articulation*' of cultural patterns which contrast with temporal '*regimes of succession'*. These two merge together in the spatial fields and combinatories, and in the temporalised nodes, categories and positions of social spatialisation. Harvey has argued that the development of capitalism is impossible without a knowledge of its geography (1982). A more subtle importance is pointed to here: the discursive role of the spatial has been shown to provide a basis for classification and, metaphorically, a groundwork and conceptual vocabulary in which social divisions and separations may be articulated. By restricting the possible social futures to those that can be imagined and represented, the 'conceptual toolkit' of spatialisation takes a part in the formation of the social imaginary. An understanding of the discursive role of spatialisation is therefore relevant to understanding not only current institutional arangements but also their potential direction of elaboration and change. In the theory of social spatialisation, this cultural aspect has been linked to the non-discursive, material, and institutional realities of geographical space so stressed by Harvey and by political economists. Both of these faces are indissolubly linked as a culturally and historically specific *dispositif* or disposition of institutionalised roles and social strategies, and legitimised practices and concepts.

Far from being a 'blurring' of analytical distinctions between the spheres of the 'base' and 'superstructure', the synthetic approach propounded in this book has been shown to reveal contingencies, local arrangements, and causative factors which are generally overlooked in the analytical theories which form the doxa of contemporary social science. The case-histories link the material and the abstracted, cultural aspects of practices to show the concrete nature of even the most arcane cultural rituals and beliefs. Against giving an a priori privilege to economic 'determination in the last instance' what has been proposed here is a *juxtastructure* of mutual, reciprocal determinations worked out on the terrain of local contingencies and historically embedded arrangements. Given that it is difficult at any time to separate empirically economic and ideological elements in any given case, political action, or social process, the base-superstructure dualism is not very meaningful and is especially problematic in studies of social representation and myth.

275

ALTERNATIVE GEOGRAPHIES OF MODERNITY: THE POSTMODERN OUTLOOK

The focus on 'marginal' spaces and places pursued in this book has been tactical. Rather than a voyeuristic tour guide of anomalies and limina, the four cases have provided critical insights into the conditions of the economic and cultural centres to which they are respectively linked. To be 'on the margin' has implied exclusion from 'the centre'. But social, political, and economic relations which bind peripheries to centres, keep them together in a series of binary relationships, rather than allowing complete disconnection. In this way, 'margins' become signifiers of everything 'centres' deny or repress; margins as 'the Other', become the condition of possibility of all social and cultural entities. In these 'centres', self-centered and entrenched groups inflate their opinions to ostensively universal proportions, glossing over the differences between centre and periphery, with the help of thought-constraints and banishment into exile if necessary (Bauman 1988: 25–26).

Contemporary Western society has continued to discover itself, its conditions of possibility and that which has been denied in the construction of a Western cultural identity. These are found in the 'otherness' of marginal groups and places, tourist rituals of liminality, the revival of 'lost', marginal works of art and the gentrification of run-down, marginal urban areas. Commercial films, documentary and otherwise, has probed this lure of the marginal (as in the older case of British realist cinema).[1] 'Marginality' is a *central* theme in Western culture and thought. Authors such as Jameson, who includes a feeling of being on a periphery amongst his seven features of postmodernity (1984), and De Certeau go even further to argue:

> Marginality is today no longer limited to minority groups, but is rather massive and pervasive; this cultural activity of the nonproducers of culture, an activity that is unsigned, unreadable, and unsymbolized, remains the only one possible for all those who nevertheless buy and pay for the showy products through which a productivist economy articulates itself. Marginality is becoming universal. A marginal group has become the silent majority.
>
> (De Certeau 1984:xvii)

'Marginality', in the words of George Yúdice (1989: 214), is a concept that straddles modernity and postmodernity; it is a central *topos* in both the modern pluralist utopias and postmodern, radical heterotopias, following a logic of exclusionary incorporation in the former and a tactics of singularity in the latter. Modern liberal pluralism has called for the incorporation of the 'marginal' into a de-politicising framework that co-opts it. Pluralism is 'accretive' and tolerant, 'allowing' other voices into the mainstream. While pluralism proclaims a controlled polyvocality which is harmonious, this must be extended to the dissonant, conflictual heteroglossia in which each voice can be heard with its full force and no position can remain outside of the exchange of voices, no interlocutor remains unchanged (Stam 1988:131). The postmodern tactician often uses the 'marginal' to make a case for his or her own subversive potential, to revise Mannheim's notion of the intellectual who is a perpetual wanderer and universal stranger, a perpetual exile who proclaims universal foundations against local values and 'regimes of truth'. In this classic reversal, the view from the margin becomes the only determinant of universally-binding truth. Simmel's attribution of greater cognitive freedom and the apprehension of truth through the 'critical distance' of the marginal stranger (1971:143–144) has continued to ground the political claims of contemporary social thought, especially in the work of the post-structuralists (Deleuze and Guattari 1976).

Margins, then, while a position of exclusion, can also be a position of power and critique. They expose the relativity of the entrenched, universalising values of the centre, and expose the relativism of cultural identities which imply their shadow figures of every characteristic they have denied, rendered 'anomalous' or excluded. Raymond Williams commented in one of his last essays,

the supposed universals belong to a phase of history which was both creatively preceded and creatively succeeded. . . . [I]t is a characteristic of any major cultural phase that it takes its local and traceable positions as universal. This, which Modernism saw so clearly in the past which it was rejecting, remains true for itself. What is succeeding it is still uncertain and precarious, as in its own initial phases. But it can be foreseen that the period in which social strangeness and exposure isolated art as only a medium is due to end, even within the metropolis.

(Williams 1985:24)

It is from a place on the margins that one sees most clearly the relativistic, so-called postmodern features of the modern. In this sense, margins have long been 'postmodern', before the growth of the popularity of this term amongst the intellectuals of the centre. This has been seen most clearly in the case of Niagara Falls where 'popular culture' was shown to have been in a century-long exchange with all forms of high or elite culture. An alternative geography begins to emerge from the margins which challenges the self-definition of 'centres', deconstructing cultural sovereignty and remapping the universalised and homogeneous spatialisation of Western Modernity to reveal heterogeneous places, a cartography of fractures which emphasises the relations between differently valorised sites and spaces sutured together under masks of unity such as the nation-state.

NOTE

1. More recently marginal characters have become a point of fascination for Hollywood studios: rape victims (*The Accused*, 1988); the poor and deformed (*Mask*, 1987); criminals (everwhere); ethnic subcultures (*Do the Right Thing*, 1989; *My Beautiful Laundrette*, 1985); religious subcultures (*Witness*, 1984) and so on. A veritable bestiary of the Western cultural Other.

BIBLIOGRAPHIES

TIIEORETICAL WORKS

Addison, W. 1953. *English Fairs and Markets* (London: Batsford)

Agulhon, M. 1982. *The Republic in the Village* J. Lloyd, trans. (Cambridge: Cambridge University Press)

Allen, J.L. 1969. *American Images of the American Northwest 1673–1806: An Historical Geosophy* PhD. dissertation, Dept of Geography, Clark University.

Altheide, D.L. 1986. *Media Power* (Beverly Hills, Cal.: Sage)

Altman, I. and Chemers, M. 1980. *Culture and Environment* (Belmont, Cal.: Wadsworth)

American Institute of Architects' Journal 1979. 'Canadian spaces: special issue' (Dec.).

Anderson, B. 1983. *Imagined Communities* (London: Verso)

Anderson, J. and Bower, G. 1973. *Human Associative Memory* (Washington DC: Winston)

Anderson, P. 1983. 'Modernity and revolution' in *New Left Review* 144 (March–April) 96–113.

Andréesco-Miereanu, I. 1982. 'Espace et temps de la magie dans un village roumain actuel' in *Cahiers internationaux de sociologie* 73:2 (July–Dec.) 251–266.

Andrews, J. 1966. *Frontiers and Men* (London: F.W. Cheshire Ltd.)

Andrews, W. 1887. *Famous Frosts and Frost Fairs* (London)

Appleton, J. 1978a. 'The urban political context of architecture' in *Edinburgh Architecture Research* 6. 87–98.

Appleton, J. 1978b. *The Poetry of Habitat* (Hull: Landscape Research Group Dept of Geography, University of Hull) Miscellaneous Series No. 20.

Appleyard, D. 1970a. 'Styles and methods of structuring a city' in *Environment and Behaviour* 2. 100–117.

Appleyard, D. 1970b. 'Notes on urban perception and knowledge' in J.

Archea and C. Eastman, eds. *EDRA 2: Proceedings of the Second Annual Environmental Design Research Association Conference* (Strodsburg, Penn.: Dowden, Hutchinson Ross) 97–101.

Archer, M.S. 1983. 'Process without system' in *European Journal of Sociology* 24. 196–221.

Ardener, S., ed. 1983. *Women and Space* (Cambridge: Cambridge University Press)

Auchlin, P. 1978. 'Ralentir enfants! Vers un approche sémiologique de l'analyse de l'espace à travers des dessins d'enfants' in *Geographica Helvetica* 33. 67–74.

Bachelard, G. 1958. *La Poétique de l'espace* (Paris: Presses Universitaires de France) translated as *The Poetics of Space* (New York: Basic)

Bailly, A.S. 1974. 'Introduction' in *L'Espace Géographique* special issue 'Paysages et sémiologie' 2 (June) 113–151.

Bailly, A.S. 1977. *La Perception de l'espace urbain* (Paris: Centre de recherche d'urbanisme)

Bailly, A.S. 1981. 'La géographie de la perception dans le monde francophone' in *Geographica Helvetica* 36 (March).

Bailly, A.S. 1986. 'Subjective distances and spatial representations' in *Geoforum* 17:1. 81–88.

Bakhtin, M.M. 1973. *Problems of Dostoevsky's Poetics* R.W. Rotsel, trans. (London: Ardis)

Bakhtin, M.M. 1981. *The Dialogic Imagination* M. Holquist, ed. C. Emerson and M. Holquist, trans. (Austin Tex.: University of Texas Press)

Bakhtin, M.M. 1984. *Rabelais and his World* H. Iswolsky, trans. (Bloomington, Ind: Indiana University Press)

Ball, D.W. 1973. *MicroEcology: Special Situations and Intimate Space* (Indianapolis: Bobbs-Merrill)

Barnbrock, J. 1976. *Ideology and Location Theory: a critical inquiry into the work of H.J.H. Von Thunen*, Doctoral dissertation, Johns Hopkins University (Baltimore, Md.: Johns Hopkins University Press)

Barnouw, E. 1970. *The Image Empire: A History of Broadcasting in the United States from 1953* (New York: Oxford University Press)

Barrell, J. 1980. *The Dark Side of the Landscape: The Rural Poor in English Painting* (Cambridge: Cambridge University Press)

Barrett, J. 1988. 'Fields of Discourse: reconstituting a social archaeology' in *Critique of Anthropology* 7:3. 5–16.

Barthes, R. 1964. 'Eléments de sémiologie' in *Communications* 4. 91–135.

Barthes, R. 1971. 'Sémiologie et urbanisme' in *Architecture Aujourd'hui* 153. 11–13.

Barthes, R. 1972. *Mythologies* translation of *La Tour Eiffel* 1965 Paris: Delpire (London: Paladin)

Barthes, R. 1980. *La Chambre claire* (Paris: Seuil)

Baudelaire, C. 1964. 'The painter of modern life' in *The Painter of Modern Life and Other Essays* J. Mayne, trans and ed. (London: Phaidon) 1–40.

Baudrillard, J. 1968. *Le Système des objets* (Paris: Gallimard)

Baudrillard, J. 1972. *Pour une critique de l'économie politique du Signe* (Paris: Gallimard)

Baudrillard, J. 1975. *Le Miroir de la production* (Paris: Telos)

Baudrillard, J. 1976. *L'Economie politique du signe* (New York: Colophon)

Baudrillard, J. 1982. *In the Shadow of the Silent Majorities* (New York: Semiotexte)

Baudrillard, J. 1983. *The Precession of Simulacra* (New York: Semiotexte)

Bauman, Z. 1988. 'Strangers: the social construction of universality and particularity' in *Telos* 78. 1–42.

Beazley, C.R. 1949. *The Dawn of Modern Geography* Vol.2 (New York: Peter Smith)

Bel, J. 1980. *L'Espace dans la société urbaine japonaise* (Paris: Publications orientalistes de France)

Bell, D. 1972. *Cultural Contradictions of Capital* (New York: Harper-Torch)

Benedetta, M. 1936. *The Street Markets of London* (London: Miles)

Benjamin, W. 1973a. *Reflections: Essays, Aphorisms, Autobiographical Writings* E. Jephcott, trans. (New York: New Left Books)

Benjamin, W. 1973b. *Charles Baudelaire: Lyric Poet of Nineteenth Century High Capitalism* Q. Hoare, trans. (London: New Left Books)

Benjamin, W. 1975a. 'The storyteller' in *Illuminations* (London: Fontana)

Benjamin, W. 1975b. 'The work of art in the age of mechanical reproduction' in *Illuminations* (London: Fontana)

Benjamin, W. 1978. 'Passagen Werk' in *Gesammelte Schriften* Vol 5. R. Tiedemann and H. Schweppenhauser, eds (Frankfurt: Suhrkamp Verlag)

Benjamin, W. 1979. 'A small history of photography' in *One Way Street and Other Writings* (London: New Left Books)

Bennet, J. 1970. 'The difference between right and left' in *American Philosophical Quarterly* 7. 175–191.

Bense, M. 1968. 'Urbanismus und Semiotik' in *Arch+* 23–25.

Bense, M. 1969. *Einführung in die informationstheoretische Aesthetik* (Reinbek: Rowohlt)

Bense, M. 1971. *Zeichen und Design. Semiotische Aesthetik* (Baden-Baden: Adis)

Bense, M. and Walther, E., eds 1973. *Wörterbuch der Semiotik* (Köln: Kiepnheurer & Witsch)

Benveniste, G. 1966. *Problèmes de Linguistique Générale* (Paris: Gallimard)

Berce, Y.-M. 1976. *Fête et Révolte* (Paris: Hachette)

Berdolay, V. 1976. 'French possibilism as a form of neo-Kantian philosophy' in *Proceedings of the Association of American Geographers*. 176–9.

Berger, P.L. and Luckmann, T. 1967. *The Social Construction of Reality: a Treatise in the Sociology of Knowledge* (New York: Anchor)

Bergson, H. 1948. *Essai sur les donnés immédiates de la conscience* (Paris: Presses Universitaires de France)

Berlyne, D.E. 1971. *Aesthetics and Psycho-biology* (New York: Appleton-Century-Crofts)

Berman, M. 1982. *All That is Solid Melts into Air* (New York: Simon & Schuster)

Berman, M. 1983. 'The signs in the streets' in *New Left Review* 144. 114–123.

Berque, A. 1982. *Vivre l'espace au Japon* (Paris: Presses Universitaires de France)

Berrong, R.M. 1985. *Every Man for Himself. Social Order and its Dissolution in Rabelais* (Saratoga, Calif.: Anma Libri Stanford French and Italian Studies 38)

Berrong, R.M. 1986. *Rabelais and Bakhtin: Popular Culture in Gargantua and Pantagruel* (London: University of Nebraska Press).

Bezzola, G. 1982. 'A Milano, La Galleria' in *Abitare* 201 Jan–Feb.

Blanchot, M. 1968. *Les Espaces littéraires* (Paris: Mouton)

Blonsky, M. 1985. *On Signs* (London: Basil Blackwell)

Boudon, P. 1979. *Essai de Sémiologie de l'architecture* (Paris: Dunod)

Bourdieu, P. 1968. 'Structuralism and theory of sociological knowledge' in *Social Research* 35. 681–706.

Bourdieu, P. 1969. 'Intellectual field and Creative Project' in *Social Science Information* 8:2. 89–119

Bourdieu, P. 1971a. 'Reproduction culturelle et reproduction sociale' in *Social Science Information* 10:2. 45–79.

Bourdieu, P. 1971b. 'Genèse et structure du champ religieux' in *Revue Française de sociologie* 12. 295–334.

Bourdieu, P. 1971c. 'The Berber house or the world reversed' in M. Douglas, ed. *Rules and Meanings* (Harmondsworth: Penguin) 98–110.

Bourdieu, P. 1971d. 'Disposition esthétique et compétence artistique' in *Les Temps Modernes* 295 (Feb.). 1,345–1,378.

Bourdieu, P. 1972. *Esquisse d'une théorie de la pratique* (Paris: Presses Universitaires de France)

Bourdieu, P. 1974. 'The school as a conservative force: scholastic and cultural inequalities' in J. Eggleston, ed. *Contemporary Research in the Sociology of Education* (London: Tavistock)

Bourdieu, P. 1977. *Outline of a Theory of Practice* R. Nice, trans. (Cambridge: MIT Press)

Bourdieu, P. 1984. *Distinction: A Social Critique of the Judgement of Taste* (London: Routledge)

Bourdieu, P. 1985. 'The social space and the genesis of groups' in *Theory and Society* 14. 723–744.

Bourdieu, P. and Passeron, J.-C. 1977. *Reproduction in Education, Society and Culture* (London: Sage)

Bristol, M.D. 1983. 'Acting out Utopia: the politics of carnival' in *Performance* I:6. 13–28

Broadbent, G. 1981. *Signs, Symbols and Architecture* (Cambridge, Mass.: MIT Press)

Bronowski, J. 1973. *The Ascent of Man* (Boston, Mass.: Little, Brown)

Burgel, G., Burgel, G. and Dezes, M.G. 1986. 'Interview with Henri Lefebvre' E. Kofman, trans., in *Society and Space* 5:1. 27–38. Orig. published in *Villes en Parallèle* 7 special issue on 'Marxisme et géographie urbaine' (1983).

Bürger, P. 1984. *Theory of the Avant Guarde* (Minneapolis, Minn.: University of Minnesota Press)

Buroker, J.V. 1981. *Space and Incongruence: The Origin of Kant's Idealism* (Boston, Mass.: D. Reidel)

Buttimer, A. 1969. 'Social space in interdisciplinary perspective' in *Geographical Review* 59. 417–426.

Buttimer, A. 1971. *Society and Milieu in the French Geographical Tradition* (Chicago: Rand McNally)

Buttimer, A. 1974. *Values in Geography* (Washington, DC: Association of American Geographers Resource Paper 24)

Callaghan, B. 1987. 'Honeymoon Suite. Niagara Falls' in *Saturday Night* (Jan.) 154–158

Canter, D.V., ed. 1975. *Environmental Interaction* (London: Surrey University Press)

Canter, D.V. and Tagg, S.K. 1975. 'Distance estimation in cities' in *Environment and Behaviour* 7. 59–80.

Cantor, J. 1981. *The Space Between* (London: Johns Hopkins University Press)

Câpek, M. 1976. *The Impact of Physics on Philosophy* (New York: Van Nostrand, Boston Studies in the Philosophy of Science)

Carignan, D. 1984. Review of *Nordicité Canadienne* in *Canadian Journal of Political Science* 17:2. 397–398.

Carpenter, E. 1973. *Eskimo Realities* (New York: Dutton)

Carpenter, E. and McLuhan, M., eds. 1960. *Explorations in Communication* (Boston, Mass.: Beacon Press)

Cassirer, E. 1945. 'Structuralism in modern linguistics' in *Word* 1. 99–120.

Castells, M. 1976a. 'Is there an urban sociology?' in Pickvance 1976.

Castells, M. 1976b. 'Theory and ideology in urban sociology' in Pickvance 1976.

Castells, M. 1976c. 'The wild city' in *Kapitalistate* 4. 2–30.

Castells, M. 1977. *The Urban Question* (London: Edward Arnold)

Castells, M. 1983. *The City and The Grassroots* (Los Angeles: University of California Press)

Chang, Ching-Yu 1984. 'Japanese spatial conceptions' in three parts in *JA* 324, 325, 326. April, May, June, resp.

Change 1983. Special issue: 'L'Espace amérique' L. Zufosky, ed. (Paris)

Chapin, F. and Brail, R. 1969. 'Human activity systems in metropolitan United States' in *Environmental Behaviour* 1:1. 107–130.

Chomsky, N. 1968. *Language and Mind* (New York: Harcourt & Brace)

Cixous, H. and Clément, C. 1975. *La Jeune née* (Paris: 10/18)

Cixous, H. and Foucault, M. 1978. 'A propos de Marguérite Duras' in *Cahiers Renaud Barrault* 89.

Clark, K. and Holquist, M. 1984. *Mikhail Bakhtin* (Cambridge, Mass.: Belknap Press, Harvard University Press)

Clark, M. 1983. *Michel Foucault: An Annotated Bibliography. Tool Kit for a New Age* (New York: Garland Publishing)

Clark, P. 1983. *The English Alehouse: A Social History 1200–1830* (London: Longman)

Claval, P. 1975. 'Contemporary human geography in France' in *Progress in Geography* 7. 268–70.

Claval, P. 1977. *Espace et pouvoir* (Paris: Presses de la Université de Paris-Sorbonne (Paris IV))

Claval, P. 1980. 'L'évolution récente des recherches sur la perception' in *Rivista Geografica Italiana* 87 (March) 28ff.

Clifford, J. and Marcus, G.E. 1986. eds. *Writing Culture. The Poetics and Politics of Ethnography* (Chicago: University of Chicago Press)

CNRS. 1981. *Espaces vécus et civilizations* (Paris: CNRS)

Cohen, A.P. 1986. *Symbolizing Boundaries* (Manchester: Manchester University Press)

Cohen, G. 1978. *Karl Marx's Theory of History* (Oxford: Oxford University Press)

Cohn-Bendt, D. 1968. *Obsolete Communism: The Left-Wing Alternative* (London: Deutsch)

Coleman, A. 1985. *Utopia on Trial* (London: Hilary Shipman)

Collège de France. 1971. *Prospectus* (Paris: Collège de France)

Collins, C.O. and Holt Sawyer, C. 1984. 'Teaching from television: M*A*S*H as geography' in *Journal of Geography* (Nov.–Dec.). 265–268

Colombo, J.R., ed. 1974. *Colombo's Canadian Quotations* (Edmonton: Hurtig Publishers)

Communications 1977. Special issue: 'Sémiotique de l'espace' (Paris: Ecole des Hautes Etudes en Sciences Sociales)

Connell, R. 1983. *Which Way is Up? Essays on Sex, Class, and Culture* (Sydney: Allen & Unwin)

Cook, R.W. 1984. 'Imagining a North American garden' in *Canadian Literature* 103 (Winter) 32–38.

Cooke, P. ed. 1984. *Locality* (London: ESRC)

Cooper, B. 1981. *Michel Foucault: An Introduction to the Study of his Thought* (Toronto: Edwin Mellen)

Cooper, G. 1961. *Festivals of Europe* (London: Percival Marshall)

Cosgrove, D. 1982. *Social Formation and Symbolic Landscape* (London: Croom Helm)

Cousin, J. 1980. *L'Espace vivant* (Paris: Ed. du Moniteur)

Cousins, M. and Hussain, A. 1984. *Michel Foucault* (London: Macmillan)

Cox, K. and Golledge, R., eds 1969. *Behavioural Problems in Geography Northwestern Studies in Geography* 17. (Evanston, Ill.: Northwestern University Press)

Craik, K.H. 1970. 'Environmental psychology' in *New Directions in Psychology* Vol. 4 (New York: Holt) 1–121.

Crewes, F. 1986. 'In the big house of theory' in *The New York Review* 33:9 (May 29) 36–42.

Cunningham, H. 1980. *Leisure in the Industrial Revolution* (London: Croom Helm)

Darke, R. and Darke, J. 1981. 'Towards a sociology of the built environment' in *Architectural Psychology Newsletter* 11:1,2. 8–16.

Davis, M. 1985. 'Urban renaissance and the spirit of postmodernism' in *New Left Review* 151, May–June. 106–114.

Davis, S.G. 1985. 'Popular uses of public space in Philadelphia, 1800–1850' in V. Mosco and J. Wasko, eds, *The Critical Communications Review Vol. 3*: 'Popular culture and media events' (Washington, DC: Ablex)

Dayan, D., Katz, E., and Kerns, P. 1984. 'Armchair pilgrimages' mimeo. Paper presented at the annual conference of the American Sociological Association, San Antonio, Tex.

Dear, M. and Scott, A., eds 1981. *Urbanization and Urban Planning in Capitalist Society* (New York: Methuen)

Debord, G. 1972. *La Société du spectacle* (Paris: Minuit) translated 1973 as Society of Spectacle (London: Black and Red Books)

De Certeau, M. 1968. *La Vie quotidienne* (Paris: Mouton) translated 1984 as *Daily Life* (Cambridge Mass.: MIT Press)

De Certeau, M. 1984. *The Practice of Everyday Life* S.F.Rendall, trans. (Berkeley: University of California Press)

De Certeau, M. 1985. 'Practices of space' in Blonsky 1985. 122–145.

Deleuze, G. 1970. 'Un nouvel archiviste' in *Critique* 274 (March) 195–209

Deleuze, G. 1986. 'Le nouveau cartographe' in *Foucault* (Paris: Minuit)

Deleuze, G. and Guattari, F. 1976. *The Anti-Oedipus* (Paris: Minuit)

Denis, M. 1975. *Représentations imagées et activité de mémorisation* (Paris: CNRS)

Derrida, J. 1974. *Of Grammatology* G.C. Spivak, trans. Orig. published as *De la grammatologie* (Baltimore, Md.: Johns Hopkins University Press)

Derrida, J. 1975. *Introduction to Husserl's 'The Origins of Geometry'* (London: Oxford University Press)

Derrida, J. 1980. *La Carte postale* (Paris: Flammarion)

Descombes, V. 1980. *Modern French Philosophy* (Cambridge: Cambridge University Press)

Dilthey, W. 1900. 'Die Entstehung der Hermeneutik' in *Gesammelte Schriften* 1921–1958. Vol. 5. (Leipzig: Teubner)

DiMaggio, P. 1979. 'Review essay: on Pierre Bourdieu' in *American Journal of Sociology* 84. 1,460–1,474.

Disher, M.W. 1950. *The Pleasures of London* (London: Hale)

Douglas, M. ed. 1973. *Natural Symbols: Explorations in Cosmology* (Harmondsworth: Penguin)

Douglas, M. 1978. *Purity and Danger: An Analysis of Concepts of Pollution and Taboo* 2nd edn (London: Routledge & Kegan Paul)

Douglas, M., ed. 1982. *Essays in the Sociology of Perception* (London: Routledge & Kegan Paul)

Downs, R. 1970a. 'The cognitive structure of an urban shopping centre' in *Environment and Behaviour* 2. 13–39.

Downs, R. 1970b. 'Geographic space perception: past approaches and future prospects' in *Progress in Geography* 2. 65–108.

Downs, R. and Stea, D., eds 1973. *Image and Environment* (Chicago: Aldine)

Downs, R. and Stea, D. 1977. *Maps in Minds: Reflections on Cognitive Mapping* (New York: Harper & Row)

Dreyfus, H.L. and Rabinow, P. 1982. *Michel Foucault: Beyond Structuralism and Hermeneutics* (Chicago: University of Chicago Press)

Duncan, S.S. 1985. 'What is locality?' University of Sussex Working Papers in Urban and Regional Studies (Brighton: University of Sussex)

Durkheim, E. and Mauss, M. 1963. *Primitive Classification* (Chicago: University of Chicago Press)

Dwyer, K. 1977. 'The dialogic of anthropology' in *Dialectical Anthropology* 2. 143–151.

Dymza, W. 1972. *Multinational Business Strategy* (New York: McGraw-Hill)

Dyos, H.J. and Wolf, M. 1973. *The Victorian City* (London: Routledge & Kegan Paul)

Eagleton, T. 1983. *Literary Theory: An Introduction* (Minneapolis, Minn.: University of Minnesota Press)

Eco, U. 1968. *La Struttura Assente Introduzione alla Ricerca Semiologica* 3rd edn (Milan: Bombiani)

Eco, U. 1977. 'A photograph' reprinted in *Faith in Fakes* (London: Secker & Warburg). 213–217.

Eco, U. 1985. *Truths and Transgression* (New York: Harper)

Eco, U., Ivanov, V.V. and Rector, M. 1984. *Carnival* (New York: Mouton)

Edel, M. 1977. 'Rent theory and working class strategy: Marx, George and the urban crisis' in *Review of Radical Political Economy* 9.

Edel, M. 1981. 'Capitalism, accumulation and the explanation of urban phenomena' in Dear and Scott 1981.

Edel, M. 1982. 'Home ownership and working class unity' in *International Journal of Urban and Regional Research* 6. 201–221.

Einstein, A. 1961. *Relativity: the special and general theory* R. Lawson, trans. Orig. published 1916 (New York: Crown)

Ellis, A. 1956. *The Penny Universities: A History of the Coffee-Houses* (London: Secker & Warburg)

Ericksen, E.G. 1980. *The Territorial Experience* (Austin, Tex.: University of Texas Press)

Eyles, J. 1985. *Senses of Place* (Warrington, Cheshire: Silverbrook Press)

Faccani, R. and Eco, U., eds 1969. *I Sistemi di Segni e la Struturalismo Sovietico* (Milan: Bompiani)

Finquelievich, S. 1981. 'Urban social movements and the production of urban space' in *Acta Sociologica* 24: 4. 239–249.

Fiske, J. 1986. *Television Culture* (London: Macmillan)

Forster, H., ed. 1983. *The Anti-Aesthetic: Essays on Postmodern Culture* (San Francisco: The Bay Press)

Forster, K. 1981. 'Residues of a dream world' in *AD* 51:6/7.

Foucault, M. 1964. 'Langage de l'espace' in *Critique* 203 (April). 378–382.

Foucault, M. 1970a. 'History discourse and discontinuity' in *Salmagundi* 20 (Summer–Fall) 225–248. A.M. Nazarro, trans. of 'Réponse à un question' in *Esprit* 371 (May 1968) 850–874.

Foucault, M. 1970b. *The Order of Things* (New York: Random House)

Foucault, M. 1972. *The Archaeology of Knowledge* A.M. Sheridan Smith, trans. of *Archéologie du savoir* 1969 (New York: Colophon)

Foucault, M. 1973a. *Discipline and Punish* (London: Allen Lane)

Foucault, M., ed. 1973b. *Moi, Pierre Rivière, ayant égorgé ma mère, ma soeur et mon frère... Un cas de parricide dans le dix-neuvième siècle* (Paris: Gallimard)

Foucault, M. 1975. *The Birth of the Clinic: An Archaeology of Medical Perception* A.M. Sheridan Smith, trans. of *Naissance de la clinique* (New York: Vintage/Random House)

Foucault, M. 1977. 'Entretien: Le jeu de Michel Foucault' in *Ornicar* 10. 63-64.

Foucault, M. 1979. *History of Sexuality Vol. 1 An Introduction* (London: Allen Lane)

Foucault, M. 1980a. 'Questions on geography' in *Power/Knowledge* (New York: Pantheon) 63–77.

Foucault, M. 1980b. 'Two lectures' in *Power/Knowledge* (New York: Pantheon) 78–108.

Foucault, M. 1982. 'Space, knowledge and power' in *Skyline* (March) reprinted in P. Rabinow, ed. 1984. *The Foucault Reader* (New York: Random House) 239–256.

Frampton, K. 1982. *Modern Architecture and the Critical Present* (New York: AD Profiles)

Frampton, K. 1983. 'Critical regionalism: towards an architecture of resistance' in Forster 1983.

Francaviglia, R.V. 1970. *The Mormon Landscape: Existence Creation and Perception of a Unique Image in the American West* PhD, University of Oregon.

Frank, M.E. 1971. 'The use and abuse of psychology in history' in *Daedalus* 100. 187–213.

Fraser, R. 1984. *In Search of a Past: The Manor House, Amnersfield 1933–1945* (London: Verso)

Gadamer, H.-G. 1975. *Truth and Method* (London: Sheed & Ward)

Gans, H. 1967. *The Levittowners* (New York: Pantheon)

Garnham, N. and Williams, R. 1980. 'Pierre Bourdieu and the sociology of culture: an introduction' in *Media, Culture and Society* 2. 209–223

Geertz, C. 1966. *Person, Time, and Conduct in Bali: An Essay in Cultural Analysis* (Detroit, Mich.: Yale University Southeast Asia Studies, Cultural Report Series No. 14 and The Cellar Book Shop)

Geertz, C. 1973. *The Interpretation of Cultures* (New York: Basic)

Geertz, C. 1983. *Local Knowledge* (New York: Basic)

Geist, J.F. 1983. *Arcades* J.O Newman and J.H. Smith, trans. (Cambridge, Mass.: MIT Press)

Gibson, F.J. 1970. 'The development of perception as an adaptive process' in *American Scientist* 58. 98–107.

Giddens, A. 1976. *New Rules of Sociological Method: A Positive Critique of Interpretative Sociologies* (London: Hutchinson)

Giddens, A. 1979. *Central Problems in Social Theory: Action, Structure and Contradiction in Social Analysis* (London: Macmillan)

Giddens, A. 1984. *The Constitution of Society* (London: Harper)

Giedion, S. 1941. *Space Time and Architecture* (Cambridge, Mass.: MIT Press)

Gilbert, A. 1986. 'L'Analyse de contenu des discourse sur l'espace: une méthode' in *Canadian Geographer* 30:1 (Spring) 13–25.

Gill, A.M. 1982. *Residents' Images of Northern Canadian Resourse*

Communities PhD, University of Manitoba.

Goffman, E. 1963. *Behaviour in Public Places* (Glencoe, Ill.: Free Press)

Goffman, E. 1973. *The Presentation of Self in Everyday Life* (Woodstock, NY: Overlook Press)

Gold, J.R. 1984. 'Behavioural geography in Western Europe. Reflections on research in Great Britain and the francophone nations. 25–31. in T.F. Saarinen, D. Seamon, and J.L. Sell, eds, 1984. *Environmental Perception and Behaviour: an inventory and prospect* (Chicago: University of Chicago Press). 25–31.

Golledge, R.G. and Zannaras, G. 1973. 'Cognitive approaches to the analysis of human spatial behaviour' in Ittleson 1973.

Golledge, R.G., Briggs, R., and Demko, D. 1969. 'The configuration of distances in intra-urban space' in *Proceedings of the Association of American Geographers* 1. 60–66.

Gorz, A. 1982. *Farewell to the Working Class* M. Sonenscher, trans. (London: Pluto)

Gottdiener, M. 1985. *The Social Production of Urban Space* (Austin, Tex.: University of Texas Press)

Gottdiener, M. 1986. 'Recapturing the centre: a semiotic analysis of the shopping mall' in M. Gottdiener and A.-Ph. Lagopoulos, eds. *The City and the Sign* (New York: Columbia University Press). 288-302.

Gould, J. 1975. *People in Information Space: The Mental Maps and Information Surfaces of Sweden* (Lund: Royal University of Lund, Dept of Geography)

Gould, J. and White, R. 1974. *Mental Maps* (Harmondsworth: Penguin)

Goux, J.J. 1973. *Economie et symbolique* (Paris: Seuil)

Grant, G. 1969. *Technology and Empire* (Toronto: House of Anansi).

Gregory, D. 1978a. 'The discourse of the past: phenomenology, structuralism and historical geography' in *Journal of Historical Geography* 4:2. 161–173.

Gregory, D. 1978b. *Ideology, Science, and Human Geography* (London: Hutchinson)

Gregory, D. 1981. 'Human agency and human geography' in *Transactions of the Institute of British Geographers* (New Series) 6 (March) 1–18.

Gregory, D. and Urry, J., eds. 1985. *Social Relations and Spatial Structures* (London: Macmillan)

Greimas, A.J. 1976. *Sémiotique et sciences sociales* (Paris: Seuil)

Guelke, L. 1978. 'Geography and logical positivism' in D.T. Herbert and R.J. Johnston, eds *Geography and the Urban Environment. Progress in research and applications* Vol. 1 (New York: Wiley) 35–61.

Guerin, J.P. and Gumuchian, H. 1977. 'Les mythologies de la montagne: étude comparée de deux textes publicitaires (application de la methode AAAD75)' in *Revue de Géographie Alpine* 65. 385–402.

Habermas, J. 1983. 'Modernity, an incomplete project' in Forster 1983.

Habermas, J. 1984. 'Les Néo-Conservateurs americains et allemands contre la culture' in *Les Temps Modernes* winter. 1111–1137

Hall, E.T. 1966. *The Hidden Dimension* (Chicago: University of Chicago Press)

Hall, S. forthcoming. *Thatcherism and Other Essays* (London: New Left Books)

Hanson, N.R. 1958. Patterns of Discovery: An Inquiry into the Conceptual Foundations of Science (Cambridge: Cambridge University Press)

Harbison, R. 1977. *Eccentric Spaces* (New York: Avon)

Harris, M. 1973. *The Dilly Boys: Male Prostitution in Piccadilly* (London: Croom Helm)

Harrison, F. 1982. *Strange Land: The Countryside: Myth and Reality* (London: Sidgewick & Jackson)

Harrison, R.T. and Livingston, D.N. 1982. 'Understanding in geography: structuring the subjective' in D.T. Herbert and R. J. Johnston, eds, *Geography and the Urban Environment* Vol.5 (Chichester: John Wiley). 1–39.

Harvey, D. 1973. *Social Justice and the City* (Baltimore, Md.: Johns Hopkins University Press)

Harvey, D. 1975. 'The geography of capitalist accumulation: a reconstruction of Marxian theory' in *Antipode* 7. 9–21.

Harvey, D. 1982. *The Limits to Capital* (Chicago: University of Chicago Press)

Hay, A.M. 1979. 'Positivism in human geography: response to critics' in R.J. Johnston and D.T. Herbert, eds, *Geography and the Urban Environment. Progress in Research and Applications* Vol. 1 (New York: Wiley) 1–26.

Heathcote, R. 1965. *Back of Bourke: A Study of Land Approval and Settlement in Semi-Arid Australia* (Melbourne: University Press)

Hechter, M. 1975. *Internal Colonialism* (London: Routledge & Kegan Paul)

Heidegger, M. 1959. *An Introduction to Metaphysics* R. Mannheim, trans. (Hartford, Conn.: Yale University Press)

Heidegger, M. 1962. *Being and Time* J. Macquarrie and E. Robinson, trans. Orig. published 1927. (New York: Harper & Row)

Heidegger, M. 1968a. 'Building dwelling thinking' in *Basic Writings of Martin Heidegger* A. Hofstadter, trans. Orig. published as 'Bauen, Wohnen, Denken' in *Vörtrage und Aufsätze 1934–1954* (New York: Academic Press) 323–339.

Heidegger, M. 1968b. *What is Called Thinking* J. Glenn Grey, trans. (New York: Harper & Row)

Hern, A. 1967. *The Seaside Holiday: The History of the English Seaside Resort* (London: Cresset Press)

Higgonnet, A., Higgonnet, M.L., and Higgonnet, P. 1984. 'Façades: Walter Benjamin's Paris' in *Critical Inquiry* 10:3, March pp.1ff.

Hill, C. 1972. *The Trinidad Carnival* (Austin, Tex.: University of Texas Press)

Hindess, B. and Hirst, P. 1977. *Modes of Production and Social Formation* (London: Macmillan)

Hirst, P.Q. 1976. 'Althusser and the theory of ideology' in *Economy and Society* 5. 385–412.

Hodgins, B.W. and Hobbs, M. 1985. *Nastawgan: The Canadian North by Canoe and Snowshoe* (Toronto: Betelgeuse)

House, J.W., ed. 1982. *The UK Space* (London: Weidenfeld & Nicolson)

Howard, A. 1964. *Endless Cavalcade: A Diary of British Festivals and Customs* (London: Arthur Barker)

Howkins, A. 1981. 'The taming of Whitsun: the changing face of a nineteenth century rural holiday' in E. Yeo and S. Yeo, eds, *Popular Culture and Class Conflict* (Brighton: Harvester)

Huizinga, J. 1924. *The Waning of the Middle Ages* (London: Edward Arnold)

Hull, C.L. 1943. *Principles of Behaviour* (New York: Appleton-Century-Crofts)

Hull, C.L. 1951. *Essentials of Behaviour* (New York: Appleton-Century-Crofts)

Hull, C.L. 1952. *A Behaviour System* (New Haven, Conn.: Yale University Press)

Husserl, E. 1907. *The Idea of Phenomenology* W.P. Alston and G. Nakhnikian, trans. 1973 (The Hague: Martinus Nijhoff)

Husserl, E. 1970. *The Crisis of European Science and Transcendental Phenomenology* (Evanston, Ill.: Northwestern University Press)

Inhelder, B.A. and Piaget, J. 1964. The Early Growth of Logic in the Child (London: Routledge)

Innis, H.A. 1950. *Empire and Communications* (Toronto: University of Toronto Press)

Institut Quebecoise de Recherches sur Culture. 1983. *Architectures: La Culture dans l'espace, questions de culture, 4* (Quebec City: Editions Lemeac)

Isard, W. 1956. *Location, The Space-Economy* (Cambridge, Mass.: MIT Press)

Iser, W. 1978. *The Act of Reading: A Theory of Aesthetic Response* (London: Routledge & Kegan Paul)

Ittelson, W.H., ed. 1973. *Environment and Cognition* (New York: Seminar Press)

Jackson, J.B. and Zube, E.H. eds 1970. *Landscapes* (Boston, Mass.:

University of Massachusetts Press)

Jackson, P. 1981. 'Phenomenology and social geography' in *Area* 13:4. 299–305

Jackson, P.J. and Smith, S.J. 1984. *Exploring Social Geography* (London: George Allen & Unwin)

Jacobs, J. 1961. *The Death and Life of the Great American Cities* (New York: Random House)

Jameson, F. 1983. *The Prison-House of Language: A Critical Account of Structuralism and Russian Formalism* (Princeton, Mass.: Princeton University Press)

Jameson, F. 1984. 'Postmodernism, or the cultural logic of late capitalism' in *New Left Review* 146. 53–92.

Jardine, A. 1985. *Gynesis* (Cambridge, Mass.: Harvard University Press)

Jauss, H.R. 1982. *Toward an Aesthetic of Reception* T. Bakhti, trans. (Minneapolis, Minn.: University of Minnesota Press)

Jaynes, J. 1976. *The Origin of Consciousness in the Breakdown of the BiCameral Mind* (Boston, Mass.: Houghton Mifflin)

Jenkins, R. 1982. 'Pierre Bourdieu and the reproduction of determinism' in *Sociology* 16. 270–281.

Jensen-Butler, C. 1981. *Behavioural Geography: An Epistemological Analysis of Cognitive Mapping and Hagerstrand's Time-Space Model* (London: Institute of British Geographers)

Johns, E. 1965. *British Townscapes* (London: Arnold)

Johns, E. 1969. 'Symmetry and asymmetry in the urban scene' in *Area* 1:2. 48–56.

Johnston, R.J. 1979. *Geography and Geographers: Anglo-American Human Geography since 1945* (London: Edward Arnold)

Kant, I. 1922. *Kant: Gesammelte Schriften* (Berlin: Suhrkamp Verlag)

Kant, I. 1952. *Critique of Judgement* J.C. Meredith, trans. (Oxford: Clarendon)

Kant, I. 1953. *Prolegomena to any Future Metaphysic* G.R. Lucas, trans. (Manchester: University of Manchester Press)

Kant, I. 1965. *Critique of Pure Reason* N.K. Smith, trans. (New York: Macmillan and St Martin's Press)

Kant, I. 1968. 'Concerning the ultimate foundations of the differentiation of regions in space' (inaugural lecture) in *Selected Pre-Critical Writings*, G.H.R. Parkinson, selector; G.B. Kerferd and D.E. Walford, trans.; G.R. Lucas, contributor (Manchester: University of Manchester Press) xii–xvii.

Karabel, J. and Halsey, A.H. 1977. 'Education research: a review and interpretation' in J. Karabel and A.H. Halsey, eds, *Power and Ideology in Education* (New York: Oxford University Press). 1–85.

Keat, R. and Urry, J. 1982. *Social Theory as Science* 2nd edn (London: Routledge & Kegan Paul)

Keifer, G.R. 1970. *Zur Semiotisierung der Umwelt. Eine exemplarische Ertürung der sekundären Architektur* PhD dissertation, University of Stuttgart.

Kennet, J. 1973. 'The sociology of Pierre Bourdieu' in *Education Review* 25. 237–249.

Kern, S. 1983. *The Culture of Time and Space* (London: Weidenfeld & Nicolson)

Kesten, J. 1959. *Dichter im Cafe* (Wein: K. Desch)

King, A. 1983. 'Culture and the political economy of building form' in *Habitat* Fall. 7:5–6. 237–248.

Kirby, A. 1982. *The Politics of Location* (London: Methuen)

Knox, P. 1982. 'The social production of the built environment' in *Ekistics* 295. 291–297.

Kockelmans, J.J., ed. 1967. *Phenomenology: The Philosophy of Edmund Husserl and its Interpretation* (New York: Anchor-Doubleday)

König, R. 1973. *The Restless Image. A Sociology of Fashion* R. Bradley, trans. (London: George Allen & Unwin)

Koffka, K. 1935. *Principles of Gestalt Psychology* (New York: Kegan Paul, Tench, Trubner)

Kohler, W. 1947. *Gestalt Psychology* (New York: Liveright)

Kolaja, J.T. 1969. *Social System and Time and Space: Introduction to the Theory of Recurrent Behavior*

Kosslyn, S. and Pomerantz, J. 1977. 'Imagery, propositions and the form of internal representations' in *Psychology Bulletin* 78. 155–158.

Kottak, C.P. 1979. 'Rituals at McDonalds' in *Natural History* 87. 75ff.

Koyré, A. 1957. *From the Closed World to the Infinite Universe* (New York: Harper)

Krampen, M. 1979. *Meaning in the Urban Environment* (London: Pion)

Kristeva, J., 'Women's time' A. Jardine and H. Blake, trans. in *Signs* 7:1. (Autumn). 13–35.

Kroker, A. and Cook, D. 1988. *The Postmodern Scene Excremental Culture and Hyper-aesthetics* (Toronto: New World Perspectives and Macmillan)

Kuhn, T.S. 1970a. *The Structure of Scientific Revolutions* 2nd edn (Chicago: University of Chicago Press)

Kuhn, T.S. 1970b. 'Second thoughts on paradigm' in *The Essential Tension* (Chicago: University of Chicago Press)

Laclau, E. 1979. *Politics and Ideology in Marxist Theory* (London: Hutcheon)

Lakoff, G. and Johnson, M. 1979. *Metaphors We Live By* (Chicago: University of Chicago Press)

Lasch, C. 1980. *The Culture of Narcissism* (New York: Warner)

Lash, S. and Urry, J. 1986. *The End of Organized Capitalism* (London: Polity)

Latimer, D. 1984. 'Jameson and post-modernism' in *New Left Review*
148. 116–128.

Lauzen, F.E. 1982. 'Marketing the image of the last frontier' in *Alaska Journal* 12:3 (Spring) 13–19.

Lavenda, R.H. 1980. 'The festival of Progress: the globalizing world-system and the transformation of the Caracas Carnival' in *Journal of Popular Culture* 14:3. 465–475.

Lawson, H. 1986. *Reflexivity: The Post-Modern Predicament* (London: Hutchinson)

Leclaire, L. 1954. *Le Roman régionaliste dans les Isles Britanniques, 1800–1950* (Clermont-Ferrand: Editions G. de Bussac)

Lee, T.R. 1970. 'Perceived distance as a function of direction in the city' in *Environmental Behaviour* 2. 40–51.

Lefebvre, H. 1939. *La Conscience mystifiée* (Paris: Gallimard)

Lefebvre, H. 1946. *Logique formelle, logique dialectique* (Paris) reprinted 3rd edn 1982 (Paris: Editions Sociales)

Lefebvre, H. 1958. *Critique de la vie quotidienne vol. 1* (Paris: Presses Universitaires de France)

Lefebvre, H. 1961. *Fondement d'une sociologie de la quotidienneté* (Paris: L'Arche)

Lefebvre, H. 1968. *La Vie quotidienne dans le monde moderne* (Paris: Gallimard)

Lefebvre, H. 1970a. *Du rural à l'urbain* (Paris: Anthropos)

Lefebvre, H. 1970b. *La Révolution urbaine* (Paris: Gallimard)

Lefebvre, H. 1972. *La Pensée marxiste et la ville* (Paris: Casterman)

Lefebvre, H. 1974. 'La production de l'espace' in *Homme et la société* 31–32. 15–32.

Lefebvre, H. 1975. *Le Droit à la ville* (Paris: Editions Anthropos)

Lefebvre, H. 1976. 'Reflections on the politics of space' M. Enders, trans. in *Antipode* 8. 31ff.

Lefebvre, H. 1978. *De l'état* vol. 4. 'Les contradictions de l'état moderne (Paris: Union Générale d'Editions)

Lefebvre, H. 1979. 'Space: social product and use value' in J. Freiberg, ed. *Critical Sociology, European Perspectives* (New York: Irvington)

Lefebvre, H. 1981. *La Production de l'espace* 2nd edn. Orig. published 1974 (Paris: Anthropos)

Le Goff, J. and Nora, P., eds 1985. *Constructing the Past: Essays in Historical Methodology* (Cambridge: Cambridge University Press)

Leitch, V.B. 1983. *Deconstructive Criticism: An Advanced Introduction* (London: Hutchinson)

Lévi-Strauss, C. 1958. 'La notion de structure en ethnologie' in *Anthropologie Structurale* (Paris: Plon). 303–351.

Lévi-Strauss, C. 1964. *Mythologiques I: Le Cru et le cuit* (Paris: Plon)

Lévi-Strauss, C. 1966. *Du Miel aux cendres* (Paris: Plon).

Lévi-Strauss, C. 1971. *Mythologiques IV: L'Homme nu* (Paris: Plon).
Lewin, K. 1935. *A Dynamic Theory of Personality* (New York: McGraw-Hill)
Lewin, K. 1936. *Principles of Topological Psychology* (New York: McGraw-Hill)
Lewin, K. 1951. *Field Theory and Social Science* (New York: Harper)
Lewis, G.M. 1962. 'Changing emphasis in the description of the natural environment of the Great Plains area' in *Institute of British Geographers Transactions* 30.75–90.
Ley, D. 1977. 'Social geography and the taken-for-granted world' in *Transactions of the Institute of British Geographers* New Series 2:4. 498–512.
Ley, D. and Samuels, M.S., eds 1978. *Humanistic Geography: Prospects and problems* (London: Croom Helm)
Lösch, A. 1954. *The Economics of Location* (New Haven, Conn.: Yale University Press)
Lowe, D.M. 1982. *History of Bourgeois Perception* (Chicago: University of Chicago Press)
Lowenthal, D., 1961. 'Geography, experience and imagaination: towards a geographical epistemology' in *Annals of the American Association of Geographers* 51. 241–260.
Lucas, G.R. 1984. *Space, Time and Causality* (London: Oxford University Press)
Lynch, K. 1956. *The Image of the City* (Cambridge, Mass.: MIT Press)
Lynch, K. 1981. *A Theory of Good City Form* (Cambridge, Mass.: MIT Press)
Lyotard, J.-F. 1974. *Economie libidinale* (Paris: Minuit)
Lyotard, J.-F. 1976. *Discours figure* (Paris: Minuit)
Lyotard, J.-F. 1979. *La Condition postmoderne* (Paris: Minuit)
Lyotard, J.-F. 1980. *The Post-Modern Condition* G. Bennington and B. Massumi, trans. (Minneapolis, Minn.: University of Minnesota Press)
Lyotard, J.-F. 1983. 'The avant garde and the sublime' in *Art Forum* (Summer)
Lyotard, J.-F. 1984. 'Le Différend' translated 'The Différend, the Referent, and the Proper Name' in *Diacritics* special issue on Lyotard (Minneapolis, Minn.: University of Minnesota Press)
Maclaren, I.S. 1984. 'David Thompson's imaginative mapping of the Canadian Northwest' in *Ariel* 15. 89–106.
MacLulich, T.D. 1985. 'Reading the land' in *Journal of Canadian Studies* 20 (Summer). 29–44
Maffesoli, M. (1985), *L'Ombre de Dionysos. Contribution à une sociologie de l'orgie* (Paris: Gallimand)
Maffesoli, M. 1988a. 'Daily Life' University of Sussex, Sociology Faculty Seminar, Jan.
Maffesoli, M. 1988b. *Le Temps du tribus* (Paris: Gallimard)

Major-Poetzl, P. 1983. *Michel Foucault's Archaeology of Western Culture.*
Toward a New Science of History (Brighton: Harvester)
Maldonado, T. 1973. 'Objekte, Waren Bedürfnisse. Zu gegenwärtigen
Diskussion um eine marxistische Anthropologie' in *Semiologie und
Theorie der Architektur* M. Krampen, ed. Berichte über ein Seminar
an der Ecole d'Architecture, Université de Genève (mimeo)
Mandel, E. 1977. *Late Capitalism* (London: New Left Books)
Manning-Sanders, R. 1951. *Seaside England* (London: Batsford)
Marchand, B. 1978. 'A dialectical approach in geography' in
Geographical Analysis 10. 105–119.
Marcus, J.T. 1960–61. 'Time and sense of history: East and West' in
Comparative Studies in Society and History 123–39.
Marin, L. 1978. *Utopiques: jeux d'espaces* (Paris: Editions de Minuit)
Markus, T.A., ed. 1982. *Order in Space and Society: Architectural Form and
its Context in the Scottish Enlightenment* (Edinburgh: Mainstream)
Markusen, A. 1978. 'Regionalism and the capitalist state: the case of the
United States' in *Kapitalistate* 7. 39–62.
Martensson, S. 1979. *On the Formation of Biographies in Space-Time
Environments* (Lund: Royal University of Lund, Dept of Geography)
Martins, M.R. 1982. 'The theory of social space in the work of Henri
Lefebvre' in R. Forrest, J. Henderson and P. Williams, eds, *Urban
Political Economy and Social Theory* (Epping, UK: Gower) 160–185.
Massey, D. 1984. *Spatial Divisions of Labour: Social Structures and the
Geography of Production* (London: Macmillan)
Massey, D.B. and Morrison, W.I., eds 1975. *Industrial Location:
Alternative Frameworks. Proceedings of a Workshop held at the Centre for
Environmental Studies* Dec. 1974.
Mattelart, A. 1980. *Mass Media, Ideologies and the Revolutionary Movement*
M. Coad, trans. Orig. published by Anthropos, Paris 1974 (Brighton:
Harvester)
McKinley, R. 1983. 'Culture meets nature on the Six o'clock News:
American cosmology' in *Journal of Popular Culture* 17. 109–114.
Meethan, K. 1989. *Welfare Policy in Brighton* D.Phil. thesis, Unit of
Anthropology, University of Sussex, Brighton.
Meinig, D.W., ed. 1979. *The Interpretation of Ordinary Landscapes:
Geographical Essays* (New York: Oxford University Press)
Merleau-Ponty, M. 1962. *Phenomenology of Perception* C. Smith, trans.
(London: Blackwell)
Merleau-Ponty, M. 1964. *Sense and Non-sense* H.L. Dreyfus and P.A.
Dreyfus, trans. (Evanston, Ill.: Northwestern University Press)
Merrell, H. 1984. 'Writing riots: representations of the riotous body'
M.A. thesis, University of Sussex, Brighton.
Meyrowitz, J. 1985. *No Sense of Place* (London: Oxford University Press)
Millington, B. and Nelson, R. 1985. *Boys from the Black Stuff* (London:

Comedia)

Mills, W.J. 1982. 'Metaphorical vision; changes in western attitudes to the environment' in *Annals of the Association of American Geographers* 72. 237–53.

Moles, A.A. 1972. *Théorie des objets* (Paris: Editions Universitaires)

Moles, A.A. 1982. *Labyrinthes du vécu. L'Espace: matière d'actions* (Paris: Meridiens)

Moles, A.A. and Rohmer, E. 1978. *Psychologie de l'espace* (Paris: Casterman)

Moore, G.T. and Golledge, R.G., eds 1976. *Environmental Knowing* (Stroudsburg, Pa.: Dowden, Hutchinson & Ross)

Moriarty, B. 1981. 'Future research directions in American human geography' in *The Professional Geographer* 33:4. 484–88.

Morot-Sir, E. 1971. *La Pensée française d'aujourd'hui* (Paris: Presses Universitaires de France)

Morris, C. 1955. *Signs, Language and Behavior* (New York: George Braziller)

Mosco, V. and Wasko, J. eds 1985. *The Critical Communications Review Vol 3*. (Washington DC: Ablex)

Mukarovsky, J. 1970. *Kapitel aus der Aesthetik* (Frankfurt aM: Edition Suhrkamp)

Mumford, L. 1934. *Technics and Civilization* (New York: Harcourt, Brace & World)

Musson, R.W.M. 1979. *The Perception of Geographic Distance and the Philosophy of Space* PhD. dissertation, Edinburgh University.

Needham, R. 1973. *Right and Left: Essays on Dual Symbolic Classification* (Chicago: University of Chicago Press)

Nerville-Havins, P.J. 1976. *The Spas of England* (London: Hale Press)

Norberg-Shultz, C. 1965. *Intentions in Architecture* (Cambridge, Mass.: MIT Press)

Norberg-Shultz, C. 1980. *Genus Loci* (New York: Rizzoli)

Olivier, B. 1977. 'Des réponses aux questions de Michel Foucault' *Hérodote* 6. 3–39.

Olson, D.R. and Bialystok, E. 1983. *Spatial Cognition: The Structure and Development of Mental Representations of Spatial Relations* (Hillsdale, NJ: Lawrence Erlbaum Assoc.)

Olsson, G. 1974. 'The dialectics of spatial analysis' in *Antipode* 6:50–62.

O'Riordan, T. 1976. *Environmentalism* (London: Pion)

Orleans, P. 1973. 'Differential cognition of urban residents: effects of social scale on mapping' in Downs and Stea 1973

Orwell, G. 1949. *Down and Out in London and Paris* (London: Secker & Warburg)

Outhewaite, W. 1987. *New Philosophies of Social Science: Realism, Hermeneutics and Critical Theory* (London: Macmillan)

Pailhous, J. 1970. *La Représentation de l'espace urbain: l'exemple du chauffeur de taxi* (Paris: Presses Universitaires de France)

Paivio, A. 1969. 'Mental imagery in associative learning and memory' in *Psychological Review* 76. 241–263.

Pastier, J. 1977. 'An evaluation: San Francisco's Hyatt Regency Hotel as a spatial landmark' in *Journal of the American Institute of Architects* (Oct.).

Paterson, J.L. 1984. *David Harvey's Geography* (London: Croom Helm)

Peet, R. 1983. 'Introduction to the global geography of contemporary capitalism' in *Economic Geography* 59:2 (April) 105–111.

Peirce, C.S. 1960. *Collected Papers* 6 vols. C. Hartshore, P. Weiss and A.W. Burkes, eds (Cambridge, Mass.: Harvard University Press)

Perec, G. 1974. *Espèces d'espaces* (Paris: Editions Galilee, collection L'espace critique)

Perrin, C. 1977. *The Politics of Zoning* (Baltimore, Md.: Johns Hopkins University Press)

Petchevsky, R. 1981. 'NeoConservatism and the New Right' in *Marxist Feminist* (Fall).

Pickles, J. 1981. *Phenomenology, Science and Geography* (Cambridge: Cambridge University Press)

Pinxten, R., van Dooren, I. and Harvey, F. 1983. *The Anthropology of Space* (Philadelphia: University of Pennsylvania Press)

Pitt-Rivers, J.A. 1971. *The People of the Sierra* 2nd edn (Chicago: Chicago University Press)

Pocock, D.C.D., ed. 1981. *Humanistic Geography and Literature: Essays on the Experiences of Place* (London: Croom Helm)

Pocock, D.C.D. 1982. 'The view from the bridge: experience and recall of landscape' Dept of Geography, Occasional Publications (New Series) 17 (Durham: University of Durham)

Pocock, D.C.D. and Hudson, R. 1978. *Images of the Urban Environment* (London: Macmillan)

Podgorecki, A. 1975. *Practical Social Sciences* (London: Routledge & Kegan Paul)

Podgorecki, A. and Shields, R. 1985. 'Sociotechnics: a paradigm for planned social action' Carleton University, Dept of Sociology Working Papers 85–8, Ottawa.

Poggioli, R. 1969. *Theory of the Avant-Garde* (New York: Belknap/Harvard University Press)

Portoghesi, P. 1982. *Post Modernism* (New York: Rizzoli)

Portoghesi, P. 1983. *Postmodern: The Architecture of the Postindustrial Society* (New York: Rizzoli)

Postel, J. 1977. *Esprit* n.s. 1. 294–296.

Poster, M. 1975. *Existential Marxism in Postwar France* (Princeton, NJ: Princeton University Press)

Poulet, G. 1977. *Proustian Space* E. Coleman, trans. (Baltimore, Md.: Johns Hopkins University Press)

Preziosi, D. 1981. *Semiotics of the Built Environment* (Minneapolis, Minn.: University of Minnesota Press)

Prieto, L.J. 1966. *Messages et Signaux* (Paris: Presses Universitaires de France)

Prieto, L.J. 1971. 'Notes pour une sémiologie de la communication artistique' in *Werk* 4. 248–251.

Prieto, L.J. 1973. 'Signe et instrument' in *Littérature, Histoire, Linguistique. Receuil d'Etudes Offert à Bernard Gagnebin* (Paris: Editions de Minuit)

Prieto, L.J. 1975a. *Etudes de Linguistique et de sémiologie générales* (Paris: Droz)

Prieto, L.J. 1975b. *Pertinence et pratique* (Paris: Minuit)

Pritchard, A. 1984. 'West of the Great Divide' in *Canadian Literature* 102 (Autumn) 36–53.

Raleigh, J.H. 1968. 'The novel and the city: England and America in the nineteenth century' in *Victorian Studies* 52. 290–328.

Rapoport, A. 1982. 'Sacred places, sacred occasions and sacred environments' in *AD* n.9–10:75–82.

Reiss, T.J. 1982. *The Discourse of Modernism* (Ithaca, NY: Cornell University Press)

Relph, E.C. 1970. 'An inquiry into the relations between phenomenology and geography' in *Canadian Geographer/Géographe canadien* 14:3. 193–201.

Relph, E.C. 1976a. *Place and Placelessness* (London: Pion)

Relph, E.C. 1976b. 'The phenomenological foundations of geography' University of Toronto, Dept of Geography Discussion Paper.

Relph, E.C. 1977. 'Humanism, phenomenology and geography' in *Annals of the Association of American Geographers* 67:1 (March) 177–179.

Relph, E.C. 1981. *Rational Landscapes and Humanistic Geography* (London: Croom Helm)

Resnikow, L. 1968. *Erkennungtheoretische Fragen der Semiotik* (Berlin: VEB Deutscher Verlag der Wissenschaften)

Richardson, W. 1963. *Heidegger through Phenomenology to Thought* (The Hague: Mouton)

Ricoeur, P. 1973a. 'The task of hermeneutics' in *Philosophy Today* 17:2–4 (Summer) 112–128.

Ricoeur, P. 1973b. 'The hermeneutical function of distanciation' in *Philosophy Today* 17:2–4 (Summer) 129–141.

Ricoeur, P. 1977. *The Rule of Metaphor* R. Czerny, trans. (Toronto: University of Toronto Press)

Rochberg-Halton, E. 1986. *Meaning and Modernity: Social Theory in the Pragmatic Attitude* (London: University of Chicago Press)

Rorty, R. 1979. *Philosophy and the Mirror of Nature* (Princeton, NJ: Princeton University Press)

Rorty, R. 1981. 'Beyond Nietzsche and Marx' in *London Review of Books* (19 Feb.). 5–6.

Rose, G. 1978. *The Melancholy Science: An Introduction to the Thought of Theodor W. Adorno* (London: Macmillan)

Rose, G. 1985. *Dialectic of Nihilism* (Oxford: Basil Blackwell)

Rossi-Landi, F. 1968. *Il Linguaggio come Lavoro e come Mercato* (Milano: Bompiani)

Rossi-Landi, F. 1972. 'Omologia della riproduzione sociale' in *Ideologia* 16/17. 43–103.

Rossi-Landi, F. 1975. *Linguistics and Economics* (The Hague: Mouton)

Rozelle, R.M. and Baxter, J.C. 1972. 'Meaning and value in conceptualizing the city' in *Journal of the American Institute of Planners* 38. 116–122.

Rudolfsky, B. 1969. *Streets for People: A Primer for Americans* (New York: Doubleday)

Saarinen, T.F. 1976. *Environmental Planning: Perception and Behaviour* (Boston, Mass.: Houghton Mifflin)

Saarinen, T.F., Seamon, D. and Sell, J.L. 1984. *Environmental Perception and Behaviour: An Inventory and Prospect* (Chicago: University of Chicago Press)

Sack, R.D. 1980. *Conceptions of Space in Social Thought* (Minneapolis, Minn.: University of Minnesota Press)

Saïd, E. 1978. *Orientalism* (New York: Vintage)

Salter, C.L. 1971. *The Cultural Landscape* (Belmont, Cal.: Duxbury Press)

Sartre, J.P. 1960. *Critique of Dialectical Reason* (Paris: Presses Universitaires de France)

Saunders, P. 1981. *Social Theory and the Urban Question* (London: Hutchinson)

Saussure, F. de 1971. *Course in General Linguistics* Wade Baskin, trans. (London: Fontana)

Sawatsky, H.L. and Lehn, W.H. 'The cultural geography of the Arctic mirage' in *Proceedings of the Canadian Association of Geographers Annual Meeting, Vancouver 1975*. 29–36.

Sayer, A. 1985. 'The difference that space makes' in Gregory and Urry 1985. 49–66.

Sayer, A. 1987. 'Realism and space' paper presented to the 2nd Annual Conference on Realism, University of Sussex, Sept.

Schleiser, R. 1988. 'Lévi-Strauss' Mythology of the Myth' in *Telos* 77 (Fall). 143–157.

Schlesinger, P. 1978. *Putting 'Reality' Together. BBC News* (London: Constable)

Schön, D. 1983. *The Reflective Practitioner: How Professionals Think in*

Action (New York: Basic)

Schrag, C.O. 1958. 'Phenomenology, ontology and history in the philosophy of Heidegger' in J.J. Kockelmans, ed., 1967. *Phenomenology: The Philosophy of Edmund Husserl and its Interpretation* (New York: Anchor-Doubleday) 277–293.

Schutz, A. 1967. *The Phenomenology of the Social World* (Evanston, Ill.: Northwestern University Press)

Schwartz, B. 1981. *Vertical Classification* (Chicago: University of Chicago Press)

Seamon, D. 1976. 'Phenomenological investigation of literature' in Moore and Golledge 1976. 273–285.

Seamon, D. 1979. *A Geography of the Lifeworld* (New York: St Martins Press)

Serres, M. 1968. 'D'erehwon à l'antre du cyclope' in *Hermès ou la communication* (Paris: Editions de Minuit). 167–206.

Serres, P. 1972. *Hermès II: La Communication* (Paris: Editions de Minuit)

Serres, M. 1982. *Hermes: Literature, Sciences, Philosophy* (Baltimore, Md.: Johns Hopkins University Press)

Sheridan, A. 1980. *Michel Foucault: The Will to Truth* (London: Tavistock)

Shields, R. 1985. 'The importance of problem stories: reflections and expansion on Schön's analysis of problem definition' in V. Subramaniam, ed., 1986. *Problem Recognition in Public Policy and Business Management* (New Delhi: Ashish) 176–188.

Shields, R. 1986. *Towards a Theory of Social Spatialisation: Henri Lefebvre, the Question of Space and the Postmodern 'Hypothesis'* MA thesis, Dept of Sociology and Anthropology, Carleton University, Ottawa.

Shields, R. 1989. 'Social spatialisation and the built environment: the West Edmonton Mall' in *Society and Space* 7:2. 147-164.

Sidro, A. 1979. *Le Carnaval de Nice et ses fous* (Nice: Editions Serre)

Silverman, K. 1983. *The Subject of Semiotics* (New York: Oxford University Press)

Simmel, G. 1971. *On Individuality and Social Forms* (Chicago: University of Chicago Press)

Skinner, B.F. 1953. *Science and Human Behaviour* (London: Macmillan)

Smith, N. 1983. *Uneven Development* (Oxford: Basil Blackwell)

Smith, P. 1974a. 'Familiarity breeds contentment' in *The Planner*. 901–904.

Smith, P. 1974b. 'Human rights in architecture' in *The Planner*. 953–955.

Smith, P. 1977. *The Syntax of Cities* (London: Hutchinson)

Soja, E.W. 1980. 'The socio-spatial dialectic' in *Annals of the American Association of Geographers* 70:2. 207–225.

Soja, E.W. 1985. 'The spatiality of social life' in Gregory and Urry 1985.90–127.

Soja, E.W. 1987. 'The reassertion of space in social theory: the next fin de siècle' ms.

Solzhenitsyn, A. 1977. *The Gulag Archipelago* (New York: Harper & Row)

Sorokin, P.A. 1943. *Sociocultural Causality, Space, Time* (Durham, NC: Duke University Press)

Spencer, S. 1971. *Space, Time and Structure in the Modern Novel* (Chicago: Swallow)

Stallybrass, P. and White, A. 1986. *The Poetics and Politics of Transgression* (London: Methuen)

Stamm, K.R. 1985. *Newspaper Use and Community Ties* (Washington, DC: Ablex)

Stam, R. 1988. 'Mikhail Bakhtin and left cultural critique' in K.A. Kaplan, ed. *Postmodernism and its Discontents* (Minneapolis,Minn.: University of Minnesota Press) 116–145.

Stedman-Jones, G. 1971. *Outcast London* (Oxford: Clarendon)

Stedman-Jones, G. 1981. 'Class and Leisure' in A. Tomlinson ed. *Leisure and Social Control* BSA and Leisure Assoc. Joint Study Group, University of Birmingham CCCS (Brighton: Brighton Polytechnic). 162–170.

Steiner, G. 1975. *After Babel: Aspects of Language and Translation* (London: Oxford University Press)

Storper, M. 1985. 'The spatial and temporal constitution of social action: a critical reading of Giddens' in *Society and Space* 3:4. 407–424.

Strauss, A. 1968. *The American City: A Source-Book of Urban Imagery* (Chicago: Aldine)

Streatfield, D.C. and Duckworth, A.M. 1981. *Landscape in the Gardens and Literature of Eighteenth-Century England* (Los Angeles: WA Clark Memorial Library, UCLA)

Sulkunen, P. 1982. 'Society made visible – On the cultural sociology of Pierre Bourdieu' in *Acta Sociologica* 25. 103–115.

Suttles, G. 1985. 'Cumulative texture of local urban culture' in *American Journal of Sociology* 90:2. 283–304.

Tafuri, M. 1976. *Architecture and Utopia* B. Luiga La Penta, trans. (Cambridge, Mass.: MIT Press)

Tafuri, M. 1980. *Theories and History of Architecture* G. Verrecchi, trans. (New York: Granada Publishing through Harper & Row)

Tedlock, D. 1979. 'The analogical tradition and the emergence of a dialogical anthropology' in *Journal of Anthropological Research* 35. 387–400.

Teymur, N. 1980. *Environmentalism* (Edinburgh: University of Edinburgh Press)

Tolman, E.C. 1932. *Purposive Behaviour in Animals and Men* (New York: Appleton-Century-Crofts)

Tolman, E.C. 1948. 'Cognitive maps in rats and men' in *Psychological Review* 55. 189–208.

Tolman, E.C. 1952. 'A cognition-motivation model' in *Psychological Review* 59. 389–400.

Tolman, E.C. 1963. 'Principles of purposive behaviour' in S.Koch, ed. *Psychology: Study of a Science* Vol. 5. (New York: McGraw-Hill)

Touraine, A. 1971. *Post-Industrial Society* (New York: Harper)

Trowbridge, C.C. 1912. 'On fundamental methods of orientation and imaginary maps' in *Science* 38. 888–897.

Tuan, Y.-F. 1976. 'Literature, experience, environmental knowing' in Moore and Golledge 1976. 260–272.

Tuan, Y.-F. 1977. *Space and Place: The Perspective of Experience* (London: Edward Arnold)

Tunstall, J. 1983. *The Media in Britain* (London: Constable)

Turner, V. 1974. *Dramas, Fields and Metaphors* (Ithaca, NY: Cornell University Press)

Turner, V. 1979. *Process, Performance and Pilgrimage* (New Delhi: Concept)

Tymiencka, A.T. 1962. *Phenomenology and Science in Contemporary European Thought* (New York: Noonday Press)

Uexküll, J. von. 1940. 'Bedeutungslehre' in *Bios* (Leipzig) 10.

Uexküll, T. von. 1973. 'Information als Mitteilung und Formung' in *Praxis der Psychotherapie* 18. 137–150.

Urry, J. 1981. 'Localities, regions, and social class' in *International Journal of Urban and Regional Research* 5. 455–473

Urry, J. 1982. 'Duality of structure: Some critical issues' in *Theory, Culture and Society* 1:2 (Sept.). 100–106.

Van Gennep, A. 1960. *The Rites of Passage* M.B. Vizedom and G.L. Caffee, trans. (Chicago: University of Chicago Press)

Van Paassen, C. 1957. *The Classical Tradition of Geography* (Groningen: J.B. Wolters) reprinted 1976.

Veblen, T. 1963. *The Theory of the Leisure Class* (New York: Mentor)

Wachtel, E.A. 1981. *Visions of Order* PhD. thesis, Dept of History, City University of New York.

Wallerstein, I. 1974. *The Modern World System* (New York: Academic Press)

Walther, E. 1969. 'Abriss der Semiotik' in *Arch+* 2. 8.

Walther, E. 1974. *Allgemeine Zeichenlehre. Einführung in die Grundlagen der Semiotik* (Stuttgart: Deutsche Verlaganstalt)

Walvin, J. 1978. *Leisure and Society 1830–1950* (London: Longman)

Ward, C. and Hardy, D. 1986. *Goodnight Campers! The History of the Holiday Camp* (London: Mansell)

Watson, J.W. 1969. 'The role of illusion in North American geography' in *Canadian Geographer* 13:1. 10–27.

Wayne, D.E. 1984. *Penshurst: The Semiotics of Place and the Poetics of History* (London: Methuen),

BIBLIOGRAPHIES

Weber, M. 1978. *Economy and Society: An Outline of Interpretative Sociology* G. Roth and C. Wittich, eds (Los Angeles: California University Press)
Werkmeister, O.K. 1982. 'Walter Benjamin, Paul Klee, and the Angel of History' in *Oppositions* 25, (Fall).
White, H. 1978. *Tropics of Discourse* (Baltimore, Md.: Johns Hopkins University Press)
Whitney, H.A. 1984. 'Preferred locations in North America: Canadians, clues, and conjectures' in *Journal of Geography* (Sept.–Oct.). 221–225.
Williams, R.H. 1982. *Dream Worlds: Mass Consumption in Late Nineteenth-Century France* (Los Angeles: University of California Press)
Williams, R. 1973. *The Country and the City* (London: Chatto & Windus)
Williams, R. 1981. *Culture* (London: Fontana)
Williams, R. 1985. 'The metropolis and modernism' in E.Timms and D. Kelley, eds, *Unreal City. Urban Experience in Modern European Literature and Art* (Manchester: Manchester University Press). 13–24.
Williams, S.H. 1954. 'Urban aesthetics' in *Town Planning Review* 25. 95–113.
Wonders, W.C. 1962. 'Presidential address: our northward course' in *Canadian Geographer* 6:3–4. 96–105.
Wonders, W.C. 1984. 'The Canadian north: its nature and prospects' in *Journal of Geography* 83. 226–233.
Worster, D. 1977. *Nature's Economy. A History of Ecological Ideas* (London: Cambridge University Press)
Wright, J.K. 1947. 'Terrae incognitae: the place of imagination in geography' in *Annals of the American Association of Geographers* 37. 1–15.
Wrightson, K. 1981. 'Alehouse, order and reformation in rural England, 1590–1660' in E. Yeo and S. Yeo, eds, *Popular Culture and Class Conflict* (Brighton: Harvester)
Yúdice, G. 1989. 'Marginality and the ethics of survival' in A. Ross, ed. *Universal Abandon? The Politics of Postmodernism* (Minneapolis, Minn.: University of Minnesota Press)
Zevi, B. 1969. *Architecture as Space* (Princeton, NJ: Princeton University Press)

BRIGHTON AND THE 'DIRTY WEEKEND'

Aitchison, G. 1926. *Unknown Brighton* (Brighton: John Lane)
Awsiter, J. undated. *Thoughts on Brighthelmstone* pamphlet (no publisher)
Bainbridge, C. 1986. *Pavilions on the Sea* (London: Hale)
Barker, P. and Little, A. 1964. 'The Margate offenders – a survey' in *New Society* 4:96 (July) 189–192.
Becker, B. 1884. *Holiday Haunts* (London: no publisher)

304

Bennett, A. 1910. *Clayhanger* (London: Methuen)

Bennett, A. 1911. *Hilda Lessways* (London: Methuen)

Beresford, P. and Croft, S. 1985. *Extracts from Patch in Brighton* (Brighton: Lewis Cohen Urban Studies Centre)

Betjeman, J. and Gray, J.S. 1972. *Victorian and Edwardian Brighton from Old Photographs* (London: Batsford)

Brake, M. 1985. *Comparative Youth Culture* (London: Routledge & Kegan Paul)

Brent, C.E. 1979. *A Short Economic and Social History of Brighton, Lewes and the Downland Region between the Adur and the Ouse 1500-1900* (Lewes: E. Sussex County Council)

Bridgeman, H. and Drury, E. 1977. *Beside the Seaside: A Picture Postcard Album* (London: Elm Tree)

Brighthelmstone Intelligence 1784 Pamphlet (Brighton: no publisher)

Brighton and Hove Gazette and Herald 1982. 'Why do they all knock Brighton?' in *Brighton and Hove Gazette and Herald* 15 Oct. (Brighton). Earlier published as *Brighton Herald*.

Brighton Borough Council 1972. *Central Whitehawk Redevelopment versus Modernization* 2 vols (Brighton: Brighton Borough Council)

Brighton Borough Council 1978. *Brighton Central Area District Plan* (Brighton: Brighton Borough Council)

Brighton Borough Council 1980/81. *Annual Report* (Brighton: Brighton Borough Council)

Brighton Borough Council 1984. *Brighton towards 2000* (Brighton: Brighton Borough Council)

Brighton Environmental Committee 1972. *Transport and the Quality of the Environment in Brighton: Some New Assumptions and Some Practical Proposals* (Brighton: Brighton Environmental Committee)

Brighton Magazine 1874. 'Our Season' in *Brighton Magazine*. 289-290.

Brighton Polytechnic, Geographical Society 1979. *Countryside Research* (Brighton: Brighton Polytechnic)

Brighton Society 1974. *Brighton Going?* (Brighton: Brighton Society)

Brighton Society 1979. *Riding out the Storm? The West Pier* (Brighton: Brighton Society)

Brighton Tourism Committee 1937-1968. *Official Guidebook to Brighton* Yearly Pamphlet (Brighton: Brighton Council)

Brighton Transport Study Group 1979. *Feet First* (Brighton: Brighton Transport Study Group)

Brighton Voice 1981. *Brighton Voice: Index 1973-1980* (Brighton: *Brighton Voice*)

Browne, T.J. and Fielding, A.J. 1986. *Brighton and Hove Census Atlas* (Research Papers in Geography 18, University of Sussex)

Burns, D. 1975. *Social Movements and Political Action*: 6 cassettes. Cassette 5: 'Brighton Voice' (Lecture, University of Sussex)

Clare, B. and Kedward, C. 1982. *The Needs of Young People* (Brighton: Brighton Council for Voluntary Service and National Council for Voluntary Organisations)
Cloud, Y. ed. 1934. *Beside the Seaside* Review in *Times Literary Supplement.* 608.
Clunn, H.P. 1929. *Famous South Coast Resorts* (Brighton: H.P. Clunn)
Clunn, H.P. 1953. *The Capital by the Sea* (Brighton: H.P. Clunn)
Cobbett, W. 1912. *Rural Rides* 2 vols (London: Dent)
Cochran, C.B. 1945. *The Showman Looks On* (London: Dent)
Cohen, S. 1972. *Folk Devils and Moral Panics* (London: MacGibbon & Kee)
Dale, A. 1947. *Fashionable Brighton 1820–1860* (London: Country Life)
Dale, A. 1950. *History and Architecture of Brighton* (London: Bredon)
Dale, A. 1976. *Brighton Town and Brighton People* (London: Phillimore)
Dale, A. 1980. *The Theatre Royal, Brighton* (Brighton: Oriel Press)
Dickens, P. and Gilbert, P. 1979. 'The state and the housing question' Urban and Regional Studies Working Paper 13, University of Sussex.
Dinkel, J. 1983. *The Royal Pavilion, Brighton* (London: Philip Wilson)
Dudeney, H. 1928. *Brighton Beach* Review in *Times Literary Supplement* 1928:360
Eliot, T.S. 1922. *The Waste Land* (London: Faber & Faber)
English Tourist Board. Research Services Branch 1984. *Brighton Tourism Study* (London: English Tourist Board)
Erlich, V. 1980. *Russian Formalism: History-Doctrine* 4th edn (The Hague: Mouton)
Evans, J. 1821. *Recreation for the Young and Old* (Chiswick: C. Whittingham)
Evening Argus 1964. 'Beats of Arch 141' in *Evening Argus* 10 Nov. (Brighton)
Evening Argus 1986. 'The unsung attractions' and 'Leave us out . . . ' in *Evening Argus* 27 Oct. (Brighton)
Farrant, J.H. 1985. *The Rise and Decline of a South Coast Seafaring Town: Brighton 1550–1750* (London: Society for Nautical Research)
Farrant, J.H. and Farrant, S. compilers 1979. *Brighton before Dr. Russell* (Brighton: The Centre)
Farrant, S. 1977. *A Guide to Printed Sources for the Study of Brighton* (Brighton: University of Sussex Centre for Continuing Education)
Farrant, S. 1980. *Georgian Brighton 1740–1820* (Brighton: University of Sussex Centre for Continuing Education)
Farrant, S., Fossey, K. and Peasgood, A.N. 1982. 'The growth of Brighton and Hove 1810–1939' (Brighton: University of Sussex Centre for Continuing Education Working Paper)
Ford, J. and Ford, J. 1981. *Images of Brighton* (Richmond-upon-Thames: St Helena Press)

Fraser, R. 1984. *In Search of the Past: The Manor House at Amnerfield 1933–1945* (London: Verso)

Friend, D.B. 1886. *D.B. Friend's Handy Guide to Brighton* rev. edn (Brighton: D.B. Friend)

Gaskell, E.D. 1966. *Letters* J.A.V. Chapple and A. Pollard, eds (Manchester: Manchester University Press)

Geographical Association 1964. *A Bibliography for Local Studies* (London: Geographical Association)

Gibbon, E. 1923. *Letters of Edward Gibbon* J.B. Holroyd and J. Murray, eds, 3 vols: Orig. published 1896 (London: Cassell)

Gilbert, E.W. 1939. 'The growth of inland and seaside health resorts in England' in *Scottish Geographical Magazine* 55. 16–35

Gilbert, E.W. 1954. *Brighton: Old Ocean's Bauble* (London: Methuen)

Granville, A.B. 1971. *Spas of England and Principal Sea-bathing Places* 2 vols. Orig. published 1841 (London: Adams & Dart)

Graves, R. and Hodge, A. 1950. *The Long Weekend: A Social History of Great Britain 1918–1939* (London: Faber)

Greene, G. 1936. *Brighton Rock* (London: Heinemann)

Hennessy, J. 1974. *Social Movements and Political Action:* 6 cassettes. Cassette 6: 'The Marina in Brighton: planning controls and democratic input' (Lecture, University of Sussex)

Herbert, A.P. 1934. *Holy Deadlock* (London: Methuen)

Hern, A. 1967. *The Seaside Holiday: The History of the English Seaside Resort* (London: Cresset)

Hindley, C. 1875. *The Brighton Murder. An Authentic and Faithful History of the Atrocious Murder of Celia Holloway* (no publisher)

Huizinga, J. 1924. *The Waning of the Middle Ages* (London: Edward Arnold)

Hume, M. 1984. *After the Brighton Bomb* (London: Revolutionary Communist Party)

Hunter, L. 1959. *The Road to Brighton Pier* (London: Barker)

Ivanov, V. 1974. 'The significance of M. Bakhtin's ideas on sign, utterance and dialogue from modern semiotics' in H. Baran, ed. *Semiotics and Structuralism* (New York)

Kimball, P. 1969. 'Coastal home for Commuters' in *The Times* (30 Apr.)

Lennard, R. ed. 1931. *The Englishman at Rest and Play: Some Phases of English Leisure 1558–1714* (Oxford: Clarendon)

Lowerson, J. and Howkins, A. 1981. 'Leisure in the Thirties' in Tomlinson 1981. 72–85.

Lustgarten, E. 1951. *Defender's Triumph* (London: no publisher)

MacCannell, D. 1976. *The Tourist: A New Theory of the Leisure Class* (London: Macmillan)

Mackenzie, S.D. 1983. *Gender and Environment: Reproduction of Labour in Post-War Brighton* D.Phil, Urban and Regional Studies, University of

Sussex, Brighton.
MacLaren, P. 1987. 'The anthropological roots of pedagogy: the teacher as liminal servant' in *Anthropology and Humanism Quarterly* 12:3–4 (Sept. and Dec.) 75–85.
MacLaren, P. 1988. *Rituals of Resistance* (Chicago: University of Chicago Press)
Manning-Sanders, R. 1951. *Seaside England* (London: Batsford)
Mawer, A. and Stenton, F.M. 1930. *The Place-Names of Sussex* Vol.VII Pt.II (Cambridge: Cambridge University Press)
Melville, L. 1909. Brighton Review in *Times Literary Supplement* 1909:187.
Merifield, M.P. *c.* 1855. *Brighton Past and Present: A Handbook for Visitors and Residents* (Brighton: Hannah Wallis)
Municipal Journal 1964. '"Beachniks" – Brighton . . . ' in *Municipal Journal* (Feb. 14) London 3.
Musgrave, C. 1970. *Life in Brighton from the Earliest Times to the Present* (London: Faber) 2nd edn 1981 (London: Rochester)
Neville Havins, P.J. 1976. *The Spas of England* (London: Robert Hale)
Nuttall, J. 1969. *Bomb Culture* (London: Paladin)
Office of Population, Censuses and Surveys, Great Britain 1981. *Census 1981: Small Area Statistics: Brighton* (London: Office of Population, Censuses and Surveys)
Pimlott, J.A.R. 1975. *The Englishman's Holiday* Orig. published 1947 (Hassocks: Faber)
Preston, H. 1928. *Memories* (London: no publisher)
Queenspark Rates Book Group 1983. *Brighton on the Rocks: Monetarism and the Local State* (Brighton: Queenspark Books)
Rackham, J. 1977. 'Foreign tourists and students . . . ' in *The Times* (London) 24 Aug. 11.
Report of the Census 1851–1852. (London: HMSO)
Repton, H. 1808. *Designs for the Pavilion at Brighton* (London: Stadler)
Rojek, C. 1985. *Capitalism and Leisure Theory* (London: Tavistock)
Ross, C.H. 1881. *The Book of Brighton, as it was and as it is* ms. (Brighton: Brighton Public Library)
Roth, C. 1941. *The Sassoon Dynasty* (London: Hale)
Royal Pavilion, Art Gallery and Museums 1971. *Follies and Fantasies: Catalogue of an Exhibition* (Brighton: Brighton Art Gallery and Museum)
Royal Pavilion, Art Gallery and Museums (De Mare, E. and Higginbottom, D.) 1977. *The Royal Pavilion, Brighton: Photographs* (Brighton: Brighton Borough Council Amenities Committee)
Southern Weekly News 26 May 1928. 'Local News' column (Brighton)
Schnyder, L. 1912. 'Le cas de Renata: Contribution à l'étude de l'hystérie' in *Archives de Psychologie* 12. 201–262.
Stevenson, J. and Cook, C. 1979. *British Historical Facts 1760–1830*

(London: Macmillan)

Stokes, A. 1947. *The Very First History of the English Seaside* (London: Sylvan Press)

Tomlinson, A., ed. 1981. *Leisure and Social Control* BSA and Leisure Studies Assoc. Joint Study Group, University of Birmingham CCCS (Brighton: Brighton Polytechnic)

Walton, J.K. 1983. *The English Seaside Resort: A Social History 1750–1914* (Leicester: University of Leicester Press)

Weiner, M. 1960. *French Exiles, 1789–1815* (London: Murray)

Willis, P. 1978. *Profane Culture* (London: Routledge & Kegan Paul)

NIAGARA FALLS

Adamson, J.E. 1985. *Niagara: Two Centuries of Changing Attitudes, 1697–1901* (Washington, DC: Corcoran Gallery of Art)

Anon. 1905. *Niagara in Summer and Winter* (no publisher)

Architectural Concepts 1979. 'Nouvel étage à la tour d'observation de Niagara Falls' in *Architectural Concepts* 35 (Jan.–Feb.) 9.

Ariès, P. 1974. *Western Attitudes toward Death: From the Middle Ages to the Present* P.M. Ranum, trans. (Baltimore, Md.: Johns Hopkins University Press)

Balliers, G. 1962. 'More tourism Niagara goal' in *Financial Post* 56 (24 Mar.) 12.

Bannon, A. 1982. *The Taking of Niagara: A History of the Falls in Photography* Exhibition catalogue (Buffalo, NY: Buffalo Media Study Group)

Barry, E. 1978. 'Herman Melville; the changing face of comedy' in *American Studies International* 16 (Summer) 22–33.

Boorstein, D. 1961. *The Image: A Guide to Pseudo-Events in America* (New York: Harper & Row)

Braider, undated. *The Niagara* (no publisher)

Butor, M. 1965. *6,810,000 litre d'eau par seconde* (Paris: Gallimard). Also available as *Niagara* E.S. Miller, trans. (Chicago: Regnery Press, 1969)

Callwood, J. and Frayne, T.G. 1950. 'Honeymoon at the Falls' in *Maclean's Magazine* 63 (1 Aug.) 10–11, 43–44.

Campbell, M. 1958. *Niagara: Hinge of the Golden Arc* (no publisher)

Campell, M.F. 1960. 'The day Niagara stood still' in *Canadian Geographical Journal* 50 (Jan.) 28–33.

Canada Magazine 1938. 'More power from Niagara' in *Canada Magazine* 89 (Jan.) 24.

Canadian Geographical Journal 1954. 'Niagara Falls remedial program' in *Canadian Geographical Journal* 49 (Sept.) 118–124.

Canfield, W.W. 1902. *The Legends of the Iroquois Told by 'The Cornplanter'* (New York: Wessels)

Catton, B. 1964. 'The thundering water' in *American Heritage* 15 (June).
C-I-L *Oval* 1966. 'New look-out for Niagara Falls (Skylon Tower) in *C-I-L Oval* 35 (Summer) 15.
Coffey, B. 1939. 'Beautiful Niagara becomes more beautiful' *Saturday Night* 54 (O 21) 27
Cohen, E., Ben-yehuda, N., and Aviad, J. 1987. 'Recentering the world: the quest for "elective" centers in a secularized universe' in *Sociological Review* 35:2. 320–346.
Commissioners for Niagara Falls Park 1886. 'Preliminary Report for 1885' in *Papers Relating to the Niagara Falls Park* (1885–6) in *Ontario Sessions Papers* v. 18 pt. 6 1886. No. 77 (Toronto: Warwick & Sons)
Conrad, P. 1980. *Imagining America* (Oxford: Oxford University Press)
Cooper, J.F. 1821. *The Spy: A Tale of the Neutral Ground* W. Haffner, ed. reprinted 1960 (New York: Hafner)
Cooper, W. 1810. *Guide in the Wilderness* (Dublin: no publisher)
'Cousin George' 1846. *Sketches of Niagara Falls and River* (Buffalo: no publisher)
Cruikshank, E.A. 1930. *Records of Niagara: A Collection of Contemporary Letters and Documents, 1790–1792* (Niagara, Ontario: Niagara Historical Society)
Curtis, G.W. 1852. *Lotus-Eating* (no publisher)
Danard, J. 1983. 'Niagara Falls aims to light up your night life' in *Financial Post* 77 (24 Dec.) 28.
Davison, G.M. 1933. *The Fashionable Tour. An Excursion to the Springs, Niagara, Quebec, and Boston* 3rd edn (Boston: no publisher)
Donaldson, G. 1979. *Niagara! The Eternal Circus* (Toronto: Doubleday)
Dow, C.M. 1921. *Anthology and Bibliography of Niagara Falls* 2 vols (Niagara Falls: no publisher)
Downes, P.G. 1943. Sleeping Island (New York)
Edwards, F. 1939. 'City behind the Falls' *Maclean's Magazine* 52 (15 Dec.) 12–13, 30–31.
Epp, A. 1964. 'Revolving dining room will top tallest tower at Niagara Falls' in *Financial Post* 58 (24 Oct.) 12.
Ewen, D., ed. 1966. *American Popular Songs from the Revolutionary War to the Present* (New York: Random House)
External Affairs 1969. 'Niagara cataract to be restored' in *External Affairs* 21 (July) 296
Financial Post 1954. 'New lighting more colours for Niagara' in *Financial Post* 51 (5 Oct.) 22.
Financial Post 1957a. 'Niagara: tourist, power and steel' in *Financial Post* 53 (23 May) 35.
Financial Post 1957b. '"New Light" on Niagara Falls' in *Financial Post* 51 (19 Oct.) 50 and 65.
Financial Post 1957c. 'Tourist lures overseas threaten honeymoon city'

in *Financial Post* 51 (23 Nov.) 15.

Financial Post 1962a. 'Tourism just one of 71 industries in Niagara Falls' in *Financial Post* 56 (3 Mar.) 55.

Financial Post 1962b. 'Record tourist influx in honeymoon capital' in *Financial Post* 56 (1 Sept.) 56.

Financial Post 1965. 'Falls still tops "must" list' *Financial Post* 59 (24 Apr.) Supp. 22–3.

Financial Post 1987. 'Boom in the frog and bust business' in *Financial Post* 81 (12 July) 3.

Forrester, G.C. 1928. *Falls of Niagara* (New York: Van Nostrand)

Frank, M. 1977. 'Niagara's fallen arch' in *Weekend Magazine* 27 (3 Dec.) 10d.

Gilman, C. 1838. *The Poetry of Travelling* (New York: Colman)

Greenhill, R. and Mahoney, T.D. 1969. *Niagara* (Toronto: University of Toronto Press)

Grenier, S. 1980. 'Niagara Story' in *L'Actualité* 5 (6 and 9 Mar.) 6,9.

Hennepin, L. 1698. *A New Discovery of a Vast Country in America* (London: British Library)

Henning Christensen Graphics 1981. *Niagara Falls* (Agincourt, Ont.: GLC Publishers)

House, A.W. 1953. 'Beauty treatment for Niagara' in *Industry Canada* 53 (Mar.) 51–53.

Howard, R.W. 1969. *Niagara Falls* (Niagara Falls, NY: Franklin Watts Inc.)

Howells, W.D. 1808. *Their Wedding Journey* (New York: Random)

Howells, W.D. 1893. *The Niagara Book* 2nd edn (New York: Doubleday)

International Joint Commission 1975. *Preservation and Enhancements of the American Falls at Niagara*

Irwin, J. 1959. 'Kings, presidents and Mr. K. are boosting Niagara Falls' in *Financial Post* 53 (26 Sept.) 35.

Jackson, B. 1968. 'Three-way plan would harvest lost power from Niagara Falls' in *Financial Post* 62 (13 July) 17.

Jacobson, D. 1971. 'The Falls' in *The Listener* 25 Nov.

Jameson, A.B.M. 1838. *Winter Studies and Summer Rambles in Canada* (London)

Jamieson, L. 1981. 'More than just the waterfall at Niagara' in *Financial Post* 75 (23 May) Supplement 10.

Katz, S.M. 1951. 'Why Red Hill did it (Attempt to shoot Niagara Fall)' in *Maclean's Magazine* 64 (1 Nov.) 7–9, 38–40.

Kendall, A. 1970. *Medieval Pilgrims* (London: Wayland)

Kilan, G. 1978. 'Mowat and a park policy for Niagara Falls, 1883–1887' in *Ontario History* 70 (June) 115–135.

Lash, S. 1987. 'Critical theory and postmodernist culture: the eclipse of aura' in *Current Perspectives in Social Theory* 8. 197–213.

Las Vergnas, R. 1956. *Mystère Niagara* (no publisher)
Lee, B. 1973. 'Farewell to Mrs. Elizabeth Henry of Niagara Falls, Ontario' in *Maclean's Magazine* 86 (3 Jan.) 40–43.
Leighton, T. 1984. 'Pandemonium inc.' in *Equinox* 4 (Jan.–Feb.) 87–94.
Levin, H. 1970. *The Power of Blackness* (New York: Alfred Knopf)
Lewis, C.O. 1971. *Niagara, Maid of the Mist, and famous Niagara News Stories* (Niagara, Ontario: Kiwanis Club of Stamford)
MacCannell, D. 1976. *The Tourist* (New York: Schocken)
McCausland, W. 1947. 'Honeymoons at Niagara Falls' in *American Notes and Queries* 6 (Jan.) 17–24.
McGreevy, P. 1985. 'Review of *Niagara Falls: Icon of the American Sublime* by E. McKinsey' in *Journal of Historical Geography* 13:1. 97–98.
McGreevy, P. 1987. 'Imagining the future at Niagara Falls' in *Annals of the Association of American Geographers* 77:1 (March) 48–62.
McKinsey, E.R. 1985. *Niagara Falls: Icon of the American Sublime* (Cambridge: Cambridge University Press)
Maclean's Magazine 1955. 'The day Niagara Falls stopped' in *Maclean's Magazine* 68 (26 Nov.) 64.
McLeod, D.W. 1955. 'Niagara Falls was a hell raising town' in *Maclean's Magazine* 68 (26 Nov.) 22–3,64.
Marshall, T. 1988. *Voices on the Brink* (Toronto: Macmillan Canada)
Martin, E.S. 1893. 'As it rushes by' in Howells *et al.* 1893
Marx, L. 1975. *The Machine in the Garden: Technology and the Pastoral Ideal in America* 2nd edn (London: Oxford University Press)
Montgomery, L.M. 1942. *Anne of Green Gables* (Toronto: Ryerson Press) Orig. published 1908.
Monthly Anthology and Boston Review 1806. 'Extracts from a journal' in *Monthly Anthology and Boston Review* 3 (Sept.) 457–458.
Neumann, E. 1955. *The Great Mother: An Analysis of the Archetype* (New York: Pantheon)
Newman, M. 1988. 'Wandering through the museum: experience and identity in a spectator culture' in *Borderlines* 12 (Summer) 20–27.
New York Historical Society 1974. *Early travels in New York State* (New York: New York Historical Society)
Niagara Falls Tourism and Convention Bureau 1949–1986. 'Niagara Falls Honeymoon Register'. Unpublished folios
Nystrom, C. 1978. 'Space and situations' in *ETC. Journal of General Semantics* 35:3 (Sept.) (Palo Alto, Calif.: State University of California Press)
Ontario Ministry of Education 1973. 'Research resources for the Niagara Peninsula' 2 vols (Toronto, Ontario: Government of Ontario)
Parsons, H. 1836. *The Book of Niagara Falls* (no publisher)
Rogerson, W. 1949. *Panorama* 2 (Aug.–Sept.) Harry Shaw Newman

Gallery, New York 1–2.

Rothman, E. 1984. *Hands and Hearts: A History of Courtship in America* (New York: Basic)

Rowell, G. 1974. *Hell and the Victorians* (Oxford: Clarendon)

Saturday Night 1945. 'Niagara enhanced by exquisite garden setting' in *Saturday Night* 60 (16 June) 4.

Schupp, P. 1960. 'Les Chutes du Niagara et la future tour Seagram' in *Arch-Bat-Constrir* 15 (Dec.) 397.

Seibel, G.A., coord. 1978. *300 Years since Father Hennepin: Niagara Falls, in Art: 1678–1978* (Niagara Falls, Ont.: Niagara Falls Heritage Foundation)

Severance J. undated. *Niagara Frontier* pamphlet.

Shepard, P. 1967. *Man in the Landscape: A Historic View of the Esthetics of Nature* (New York: Knopf)

Smith, L. *et al.* 1950. 'Falls: roaring trade; Niagara–St. Catharines–Welland' in *Saturday Night* 66 (14 Nov.) 8–10,31.

Thompson, G.R., ed. 1974. *The Gothic Imagination: Essays in Dark Romanticism* (Pullman, Washington: Washington State University Press)

Tocqueville, A. de 1983. *Oeuvres complètes* Part 1. Correspondance. J.P. Mayer, ed. (Paris: Gallimard)

Tovell, W.M. 1966a. 'Beauty and the Falls' in *Canadian Auditing* 28 (March–April) 46–47.

Tovell, W.M. 1966b. *Niagara Falls: Story of the River* (Toronto: Royal Ontario Museum)

Turner, V. 1973. 'The centre out-there: the pilgrim's goal' in *History of Religion* XII. 191–230.

Turner, V. 1988. *The Anthropology of Performance* (New York: Performing Arts Journal Publications)

Turner, V. and Turner, E. 1978. *Image and Pilgrimage in Christian Culture: Anthropological Perspectives* (New York: Columbia University Press)

Tyler, S. 1986. 'Post-Modern Ethnography: From Document of the Occult to Occult Document' in J. Clifford and G.E. Marcus eds. *Writing Culture. The Poetics and Politics of Ethnography* (Chicago: University of Chicago Press)

Urry, J. 1987. 'Cultural change and contemporary holiday-making' Lancaster Regionalism Group Working Paper (University of Lancaster)

Van Steen, M. 1962. 'Ask booster button men where to go, what to do' in *Financial Post* 56 (26 May) 28.

Weber, E. 1963. 'Niagara Falls in history; a bibliography' in *Ontario Library Review* 47 (Aug.) 107–111.

Wells, H.G. 1908. *The War in the Air* (London: Bell & Sons)

313

Willis, N.P. 1840. *American Scenery* (London: Virtue)
Wilson, A. 1818. 'The Foresters: A Poem descriptive of a pedestrian
  journey to the Falls of Niagara, in the Autumn of 1804' in *Port Folio*
  New Series 1–3 (June 1909–March 1910), reprinted in Grosart, A.B.
  ed. 1876. *The Poems and Literary Prose of Alexander Wilson, American
  Ornithologist* (Paisley, NY: Gardner)
Wilson, A. 1988. 'The view from the road: tourism in the interwar years'
  in *Borderlines* 12 (Summer) 10–14.
Wood, E.B. 1873. *Royal Commission Report on the State of Niagara Falls*
  (Ottawa: Government of Canada)

THE TRUE NORTH STRONG AND FREE

Armour, L. 1981. *The Idea of Canada* (Ottawa: Steel Rail)
Atwood, M. 1973. *Surfacing* (Don Mills, Ont.: Paperjacks)
Atwood, M. 1979. *Survival* (Toronto: Anansi)
Atwood, M. 1987. 'True North' in *Saturday Night* (Jan.) 141–148.
Becker, B.K. 1986. 'Signification actuelle de la frontière: une
  interprétation géopolitique à partir du cas de l'Amazonie
  Brésilienne' in *Cahiers des Sciences Humaines* 22:3–4. 297–317.
Berger, C. 1966. 'The True North Strong and Free' in Russell 1966.
  4–19.
Berger, C. 1971. 'An introduction' in Goldwin Smith, *Canada and the
  Canadian Question* M. Bliss, ed. (Toronto: University of Toronto
  Press)
Berger, C. 1976. *The Writing of Canadian History* (Toronto: Oxford
  University Press)
Berger, C. and Cook, R., eds 1976. *The West and the Nation: Essays in
  Honour of W.L. Morton* (Toronto: McClelland & Stewart)
Berger, T. 1977. *Northern Frontier, Northern Homeland: The Report of the
  Mackenzie Valley Pipeline Inquiry* (Ottawa: Supply and Services Canada)
Berton, P. 1956. *The Mysterious North* (Toronto: McClelland & Stewart)
Berton, P. 1975. *Hollywood's Canada: The Americanization of Our National
  Image* (Toronto: McClelland & Stewart)
Berton, P. 1982. *Why We Act like Canadians* (Toronto: McClelland &
  Stewart)
Brimelow, P. 1986. *The Patriot Game* (Toronto: Key Porter)
Burpee, L.J. undated. *Henry Hudson Ryerson Canadian History Readers
  Series* (Toronto: Ryerson)
Campbell, J. 1956. *The Hero with a Thousand Faces* (New York)
Catholic World 1865. 'A vanishing race' 1:5 (Aug.) 1865. 705–711.
Christy, J. 1980. *Rough Road to the North* (Toronto: Doubleday)
Clement, W. 1983. 'Canadian class cleavages: an assessment and

contribution' in W. Clement, *Class, Power and Property* (Agincourt, Ont.: Methuen), 134–171.

Coates, K. 1985. *Canada's Colonies* (Toronto: Lorimer)

Cook, R. 1984. 'Imagining a North American garden' in *Canadian Literature* 103 (Winter) 10–21.

Creighton, D. 1957. *Dominion of the North*, 2nd edn (Toronto: Macmillan)

Creighton, D. 1970. *Character and Circumstance* J.S. Moir, ed. (Toronto: Macmillan)

Creighton, D. 1974. *Towards the Discovery of Canada: Selected Essays* (Toronto: Macmillan)

Creighton, D. 1980. *The Passionate Observer* (Toronto: McClelland & Stewart)

Cruikshank, J. 'Myths and futures in the Yukon Territory: the inquiry as a social dragnet' in *Canadian Issues* 2:2. 15–19.

Curwood, J.O. 1913. *The Honor of the Big Snows* (New York: A.L. Burt)

Dacks, B. 1981. *A Choice of Futures* (Toronto: Methuen)

Dagenais, P. 1959. 'Le mythe de la vocation agricole du Québec' in R. Blanchard *Mélanges* (Québec) 193–201.

Davey, F. 1986. 'Critics' folly', in *Canadian Forum* 66 (Nov.) 40–41.

Davis, A. 1982. *A Distant Harmony* (Winnipeg: Winnipeg Art Gallery)

Department of Northern Affairs and Natural Resources 1958. *This is the Arctic* (Ottawa: Crown Printer)

Dickens, C. 1855. 'Comments' in *Household Words* (5 Feb.) 1–2.

Diubaldo, R.J. 1978. *Stefansson and the Canadian Arctic* (Montreal: McGill-Queen's University Press)

Dorfman, A. and Mattelart, A. 1975. *How to Read Donald Duck* (New York: International General)

Dorion, H. 1962. 'Connaissances des frontières canadiennes' in *Cahiers de géographie de Québec* 11. 147–148.

Downes, P.G. 1943. *Sleeping Island* (New York)

Doxman, E.J. 1976. *The Arctic in Question* (Toronto: Oxford University Press)

Drew, W. 1973. *The Wabeno Feast* (Toronto: University of Toronto Press)

Dunbar, G.S. 1985. 'Innis and Canadian geography' in *Canadian Geographer* 29:2. 159–164.

Dunn, R. 1904. 'The spirit of the north' in *Outing* 45:3 (Dec.) 320.

Eggleston, W. 1957. *The Frontier and Canadian Letters* (Toronto: Ryerson)

Elkins, D.J. and Simeon, R. 1980. *Small Worlds* (Toronto: Methuen)

Ferres, J. 1986. Review of *The Wacousta Syndrome* by Gaile McGregor in *American Review of Canadian Studies* 16:3 (Autumn). 371–3.

Frye, N. 1971. *Stubborn Structure: Essays on Criticism and Society* (London: Methuen)

Frye, N. 1977. 'Haunted by lack of ghosts: some patterns in the imagery of Canadian poetry' in D. Staines, ed. *The Canadian Imagination: Dimensions of a Literary Culture* (Cambridge, Mass.: Harvard University Press).

Geddes, G., ed. 1975. *Skookum Wawa* (Toronto: Oxford University Press)

Gold, G.L. 1984. *Minorities and Mother Country Imagery* (St John's, Nfld: Institute of Social and Economic Research, Memorial University)

Government of Canada 1963; 1968. *Canada Pent-annual Report* (Ottawa: Supply and Services Canada)

Government of Canada 1983. *Tourism in Canada: Past, Present and Future* Canadian Government Office of Tourism, Policy, Planning and Coordination Group (Ottawa: Supply and Services Canada)

Government of Canada 1987. 'Canadian travel survey' Mimeo, Canadian Government Office of Tourism, Policy, Planning and Coordination Group (Ottawa: Supply and Services Canada)

Government of the Northwest Territories 1986. 'Sale of NWT Sport Fishing Licences' Mimeo, Dept of Economic Development and Tourism Dec. 1986 (Yellowknife: Government of the Northwest Territories).

Government of the Northwest Territories 1987. *Growth in the Northwest Territories Tourism Facilities,* Dept of Economic Development and Tourism (Yellowknife: Government of the Northwest Territories)

Griffiths, F., ed. 1987. *Politics of the Northwest Passage* (Toronto: McGill-Queen's University Press)

Hamelin, L.-E. 1974. 'Perception et géographie: le cas du Nord' in *Canadian Geographer* 18:3. 185–200.

Hamelin, L.-E. 1977. *Le Mot Nord et son language* (Québec: Editeur officiel, Office de la langue française)

Hamelin, L.-E. 1979. *Canadian Nordicity* (Montréal: Hurtubise HRH)

Hamelin, L.-E. 1980. *Nordicité Canadienne* 2nd edn (Montréal: Hurtubise HRH)

Hamelin, L.-E. 1984. 'Managing Canada's north: challenges and opportunities: rapporteur's summary and comments' in *Canadian Public Administration/Administration Publique du Canada* 27:2 (Summer) 165–181.

Hamilton, R.M. and Shields, D. 1979. *The Dictionary of Canadian Quotations and Phrases* (Toronto: McClelland & Stewart)

Hare, F.K. 1972. 'Introduction' in J.B. Bird, *The Natural Landscapes of Canada* (Toronto: Wiley)

Harris, L. 1926. 'Revelation of art in Canada' in *The Canadian Theosophist* 7:15 (July) 85–86.

Harris, L. 1948. 'The Group of Seven in Canadian history' in *Report of the Canadian Historical Association* 29. 1–12.

Hawthorn, H.B. 1973. 'Northern views' in K.R. Greenaway, ed. *Science and the North* (Ottawa: Department of Indian and Northern Affairs)

Hearne, S. 1795. *A Journey from Prince of Wales Fort in Hudson's Bay to the Northern Ocean in the Years 1769-70-71* (London: no publisher)

Hinz, E.J. 1978. 'The masculine/feminine psychology of American/Canadian primitivism: deliverance and surfacing' in R.W. Winks, *Other Voices, Other Views: An International Collection of Essays from the Bicentennial* (Westport, Conn.: Greenwood Press) 75-96.

Hodgins, B.W. and Hobbs, M. 1985. eds *Nastawagan: The Canadian North by Canoe and Snowshoe* (Toronto: Betelgeuse)

Hopkins, C. 1904. *Canadian Annual Review 1903* (Toronto: Canadian Press)

Ibsch, E. 1982. 'Historical changes of the function of spatial description in literary tests' in *Poetics Today* 3:4 (Autumn) 97-114.

Irvine, L. 1986. 'The real Mr. Canada' in *Canadian Literature* 108 (Spring) 68-79.

James, P.E. 1967. 'On the origin and persistence of error in geography' in *Annals of the Association of American Geographers* 57. 1-24.

James, W.C. 1985. 'The quest pattern and the canoe trip' in B.W. Hodgins and M. Hobbs eds. *Nastawagan: The Canadian North by Canoe and Snowshoe* (Toronto: Betelgeuse) 8-20.

Kemp, D.D. 1987. 'Attitudes to winter in the northwest fur trade' in *Canadian Geographer* 31:1 (Spring) 49-56

Keon, D.J. 1975. *The New World Idea in British North America: An Analysis of some British Promotional, Travel and Settler Writings 1784 to 1860* MA thesis, University of Toronto.

Kilbourn, W. 1970. *Canada: A Guide to the Peaceable Kingdom* (Toronto: Macmillan)

Kline, M. 1970. *Beyond the Land Itself: Views of Nature in Canada and the United States* (Cambridge, Mass.: Harvard University Press)

Klinge, M. 1987. 'Nord, nature et pauvreté, facteurs fondamentaux de l'identité nordique' in *Lumières du Nord* (Paris: Association français d'action artistique)

Knelman, M. 1983. 'It's the new Bob and Doug movie, eh?' in *Atlantic Insight* 5 (Oct.) 28-29.

Konrad, V. guest ed. 1986. 'Nationalism in the landscape of Canada and the United States' in *Canadian Geographer* 3:2. 167-180.

Kroetsch, R. 1966. *But We Are Exiles* (Toronto: Macmillan)

Lacombe, M. 1982. 'Theosophy and the Canadian idealist tradition: a preliminary exploration' in *Journal of Canadian Studies* 17 (Summer) 100-118.

Lauzen, R.E. 1982. 'Marketing the image of the last frontier' in *Alaska Journal* 12:3 (Spring) 13-19.

Leacock, S. 1938. 'Introduction' in V. Stefansson *The Standardization of Error* (London: Kegan Paul)

Leacock, S. 1957. 'I'll stay in Canada' orig. published 1936 in J. Klinck and S. Watters, eds, *Canadian Anthology* (Toronto: McClelland & Stewart) 210–216.

London J. 1977. 'The White Silence' in *Irving Stone's Jack London: His Life – Sailor on Horseback and 28 Selected Jack London Stories* I. Stone, ed. (Garden City, NY: Random House)

Luste, G. 1985. 'History, travel and canoeing in the barrens' in B.W. Hodgins and M. Hobbs eds. *Nastawagan: The Canadian North by Canoe and Snowshoe* (Toronto: Betelgeuse)

McGregor, G. 1985. *The Wacousta Syndrome* (Toronto: University of Toronto Press)

McGregor, J.G. 1984. 'North west of sixteen' (Tokyo, Japan and Rutland, Vermont: C.E. Tuttle & M.G.Hurtig)

McKay, I. 1988. 'Twilight at Peggy's Cove: towards a genealogy of "Maritimicity"' in *Borderlines* 12 (Summer) 30–37.

Mackenzie, A. 1801. *Voyages from Montreal on the River St. Lawrence, through the Continent of North America, to the Frozen and Pacific Oceans; in the Years 1789 and 1793. With a Preliminary Account of the Rise, Progress and Present State of the Fur Trade of that Country* (London: T. Cadell)

MacLaren, I.S. 1977. *The Influence of Eighteenth-Century British Landscape Aesthetics on Narrative and Pictorial Responses to the British North American North and West 1769–1872* PhD. thesis, University of Manitoba.

Maclean's 1964. 'The double image: the vision, the reality' special issue 77 (17 Oct.)

McCleary, R. 1981. *Beyond Survival: The Making of an Artist out of the North in Men* MA thesis, Dept of English Literature, University of Manitoba.

Milne, G., Sheridan, W., and Shields, R. 1982. *Beaufort Sea Regulatory Issues* Mimeo (Ottawa: Nepean Development Consultants)

Mitcham, A. 1974. 'Northern mission: priest, parson and prophet in the north: a study in French and English-Canadian contemporary fiction' in *LUR* 3 (Nov.) 25–31

Morisset, J. and Pelletier, R.-M., eds 1986. *Ted Trindell. Métis Witness to the North* Prose Series, Vol. 3 (Vancouver, BC: Tillacum Library)

Morrissonneau, C. 1978. *La Terre promise: le mythe du Nord québecois* (Montréal: Hurtubise HMH)

Morton, W.L. 1961. *The Canadian Identity* (Madison, Wisc.: University of Wisconsin Press)

Morton, W.L. 1969. *The Kingdom of Canada* 2nd edn (Toronto: McClelland & Stewart)

Morton, W.L. 1970. 'The "North" in Canadian historiography' in *Transactions of the Royal Society of Canada* Series IV:8. 31–40.

Morton, W.L. 1971. 'The relevance of Canadian history' in Eli Mandel, ed. 1971 *Contest of Canadian Criticism* (Chicago: University of Chicago Press)

Morton, W.L. 1976. *The West and the Nation* (Toronto: McClelland & Stewart)

Moss, J.G. 1973. 'Canadiana frontiers: sexuality and violence from Richardson to Kroetsch' in *Journal of Canadian Fiction* 3 (Summer). 36–41.

Moss, J.G. 1974. *Patterns of Isolation in English Canadian Fiction* (Toronto: McClelland & Stewart)

Mowat, R. 1976. *Canada North Now* (Toronto: McClelland & Stewart)

Neatby, L.H. 1966. *The Conquest of the Last Frontier* (Athens, Ohio: Ohio University Press)

New, W.H. 1972. *Articulating West: Essays on Purpose and Form in Modern Canadian Literature* (Toronto: New Press)

Newbigin, M. 1927. *The Great River, the Lands and the Men* (New York: Harcourt, Brace, Jovanovich)

O'Malley, M. 1976. *The Past and Future Land* (Toronto: PMA)

Ornstein, M. 1983. 'The development of class in Canada' in J.P. Grayson, ed. *Introduction to Sociology* (Toronto: Gage) 216–258.

Page, R. 1986. *Northern Development: The Canadian Dilemma* (Toronto: McClelland & Stewart)

Panitch, L. 1981. 'Dependency and class in Canadian political economy' in *Studies in Political Economy* 6 (Autumn) 7–33.

Parr Traill, C. 1836. *The Backwoods of Canada* (London: C. Knight)

Porteous, J.D. 1986a. 'Bodyscape: the body-landscape metaphor' in *Canadian Geographer* 30:1 (Spring) 2–12.

Porteous, J.D. 1986b. 'Inscape: landscapes of the mind in the Canadian and Mexican novels of Malcolm Lowry' in *Canadian Geographer* 30:2 (Summer) 123–131.

Purdy, A. 1967. *North of Summer* (Toronto: McClelland & Stewart)

Puxley, P. 1986. 'Review of B. Lopez *Arctic Dreams* and F. Daniel *Discovery of the North* and R. Page *Northern Development: The Canadian Dilemma*' in *Canadian Forum* (Aug./Sept.) 1986. 25–27.

Rae, J. 1855. 'Report on the fate of the Franklin Expedition' in *Journal of the Royal Geographical Society* 25. 246–270.

Rasmussen, K. 1927. *Across Arctic America* (New York: G.P. Putnam & D. Meakin)

Rasmussen, K. 1931. *The Netsilik Eskimos: Social Life and Spiritual Culture: Report of the Fifth Thule Expedition 1921–24* Pamphlet (Ottawa: National Library of Canada)

Reany, J. 1979. *Wacousta!* (Toronto: Press Porcépic)

Rich, E.E. 1953. *John Rae's Correspondence 1844–1855* (London: Hudson Bay Record Society)

Richardson, J. 1964. *Wacousta* (Toronto: University of Toronto Press)

Rimbert, S. 1971. 'Essai méthodologique sur des stéréotypes régionaux au Canada' in *Cahiers de géographie du Québec* 36. 523–536.

Roberts, D. 1980. 'Dickens and the Arctic' in *Horizon* (Jan.) 70–71.

Rohmer, R. 1970. *Essays on Mid-Canada* (Toronto: Anansi)

Russell, P. 1966. *Nationalism in Canada* (Toronto: University League for Social Reform)

Salutin, R. 1981. 'The Great White North' in *This Magazine* 15 (Dec.–Jan.). 28–29.

Sanderson, M. 1982. 'Giffith Taylor: a geographer to remember' in *Canadian Geographer* 26. 293–299.

Savard, P. dir. 1980. *Aspects de la civilisation canadienne-française* (Montréal: CRCCF / Presses de l'Université d'Ottawa)

Sawatsky, H.L. and Lehn, W.H. 1975. 'The cultural geography of the Arctic mirage' in *Proceedings, Canadian Association of Geographers Annual Meeting Vancouver 1975* (Toronto: University of Toronto Press) 29–36.

Schmitt, P.J. 1969. *Back to Nature: The Arcadian Myth in Urban America* (New York: Oxford University Press)

Schwartz, M.A. 1967. *Public Opinion and Canadian Identity* (New York: University of California Press)

Scott, F.R. 1981. *The Collected Poems of F.R. Scott* (Toronto: McClelland & Stewart)

Senate 1888. *Report of the Select Committee Appointed to Inquire into the Resources of the Greater Mackenzie Basin* (Ottawa: Crown Printer).

Service, R. 1907. *The Collected Poems of Robert Service* (New York: Harper)

Service, R. 1911. *Songs of the Sourdough* 30th edn Orig. published 1906 (New York: Hunt)

Shields, W.R. 1982. *Some American Perceptions of the Canadian North, 1850–1915* MA thesis, Dept of History, Queen's University, Kingston, Ontario

Sitwell, O.F.G. 1981. 'Elements of cultural geography as figures of speech' in *Canadian Geographer* 25:2. 167–179.

Smith, G. 1971. *Canada and the Canadian Question* M. Bliss, ed. (Toronto: University of Toronto Press)

Statistics Canada 1985. *Canada Yearbook 1985* (Ottawa: Supply and Services Canada)

Stefansson, V. 1923. *The Northward Course of Empire* (London: Harrap)

Stefansson, V. 1938. *The Standardization of Error* (London: Kegan Paul)

Stefansson, V. 1945. *The Arctic in Fact and Fable* (New York: no publisher)

Stratton, J. 1989. 'Deconstructing the territory' in *Cultural Studies* 3:1 (Jan.) 38–57.

Thompson, D. 1962. *David Thompson's Narrative 1784–1812* R. Glover, ed. (Toronto: The Champlain Society).

Thompson, D. 1971. *Travels in Western North America 1784–1812* V.G. Hopwood, ed. (Toronto: Macmillan)

Underhill, F.H. 1964. *The Image of Canada* (Toronto)

Wadland, J. 1985. 'Wilderness and culture' in B.W. Hodgins and M. Hobbs eds. *Nastawagan: The Canadian North by Canoe and Snowshoe* (Toronto: Betelgeuse)

Warburton Pike. 1896. *Through the Subarctic Forest. A Record of a Canoe Journey from Fort Wrangel to the Pelly Lakes and Down the Yukon River to the Bering Sea* (London: Edward Arnold).

Warwick, J. 1968. *The Long Journey: Literary Themes of French Canada* (Toronto: University of Toronto Press)

Watson, J.W. 1969. 'The role of illusion in North American geography' in *Canadian Geographer – Le géographe canadien* 13:1. 10–27.

Weiss, K. and Goodgold, E. 1972. *To Be Continued . . .* (New York: Crown)

White, H.S. 1910. *The Great White North: The Story of Polar Exploration* (New York: Macmillan)

White, P.J. 1979. *A Heartland–Hinterland Analysis of Images of Northern Canada as a Frontier, Wilderness, and Homeland* MA thesis, Canadian Studies, Carleton University, Ottawa.

Whittington, M.S. 1985. *The North Research Report for the MacDonald Commission* (Ottawa: Government Publications Centre, Supply and Services Canada)

Willson, B. 1915. *Life of Lord Strathcona and Mount Royal* (London: Cassell)

Winks, R.W., ed. 1966. *The Historiography of the British Empire-Commonwealth* (Durham, NC: Duke University Press)

Wonders, W.C. 1962. 'Presidential address: our northward course' in *Canadian Geographer* 6:3–4. 96–105.

Wonders, W.C. 1984. 'The Canadian North: its nature and prospects' in *Journal of Geography* (Sept.–Oct.) 226–233.

Wrightman, W.R. 1982. *Forever on the Fringe: Six Studies in the Development of the Manitoulin Island* (Toronto: University of Toronto Press)

Zaslow, M. 1971. *The Opening of the Canadian North, 1870–1914* (Toronto: McClelland & Stewart)

THE 'NORTH–SOUTH DIVIDE' IN ENGLAND

Barthes, R. 1972. *Critical essays* (New York: Northwestern University Press)

Barthes, R. 1981. 'Narrative space' in Heath 1981. 22–30.

Benevolo, L. 1977. *History of Modern Architecture* 2 Vols (Cambridge, Mass.: MIT Press)

Bennett, A. 1917. *Anna of the Five Towns* Orig. published 1902 (London: Methuen)

Bordwell, D. and Thompson, K. 1976. 'Space and narrative in the films of Ozu' in *Screen* 17:2 (Summer) 42.

Brunsdon, C. and Morley, D. 1978. *Everyday Television: 'Nationwide'* (London: British Film Institute)

Dear, M.J. 1986. 'Postmodernism and planning' in *Society and Space* 4:3. 367–384.

Dennis, R.J. 1984. *English Industrial Cities in the Nineteenth Century* (Cambridge: Cambridge University Press)

Dickens, C. 1966. *Hard Times* Orig. published 1854 (London: Norton)

Disraeli, B. 1904. *Sybil: The Two Nations* in *The Collected Works* (London: Dunne)

Dorfman, A. and Mattelart, A. 1975. *How to Read Donald Duck* (New York: International General)

Dyer, R., ed. 1980. *Coronation Street* (London: British Film Institute Television Monograph)

Gaskell, E. 1973. *North and South* A. Eason, ed. Orig. published 1855 (London: Oxford University Press)

Gaskell, E. 1976. *Mary Barton: A Tale of Manchester Life* S. Gill, ed. Orig. published 1848 (Harmondsworth: Penguin)

Granada Television 1985. *Coronation Street: 25 Years* (Manchester: Granada Publishing)

Heath, S. 1981. *Questions of Cinema: Communications and Culture* (London: Macmillan)

Higson, A. 1984. 'Space, place, spectacle' in *Screen* 25:4–5 (July–Oct.) 2–21.

Hoggart, R. 1957. *The Uses of Literacy* (London: Chatto)

Hudson, B. 1982. 'The geographical imagination of Arnold Bennett' *Transactions of the Institute of British Geographers* New Series 7. 365–379.

Kirk, N. 1984. *The Growth of Working Class Reformism in Mid-Victorian England* (London: Croom Helm)

Krieger, M.H. 1986. 'Ethnicity and the frontier in Los Angeles' in *Society and Space* 4:3. 385–389.

Krish, J. 1963. 'Introduction' in *SFTA Journal* special issue on The New Realism in British Films (Spring) 1–15.

Laing, S. 1986. *Representations of Working-Class Life 1957–1964* (London: Macmillan)

Läpple, D. 1985. 'Internationalization of capital and the regional problem' in J. Watson, ed. *Capital and Labour in the Urbanized World* (London: Sage) 43–75.

Lawrence, D.H. 1929. *Sea and Sardinia* (London: Martin Secker)

Lawrence, D.H. 1930. 'Nottingham and the mining country' in The New Adelphi (June–Aug.)

Leclaire, L. 1954. *Le Roman régionaliste dans les Isles Britanniques, 1800–1950* (Clermont-Ferrand: Editions G. de Bussac)

Massey, D. 1978. 'Survey: regionalism: some current issues' in *Capital and Class* 6. 106–125.

Massey, D. 1988. 'A new class of geography' in *Marxism Today* (May) 12–17.

Maugham, S. 1952. *The Razor's Edge* (London: Vanguard)

Morton, H.V. 1934. *In Search of England* (London: Methuen)

Nicholls, T. and Armstrong, P. 1976. *Workers Divided* (London: Fontana)

Orwell, G. 1949. *Down and Out in London and Paris* (London: Secker & Warburg)

Orwell, G. 1959. *The Road to Wigan Pier* (London: Secker & Warburg)

Parkinson, C.N. 1967. *Left Luggage: From Marx to Wilson*

Paterson, R. and Stewart, J. 1980. 'The production context of *Coronation Street*' in R. Dyer ed. 1980. *Coronation Street* (London: British Film Institute Television Monograph): 55–69.

Pocock, D.C.D. 1974. 'The nature of environmental perception' Dept of Geography, University of Durham, Occasional Publications (New Series) 4.

Pocock, D.C.D. 1978. 'The novelist and the North' Dept of Geography University of Durham, Occasional Publications (New Series) 12.

Priestley, J.B. 1934. 'Journey through Britain' in *English Journey* (London: Heinemann)

Raleigh, J.H. 1968. 'The novel and the city: England and America in the nineteenth century' in *Victorian Studies* 52. 290–328.

Savage, M. 1987. 'Understanding political alignments in contemporary Britain: do localities matter? Both high and low' in *Political Geography Quarterly*.

Savage, M. 1988. *The Dynamics of the Working Class* (Cambridge: Cambridge University Press)

Schlereth, T. 1983. 'Material culture studies and social history research' in *Journal of Social History* 16. 111–432.

Schlereth, T. 1985a. *Material culture: a research guide* (Lawrence, Kansas: University Press of Kansas)

Schlereth, T. 1985b. 'Review of views and view makers of urban America. Winterthur Portfolio: A' in *Journal of American Material Culture* 20. 205–207.

Shankman, P. 1984. 'The thick and the thin: on the interpretive theoretical program of Clifford Geertz' in *Current Anthropology* 25. 261–279.

Sharp, T. 1938. 'Hills and hells' in C. William-Ellis, J.W. Keynes *et al. Britain and the Beast* 2nd edn (London: Dent) 141–159.

Tillotson 1954. *Novelists of the 1840s* (London: Oxford University Press)

Urry, J. 1990. *The Tourist Gaze* (London: Routledge)

Walmsley, D.J. 1980. 'Spatial bias in Australian news reporting' in *Australian Geographer* 14. 342–349.

Watney, S. 1983. 'Gardens of speculation: landscape in *The Draughtsman's Contract*' in *Undercut* 7–8 (Spring) 4–9.

Whipple, E.P. 1966. 'On the economic fallacies of *Hard Times*' in C. Dickens, *Hard Times* (London: Norton) 323–330.

White, B. 1974. 'Interview with Walter Lassally' in *Journal of the University Film Association* (USA) 26:4.

Wilkinson, E. 1939. *The Town that was Murdered* (London: Gollancz)

Williams, R. 1973. *The Country and the City* (London: Chatto)

Wollen, P. 1980. 'Introduction: place in the cinema' in *Framework* 13. 10–25.

NAME INDEX

Anderson, B. 4, 5, 58, 65, 198, 221
Anderson, P. 4, 5, 58, 64, 198, 221
Ardener, S. 62
Atwood, M. 183, 185, 204

Bachelard, G. 30
Bailly, A.S. 14
Bakhtin, M. 73, 91–3, 152, 199
Barker, P. 104
Barry, E. 132
Bartes, R. 118
Bauman, Z. 273
Beazley, C.R. 27
Becker, B. 88
Bel, J. 63
Bennett, A. 101
Benveniste, G. 62
Berger, C. 178, 204
Berger, T. 193
Berman, M. 58
Berque, A. 63
Boorstein, D. 126
Bordwell, D. 217
Bourdieu, P. 32–4, 36, 38, 58–9 63–4
Braider 140
Brake, M. 104
Brighthelmstone Intelligence 78, 79

Callwood, J. 149
Campbell, J. 191
Canfield, W.W. 144
Clifford, J. 18, 19, 21, 22
Coates, K. 164, 186, 193
Cobbett, W. 76, 79
Cochran, C.B. 100
Cohen, A.P. 4, 21, 63, 221
Cohen, E. 154–5

Cohen, S. 104
Colombo, J.R. 118, 125
Cook, C. 101
Cook, R. 189
Cooke, P. 48
Cooper, B. 43
Cosgrove, D. 189
Cousins, M. 38, 39, 42, 45, 59
Curtis, G.W. 133

Derrida, J. 15
Dickens, C. 211
Dilthey, W. 17
Diubaldo, R.J. 178
Dorfman, A. 197
Dow, C.M. 128, 150, 158
Downes, P.G. 173
Doxman, E.J. 178
Drew, W. 194
Dreyfus, H.L., 25, 40, 45
Dunbar, G.S. 202
Duncan, S.S. 48, 53
Durkheim, E. 11, 29, 62, 83
Dwyer, K. 19

Eco, U. 55
Ewen, D. 139

Fiske, J. 95
Foucault, M. 40, 44, 58, 59, 63, 67, 149
Frampton, K. 58
Frayne, T.G. 149
Frye, N. 183, 184, 204, 257

Gadamer, H.-G. 19
Garnham, N. 36, 67
Gaskell, E. 210, 214

325

Geertz, C. 20–1
Geist, J.F. 53
George IV 73, 75–7, 196, 254
Gibbon, E. 75
Gibson, E.J. 27
Giddens, A. 37, 48, 270
Gilbert, E.W. 76, 100, 101
Gorz, A. 58
Gottdiener, M. 1, 55
Granville, B. 76
Graves, R. 107
Greene, G. 100

Hall, E.T. 4
Hamelin, L.-E. 61, 166, 169, 171–3, 176
Hamilton, R.M. 179, 197
Harris, L. 172, 190
Harvey, D. 6
Hearne, S. 173, 202
Heath, S. 220
Hechter, M. 193, 197
Herbert, A.P. 107, 108
Hern, A. 73, 79, 85, 106, 114
Higson, A. 216, 220, 221, 247
Hindley, C. 102
Hobbs, M. 166
Hodge, A. 107
Hodgins, B.W. 166, 170, 190
Hopkins, C. 177
Howells, W.D. 135, 150–1
Hudson, R. 15, 48, 207, 211–13, 231
Huisinga, J. 96
Hurley, G. 203
Hussain, A. 38, 42, 59

Ivanov, V. 92

Jacobs, J. 226
Jacobson, D. 132
James ,W.C. 174, 191
Jameson, F. 58
Jameson, A.B.M. 128
Jardine, A. 248
Jenkins, R. 37, 67
Jensen-Butler, C. 270
Johns, E. 27

Kirk, N. 214
Kline, M. 187
Knelman, M. 172
Krampen, M. 22, 23
Kroetsch, R. 191

Kroker, A. 267, 268
Lacombe, M. 190
Leacock, S. 188
Leclaire, L. 230
Lefebvre, H. 6, 30, 51, 58–9, 63
Leighton, T. 144
Levin, H. 160
Little, A. 104
Lowe, D.M. 63
Lowenthal, D. 12, 13, 65
Lustgarten, E. 102

MacCannell, D. 119
McGreevy, P. 146, 160
McGregor, G. 184, 185, 195
McKinsey, E.R. 125, 128, 131, 133,
   135, 138, 143, 144, 146, 151, 158,
   159
MacLaren, I.S. 202
MacLaren P. 95, 114
Major-Poetzl, P. 39, 67
Manning-Sanders, R. 76–9, 86, 88, 113
Marcus, G.E. 18, 19, 21, 22
Marshall, T. 147, 152
Marx, L. 119
Massey, D. 4, 244, 245
Mattelart, A. 197
Mauss, M. 62, 83
Mawer, A. 75
Montgomery, L.M. 154
Morton, W.L. 182, 191
Moss, J.G. 183, 185, 191, 204
Musgrave, C. 100

Needham, R. 62
Neumann, E. 145
Newman, M. 126, 148
Nutall, J. 104

Orwell, G. 212

Page, R. 178, 181, 193
Passeron, J.-C. 33, 34, 36
Pimlott, J.A.R. 77, 81, 86, 100, 113
Pocock, D. 15, 48, 207, 209, 211–13,
   231
Preston, H. 99, 100

Rabinow, P. 26, 40, 45
Rae, J. 175
Raleigh, J.H. 230
Rasmussen, K. 202

NAME INDEX

Rich, E.E. 175
Richardson, J. 185
Roberts, D. 176
Rojek, C. 90
Rothman, E. 139
Rowell, G. 160

Salutin, R. 172
Sanderson, M. 202
Savage, M. 211, 244
Sharp, T. 213
Shepard, P. 141
Shields, D. 179, 197
Shields, W.R. 165, 187, 188
Stallybrass, P. 85, 91, 92
Stefansson, V. 176, 179, 180, 188, 203
Stenton, F.M. 75
Stevenson J. 101
Stokes, A. 78
Stratton, J. 163

Thompson, D. 175, 202

Thompson, G.R. 160
Thompson, K. 217
Tomlinson, A. 111
Turner, V. 128, 150
Tyler, S. 124

Urry, J. 119

Wadland, J. 194
Walton J.K. 81, 87
Warwick, J. 165
Weiner, M. 82
Whipple, E.P. 211
White, A. 85, 91, 92
White, B. 216
Wilkinson, E. 213
Williams, R. 36, 214
Willis, P. 104
Willson, B. 182
Winks, R.W. 203
Wood, E.B. 134

SUBJECT INDEX

215–16, 218–21, 229–31, 243, 247;
langscape 184
language 4, 10, 15, 17, 19, 25, 31, 34,
43, 46, 48, 57, 58, 67–9, 127, 131,
158, 159, 195, 214, 234, 248
leisure 4, 9, 23, 25, 75, 81–3, 90, 95–7,
111, 137, 190–2, 257, 262
lifeworld 15
liminal zone 9, 81, 82, 84, 89, 93,
102–3, 109, 111, 150, 163, 174, 194,
256
liminality 73, 83, 84, 89, 93, 95, 110,
111, 125, 148, 150, 255, 276
linguistics 21, 22
localism 58
locality 56, 58, 146, 224
London 2, 68, 74–9, 85, 90, 100,
103–8, 110–15, 122, 129, 158, 160,
176–7, 187–8, 204, 207–9, 211,
214–21, 224, 228–30, 232–4, 237,
241–8, 256, 259
ludic 152, 260–2, 271

Manchester 177, 207, 210, 223, 240
Manitoba 202, 203, 205
marginality 39, 274, 277; marginal
places 1–2, 261; periphery 1
markets 151, 155, 181, 184
Marxism 23–4, 31
masculinity 141, 144
mass consumption 100
material culture 258
materialism 24
media 9, 19, 23, 27, 61, 104, 108, 110,
146, 148, 174, 176, 181, 191–4, 209,
223, 228, 231, 232, 234, 239, 240,
243, 245, 267–9; British realist
cinema 208, 215–21, 274;
newspapers 106, 177, 192, 195, 204,
243; television 9, 167, 192, 195, 202,
204, 208, 216, 222–4, 228, 231, 239,
243, 248
men 35, 78, 88, 102, 103, 106–7, 158,
163, 165, 174, 175, 179, 184, 187,
194, 199, 212, 229, 237
mental maps 11, 66, 263; cognitive
maps 29, 24, 25, 27, 263
metaphor 21, 33, 47, 66, 97, 114, 121,
143, 145, 184, 216, 232, 241, 257,
263, 267, 269, 271
method 170–1, 247, 260, 263, 278
Middle East 17, 19, 20, 24, 42
modern 1, 11, 17, 23, 39, 44, 51, 55,

97, 100, 121, 126–7, 137, 139, 148,
198, 209, 225–6, 228, 272, 275, 276
modernism 275
modernity 1, 4, 10, 77, 272, 274–6
Mods 101, 103–5, 110, 260
Montreal 166, 203, 205
morality 43, 86, 91, 93, 94, 112, 149;
immorality 106, 108, 109
myths 3–5, 22, 27, 32, 35, 47, 61, 62,
64, 68, 106, 109, 112, 118, 156,
162–3, 171–2, 178, 181–2, 185, 192,
194, 203, 213–14, 221–2, 232, 244,
246, 255–7, 260–4, 266, 268; Cree
Windigo 194; Manitto 144

nation-state 2, 45, 63, 68, 256, 278
National Film Board of Canada 195
nationalism 4, 164, 185, 186, 221
nationwide 197, 222, 243
native 101, 118, 120, 126, 144–5, 175,
181–2, 184, 188, 194–5, 202, 211,
258; Inuit 193
New York 122–5, 134, 136, 158–61, 203
nineteenth century 76, 86–8, 94, 100,
120, 126, 127, 129, 189, 207, 208,
210, 214, 223, 229, 230, 245, 246,
257, 268
nordicity 166–8, 170, 193
norms 16, 42, 68, 75, 90, 92, 94, 95,
108, 109, 111, 150, 194, 202, 247,
256, 263, 272
North: Far 61, 167, 170; of England
207, 210, 222, 229, 232; Near 191;
Real 186, 195, 199; True 162–5,
171–2, 174, 176, 180, 182, 184, 186,
188, 190–9, 201, 205, 207, 246, 258,
259, 262; see also image
North–South Divide 9, 208, 211–12,
231–4, 239–45, 247, 249, 259, 260,
262
northern frontier 9, 183–5
northern images 172, 188, 209, 213
northern nation 8, 178, 186, 198
northern development 165, 179, 195,
205
Northwest Territories 165–7, 170, 201,
202
nostalgia 1, 189, 224, 226, 228, 260
Nottingham 211, 247

objectivity 7
Ontario 121, 122, 134, 136, 138, 192,
201, 202, 204

Printed in the United Kingdom
by Lightning Source UK Ltd.
120088UK00001B/329